Facing the Music

CHARLES BAEYERTZ
AND THE *TRIAD*

*To the late Dr John Baeyertz, F.R.C.O.G.
who contributed so much to this book*

To Jossy and Don with much love from Joanna

Facing the Music

CHARLES BAEYERTZ
and
The Triad
A Journal Devoted to Literature, Art, Science & Music

Joanna M. Woods

JOANNA WOODS

OTAGO

Published by Otago University Press
PO Box 56/Level 1, 398 Cumberland Street, Dunedin, New Zealand
Fax: 64 3 479 8385
Email: university.press@otago.ac.nz
Website: www.otago.ac.nz/press

First published 2008
Copyright © Joanna Woods 2008
ISBN 978 1 877372 55 1

Cover image: Charles Baeyertz, *c.*1908. (Private collection)

Printed in New Zealand by Astra Print Ltd, Wellington

Published with the assistance of

creative nz
ARTS COUNCIL OF NEW ZEALAND *TOI AOTEAROA*

Contents

Foreword *Hamish Keith*	7
Preface	9
Acknowledgements	11
1. An Accident in a Paddock	13
2. The Preacher's Son	19
3. Marvellous Melbourne	29
4. Dunedin	38
5. The *Triad*	49
6. The Fighting Editor	61
7. The Critic in Maoriland	75
8. Walking with the Stars	88
9. New York	101
10. A Splendid Enemy	114
11. Empire City	129
12. A Leap of Passion	143
13. The Australasian *Triad*	156
14. The Abomination of War	171
15. The Wages of Sin	184
16. The End of an Old Adventuress	196
17. The Last Crusade	208
Epilogue	217
Notes	220
Selected Bibliography	230
Index	235

FOREWORD

Like Joanna Woods, I too came across the *Triad* and its extraordinary editor, Charles Nalder Baeyertz, by chance. In 1977 I began to research *New Zealand Yesterdays*, a popular social history of this country in the first seventy years of the twentieth century, and, casting about for a serial or two which might give me some flavour of the first few decades, I sat down to read through the whole of the *Triad* – a magazine I had never heard of.

To say I was astonished by the New Zealand I encountered in its pages would be an understatement. This was not the dull, grey, humourless, uncultivated wasteland in which I had been led to believe our unfortunate grandparents lived their dull, grey, humourless, and uncultivated lives. To the contrary, it would have been at the edge of things had it been written when I was reading it – well almost.

Certainly its critical voice was as intelligent and outspoken as anything my contemporaries were writing and, more to the point, better informed; its contributors did not seem on the fringe of anything or out of touch with the world. They may not have approved of contemporary events in European art, but they knew what was going on and fully engaged with it as they did with the art and music going on around them. Baeyertz was a remarkable man, of course, and would have been remarkable anywhere, but he was not some isolated genius. He spoke to and about his culture – the *Triad* was a reflection as much as a beacon.

My initial astonishment gave way to an outrage – as warm now as it was three decades ago – that our rich and lively past had been dismantled and obscured. There are a lot of possible reasons for that – among them the shift of political and economic élites away from a metropolitan to a rural focus, and the abandoning of our Tasman world for some made-up English fiction – but there is no excuse that I can see.

This biography restores to our contemporary imagination one of the great characters of our Victorian past. There are many more people and works in need of a similar resurrection and we will all be the richer for it being done.

Hamish Keith
Auckland 2008

PREFACE

The origins of this book date back to 1999 when I was researching Katherine Mansfield's early life in Wellington. My focus was on her cultural environment and as I combed the newspapers and journals of the period for evidence of artistic activities, I soon realised that contrary to what Mansfield would have us believe, the cultural life of early twentieth-century New Zealand was remarkably vigorous.

At a professional level, theatrical performances and concerts abounded, often featuring international stars who were ably supported by local actors and musicians. At an amateur level, orchestras and art societies flourished in all the main centres and almost every settlement boasted a choir or a play-reading group.

Amongst the dozens of publications that I encountered, however, one magazine stood head and shoulders above the rest, in terms of both authoritative critical commentary and sheer entertainment value. This was the *Triad*. Dominated by the larger-than-life personality of its editor, Charles Baeyertz, the *Triad*'s pages not only resound with thunderous criticisms and biting wit, but also constitute a fascinating chronicle of over three decades of New Zealand's cultural life. Moreover, unlike most home-grown journals at the time, the *Triad*'s coverage was consciously cosmopolitan, with reviews of the latest musical performances in London and New York rubbing shoulders with essays on Russian literature and verses in sixteenth-century French. Small wonder, then, that even the disdainful Mansfield deigned to send it one of her offerings.

For Mansfield, the *Triad* was little more than a footnote. But for me it was a tantalising glimpse of an unexplored world and five years later, when I was awarded a generous research fellowship by the National Library, I was finally able to return to it.

Charles Baeyertz and the *Triad* are inseparable. It was his life work and every issue bears the imprint of his extraordinary mind, which in turn reflects his exotic background and unconventional education. But the decision to tell the story of the *Triad* through the biography of its creator has inevitably produced a number of challenges, not least the task of discerning the real man beneath the veneer of editorial bombast. In addition, his activities beyond the *Triad* are largely undocumented and it is only thanks to the extensive family research done by his grandson, the late Dr John Baeyertz, that I have been able to piece together a private life that was quite as colourful as the public one.

In the course of his editorial career, Charles interacted with many of New Zealand's most celebrated writers, musicians and artists. Some, like Mansfield, appear only fleetingly, while others like Frances Hodgkins, Jessie Mackay and Alfred Hill feature regularly. Several international figures also take a bow (or a blow) in the *Triad*. Amongst them are Dame Nellie Melba, whose singing Charles famously described as 'liquid as a crystal snow-fed brook – and as cold', and Ezra Pound, whose Modernist poetry reduced Charles and his co-editor to uncomprehending fury. Away from the spotlight, Charles conducted his personal affairs with as much verve as he directed his magazine – and both dealt him an equal measure of triumphs and disasters.

Throughout the book, two powerful factors have motivated my writing. The first was a burning desire to set the record straight and, with the eloquent evidence of the *Triad*, to banish the myth that New Zealand had no viable cultural life before the 1930s. The second and perhaps less worthy factor was my longing, in a politically correct age, to share the delight of Charles's irreverent humour and refreshing honesty with others.

If I have even partially achieved these aims, the long hours of writing and research will have been worthwhile.

Joanna Woods
March 2008

Acknowledgements

To Sir Francis Drake for a prayer that every writer should know:

Lord God, when Thou givest to Thy servants to endeavour any great matter, grant us also to know that it is not the beginning, but the continuing of the same unto the end until it be thoroughly finished which yieldeth the true glory.

In writing this book, I am indebted to a great many individuals and institutions, but foremost amongst these are the National Library and Creative New Zealand. Without their financial support I could not have undertaken the project. Similarly, without the peerless staff and collections of the Alexander Turnbull Library, where much of my research took place, this book could never have been written.

I would like, therefore, to begin by extending my heartfelt thanks to Penny Carnaby, Chief Executive and National Librarian, Margaret Calder, former Chief Librarian of the Alexander Turnbull Library, and to every member of the Turnbull staff for their unfailing courtesy and competence. During the past three years, the Turnbull has been my second home where, despite my endless requests for materials and photocopies, I have always been made to feel welcome.

Amongst those who were particularly helpful are Jill Palmer, the former music archivist, and Roger Flury, Team Leader of the National Library's Music Services. Special thanks are also due to Philip Rainer and Joan McCracken for their generous support over illustrations. In addition I would like to mention: James Ashwell, Peter Atwell, Susan Bartel, Ann Breen, Barbara Brownlie, Mary Cobeldick, Tania Connelly, Walter Cook, Jill Goodwin, Rhonda Grantham, David Jones, Shaun McGuire, Marion Minson, Nigel Murphy, David Retter, Collen Slater, Helen Smith, Danny Sue, John Sullivan, Diane Woods and all the smiling staff on the ground floor reception desk. Needless to say, there are countless others in both the National and Turnbull Libraries whom space does not permit me to mention.

I would also like to thank Rosemary Wildblood, former Arts Adviser for literature at Creative New Zealand, who encouraged me to persevere with my application for funding, and Hamish Keith for his enthusiastic support of the *Triad*. His willingness to write the foreword not only represents a great act of kindness, but also adds the lustre of his own cultural eminence to this humble endeavour.

On the academic side, I am especially grateful to Greg Baughen for taking the time to meet me and discuss the project. His meticulously researched thesis, *C.N. Baeyertz and The Triad 1893–1915* (1980), reads as if it had been written yesterday and I have referred to it constantly. I would also like to thank soprano, Göknil Biner, for her intelligent commentary on Charles's *Voice Culture*.

Another figure to whom I am greatly indebted is Catherine Baeyertz for the unfettered access she has given me to her late husband's papers. Dr John Baeyertz spent the last six years of his life assembling material for a family biography of his grandfather, but died while his manuscript was still in draft. This kindly and dedicated physician, whom I have come to know through his writing, has been one of my key collaborators and it is in acknowledgement of his important contribution to my work that I have dedicated this book to him.

Across the Tasman, I would like to thank another grandchild of Charles's, Leone Flemons, for the frankness and eloquence of her letters and for the delightful photographs. My warmest thanks must also go to Dawn Peel of the Professional Historians' Association, who provided me with most of the material on Charles's early life in Colac.

Most fittingly it is in Dunedin, where the whole *Triad* adventure began, that some of my most important thanks are due: First to Anne Jackman, Reference Librarian of the Hocken Collections, and to all the staff who helped to make my week at the Hocken Library so fruitful, and second to George Griffiths for his guidance on 'Civis' and for his many insights on early Dunedin.

The single person to whom I owe the most, however, is my publisher Wendy Harrex of Otago University Press who, together with editor Richard Reeve, designer Fiona Moffat and indexer Andrew Parsloe, has coped with my recalcitrant commas and my rambling emails to produce a beautiful book. My joy at seeing it in print is matched only by my pride in sharing a publisher with the most illustrious of New Zealand's cultural magazines, *Landfall*.

Finally I should thank my husband, Richard, for sharing his home for so long with Charles Baeyertz. I suspect he will be glad to see the back of him.

Chapter 1

An Accident in a Paddock

Charles Nalder Baeyertz, who featured regularly in the New Zealand press for over thirty years, made his first bow to the media at the age of four. The year was 1871 and the occasion was the burial of his father, whose tragic shooting accident and well-attended funeral made front page news in the little township of Colac:

> *No more reliable testimony could be adduced of the respect and esteem felt towards the deceased than the large assemblage which followed his remains to their last resting-place on Thursday … The cortege left shortly after one o'clock, there being thirty or forty conveyances and a large number of horsemen … One of the most touching spectacles was the deceased's little son, who, while the service was being proceeded with, sprinkled a basket of flowers into the grave.*[1]

Like many notable figures in nineteenth-century New Zealand, Charles spent his early life in Australia. He was born at his parents' house at Bridge Road in Melbourne on 15 December 1866, fourteen months after their clandestine marriage. Both families had opposed the match and the couple eloped to marry in an empty church where the officiating priest had to summon his gardener and maid to sign the marriage register.

Charles's mother, Emilia, was Jewish and when his father (after whom he was named),* told his parents that he wanted to marry her, they found the prospect of a Jewish daughter-in-law so unacceptable that they threatened to banish him from the house for ever. Such anti-Semitic attitudes were typical of the era and are recorded by the Melbourne diarist, Samuel Candler, who claimed that the downfall of the Governor, Sir Henry Barkly, stemmed from the anger of Victoria's Anglo-Saxon establishment over his hospitality to the Jews:

> *Sir Henry Barkly once invited some decent Hebrews to a 'Lawn Party'. This not only offended the Faubourg de South Yarra, but excited hatred, malice,*

---

* Charles's father and grandfather were also named Charles, making three generations of Baeyertz males with the same name. Charles perpetuated this tradition – and went one better – by christening both his first and his third sons Charles.

envy and jealousy in the tribe itself… I found a new source of pleasure in flirting with the Rebeccas. But the Governor estranged himself from all the rococo folk and the swells in the country. When a political crisis came, his sins were had up for judgement. The haut ton joined the 'roughs' and Sir Henry (although right) had to retire a year before his time.[2]

Despite his foreign-sounding surname, Charles's paternal grandfather considered himself quite as staunchly British as the gentry of South Yarra. His portrait fully supports this claim and shows him as an archetypal Victorian gentleman, soberly dressed, with a fine head and an air of great dignity. Before emigrating to Australia with his wife and two children in 1852, he had served in the Royal Navy followed by a term as private secretary to the Governor of the West Indies. In Melbourne, he was appointed by the newly established Government of Victoria as Warehouse Keeper of the Trades and Customs Department, where his generous salary of £500 a year reflected his considerable responsibilities. The Victorian gold rush of the 1850s was already in full swing; in the heady atmosphere of a rapidly expanding economy, the warehouse of the busy port of Melbourne needed close oversight and a safe pair of hands.

The careers of earlier forbears are less well documented. By the mid nineteenth century, the Baeyertz family had been in England for at least three generations, but all that is known of Charles's great grandfather, Peter Baeyertz, is that he married a Miss Elizabeth Tanner in London and described his occupation as 'gentleman'. During World War I, when German-sounding names became unfashionable, Charles claimed that his family was of Flemish origin and suggested, with typical linguistic ingenuity, that his ancestors had given the name 'Lombaeyertzyde' to a whole town and district eight miles from the Belgian port of Ostend. Without access to records and indexes, Charles quite possibly believed this claim, but more recent research indicates that the name Baeyertz is German and that during the eighteenth century some unknown twist of history or fortune prompted a member of the family to move from what is now Germany to settle in England.

The family of Charles's paternal grandmother, Mary, also had European connections, for although her father, John Treleaven, was of Cornish stock and claimed to have served in the Royal Navy, her mother's maiden name of Roscorlitz was certainly not English and she herself was born in Spain. A photograph of Mary shows a sharp-faced woman, in an elaborate bonnet, whose stern expression is at odds with the tender picture later drawn of her in Emilia's biography.

Thus, on the paternal side, Charles's lineage included 'gentlemen', naval officers, a civil servant and, once Charles's father started working for the

National Bank of Australasia, a banker. All were conservative, middle-class citizens whose national loyalties lay with England, but who had European links that could have contributed to Charles's distinctly cosmopolitan bias. On the maternal side, his connections with a wider cultural perspective are far more clearly discernible. Both his mother's parents, John Aronson and Maria Lazarus, sprang from 'unblemished Hebrew stocks'[3] and, although Emilia was born and raised in Wales, her family's cultural and intellectual outlook stretched far beyond her home town of Bangor.

From the pious and respectful biography of Emilia by Sydney Watson, which is largely based on her personal recollections, a vivid picture emerges of her early life as the pampered and supposedly delicate child of a wealthy jeweller. She left school at thirteen, but her education continued at home and she later attributed her gifts as a public speaker to the many hours she spent reading aloud to her mother from the great works of English literature. Throughout her subsequent career, the perfection of Emilia's diction and the charm of her speaking voice were remarked on in the press and were perhaps the origin of Charles's own well-modulated tones and his exacting standards of pronunciation.

Watson's biography also reveals other characteristics which Emilia may have bequeathed to her son, such as the pragmatism with which both she and her parents approached the breaking-off of her first engagement. Even Watson's sentimental prose cannot disguise the business-like fashion in which, as soon as it was discovered that he had tuberculosis, Emilia's unfortunate fiancé was summarily dismissed to die in the French Riviera. Pragmatism and a shrewd sense of business were salient features of Charles's make-up which, together with his entrepreneurial flair, may well have been inherited from the Aronsons.

Watson also glosses over the real reasons for Emilia's despatch at the age of twenty-two to Australia, claiming that it was to regain her health after the shock of her broken engagement. In fact, what seems far more probable is that her parents decided that her chances of finding a husband would be better in Australia. There, her past history was unknown and a married sister, resident in Melbourne, could provide a home and act as a chaperone. In this last role, however, her sister failed abysmally, for within a short time of her arrival in Melbourne in 1864, Emilia – perfectly restored to health – had committed the unpardonable crime of falling in love with a Gentile.

By the 1860s, the Jewish business community in Melbourne had formed a powerful* and closely-knit group whose members were quite as wary of inter-faith marriages as Charles's grandparents. Although Emilia told Watson

---

* In 1862 a member of the group, Edward Cohen, became Melbourne's first Jewish mayor.

that her sister 'lived in great style, moving in the most fashionable society'[4] (which may well have included non-Jews), she also stressed her sister's strong disapproval of marriage to non-Jews. As a result, Emilia told no one about her passion for the young banker, Mr Baeyertz. Early on the morning of 16 October 1865, after months of soul-searching, she stole away from her sister's house and married him in secret.

Within a few hours, Emilia's sister discovered what had happened. Furious at the disgrace that had been brought on the family, she gathered up Emilia's belongings, together with any household objects that were tainted by some association with her, and despatched them to her without a word. Before long, the Baeyertz family relented. Emilia's mother and her favourite brother, George, also forgave her. But her father disinherited her and Emilia never heard from him again. Similarly, for many months after her marriage, a number of earlier friends made a point of 'cutting' her on the street.

When Charles was a few months old, his father was appointed as manager of the National Bank of Australasia's recently opened branch in Colac, a small township with a population of one and a half thousand that lay two days' travel from Melbourne. Towards the end of 1867, the family moved there and took up residence in the plain, two-storey brick building on the main street that had been built to house the bank and its manager. This was Charles's home for the next four years and would have been the first place that he remembered.

An early photograph of Colac's business district, taken two years before the erection of the bank, shows a wide, unpaved street with a line of single-storey cottages down one side. Except for two horse-drawn wagons, the street is completely deserted. Judging from the modesty of the architecture, the comment by Colac's nineteenth-century historian, Isaac Hebb, that 'at the time the new bank was considered quite an addition to the architectural adornment of the town'[5] has a ring of truth. Despite its architectural shortcomings, however, Colac already had a sense of civic pride. In 1865 thirty-eight acres on the foreshore of Lake Colac had been consecrated to the creation of a botanical garden, and by 1871 residents had a free library and a hall for public functions.

None of these amenities would have made much impression on the infant Charles. At this early stage, his world would have been circumscribed by the nursery and the main figures in his life would have been his parents, the household servants and later his baby sister, Marion. But as he grew older he could not have failed to notice Colac's magnificent 1820-hectare lake or the small boat which his father built to row on it. He may also have observed, far across the lake, the lunar contours of the volcanic Warrion Hills flanked by the rich pastureland that had lured the first settlers to the district.

According to Watson, Emilia was delighted by the natural beauties of her new surroundings and the active social life which she enjoyed with the neighbouring 'squattocracy'. Within the township, the population was more mixed. The 1868 Post Office directory lists no fewer than nine hotel keepers and numerous butchers and blacksmiths. But it also mentions a professor of music, an accountant and a barrister with whom the bank manager and his wife would have consorted. For Charles's father, however, the social high point of his time in Colac would have been when his two well-trained gun dogs were summoned in December 1867 for use by the first royal visitor to Australia, Queen Victoria's second son, Prince Alfred. The Prince had been invited to shoot by the most important landowner in the district, William Robertson, and as a keen sportsman, Charles's father probably participated in the shoot – especially as in these early days his trigger-happy habits would not have been common knowledge. Whether or not he joined the royal party, the occasion passed without mishap – unlike several months later when the Prince was shot in the back at a public picnic in Sydney.*

Apart from Emilia's biography, the scant material on Charles's father makes it hard to assess his abilities or to pinpoint characteristics that he might have passed on to his son. Even the detection of physical similarities is ruled out by the absence of a single photograph. Emilia's image of her husband is heavily tinted with rose. She depicts him as a paragon of Christian virtue and uxorial rectitude, who 'was passionately fond of outdoor pursuits, yet he combined with this the intensest love of home' and 'a most ardent'[6] love of music. Yet from other sources, a distinct impression remains that while Charles's father was clearly 'a thorough good fellow',[7] his behaviour sometimes lacked caution. Quite apart from his carelessness with firearms, which is all too well documented, the following extract from a newspaper article, based on material in the National Bank archives in Melbourne, suggests that his professional life was also characterised by a certain negligence:

> *One of Colac's early bank managers distinguished himself by burying the duplicate keys of the bank's main safe, because he did not want them in his house, then forgetting where they were interred. This fact ... is recorded in a letter written by the manager, Mr. Charles Baeyertz, to the assistant accountant in Melbourne.*[8]

Such snippets, combined with the copious newspaper coverage of his death, make it possible to deduce that some of the more flamboyant aspects of Charles's character, including his willingness to take risks, may have come from his father.

---

*   The Prince made a full recovery, but his would-be assassin, a disaffected Irishman named James O'Farrell, was hanged.

Charles's father died after less than four years in Colac as the result of a shooting accident. It occurred while he was out shooting quail when, with a fatal disregard for safety, he stood his loaded gun against a fence and leant over it to shake hands with a friend. The gun went off, sending a charge through his shoulder at point blank range and wounding him so seriously that he had to be transported home on the floor of a cart. The local doctor was called but, once he saw the gravity of the case, he telegraphed for assistance from his closest colleague, whose practice was over forty miles away in Geelong.

As Colac's only bank manager, Charles's father was one of the leading lights of the town and the news of his accident spread like wildfire. Throughout the night, the residents of Colac maintained an anxious vigil. When the second doctor arrived at 3 a.m., he found all the houses ablaze with light as their occupants waited up for his arrival. By first light, the two doctors had decided that the only hope of recovery lay in amputation, and at 8 a.m. the patient's arm was removed, close to the joint of the shoulder. According to a report in the *Colac Herald,* he 'bore the operation with great fortitude',[9] but his condition continued to deteriorate and two days later, at 11 p.m. on 6 March 1871, he died.

For the isolated population of Colac, the untimely death of Charles's father at the age of only twenty-eight was a major event and prompted a noisy but short-lived outpouring in the local press – including the revelation that 'the unfortunate gentleman' had 'on a previous occasion shot off two of his toes.'[10] For Emilia and her two small children, however, the impact of the tragedy was far more enduring. Emilia was driven by her grief to embrace a new vocation and, although Watson states blithely that 'her children were quite happy without their father … and everything went on just the same without him',[11] his death drastically changed their lives.

Charles's blend of German, English and Jewish ancestry is a mixture that has produced much brilliance in the worlds of business and letters,* but in the formation of character, environment, education and chance are quite as important as inheritance. At the age of four, Charles was robbed of the privileged life of a banker's son by a chance shooting in a paddock. From then on, the principal arbiter of his education was Emilia and the atmosphere of crusading zeal in which she raised him played a key role in his destiny.

---

* In New Zealand notable examples are the poet, Charles Brasch, founding editor of the literary magazine, *Landfall,* and the co-founder of the *Otago Daily Times,* Julius Vogel, although his forbears were Dutch rather than German.

CHAPTER 2

THE PREACHER'S SON

On the night after the funeral, only the timely arrival of a neighbour prevented Emilia taking an overdose of laudanum. A few days later, she and the children moved from their comfortable home at the bank forever. For the first few weeks they stayed with Charles's paternal grandparents, who had recently retired to a house just outside Colac. But despite the support of her parents-in-law, Emilia continued to be overwhelmed by her loss. She spent much of her time walking alone beside the lake or lying on the grave of her late husband, weeping.

Throughout this unhappy period, Emilia believed that, apart from her mother-in-law, she was largely alone in her suffering, but at four Charles would certainly have been aware of his mother's distress and the changes in their domestic life. Within a few weeks, Emilia and the children moved again to a small cottage in Colac which she furnished with her belongings from the bank. By now her mental state was causing widespread concern in the family and her talk of a 'Divine revelation'[1] and the hours she spent studying the New Testament were seen, at least by her sister in Melbourne, as symptoms of increasing instability.

On her marriage, Emilia had become a Christian, but her adoption of her husband's faith was largely a matter of convenience and she did not bother with baptism until after the birth of her daughter in 1869, when mother and daughter were christened on the same day. In Colac's overriding atmosphere of 'middle-class religious respectability',[2] being a member of the Anglican or Presbyterian Church carried a certain social status, and once Colac's Anglican church was opened in 1870, Emilia busied herself with organising a choir and helping with the Sunday school. But while she paid lip service to Christianity, she remained unconvinced.

There can be no doubt that Emilia's dramatic religious conversion within a few months of becoming a widow was prompted by grief. Many years later, the original motive for her conversion was bluntly stated by a Los Angeles newspaper which presented her to its readers as 'a Converted Jewess' who 'Became a Christian Out of Her Desire to Be Reunited to Her Deceased Husband'.[3] Whatever the starting point of her faith, however,

Emilia's conversion was genuine and enduring and launched her on a path of itinerant evangelism which she pursued for the rest of her life.

The consequences of Emilia's newfound faith were soon felt by her children. Late in 1871, they moved house again, this time to neighbouring Geelong where her sister hoped she would find it easier to recover from her bereavement. For Emilia the chief attraction of Geelong, which was the second largest town in Victoria, was not its greater amenities or its picturesque location but rather 'its thousands of precious souls, many of whom were without God or hope in the world'.[4]

The earliest known photograph of Charles dates from this time, taken on 16 February 1872 in Turner's Portrait Rooms on Geelong's fashionable Moorabool Street. He is expensively dressed in a Tyrolean-style suit decorated with buttons and topped by a slightly lop-sided bow tie, but he is small for his age and his expression is watchful. Although smiling for the camera was not customary in early photography, Charles's demeanour does not suggest a carefree child. Perhaps the burden of his mother's fervour was already taking its toll, for Watson claims that when Emilia moved to Geelong 'her boy was her constant companion, when not working for God, and a great comfort to her.'[5]

Watson is at pains to point out that Emilia never neglected her children – despite her self-imposed regime of hospital and prison visiting, door-knocking and a large Sunday school class for teenage boys. Nevertheless, her single-minded pursuit of souls and her burning religious zeal must have created an unusual home environment. Nor did Charles have any outside schooling to redress the psychological balance, for, although Geelong had several excellent schools, his early education took place at home. Exactly how much of the teaching was undertaken by his mother is not clear. Her own education had been brief and the range of subjects would have been limited. On the other hand, she was well read and highly musical and she may well have laid the foundations of Charles's interest in literature and his extensive knowledge of music.

Compared with Colac, Geelong was a metropolis. Like Melbourne, its population had exploded during the 1850s gold rush, increasing from 9000 in 1851 to 23,000 in 1854. By mid 1857, it had a railway link with Melbourne and in 1858 it opened its famous Grammar School. By the 1860s, the town centre boasted a number of substantial public buildings, including an imposing neo-classical town hall, and the streets and shops were lit by gas. Geelong's economy, however, was not solely dependent on its position as a gateway to the goldfields. The surrounding countryside encompasses some of the finest wool-grazing areas in Australia and when the boom years had passed, the town continued to flourish as an important centre for the wool trade. By 1870,

Moorabool Street was lined by two-storey buildings and shops and had a distinct air of elegance. Beyond it lay Corio Bay where Emilia, who was a keen bather, was delighted to find several well-appointed bathing establishments.

Watson provides no details of the domestic circumstances of Emilia and her children. His chapter on their five years in Geelong is focused on the spiritual development of his subject and never touches on anything as indelicate as money. Yet, for Emilia, the financial implications of widowhood were considerable. Disinherited by her father and without her husband's salary (and before the era of pensions), she was now dependent on the generosity of her parents-in-law and her siblings for a livelihood. She must have received some financial assistance from the Baeyertz grandparents, with whom she now had a close relationship, but the modest sum of £94 15s 11d that she left on her death suggests that her means were slender and that, from an early age, Charles had every reason to be interested in making money.

In normal circumstances, Emilia's brothers would certainly have been generous to their sister and her fatherless children – especially George who was one of the first members of the family to accept her marriage and gave her a white marble clock as a wedding present. Moreover, in Melbourne the Aronsons' flair for business was paying handsome dividends. By 1874 Emilia's younger brother, Saul, was already a partner in a successful firm of jewellers, and in 1878 he was joined by George. Their business later expanded to London, Brisbane and Perth, and in 1884 another brother, Frederick, became a partner in a major jewellery business in Sydney. But while it was possible for Emilia's brothers to overlook her marriage to a Christian, her evangelistic activities were less easy to ignore. In particular, the direction that these took in early 1877 must have caused them intense embarrassment and would have discouraged them from helping her.

Meanwhile, by 1876 Emilia had decided that Charles needed to go to school. Her choice fell on a distinguished Methodist foundation in Melbourne, Wesley College, at which Charles was enrolled as a 'Day Boarder'. Since Geelong was forty-five miles from Melbourne, he had to board locally, but he was nine years old and, by the standards of the day, quite old enough to leave home.

Charles's entry to Wesley College marks an important turning point in his childhood. Up to this time, the dominant figure in his life had been his mother, and the lasting impact of Emilia's intensity, and the extent to which Charles followed her example, are demonstrated by the 'Apostolic fire'[6] which imbued his cultural mission to New Zealand and prompted him to found his critical magazine, the *Triad*. Strains of his mother's evangelism resound through its pages, not only in his exacting musical and literary reviews, but also in his many pronouncements on the moral dangers of 'a prevalence of bad English'[7] and his dire warnings on the evils of faulty diction. Emilia continued to play a central role in Charles's development, but once he went to Wesley College he was exposed to a second important influence – to which she was also closely aligned – the teachings of Methodism.

The school admission register for 1876 shows Charles's entry date as 8 September and his religion as 'Brethren', which was a general term sometimes used to denote non-conformist Protestants, such as Baptists, Congregationalists and Methodists. Although Emilia and her children were officially Anglicans, she was strongly attracted by Methodism and, in registering Charles as 'Brethren', she probably meant non-conformist rather than the exclusive Plymouth Brethren with whom she had no recorded contact.

Emilia was not alone in her admiration of the Methodists. In Victoria they had been making significant gains over other denominations for some time. Part of their success may be attributed to their activity in establishing schools; their claim to have contributed more to education in the early years of the colony than any other denomination is borne out by the many schools of Methodist foundation in Melbourne today. In his 1986 thesis, however, Graham Evans makes the additional point that 'the stern and uncompromising doctrines of the Methodist Church had a strong appeal to those seeking a set of values by which they could shape their lives in the New World'.[8]

Apart from a brief interlude at a German Lutheran school outside Adelaide, Charles's formal education was entirely at the hands of Wesleyan Methodists and the notorious bluntness of his critical judgements in the *Triad* is not merely a reflection of his caustic pen, but also bears witness to the system in which he was educated. As an adult, Charles's evaluations of writers and performers permitted no shades of grey. He demanded nothing less than excellence and, in the pages of the *Triad*, his most constant refrain was that this could only be achieved by hard work and dedication. As a schoolboy, however, his own approach was rather less rigorous and he took full advantage of his photographic memory to cut corners. In his reminiscences of his father, Rudolph Baeyertz records Charles's admission that he rarely bothered to do his homework in the evenings because he could learn all he needed by running his eyes over the relevant pages of his schoolbook on his way to school in the morning.

Throughout his life, Charles's extraordinary ability to memorise a page at a glance greatly enhanced his reputation for brilliance. His capacity to read and absorb large quantities of material at high speed enabled him to display an apparently inexhaustible fund of knowledge and to acquire several languages. He mastered French, German and Italian with ease, and although the suggestion that he was able 'to converse fluently in 17 different tongues'[9] is open to question, his claim to have learnt Maori in a few months simply by memorising the dictionary is quite credible. Such a feat would have been well within the grasp of a man whose favourite party trick was reading a column from a newspaper and then reciting it backwards. But while Charles's prodigious memory was a formidable asset, it enraged his detractors and fuelled their accusations that he was less intelligent than he appeared.

No records survive of Charles's academic performance at Wesley, but he must have been favourably impressed by the teaching because, in 1904, he sent his eldest son from New Zealand to study there. Several years later, on a visit to Melbourne, he told the headmaster with his customary jocularity that he could still pass the matriculation exam with ease – and he did.

In March 1877, Emilia moved to Melbourne in response to an invitation from the vicar of St Mary's, Caulfield. Her years in Geelong had served as a time of apprenticeship during which she had only gradually discovered her charismatic powers, but her reputation as an evangelist was growing and her speaking engagements multiplied. Emilia's outside commitments left little time for home life, and, even after she moved to Melbourne, it seems likely that Charles remained boarded out during the term. At a time when little value was attached to the academic education of girls, no mention is made of schooling for Charles's sister, Marion.

When the Rev. Macartney of Caulfield wrote to Emilia inviting her to lead a mission to convert Melbourne's Jewish community to Christianity, his belief that her family background made her ideally suited to the task could hardly have been more mistaken. Emilia's well-meaning efforts only aroused the fury of her intended converts, who hounded her from their homes with cries of 'Meshumad'* and death threats. Her activities must also have infuriated the Aronsons, which could explain why Charles was never taken under the wing of one of his wealthy uncles.

Undaunted, Emilia turned to pastures new and before long she was holding lunch-time prayer meetings for Melbourne's factory girls. They were spellbound by the tale of her conversion and listened with awe as she prophesied, with chilling accuracy, that one of their number would 'never hear the Gospel again'.[10] Two hours later, a woman who had attended the meeting dropped dead and Emilia's credibility soared. She continued to foretell deaths on a regular basis and her meetings and Bible classes were soon packed by hundreds of women.

Throughout 1878, Emilia preached continually. At her first big mission, which took place in 1879 in the gold mining town of Sandhurst,† the theatre

---

* Apostate.
† Present-day Bendigo.

was crammed for every meeting and people had to arrive an hour and a half beforehand to secure their seats. Encouraged by her success, Emilia proceeded to Ballarat where her second mission enjoyed even greater popularity. Watson reports that 'over a thousand persons gathered every afternoon at the Bible readings,'[11] and that the numbers at her nightly meetings in the theatre were so great that the local authorities had to close the street to traffic.

Emilia's career had taken off. Shortly after her mission to Ballarat, she embarked on a three-month mission to Adelaide, which eventually lasted for three years. Charles, meanwhile, was removed from Wesley and sent to a boarding school in a German Lutheran settlement in the Adelaide Hills, named Hahndorf. The school had been founded in 1857 by T.W. Boehm who had come to Australia with his parents at the age of two to escape religious persecution in Prussia. When Charles arrived at Hahndorf, it still had a distinctly German air and the College, which stood on its main street, was flanked by thatched cottages and quaint, half-timbered houses with high pitched roofs. Many of the settlers spoke only limited English, but Boehm, who realised that fluency in English was essential in Australia, had established the College along the lines of an English boarding school with instruction in English. Despite his best efforts, however, Hahndorf's scholars soon became notorious for the guttural-sounding Latin which they picked up from their Prussian-born Latin master, Pastor Strempel.

Nevertheless, the College enjoyed a high reputation – especially for music. Boehm was a gifted piano teacher; one of his early pupils, Adolph Reimann, went on to found the Adelaide College of Music and later became known as the 'Father of South Australian music'. At the College, Boehm installed what is reputed to have been one of the first pipe organs in South Australia, and he kept an elaborate harpsichord in his classroom. He also maintained the German tradition of choral music and developed a 'juvenile orchestra' to accompany the school choir.

Charles's keen interest in choral music and enthusiasm for the organ may well stem from his time at Hahndorf, but he would have found other aspects of the school less enjoyable. For the boarders, living conditions were Spartan. They slept in long narrow dormitories on iron bedsteads with flock mattresses. A small table stood between each bed and the boys kept their clothes in tin trunks under their beds. The adjoining bathroom block had running water, and in summer cold showers were compulsory, but there were no other facilities and, before they went to bed, the boys were taken out by the master on duty to relieve themselves in the nearby creek.

In later life, Charles hardly mentions Hahndorf. In the *Triad* he refers to it only fleetingly as 'a German school', and he seems to have spent only a short time there before being admitted, in August 1881, to a prestigious

Methodist establishment in Adelaide named Prince Alfred College. Once again, he was boarded out, this time with a Mrs Haldane who lived just behind the school in Little Young Street. The Admissions Register shows that Charles was enrolled for three extra subjects – drawing, music and gymnastics* – but his previous school is given as Wesley, which arouses the suspicion that he may have left Hahndorf under a cloud. A further detail on the Register hints teasingly at some undisclosed irregularity, for beneath his extra subjects in the 'Extras & Remarks' column is written: 'Re-entry Preacher's son'.[12]

The reticence about Charles's brief interlude at Hahndorf is not the only indicator that his time there may not have been a success. Given his abilities, his dismal academic performance during his first term at Prince Alfred suggests that he was seriously disrupted when he arrived and had learnt little at his previous school. In the term order book, his marks hover close to the bottom in almost every subject. Even in German, which he claimed was one of his strengths, he only reaches twenty-sixth place out of a class of thirty-six. The examinations book tells a similar sorry tale and Charles occupies an inglorious position, two from the bottom.

Despite consistently low marks, however, Charles's two years at Prince Alfred were outstandingly happy, and there is plenty of evidence of his evolution from an unfocused fourteen-year-old who had barely scraped by in his first term to an active participant in the life of the school. His knowledge of music and love of teaching soon emerged and he went on to form and conduct a school choir. Similarly, his first recorded foray into the editorial world occurred at Prince Alfred when he founded a short-lived school magazine.

The *Collegian Herald*, with its ready wit and scant regard for the feelings of others, bears an unmistakable resemblance to the *Triad* and reads like an introduction to his future career – even to the extent of bringing the threat of a libel action. The chief butt of his schoolboy humour was the German master, Herr Drew, who invariably wore a thick overcoat and muffler and treated the boys to unlikely endearments when he was angry. In a mock police court column, Herr Drew's lapses in hygiene were ruthlessly lampooned:

> *Herr X was charged at the Police Court this morning before Mr Beddome, P.M. with having a wash before six months had elapsed. His Honour decided by ocular demonstration that the prisoner was not guilty. Herr X left the Court without a stain on his character, though there were many on his person.*[13]

---

*   According to family tradition his father's sister, Suzette, whose first husband was a successful businessman in Ballarat, helped to pay the fees.

Even as a teenager, Charles's wits were as sharp as his tongue. As editor of the rag, he reputedly made enough money to buy himself a pair of trousers.

The headmaster Frederic Chapple's handling of the affair is a tribute to his understanding of the boys under his charge. Instead of punishing Charles for his disrespectful portrayal of the staff, he conceded that the idea of a school magazine was good, but insisted that in future the school should produce it. Its successor, the *Prince Alfred College Chronicle*, first appeared in 1884 and survives to this day.

Charles was fortunate in getting off so lightly. In Hahndorf, a similar escapade a few months earlier had ended up with the seventeen-year-old culprit, who had recently left the school, being dragged down the main street at the end of a rope and horsewhipped. While this punishment was being meted out by a former scholar and three of his friends, Boehm applauded loudly from his balcony.

An 1882 photograph of Prince Alfred's Class V shows Charles as a lanky fifteen-year old who sits, with angular shoulders, half a head taller than most of his fellows. The impressive physique for which he was later noted had not yet developed, but, in the midst of his round-cheeked classmates, his face shows an unusual maturity and his gaze is penetrating. To the left of the group stands Chapple, an authoritative figure resplendent in mortar board and gown who sports a luxuriant beard. A later picture, taken at the celebrations for Prince Alfred's twenty-fifth anniversary in 1894, shows Chapple in a more festive mood with a carnation in his buttonhole and surrounded by a crowd of parents and staff. In contrast with the sober attire of the other men, he wears a pair of check trousers under his dark frock coat, and in his left hand he is holding a large cigar.

Many echoes of Chapple, both in dress and demeanour, are discernible in Charles as an adult. For Charles he probably came closer to a father figure than anyone else and, apart from Emilia, exerted the greatest influence on his development. According to Charles, he was 'a model manager of boys'[14] who trusted in their honour and never used the cane. Despite having eight children of his own, he still found time to play cricket and tennis with his pupils and, on at least one occasion, Charles spent his Christmas holidays with him at the seaside resort of Port Elliot, exchanging pedantic classical witticisms and reading the odes of Horace.

In the *Triad*, Charles gave great credit to the 'wisdom and tact of the masters' at Prince Alfred, especially Chapple. In 1912 he wrote of the school in the following glowing terms: 'If any boy goes to a school like P.A.C. and does not leave it with a good grounding for the University, and a sane and generous outlook on life, he must have been abnormally lazy or extremely dull.'[15] A warm exchange of letters in 1915 is yet further evidence of Charles's enduring admiration for Chapple and of their mutual affection and respect.

Under such sympathetic tutelage, Charles blossomed. The only cloud was an almost complete absence of family life. Faithful to the lay preaching tradition established by John Wesley, who travelled continuously, Emilia spent much of her time on the road, moving from church to church throughout Adelaide and its outlying townships. The constant preaching and travelling took its toll of her – on one occasion she was described as being so weak that she was 'scarcely able to stand'[16] – and left her too drained to create a proper home for her children.

An article in the Baptist monthly, *Truth and Progress*, gives a rare glimpse of mother and son together. It is dated November 1882, when Charles was nearly sixteen and Emilia was holding a series of services at the Congregational Church in Adelaide's seaside suburb of Glenelg. The services took place in the evenings and the format was always the same:

> *Punctual to the moment, Mrs Baeyertz went on the platform and began the service with prayer, and preached from those wonderfully beautiful words – 'Ye must be born again.' She at once gained the attention of the vast congregation, and it was soon evident how anxiously they were, one and all, receiving the Word of Truth. Oh, the earnestness of this little woman, and the touching stories she related which brought tears to the eyes of strong men as well as women. She has a bright face and a very pleasant manner, but oh, so honest – the plain unvarnished Gospel – out of Christ, lost; in Christ, saved. No halfway, all or none.*[17]

At the back of the crowded hall, Charles sat at the organ, waiting for the final words of the sermon and the signal to play the hymn. He had attended dozens of Emilia's services and he knew most of her sermons, with such titles as 'The Great White Throne' and 'The Demoniac of Gadara', by heart. On the platform, the familiar figure of his mother in her modest black dress and bonnet stood motionless. Her expression was composed and serene, but her large dark eyes glowed with inner fire. Once the hymn was over, a hush fell on the congregation and Emilia made her appeal to those who wished to be saved. As her words died away, a frisson of excitement hung in the air. This was the moment they had all been waiting for and then, like a breaking wave, the congregation started to pour from their seats, some sobbing uncontrollably, and made their way up the aisle to offer their souls to God.

At some of the services, Charles's musical duties were more arduous. For example, on Friday 1 December, in addition to playing the hymn, he probably played the piano accompaniment for a Miss Stephens who favoured the congregation with two solos, 'Where is my boy tonight', and 'Ye must be born again'. When the services were over, Emilia invariably stayed behind to pray with the new converts. Charles watched her as she moved quietly among the seated groups, Bible in hand, listening and responding to questions. She would be there for many hours, but Charles had no interest in saving souls and he gathered up his music and made his way back to his lodgings alone.

During 1883 Charles became seriously ill and in September *Truth and Progress* reported that the 'public work of Mrs Baeyertz' had been interrupted for some time 'by the alarming position of her son through typhoid fever.' The illness must have struck during the term time because Charles later related that he was banished from the school sick-room to a hotel in Norwood where he was cared for by a mysterious Lady Colton. For weeks, his life hung on a thread and although 'the Lord' was 'pleased to restore him',[18] his final term at Prince Alfred was marked by extensive absences and in the school records the results of his partially completed examinations have been crossed out.

On this undistinguished note, his formal education appears to have ended, and he spent much of the following year accompanying his mother on her travels. Given her frequent state of 'physical and mental prostration',[19] she would have found his musical and filial support invaluable, especially as she was no longer enjoying a universally favourable press. By December 1883, her urgings to new converts to shun 'worldly amusements' and give up theatres, dancing parties and concerts provoked the following comment:

> *We are willing to admit that the previous services held here were to us in a measure disappointing, the wholesale denunciation of many things which are enjoyable, and her teaching would, if pushed to its logical conclusions, destroy much which goes to expand the soul, and magnify the powers which the Creator has bestowed upon us.*[20]

Although her mission in Adelaide had clearly run its course, Emelia's vocation was as strong as ever. During 1884 she undertook a series of pastoral visits to the aboriginal tribes, taking Charles with her. Several years later, Charles wrote an account for the *Otago Witness* of the three months he spent at the Maloga Mission Station on the Murray River, in which he combines a description of aboriginal customs with Darwinian musings on their place in evolution. His article also reveals, however, that much of his time was devoted to learning the Yorta Yorta dialect and gathering myths and legends from the local elders. In his opening paragraph, Charles refers to other contacts with the tribes, including 'in all their untamed *aboriginality* in the northern areas',[21] but these must have been brief trips for, by the end of the year, Emilia and her family had returned to civilisation and were living in the city that boasted the richest cultural life and the greatest number of 'worldly amusements' in Australia.

Chapter 3

Marvellous Melbourne

Thanks to the fortunes made in the gold rush, the booming metropolis to which Charles returned in late 1884 had become the seventh largest city in the British Empire and styled itself 'Marvellous Melbourne'. Its central business area was adorned with magnificent new buildings, many rising eight or nine storeys high, which established its reputation as one of the grandest cities of the era. The young British immigrant, Richard Twopeny, who later became editor of the *Otago Daily Times*, was captivated by its atmosphere of vitality:

> *There is a bustle and life about Melbourne which you altogether miss in Sydney. The Melbourne man is always on the look-out for business, the Sydney man waits for business to come to him ... And as it is with business, so it is with pleasure.*
>
> *If you are a man of leisure you will find more 'society' in Melbourne, more balls and parties, a larger measure of intellectual life – i.e. more books and men of education and intellect, more and better theatrical and musical performances ... all public amusements are far better attended in Melbourne; the people dress better, talk better, think better ... There is far more 'go' and far more 'life'.*[1]

A photograph of Melbourne's busy Collins Street, taken in the 1880s, confirms Twopeny's impressions. The pavements teem with life as streams of prosperous-looking citizens go about their daily business. Most of the men are in dark suits topped by neat Panama hats, while the women wear floating white dresses and elaborately decorated broad-brimmed hats. In the centre of the street, passengers are alighting from one of Melbourne's recently installed cable trams, while by the kerbside hansom cabs lurk like relics from a bygone age.

Perhaps the most potent symbol of Melbourne's prosperity and self-assurance was the extravagant new exhibition building, completed in 1880 to house an international exhibition on a grand scale. For nine months, Victoria's manufacturing achievements were displayed to the world, while exhibits from a number of European countries introduced Melburnians to the latest in world fashions. The Exhibition Gallery was hung with pictures by European artists, giving thousands of people their first taste of world-class painting – and a chance to ogle Jules Lefebvre's provocative nude, 'Chloe'.

In 1882 'Chloe' was hung in the National Gallery and triggered a heated dispute between Melbourne's powerful Sabbatarians – who condemned the picture and were opposed to gallery openings on Sundays – and the more liberal majority. The Sabbatarians won the day, and doubtless Emilia would have agreed with them and shared in their general disapproval of Melbourne's headlong pursuit of pleasure.

Meanwhile, against all the odds, Charles had emerged from his extraordinary childhood with a mind of his own. His enduring respect for his mother is demonstrated by the dedication of his first book in which he describes her as 'a true noblewoman',[2] but he never allowed her puritanical views to interfere with his enjoyment of the theatre and the concert hall – or his appreciation of worldly pleasures. Given the atmosphere of high seriousness in which he was raised, it is astonishing that his sense of humour had also survived intact. Humour, often verging on ridicule, became one of his preferred journalistic weapons, and in later life his well-turned sallies were seized on with delight by readers of the *Triad*.

At this stage, Charles seems to have had few career plans. With no one but his unworldly mother to advise him, he undertook no professional training nor did he attend university. Instead he read voraciously and indulged his passion for music by acting as choirmaster in various churches and playing the organ at Melbourne Cathedral. Most of his activities are undocumented, but his passing reference to being hailed on the street by a German importer and invited to try out a newly arrived organ suggests the leisurely life of a man about town with an established musical reputation. Despite the absence of formal study, his intellectual growth continued apace. In the rich cultural environment of Melbourne, his exposure to some world-class musical and dramatic performances equipped him with a standard of excellence on which many of his future judgements were based.

Throughout the 1880s, Melbourne's musical public was catered for by a succession of visiting soloists of whom so many were European that for Australians and New Zealanders a European name – preferably German – became almost as a requirement for anyone claiming to be an authority on music. Thus, when Charles was seeking to establish himself as a music critic in Dunedin, his German-sounding surname – which later created such difficulties – was initially a distinct professional advantage. Furthermore, his familiarity with the many international artists who visited Melbourne in the 1880s and continued to tour Australia and New Zealand during the

1890s and 1900s gave his reviews in the *Triad* an edge over those in the local newspapers.

Melbourne also offered a wide selection of light opera and theatre, building on a tradition that stretched right back to February 1842 when the first dramatic performance was given in a ramshackle wooden structure, optimistically named the Theatre Royal. During the gold rush years, the theatrical life of Melbourne flourished as aspiring impresarios and artists poured into the colony to share in the spoils. Some of the more daring, such as the Irish-born adventuress Lola Montez, even took their talents to the goldfields. Lola's suggestive 'Spider Dance', which was no more Spanish than she was, was described by the *Argus* as 'the most libertinish and indelicate performance'.[3] But it went down well with the diggers of Ballarat.

Throughout the 1860s and 1870s, William Lyster and his Melbourne-based troupe produced a steady stream of operatic performances from their French, German and Italian repertoire. After Lyster's death, his mantle was assumed by his nephew, George Musgrove, who joined forces with the American impresario, James Cassius Williamson, and introduced Australasian audiences to a host of contemporary light operas, including the works of Gilbert and Sullivan.

Williamson's and Musgrove's opera companies toured regularly and remained a feature of Australasia's cultural life for over thirty years. Initially most of their singers were British or European, but by the 1880s some of the most popular and talented artists were local, such as Sydney-born Nellie Stewart who in 1886 was taking Melbourne audiences by storm with her performance as Yum Yum in *The Mikado*. Meanwhile in distant Brussels, the daughter of a Melbourne building contractor, who had adopted the name of Nellie Melba in honour of her native city, was poised to embark on her meteoric career in grand opera with a performance in *Rigoletto*.

But life in Melbourne was not all culture and concerts. The city also had a seamy side, with prostitutes operating so blatantly at nights on such major thoroughfares as Collins, Bourke and Flinders Streets that pious churchgoers abandoned their attempts to attend evening service, for fear of being accosted. In 1884, sixty-nine brothels were known to the police and the number of prostitutes was estimated to be the highest of any Australian city. Imbued with his mother's teaching and the strictures of Methodism, it is unlikely that Charles succumbed to Melbourne's 'social evil'. But as a tall, well-developed eighteen-year-old, who was a useful member of a local football team,* his custom may well have been solicited – and he was certainly well aware of

---

* An unidentified newspaper cutting describes him as: 'Baeyertz – Fine Kick; renders good service to the forwards; rather slow, but has improved.' (Newspaper Cutting Book, Hocken MS-0464-3)

women. Even at Prince Alfred College, he and his classmates had taken an interest in the girls at a nearby school.

In an age when sexual abstinence was the only morally permissible alternative to matrimony, Charles's early marriage, at barely twenty, comes as no surprise. His choice of bride, however, was unexpected. Isabella Delgarno Johnston was eight years his senior, and beside his youthful good looks she cut a homely and dumpy figure. For Charles, however, her homeliness may have been one of her greatest attractions. After a nomadic childhood, much of which was spent as a boarder, Charles must have longed for a place that he could call home. His description of the kindly, competent Isabella – whose eyes twinkled with humour and whose upturned mouth seemed permanently disposed to smile – as the most beautiful woman he had ever seen may also have reflected his desire for someone who would combine the qualities of a mother with a wife.

They were married on 21 December 1886 at the Baptist Church in Kew by the Rev. James Blaikie, assisted by Isabella's father, the Rev. Kerr Johnston, who was the Port of Melbourne's first Missioner to Seamen. The wedding, which was reported in the 'Society News' of the local paper, was a traditional affair with the bride in white Indian silk and a wreath of orange blossom and the three bridesmaids in white muslin carrying baskets of white flowers. After the ceremony, the seventy-odd guests were treated to a wedding breakfast in the schoolroom adjoining the church, where Charles responded with 'a few well-chosen words' to the toast in honour of the bride and groom.

Judging from the guest list, the Baeyertz family was thin on the ground. Charles's grandfather had died in 1879 and the only Baeyertz uncle, John, had long since emigrated to California. But his paternal aunt, Suzette, and her husband were present, as were Emilia's brother George Aronson and his wife, together with his partner in the jewellery business, David Rosenthal. When the meal was over, all the guests trooped over to the bride's house 'to view the numerous and handsome presents',[4] before the newly weds departed by train for their honeymoon in Ballarat. On their return, Charles and Isabella settled down to married life at 3 College Parade, Kew, not far from the homes of Emilia and Isabella's parents.

Emilia would have approved of Isabella's clerical connections and probably regarded the union as a happy deliverance for Charles from the temptations of the flesh. She may even have had a hand in the match. Isabella certainly made a point of getting on with her mother-in-law. After her marriage, she is reported as singing the hymn 'I know that my Redeemer liveth' 'with thrilling pathos and inimitable expression'[5] before one of Emilia's religious addresses.

Charles's marriage gave him, for the first time in his life, a sense of domestic security. From all accounts, Bella (as Charles always called her) was a good homemaker and an excellent cook. She was also an accomplished pianist who, before her marriage, had spent many hours playing accompaniments for sailors at the Mission to Seamen – an experience that would certainly have broadened her mind. Like Charles, she was born in Australia, although only just. Her mother had gone into labour at the end of the long sea voyage from Britain and had to be rushed ashore just short of Melbourne at the port of Williamstown to give birth in the home of a retired sea captain named Delgarno. Bella's middle name was an acknowledgement of his wife's assistance at her birth.

Within a few months, Bella was expecting a baby and the need for Charles to provide for his expanding family became pressing. He was without regular employment, but money-making opportunities were plentiful and he plunged, with all the incautiousness of his late father, into Melbourne's feverish property market. The Melbourne land boom of the 1880s was an extraordinary phenomenon that was fuelled by the need to house the exploding population and the large sums of capital that were being poured into the economy by domestic and British investors. From 1882 onwards new buildings were being rushed up all over the city in a frenzy of buying and selling. Between 1886 and 1888, the pace became more frenetic still as the population of Victoria rose by ten per cent through immigration alone. Most of the new arrivals settled in Melbourne, where land prices spiralled to dizzy heights. In the inner city, a corner of Collins and Elizabeth streets was sold at £2300 a foot, and in the suburbs fortunes were made overnight as land that was bought by the acre was sold by the yard.

In the prevailing atmosphere of wild optimism, banks and building societies leapt on the bandwagon with offers of loans at generous rates in return for cash deposits. Huge capital gains were made as properties changed hands, and even though the profits were largely on paper, the prospect of untold wealth lured thousands of small investors into the property market. No records of Charles's property speculations survive, but they would hardly have kept him fully occupied. Between deals, he probably continued to pursue his musical interests and add to his encyclopaedic knowledge by reading.

Despite his editorial escapades at Prince Alfred College, nothing suggests that, during these palmy days in Melbourne, Charles exercised his journalistic talents. Like many others, his hopes were pinned on the property market and the dazzling rewards that it seemed to offer. Nevertheless, with his lively mind and intellectual interests, he would certainly have been familiar with leading local periodicals, such as the famous Sydney *Bulletin*; the more literary *Australian Journal*, in which Marcus Clarke's outback classic *For the term of his Natural Life* first appeared as a serial; *Melbourne Punch* with all its echoes of its British counterpart; and *Table Talk*, whose columns of political commentary were interspersed with social gossip.

Jostling these homegrown publications were British and American magazines with far greater financial resources and, in the case of the British ones, a postage rate of one penny which made it as cheap to mail a magazine from England as from within Australia – or New Zealand. In addition, the British publications had the advantage of a strong sentimental appeal to the many colonists who were eager for news of the motherland. For such readers, the intellectual and literary standing of periodicals like the *Edinburgh Review* and *Blackwood's Magazine* far surpassed anything that was locally produced. Even the most homely of the British publications, *Household Words*, with its hints on cooking and gardening (and how to look after your piano), had the huge cachet of being edited by Charles Dickens.

Despite the strong competition from overseas, however, local periodicals had a trump card in Australia's growing sense of nationalism, which the *Bulletin*'s pugnacious editor, Jules François Archibald, exploited to the full. With its strongly anti-British stance and its championship of the underdog, Archibald's modest weekly soon became the region's most influential publication and a forum for local writers like Henry Lawson, whose authentic 'outback' style appealed to Archibald's nationalist sentiments. Within two years of its first issue on 31 January 1880, the *Bulletin*'s circulation had reached 22,000; by 1889 this figure had risen to 80,000 and the magazine had acquired such a following amongst workers in the outback that it was known as 'the bushman's bible'.

The effectiveness of Archibald's punchy editorial style and his insistence on short, sharp paragraphing were not lost on his competitors. When Maurice Brodsky founded *Table Talk* in 1885, he modelled his layout on the *Bulletin* and copied its bright pink cover. But Charles's reactions to the *Bulletin* would have been mixed, for despite his birth in provincial Colac and his exclusively Australian boyhood, his outlook was innately cosmopolitan. His focus was always more European than Antipodean, and the *Bulletin*'s aggressive nationalism (which some claimed mistook parochialism for patriotism) would have struck few chords with him. Far closer to his heart would have been the objectives set out in the first issue of the *Australian Journal* in 1865 'to interest and amuse and, if possible, instruct everybody who will read us'. Moreover, a distinct echo of the *Journal*'s stated aim of directing attention to 'the triumphs of art … until these pages reflect the literature, art, and science of Australia'[6] can be found in the early issues of the *Triad*.

Shortly before the birth of their first baby, Charles and Bella moved a few houses up the street to 44 College Parade, where their son was born on 12 February 1888. He was christened Charles – although he was always known as Carl – and, with three grandparents and his Baeyertz great-grandmother all living in the vicinity, his arrival must have prompted some family celebrations. For Charles this was a golden period and his self-confidence and ebullience knew no bounds. He was living in one of the most exciting cities of the epoch; he was young and bursting with energy and, according to those who knew him well, he was maddeningly good at everything.

In a letter written many years later, the New Zealand lawyer and journalist Richard Singer complained to fellow journalist, Pat Lawlor, that Charles's reputation was based on the fact 'that he was able to do all sorts of things, from writing to playing cards and billiards, a little bit better than the average person.'[7] Rudolph's reminiscences reinforce this view and describe him as 'a good rifle shot … a heady chess player … a master at whist and other card games' and 'one of the best snooker players in New Zealand'.[8]

Outside the family circle, the mood was similarly upbeat as Melbourne's joy ride of civic extravagances roared on. In 1887 Queen Victoria's Golden Jubilee had been celebrated by a grand illumination of the streets, and on 1 August 1888 the most ambitious enterprise ever undertaken by the city was marked by the elaborate opening of the Centennial International Exhibition. The exhibition, which was to celebrate Australia's first centenary, ran for six months and cost the Government of Victoria more than £250,000. Its scope was far wider than the exhibition of 1880 and was intended to embrace not only the manufacturing achievements of the Australian colonies and other countries, but also all major aspects of culture, including art and music.

For the princely sum of £5000, the eminent conductor, Frederic Cowen, was enticed from London to take up a ten-month engagement and form Melbourne's first full orchestra by bringing fourteen special instrumentalists with him. He also made up a choir of 700 voices from local volunteers and performed over 250 concerts during the course of his visit. The memoirs of a contemporary writer, Ada Cambridge, reflect the intense excitement that the exhibition generated:

> *It was the high tide in the fortunes … generally speaking of the whole community … It was now that I heard so much good music, saw so much good acting, met so many interesting travellers … enjoyed the most memorable entertainments of a time when nothing but the first rate was tolerated.*
>
> *Ah, those days! … Scores and scores of those orchestral concerts (under Frederick Cowen's conductorship) I must have attended, first and last; there were two a day and they gave you the best music of all countries, and you only had to stroll into the hall and sit down and listen, as if in your own house.*

Ada's enthusiasm for the free concerts was only exceeded by her enjoyment of the Exhibition Gallery, where a display of 2000 pictures was on loan from important collections in Britain, France, Germany, Belgium and Austro-Hungary:

> *The Art Galleries of the Exhibition were more to us than the Concert Hall, for we were more in them. Amongst the Loan Pictures, of one country or another, we met our friends; here we sat on soft lounges to muse upon our favourites ... You could live there all day long ... When the place was shut at last, we wandered forlorn and lost for a long time. We were spoiled for humdrum life.*[9]

The closing of the Centennial Exhibition was not the only reason for gloom in early 1889. It was also the moment when the seemingly unstoppable land boom began to falter. Land prices had reached unsustainable levels and two major speculators were already in financial difficulties. Over the months that followed, public concern grew and the more nervous investors rushed to withdraw their deposits. Banks and building societies retrenched by raising the deposit rate and restricting advances on property, but the economy was already out of control and heading into a dangerous downward spin. By 1891, land prices had plummeted and the buildings and properties which had formed the major assets of the banks and building societies had become almost worthless. Many of Melbourne's financial institutions were no longer solvent and thousands of people lost not only their deposit, but also their savings. In August 1891, four of Melbourne's major banks closed their doors and many others followed.

Charles must have been one of the earlier victims of the crash. In later life, he never spoke about his disastrous property speculations, but according to family sources, his losses were heavy. Nor could they have been more ill timed, for with the birth of his daughter, Maida, in December 1889, the number of his dependents had increased to three. By now he and Bella were living in Burke Street, Hawthorn, but a few months later they moved again – perhaps for reasons of economy – to the small house in which Emilia had lived at 9 Studley Park Road in Kew. In an attempt to salvage his finances, Charles tried to set up a business; in a couple of 1891 Melbourne trade directories his name appears under the unlikely guise of Tea Merchant. His efforts, however, were short-lived and apparently met with little success. Business confidence was at zero, unemployment was rife, and as Melbourne's population dwindled, the swashbuckling metropolis which had seemed to promise so much became a ghost town of empty office blocks and abandoned suburbs. Life in 'Marvellous Melbourne' now spelt nothing but financial ruin and, like thousands of others, Charles and Bella decided to leave.

Their decision to move to New Zealand was probably influenced by several factors. It was closer and more culturally compatible than either Perth or California, to which many of the other refugees from the crash were fleeing. In addition, the southern city of Dunedin – on which Charles had set his sights – was the main New Zealand port of entry from Victoria and had a long tradition of links with Melbourne. Whether or not he was aware that the country was in the throes of a serious economic depression, or that in 1889 the net emigration of New Zealanders to Australia exceeded arrivals, is not recorded.

Another consideration may have been Emilia's recent nine-month tour of New Zealand, which had started in January 1890 in Dunedin and by any standards had been a spectacular success. Throughout the country she enjoyed the constant and flattering attentions of the press. In Christchurch she was described as 'one of the finest platform speakers we have been privileged to listen to',[10] in Wellington she was called 'an elocutionist of the first order',[11] and in Auckland her audience of men and boys was so carried away by her eloquence that they responded to her earnest appeal 'not to give way to the devil of passion'[12] with repeated applause.

In 6 October, she and Marion (who acted as her private secretary) sailed from Auckland for an extended tour of the United States and Canada, where she often drew such large audiences that it was impossible to find a hall to accommodate them. But although her American mission was on a far greater scale, her impressions of New Zealand were particularly favourable and she probably conveyed this to Charles and Bella.

In March 1891, the following notice seeking employment appeared in the educational columns of the *Otago Daily Times*: 'Organist, from Melbourne, First-class, open Engagement'.[13] This may well have been inserted by Charles who, with little more than the clothes on his back and a generous measure of chutzpah, set sail on 24 February 1891 for a new life in New Zealand.

Chapter 4

Dunedin

Charles departed from Melbourne aboard the SS *Hauroto*, which plied the so-called 'Horse Shoe' run between Port Chalmers,* Sydney and Melbourne. Although he was without his family, who were to follow later, he had every reason to believe that this would be an enjoyable trip. The *Hauroto* was well-appointed and, as a saloon passenger, he would have access to a library of 'two hundred select volumes all uniformly bound'[1] and a comfortable smoking room where he could indulge his taste for cigars.

Since this was his maiden voyage across the Tasman, as well as his first journey outside Australia, the full significance of the tightly screwed footcaps and plates that secured the dining room tables and chairs to the decks may have eluded him. But his first taste of the Tasman was not slow in coming. Within a few hours of leaving Melbourne, the *Hauroto* was ploughing into strong southerly winds and a heavy sea. Her first port of call was Hobart, where the passengers had a brief respite before heading for Bluff. In the meantime, sailing conditions had deteriorated still further. The shipping reports in the *Otago Daily Times* describe them as 'strong S. and S.W. winds with high sea and rain squalls,'[2] but Charles's account of the shipboard Sunday service paints a rather more vivid picture: 'We had a shocking passage from Hobart to the Bluff. The hatches were battened down for three days and on the Sunday Captain Neville came down and preached to a visible audience of stewards and an invisible audience of seasick passengers.' In mountainous seas, the captain's choice of hymns – 'For those in peril on the sea' and 'I triumph still in death if Thou be near' – may have been apt, but, according to Charles, after 'three fearsome days and nights'[3] they reduced the passengers to a state of terror.

By the time the *Hauroto* reached Bluff, Charles had had enough and he and a fellow passenger decided to forfeit their boat tickets to Port Chalmers and take the train. Both men were ravenously hungry and at neighbouring Invercargill they alighted to sample two dozen oysters and a bottle of stout before continuing northwards to Dunedin. Charles's first view of New

---

* The port of Dunedin.

Zealand would have been of rolling pastureland and rounded hills, that gave little hint of the spectacular scenery of the Southern Alps. But even in the quieter landscape of Southland, he could not have failed to notice the striking contrast between the countryside of New Zealand and that of his native Australia.

Several years earlier the British novelist, Anthony Trollope, who had made the same voyage from Melbourne and had also disembarked at Bluff, commented on the differences:

> It would be impossible to imagine any country more unlike Australia ... a remark which I may as well make once for all, and which may be applied to everything in New Zealand. The two countries both grow wool, and are both auriferous. Squatters and miners are common to them. But in all outward features they are dissimilar, – as they are also in the manners of the people, and in the forms of their government.[4]

To Trollope's Eurocentric eye 'all New Zealand towns are more like England than are the towns of Australia' and he found the native bush infinitely preferable to 'the everlasting gum forests'.[5] No similar record of Charles's first impressions survives, but later, when he had seen more of the country, he was quite explicit about his scenic preferences: 'We have nothing of its kind to equal Sydney Harbour ... Otherwise, our scenery is incomparably finer than that of Australia. There is nothing in Australia at all comparable with our Southern Lakes, Milford Sound, Mount Cook, the West Coast, the Wanganui River, or our thermal district.'[6] On the other hand, until he reached Dunedin, he may have found New Zealand's towns, such as the little settlements of Mataura, Gore and Balclutha which lay along his route, rather modest in comparison with their Australian counterparts. But Dunedin was a major city, and although his first impressions are once again undocumented, he would doubtless have agreed with Trollope that it was 'a remarkably handsome town'.[7]

Dunedin was New Zealand's first great commercial centre, transformed by the discovery of gold in 1861 from a modest settlement of Scottish Presbyterians to a bustling city. By 1871 the Otago goldfields had produced £23,000,000 and Otago had become the wealthiest province in New Zealand, with a population of 70,000 at a time when the total European population of the country was only 300,000. As in Melbourne, much of Otago's new-found wealth was invested in Dunedin, whose straggling, muddy streets were soon paved and lit with gas, and lined with imposing buildings.

At the time of Trollope's visit in 1872, many of Dunedin's most notable landmarks, such as the university and the Municipal Chambers, had yet to be built, and its elegant First Church was still under construction. But the magnificent Provincial Building in Princes Street (which also housed the post office), flanked by the classical facades of banks and insurance companies, already gave the city an air of self-importance which Trollope, with his unerring knack for pinpointing human vanity, gently ridicules:

> *The Provincial Chambers was not sitting, but I was shown the chamber in which it is held. The members sit, like Siamese twins, in great arm-chairs, which are joined together, two-and-two, like semi-detached villas ... The architecture, furniture, and general apparel of these Houses ... struck me as being almost grander than was necessary. The gentlemen as they sit are very much more comfortable than are the members of our own House at home, and are much better lodged than are the legislators in the States of the American Union. The congress of Massachusetts sits in a building which has indeed an imposing exterior, but the chamber itself inspires less awe than does that of Otago.*[8]

Perhaps it was just as well that he was eight years too early to see the Municipal Chambers rising in the Octagon with its unabashed echoes of Michelangelo's Capitoline Palace in Rome.

When Charles arrived in 1891, Dunedin was no longer New Zealand's largest city. According to the census taken in April 1891, the urban populations of Auckland and Wellington were slightly larger, but despite the drift of business to the North Island, Dunedin could still lay claim to being the country's leading industrial and commercial centre. Many of New Zealand's foremost businesses were based there, and even the long depression of the 1880s, when a dramatic fall in export prices for wool and wheat plunged New Zealand into an economic recession, had not extinguished the city's entrepreneurial spirit. In late 1889, less than a year after the closing of Melbourne's grandiose Centennial International Exhibition, the citizens of Dunedin mounted an elaborate international exhibition of their own, which attracted 600,000 visitors and, against all the odds, proved to be a resounding financial success.

From the mayhem of the Melbourne crash, *The Strangers' Vade-Mecum or South Land Guide* – which was specially published for visitors to the New Zealand and South Seas Exhibition – would have made encouraging reading. Furthermore its references to Dunedin as 'the largest, best built and most important commercial city in New Zealand'[9] suggest that the civic pride, so acutely observed by Trollope nearly two decades earlier, had survived intact.

The *Vade-Mecum*'s ninety-three pages are packed with useful tourist information, illustrated with attractive engravings of the city's finest buildings and interspersed with frequent reminders that 'Joel's Bottled Ale is the Best in the Market' and that 'Reingold Cigars are Delicious'.[10] Thanks to the championship of the *Otago Daily Times*, now edited by Richard Twopeny,* the business community had quickly grasped the commercial opportunities of the exhibition. But Twopeny also enlisted the support of Dunedin's art lovers and intellectuals to ensure that the city's cultural life, like that of Melbourne, was enhanced by concerts and a display of art. Amongst the members and chairmen of the various organising committees were the eminent collector and bibliographer, Dr Hocken, the ex-premier Sir Robert Stout (who had lost his seat in the 1887 elections and was temporarily outside Parliament), and William Hodgkins, the founder of New Zealand's first art society whose daughter, Frances, became one of New Zealand's most celebrated artists.

The exhibition ran for six months. By the time it closed on 19 April 1890 it had not only raised business confidence in New Zealand, but had also furthered the causes of music and art by attracting two talented Italians to settle in Dunedin. The first was the violinist and conductor, Raffaello Squarise, who had been lured from Adelaide to lead the exhibition orchestra and decided to stay permanently. The second was an accomplished artist named Girolamo Nerli, who had several paintings in the exhibition gallery and enjoyed his visit so much that in 1893 he returned to live in New Zealand.

But behind its prosperous face, particularly in the squalid suburbs of Caversham and South Dunedin, the city offered glimpses of poverty and degradation that were quite as shocking as those of industrial England. Streetwalkers may have been less common than in Melbourne, but Dunedin's vaunted commercial enterprises were making their profits at a terrible human cost. Many of the victims were employed in the clothing industry and the practice of 'putting out' tailoring work to women who worked at home – or in sweat shops – for pitiful wages was widespread.

In October 1888, a fiery Irish cleric named Rutherford Waddell startled his well-heeled Dunedin congregation by delivering a damning sermon on 'The Sin of Cheapness' in which he exposed the evils of 'sweating'. His revelations created an uproar and eventually led to the passing of pioneering legislation for the protection of workers. In early 1891, in the aftermath of a bitter maritime strike, a new Liberal Government came to power, which over the next decade established New Zealand's reputation as a world leader in social reform.

In Charles's case, the social agenda of the new Liberal Government would not have been foremost in his mind. His most pressing need was to find

---

* Twopeny, who edited the *Otago Daily Times* from 1883–90, had previously worked with the general manager of the South Seas Exhibition, Jules Joubert, on exhibitions in Adelaide, Perth and Christchurch.

work and a place to live. After the urban sprawl of Melbourne, he would have found Dunedin very compact, with its cluster of public and commercial buildings on the flats beside the harbour enclosed by the semicircle of the surrounding hills. From the main commercial area, the streets rose steeply, lined with modest wooden buildings perched precariously on narrow ledges cut into the hillside. Above them on the hilltops – or wherever the terrain was less rugged – stood the larger houses of the rich with commanding views across the harbour to the peninsula and out to the Pacific beyond.

His choice of lodgings fell on London Street, which lay just below the Town Belt* and was considered a most desirable location. Several local dignitaries such as Sir Robert Stout and Bendix Hallenstein, the founder of the Hallenstein clothing empire, had lived in London Street for years, and recently Hallenstein's son-in-law, Willi Fels, had also moved there. Adjoining it was Royal Terrace, where Frances Hodgkins was born and spent much of her childhood. By 1891 the Hodgkins were living in the neighbouring suburb of Melrose, but many of their wealthy neighbours, including the intellectual and cultured Theomins, were still in residence.

For any newcomer wishing to establish himself professionally and socially, London Street was an excellent address. Charles had been fortunate and shrewd. But the search for suitable employment was less straightforward. In the first place, he had no professional background and his abortive efforts as a tea merchant, and his losses in the Melbourne property market, had left him wary of going into business. More importantly, however, in this new environment, he was determined to find an occupation that was closely associated with his greatest interest – music.

Ever since his schooldays, Charles's love of music had been a driving force in his life. By the time he reached Dunedin, he possessed a degree of musical knowledge and expertise that already far exceeded the high musical expectations of his generation. In an era when domestic and social amusements often revolved around music and singing, Charles's accomplishments on the organ and piano were nothing exceptional, especially given his mother's links with the church. What was unusual, however, for someone without any formal musical qualifications, was the depth of his understanding of music, in all its forms, and his grasp of the technical aspects of singing and voice production.

Much of his knowledge of composition and musical history was self-taught and could have been gleaned from memorising great chunks of Grove's musical dictionary, which was one of his treasured possessions.

---

* A 500-acre swathe of grass and trees, which had been designated as a scenic reserve by Dunedin's progressive Scottish planners before the settlement began.

Thanks to his experience as a choirmaster, he was also familiar with a large number of contemporary works on singing and the vocal exercises of such well-known teachers as Cherubini, Concone, Lamperti, Garcia and Balfe. But as his precise and authoritative music criticism later demonstrates, in addition to his wide-ranging interest in music (and his prodigious memory), he possessed an extraordinary ear. When he first considered music as a career, Charles thought of himself simply as a musician, and in *Stone's Otago & Southland Directory* for 1892, this is how he is described. It took him two years to realise that his ability to distinguish every nuance of a singer's or musician's performance was the key to his true vocation.

In the meantime, he pinned his hopes on the glowing reference that he had obtained from the Dean of Melbourne, extolling his talents as an organist. But no engagements were forthcoming. Dunedin had more than enough organists, and with Bella and the children waiting anxiously for news that he had found a job, Charles turned to one of the few occupations for which his unconventional upbringing had prepared him – music teaching. Here too, however, he was out of luck, for in 1891 New Zealand was awash with registered music teachers. Dunedin alone had over twenty and furthermore, only a year earlier, Squarise had opened his impressively named Otago Conservatorio of Music, with a staff of three, leaving few pickings for an unknown newcomer.

By the time Bella and the children arrived in May, after a rather more comfortable crossing on the *Manapouri*, Charles had his back to the wall and was ready to try his hand at anything. He started giving singing lessons at home and even passed himself off as a lecturer in German and French at the university, but judging from the tales that have survived, this foray into academia was not a success. In later life he admitted to being relieved of his duties for choosing Mark Twain's 'Dreadful German Language' as the subject of his first lecture. According to Charles, the dour Scottish professor informed him that 'there was to be no lawkin' arroond in the lecture rrroom',[11] but the students loved him and followed him to a local hotel where he continued his lessons privately.

Another anecdote dating from this precarious period concerns a tram conductor who asked Charles to teach him classical Greek. After many months of tuition, it eventually emerged that his objective was 'to read the new Testament in the language which was spoken by our Saviour'.[12] When Charles explained that 'our Saviour' spoke Aramaic rather than Greek, his pupil stormed out of the house and never returned.

In Dunedin, the influence of the city's Presbyterian founders was still all-pervasive. Coming from the more liberal atmosphere of Melbourne, Charles soon discovered that his own secular and irreverent outlook was very much at odds with the piety and high seriousness of his fellow townsmen. He was not a religious man, and although he attended church on Sundays, his sincerest devotions were offered at the altars of music and literature.

But he took cultural matters very seriously, and he would have shared in the distaste of Dunedin's 'old identities' for the tawdry musical and theatrical fare served up during the gold-rush years by such shady figures as the 'impresario' Shadrach Jones and his sidekick, Henry Farley. Nor would he have had a good word for most of the entertainments provided at the notorious Vauxhall Gardens, which were created above Andersons Bay on the far side of the harbour and became a favourite haunt of the diggers – and the young women who helped them to empty their pockets. Unlike Dunedin's founding fathers, however, Charles's disdain for second-rate vaudeville was not based on moral disapproval. It was simply that, as a discerning consumer, he had little tolerance of any performance that fell below his standards.

During these early days, as he listened to the thunderous sermons delivered weekly by the Rev. Stuart from the pulpit of fashionable Knox Church, it must sometimes have seemed to Charles that little had changed in Dunedin since the private life of Robbie Burns had been subjected to moral scrutiny before the more righteous members of the public would subscribe to his statue in the Octagon. Cleanliness still came next to Godliness, closely followed by social conscience, business acumen and thrift.

In this staid society, Charles's cosmopolitan swagger, as he strode around the streets resplendent in his pin-stripe suit, fooled no one. What he most needed were solid credentials, and his decision to write a series of articles on singing for Dunedin's weekly paper, the *Otago Witness*, was a timely promotional exercise aimed at establishing himself as a teacher.

For this first attempt at serious journalism, Charles wore his knowledge lightly and adopted a slightly avuncular tone that was carefully pitched at his target audience of aspiring young singers and their mothers. Even the rather alarming diagram of the larynx, which appeared with the opening article on the 'Mechanism of the Voice and the Art of Singing', was tempered by the reassuring statement that 'if the reader resolves not to be frightened by physiological terms ... he ought to experience no great difficulty in obtaining a clear notion ... of the human voice-box.'[13] The articles that followed were packed with practical tips and frank advice against wasting money on 'the silly songs which many English composers are writing today'.[14] The series concluded with a homily on the merits of hard work and training and 'the low ebb at which the art of singing now lies in this country'.[15]

His articles must have been well received because the *Witness* promptly accepted six more in which Charles gave a sweeping panorama of musical history and ranged effortlessly over the origins of dance music, symphonies, sonatas and oratorio. Their more academic tone would have pleased the *Witness*, which prided itself on being the cultural arm of its daily counterpart, the *Times*. In the Christmas number, Charles's contributions were more light-hearted, consisting of a dig at Dunedin audiences for their unseemly behaviour at concerts and his article on the Australian aborigines.

Publication with the highly respected *Witness* undoubtedly improved Charles's prospects. Once the Christmas holidays were over, he placed a notice in the *Times* informing the public that he had resumed tuition in 'Singing, Voice Production and Voice Cultivation' at his 'Residence, London Street'.[16] He also capitalised on the success of his first four articles by prefacing them with an additional chapter and, 'at the request of several pupils and friends',[17] sending them off to be printed in a slim volume called *Voice Culture*, which was priced at one shilling. Meanwhile to fill in his spare time, he took part in a number of fundraising concerts where he played the organ and recited humorous pieces. In July, his journalistic apprenticeship with the *Witness* bore further fruit when he was engaged by George Fenwick,* who had recently taken over as Editor of the *Times*, to write music and theatre reviews.

This was Charles's first opportunity to exercise his critical skills and he wielded his pen with gusto. But his views did not always coincide with those of Dunedin's closely knit intellectual élite. Before long he had picked an unseemly quarrel with the author of a weekly column in the *Witness* entitled 'Passing Notes', who wrote under the name of 'Civis'. 'Passing Notes' had been a feature firstly of the *Times* and then also of the *Witness* for over three decades and were traditionally written by a prominent citizen whose identity was kept secret. By 1892, the role of 'Civis' had been assumed by Frederick Fitchett, a notable scholar whose witty and provocative column ranged over any subject of topical interest that took his fancy. On 7 July, the target of his pen was the programme offered by a visiting organist named Mr Jude:

> *We may assume that Mr Jude could play a Bach fugue if he liked, and ... we must believe that he is capable of better things at the organ than the imitating of harps and hurdy gurdies, the rattle of rain on a tin roof and the rumblings of stage thunder among the lower pedals. 'Descriptive organ music', forsooth! A single overture of Handel's were worth the whole lot of it.*[18]

Charles seized upon Fitchett's remarks with glee. He knew him well and admired his writing on political and economic matters, but the temptation to flex his musical muscles and score off a successful columnist fourteen years

---

* George Fenwick was also the managing director of both the *Times* and the *Witness*, which were under the same management.

his senior was irresistible. In the following week's *Witness*, he threw down the gauntlet:

> *What a pity it is that when a great musical genius visits us and tries to entertain and instruct us, musically ignorant cavillers, knowing nothing whatever about the subject, should rush in and criticise a performance at which they were probably not present, and talk glibly about fugues and Händel overtures for the organ – the former utterly beyond their comprehension, the latter nonexistent. – I am &c., C.N. Baeyertz.*[19]

'Civis' hit back hard. Charles's tone was insufferably arrogant and he needed to be taken down a peg. But Charles never embarked on a fight that he was not sure of winning and his claim that Handel never wrote an overture for organ was correct. All 'Civis' could do was to rebut a gratuitous aside that Charles had made on his grammar and suggest, with heavy sarcasm, that while 'Mr Baeyertz is at liberty to talk in any form of broken English that may be agreeable to him ... where he becomes absurd is in wanting to set up the Baeyertz dialect as the standard of grammatical propriety.' A further reference to Charles's 'imperfect knowledge of English'[20] made the slur on his non-British origins explicit. Charles reacted furiously and fired off a long-winded reply. At the end of September, the correspondence flared up again when 'Civis' made some further unflattering comments about a visiting performer.

Charles opened the engagement with a letter to the *Times* which began: 'Civis is once again consumed with the desire to figure as a musical critic, and with as little success as on the former occasion.' As usual, Charles was completely sure of his musical ground and deftly overturned Civis's criticisms. Possibly aware, however, that he had overstepped the mark in his earlier correspondence, he concluded on a conciliatory note: 'Now, Sir, believe me to be when you are seated, and clothed, and in your right mind, an admirer of Civis.'[21]

The response from 'Civis' was withering:

> *If Mr Baeyertz ... desired to be mentioned once more in 'Passing Notes', he has attained his object. I cannot afford him a note all to himself, but I have put him in the common sink, with which degree of honour I hope he will be content.*[22]

The Johnsonian reference* would not have been lost on Charles, but he still got the last word in his reply that 'nothing better could be expected from one

---

* The reference is to Samuel Johnson's quip that literary men were 'fittest for the common sink'.

who frankly confesses that a portion of his column is nothing more than a common sink.'[23]

The encounter, largely provoked by Charles, was New Zealand's first glimpse of him as a fearless disrespecter of persons, fighting his corner with his sleeves rolled up. But it was also a symptom of his growing frustration at having nothing more challenging to do than teach singing and produce toothless reviews for an audience 'rather difficult to realise for critical purposes, in a paper traditionally unwilling to offend'.[24] Fortunately, a fresh outlet for his energies soon presented itself, and by November he had been appointed as musical director for a forthcoming series of popular concerts. The venture was the brainchild of a committee of local worthies, aimed at raising support for the Saturday half-holiday movement – a topic of fierce debate throughout New Zealand, which had enflamed the social consciences of Dunedin.

Over the next five months, Charles directed nineteen concerts. He also performed himself and played many of the accompaniments. Each concert opened with an organ and piano duet executed by Charles and a pianist. His standard piece was the overture to Rossini's grand opera, *William Tell*, but he also played the 'March of the Israelites' from Costa's oratorio, *Eli*, William Hill's 'March in G', and a selection of piano and organ solos including the celebrated 'Preghiera' from Rossini's *Moses in Egypt*. The role that Charles most enjoyed, however, was that of an entertainer. Reviews in the *Times* were enthusiastic: 'Mr Baeyertz ... put the audience in a merry mood with the humorous recitation "A masher's story"';[25] 'Mr Baeyertz recited the "Three Parsons" ... [A]t the conclusion the applause was so continuous that Mr Baeyertz reappeared and delivered a short story by Mark Twain';[26] 'Mr Baeyertz besides playing a minuet as a piano solo, contributed a couple of recitations by Thomas Hood.'[27]

Not every performance went smoothly. On one occasion, Charles's accompaniments were described as 'distinctly unsatisfactory'; on another, when the venerable Rev. Wallace tried to make 'a few remarks on the maintenance of the Saturday half-holiday movement', the audience shouted 'time' and 'the rev. gentleman' was compelled to retire.[28] Similarly, on 13 January, some undisclosed scandal prompted the committee to insert a public apology in the *Times* expressing its regret to Mr Baeyertz 'for the annoyance which has been caused him by the false reports which reached them.'[29] Charles retired temporarily with flu, but whatever the trouble was, it soon blew over and at the end of January the Saturday concert was honoured by a vice-regal party, with the mayor of Dunedin in attendance.

With Charles bringing all his entrepreneurial flair and showmanship to bear, the attendance at the Popular Concerts continued to grow. By the end of February, in addition to music, the concerts were featuring 'the famous American mystifiers, THE WONDERFUL STEENS' with 'AN IMMENSE PROGRAMME' of 'Second Sight Performances, Thought Reading and other new *exposés* of Spiritualism'.[30] On 11 March, the 'Galaxy of Novelties' included the 'Clever Lightning Sketcher, Mr F.R. Rayner' and a demonstration of 'Edison's Wonderful PHONOGRAPH'.[31] By now the concerts had expanded to a second venue in populous South Dunedin where a yodelling song ('with banjo accompaniment') and a 'double clog dance'[32] brought the house down.

Charles's introduction of popular elements, while still insisting on a high musical standard for the main programme, was typical of the sort of balancing act between high-brow and low-brow that he later did in the *Triad*. The clog dancers and yodellers would certainly have given the evenings a less serious character, but even Charles's critics acknowledged that they helped the concerts to reach the mass audiences for which they were intended.

By the end of the series, Charles's energetic directorship and his musical talents had not only won him the respect of Dunedin's philanthropic Establishment, but had also transformed him into something of a celebrity for the hundreds who had paid their sixpences to attend the concerts. The final concert took place on 22 April 1893. Charles and Miss Lily Cameron – a stalwart of the series – opened with the usual organ and piano duet, but Charles's mind may well have strayed from the music because, just a week earlier, he had launched his first issue of the *Triad*.

Clockwise from top left: Emilia Baeyertz, Charles's mother, portrayed at the height of her evangelistic career, c. 1900 *(Alexander Turnbull Library B-K 820-frontis)*; Charles Baeyertz Senior, Charles's grandfather, who had a well-paid position with the government of Victoria; Isabella Baeyertz, a homely figure, whom Charles married when he was barely twenty; Charles aged five, photographed in Geelong not long after his father's death.
(All private collection)

Top: The SS Hauroto *on which Charles sailed to New Zealand. She later sank in the South China Sea.* (Museum of Wellington City and Sea Collection).
Above: Princes Street, Dunedin, in all its Victorian splendour. (Alexander Turnbull Library 092614)

The Dutch artist, Petrus van der Velden, in 1909. (Alexander Turnbull Library, G-14988-1/1)

Girolamo Nerli (right) in a jaunty boater chatting with James Nairn. Dunedin 1896. (Hocken Collections, Uare Taoka o Hakena, University of Otago, Dunedin)

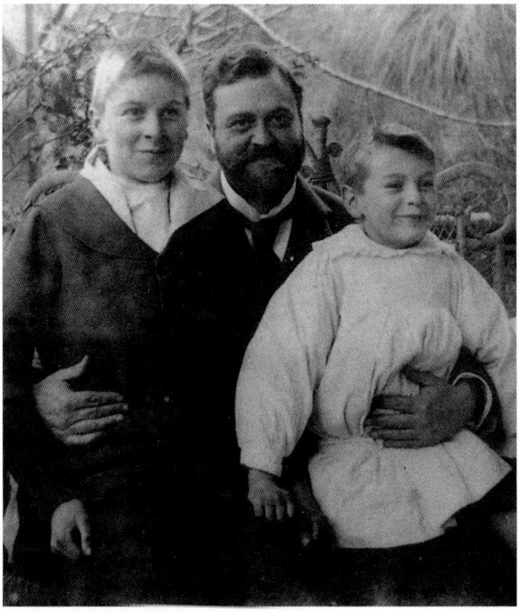

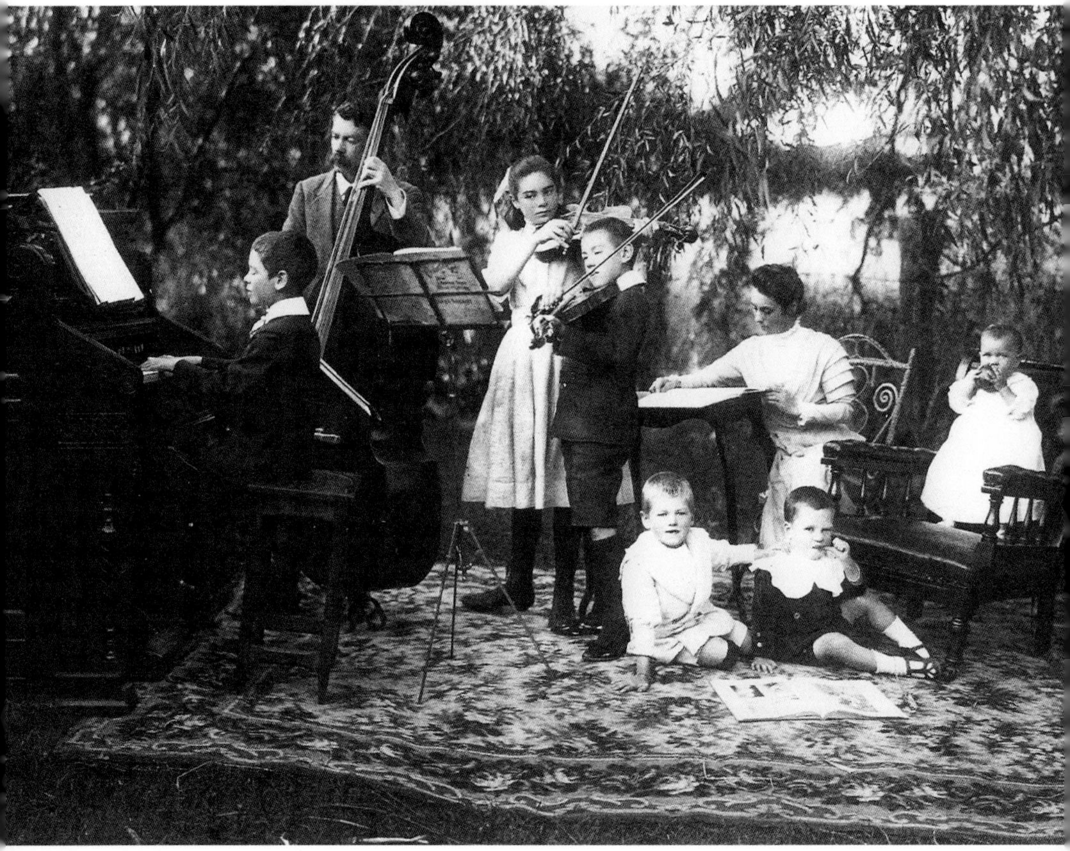

Charles in his element as chief elocutionary judge at the 1906 Dunedin Competitions. (Triad, *1 Nov 1906, p. 22, Alexander Turnbull Library S-L 805-22*)

Facing page, top: *An affectionate father: Charles with his two sons on the balcony of the house in Mornington, c. 1900. From left: Carl, Charles, Rudolph.* (Private collection)
Opposite: *A photograph of the McAllister family of Taranaki in 1912, which typifies the level of musical accomplishment in many New Zealand households.* (Alexander Turnbull Library G-12890-1/1)

Charles at the 1906 Dunedin Competitions letting his hair down with some of the competitors. (Triad, *1 Nov 1906, p. 21, Alexander Turnbull Library S-L 805-21*)

Facing page, top left: *Alfred Hill, New Zealand's first significant composer, whom Charles hailed as a possible founder of a New Zealand school of opera.*
(Alexander Turnbull Library F-83979-1/2)

Facing page, top right: *Arthur Adams, the golden boy of New Zealand poetry. In 1906 he became editor of the Sydney* Bulletin's *famous 'Red Page'.*
(Alexander Turnbull Library F-2694-1/2)

Opposite: *The Grand Opening of the 1906 Christchurch Exhibition. In the foreground is the full orchestra for which Charles lobbied so effectively.*
(Alexander Turnbull Library G-5291-1/1)

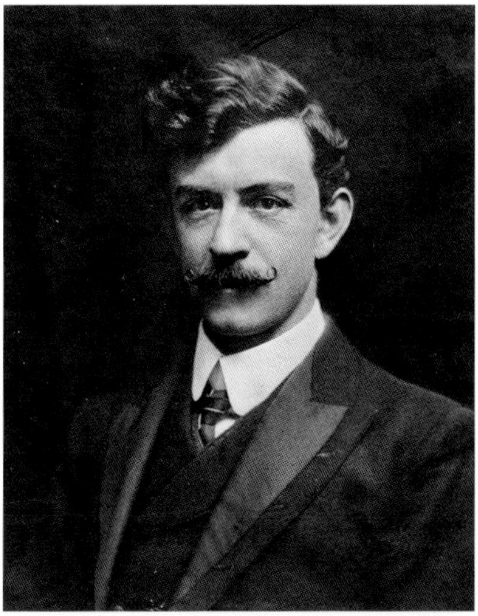
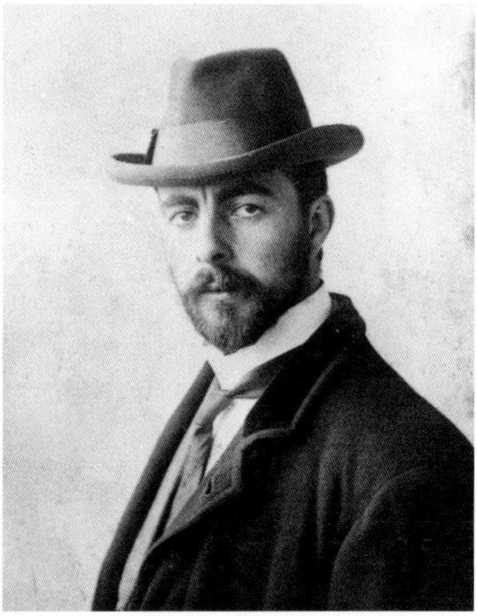
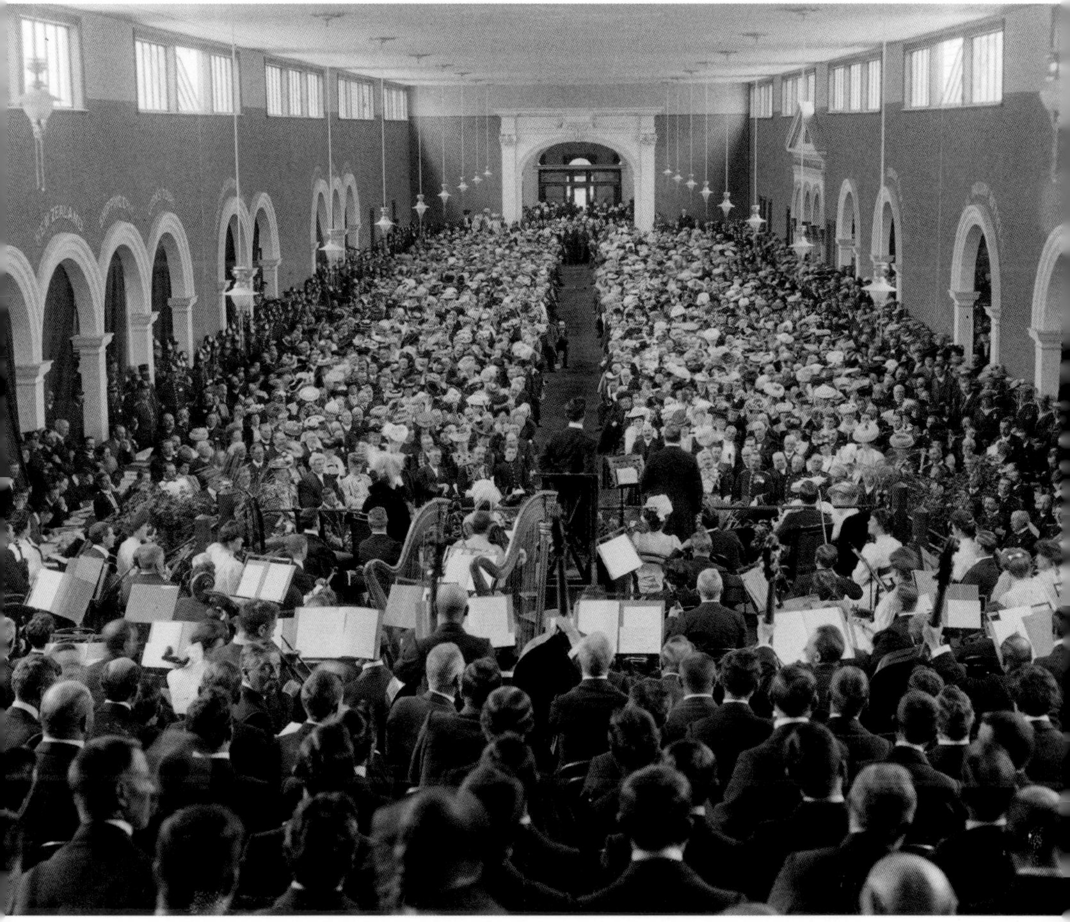

Every inch the critic. Charles appraising one of C.N. Worsley's paintings with the artist and his wife in attendance, c. 1910. (Private collection)

Chapter 5

The Triad

When Charles launched the *Triad*, he could not have foreseen New Zealand's approaching prosperity or the golden age of visiting opera companies and international musical stars that lay ahead. Nevertheless he was astute enough to sense that middle New Zealand had a keen interest in the arts and represented an untapped market for a completely new sort of cultural magazine.

Ever since Charles's arrival in New Zealand, the Liberal Government had been pushing through a series of constitutional reforms. But in April 1893, the pace of reform suddenly accelerated when the death of the first Liberal Prime Minister, John Ballance, enabled his Minister for Public Works, Richard Seddon, to manoeuvre himself into the premiership. Under Seddon and his brilliant Minister of Labour, William Pember Reeves, the Liberals embarked on the most audacious social programme in New Zealand's history. By the end of the 1890s, a dazzling array of new acts had passed into law, ranging from the protection of factory workers to the establishment of the old age pension. But the most ground-breaking piece of legislation – to which Seddon was a reluctant party – was signed on 19 September 1893 and made New Zealand the first country in the world to give the vote to women.

At the same time, the economic tide was also turning. Refrigerated shipments of meat and butter had opened up new markets and as the gloom of the recession receded and the benefits of the reforms started to filter down to the population, New Zealanders began to enjoy a growing sense of well-being. For two leading members of the Fabian Society,* Sidney and Beatrice Webb, who visited the country in 1898, New Zealand came closer than anywhere else in the world to the socialist paradise of their dreams:

> *New Zealand and its people have left in our mind an agreeable impression ... It is delightful to be in a country where there are no millionaires and hardly any slums, among a people characterised by homely refinement, and*

---

* The London-based Fabian Society, whose aim was to reconstruct society 'in accordance with the highest moral possibilities', started as a Socialist debating group in 1883. In 1895, a legacy left to the Society was used to found the London School of Economics.

by a large measure of vigorous public spirit ... Taken all in all if I had to bring up a family outside of Great Britain I would choose New Zealand as its home.[1]

A further spin-off of the social and economic changes was that a far greater number of people now had enough money and leisure to pursue their cultural interests. Thus, through a happy combination of circumstances, Charles could hardly have chosen a more auspicious moment to embark on his new enterprise.

The *Triad* was far from being New Zealand's first cultural magazine. Since the earliest days of European settlement, a number of efforts had been made to establish local equivalents to Britain's many intellectual and cultural periodicals. Most of them lasted for a few issues, but one or two such as the *New Zealand Magazine*, which was published in Dunedin from 1876–7, and the *Monthly Review*, which was published in Wellington from 1888–90, managed to survive a little longer. The *New Zealand Magazine* catered strictly for the serious-minded, and although it described itself as 'A Quarterly Magazine of General Literature', most of its articles were on education or religion. The contents of the *Monthly Review* were equally earnest and included the minutes of the local philosophical society.

One of the most admirable attempts to produce a local cultural publication was a monthly magazine dedicated to New Zealand literature called *Zealandia*. The first issue, dated July 1889, opened with a courageous statement:

Colony though it may be, New Zealand is a nation ... and to the realisation of this truth is due the fact that Zealandia *has been established as a distinctively national literary magazine. Its contributors will be all New Zealanders, and no subject will be dwelt upon it its pages that is not of interest, directly or indirectly, primarily to New Zealanders. It is nothing to us that it may prove of interest, secondarily, to all the world beside. But whilst it is intended to assist New Zealand authors ... rigid care will be exercised as to the quality of the literary pabulum provided in* Zealandia's *pages.*[2]

The first few numbers appeared to live up to these lofty ideals, with contributions from New Zealand's foremost poet at the time, Thomas Bracken, and a short story by the multi-talented William Pember Reeves, who was also a gifted writer. Unlike earlier magazines, *Zealandia* tried to make some concessions to popular tastes with a 'Ladies Page' by 'Annette', fashion notes, book reviews and articles for children. But the momentum did not last, and after twelve issues *Zealandia* too was forced to close. The editor faced defeat gallantly:

Losses are hard to bear, but from the briar of defeat wise men pluck the red rose of victory; and we heartily wish our successor all the long life and prosperity we merited – but missed.[3]

Three years later the red rose of victory was plucked by Charles, but his editorial approach was very different from that of his New Zealand predecessors, who had seldom combined business acumen with their literary aspirations. In outlook he was far closer to the latest generation of American magazine editors for whom publication was a business enterprise inspired by the editor's personal vision, but driven by what would sell.

The business-like tone of the first page of the *Triad* was in striking contrast to the opening statement of *Zealandia*:

This magazine, in common with all other magazines, is made to sell ... [A]t the same time we make bold to hope that it may be the means of disseminating a small modicum of musical, artistic and scientific information throughout New Zealand.

The second paragraph was equally unassuming:

It has often been represented to us that there would be scope for a monthly paper which might give the latest information from the English and European journals and at the same time contain reliable reports of music etc., in Australasia. It is our intention to give the enterprise twelve months' trial; and to popularise the Triad *we have determined to offer a prize, well worth winning, to any of our readers who will obtain four yearly subscribers to the magazine.*[4]

Unlike the editor of *Zealandia*, Charles made no appeals to his readers' nationalist sentiments. On the contrary, the *Triad*'s perspective would be consciously international and he announced his intention of 'quoting copiously'[5] from a long list of European and American journals. This included several of the most prominent representatives of Britain's musical press, such as the *Musical Times* and the *Monthly Musical Record*, the long-established French musical weekly *Le Ménestrel*, and W.T. Stead's widely respected *Review of Reviews*, which had recently launched an Australasian edition. Furthermore, since this was to be a critical magazine, whose main function was to comment on the arts and provide well-informed reviews of local performances, local literary contributions were not encouraged.

Not surprisingly, the main emphasis of the *Triad* was on music and, although Charles never referred to it, he may well have been aware that the demise of another local venture had created a gap in the market. From 1888 to 1890, the interests of New Zealand's music lovers had been catered for by a dignified little magazine called the *New Zealand Musical Monthly*, which hailed rather unexpectedly from Balclutha and accurately claimed to be 'the First and Only Journal in the Colony devoted to the interests of Music and Musicians'.[6] But its unworldly editor, J. Stewart Algie, understood little of the realities of magazine publishing. He attracted few advertisers and the journal's principal focus on brass bands limited its appeal to professional bandsmen. Despite its well-presented contents, the *Musical Monthly* failed to cover its costs and after, less than three years, it went the same way as *Zealandia*.

Charles's Dunedin neighbours were quick to point out the risks of his new undertaking, informing him gleefully that 'the prevailin' opeenion in Dunedin' is that the '"Triadh" will last aboot three months.'[7] But, as a later comment in the *Triad* shows, Charles needed no reminding of what a gamble he was taking:

> *It was a bold venture, for the* Triad *was to be a musical and literary monthly for Dunedin, and I was to live on the fruits of it. Few men have ever fluttered a pennon in a forlorner hope ... It was much as though one should attempt to found a magazine in the interest of Bimetallism in Timbuctoo.*[8]

These words, of course, were spoken partly in jest, for Charles was well aware that in Dunedin cultural refinement was a much sought-after commodity, and if he could capture the interest of all those young ladies who sang 'Home Sweet Home' and 'Come into the Garden Maud' so charmingly around the family piano – and that of their admiring parents and friends – he would be assured of a sizeable readership. Moreover, even those of his fellow townsmen who had few cultural aspirations could be counted on for their legendary thrift. For them, Charles's assertion that 'people were entitled to be told the truth about any entertainment for which they paid'[9] would be a strong selling point. He was also confident that his initiative would find support among Dunedin's cultural élite because one of its leading members, his neighbour David Theomin, had already agreed to sponsor the first twelve months of the *Triad* through his piano business.

The Theomin family were pillars of Dunedin's thriving Jewish community, to which both the Hallensteins and the Joels belonged. Earlier the former Premier and founder of the *Otago Daily Times*, Julius Vogel, had also been part of the same group. David Theomin, like the Aronsons, had originally made his fortune in the jewellery business, but his keen interest in music, and membership of Dunedin's male choir,* had led him to establish the Dresden

---

* The Dunedin Liedertafel, later the Royal Dunedin Male Choir.

Piano Company. Even if he was unaware of Charles's Jewish ancestry, Theomin must have felt some sympathy with him to have given his financial backing to an undertaking whose chances of success seemed so questionable.

The *Triad*, however, was quite unlike the doomed periodicals that had gone before it, most of which were aimed at a small circle of intellectuals. From the outset, Charles's chief objective was to preach the gospel of culture to the widest possible audience with a zeal that was strongly reminiscent of his mother's evangelism.

The first number of the *Triad* had sixteen pages and cost sixpence. Below its amateurish masthead, optimistically dotted with symbols of art and science, it described itself as 'A Monthly Magazine of Music, Science & Art'. On the back page, the word 'Triad' was helpfully explained as meaning 'three in one' and as 'a technical word for harmony'. The editorial voice was circumspect, even modest, and the contents comprised a judicious mix of international musical gossip – the new Wagner theatre in Bayreuth and Madame Melba's latest triumphant tour of Britain – with local musical news. Signor Squarise was reported to be 'actively rehearsing' Rossini's *Barber of Seville* with the recently revived Operatic Society, and the members of the Dunedin Orchestral Society were gently chided for overreaching themselves with a programme that included Wagner's 'Kaiser March' and MacCunn's 'Overture'. But even in this careful first issue, Charles's sense of humour sometimes got the better of him: he described the leader of the first violins, Mr Parker, as being the only violinist who 'remained steady and true amidst the battle howls and shrieks of the slain'.[10]

From further afield, he noted that the Wellington Orchestral Society was said to have 'improved greatly' under the careful training of Alfred Hill,* who had recently returned home from the Leipzig Conservatorium of Music. True to his word, Charles also quoted at length from an article (that was bound to appeal to his female readers) on the legendary Polish pianist, Paderewski, taken from 'that most admirable paper, *The Magazine of Music*'.[11]

On page twelve, Charles's mischievous side resurfaced in his review of the Easter service at First Church – a feature of the *Triad* which may have seemed less surprising in a city where church services were a principal form of entertainment:

> *On Easter morning I heard an intelligent sermon preached by the Rev. Jas. Gibbs ... I was delighted to hear the Rev. Gentleman say that it is better to be an honest doubter than an unthinking and unreasoning believer.*[12]

---

* Twenty-three year old Hill was a brilliant violinist and had just become the conductor of Wellington's amateur orchestra.

The only literary item was an ode to music by Swinburne, while most of the scientific coverage consisted of clippings from British medical magazines – although a paragraph on sanctuaries for New Zealand's native birds and the need to protect the tuatara added a local touch. The 'Art Notes' contained a similar mix of international and local subject matter, with an embarrassing misspelling of Burne-Jones and congratulations to David Con Hutton on his appointment as Vice-President of the Dunedin School of Art. There was also warm praise for 'several very clever studies by Mr O'Keefe' (sic), who was 'about to try his fortune as a professional artist'.[13]

Alfred O'Keeffe would have welcomed this public support. He had spent years running a Dunedin pub in order to provide for his family and despite his artistic talents had never been more than a part-time painter. Now he was hoping to finance himself as a professional by giving art classes. Charles, who was all too familiar with the difficulties of setting up as a teacher, concluded flatteringly: 'If he can teach them to draw and paint as well as he does himself, he should have no lack of pupils.'[14]

In Dunedin society – and throughout New Zealand – artistic accomplishments, like musical ones, were keenly pursued by those who had the means and the leisure to acquire them. In most places, the amateurs led the field, but in Dunedin the Otago Provincial Council had opened the country's first professional art school in 1870, six years before William Hodgkins helped to found the Otago Art Society. O'Keeffe had done some part-time study at the art school and had exhibited at the Art Society's exhibition, but he did not share the general enthusiasm for romantic landscapes. For him, the carefully executed watercolours of William Hodgkins aroused none of the excitement that he had felt when he first saw the swirling brushwork of Nerli's *Bacchanalian Orgie* hanging in the art gallery at the South Seas Exhibition.

Nerli, meanwhile, had recently returned to Dunedin bringing with him an arresting portrait of Robert Louis Stevenson,* which he had painted in Samoa and was hoping to sell in New Zealand. So far it had failed to find a buyer, but Charles had seen it on display in McGregor Wright's Gallery in Princes Street and informed his readers that the drawing and modelling were 'really excellent'.[15]

Over the following months, Nerli's bold technique and the spontaneity of his sketching transformed the outlook of Dunedin's small circle of serious artists. His classes attracted a stream of pupils, including twenty-four-year-old Frances Hodgkins who revealed in a letter to her sister, Isabel, that Signor

---

* This painting, which now hangs in the Scottish Portrait Gallery, remained unsold for many months and was eventually purchased locally for £8.

Nerli was being 'most awfully good to me and gives me an extra lesson on Saturdays.'[16] Later, however, she admitted to Isabel that it had come as 'a bit of a shock' to discover that her father had been attending 'a nude class at Nerli's studio'.[17] Nerli also encouraged O'Keeffe to enrol at one of Europe's most prestigious art schools, the Académie Julian in Paris, and formed part of the group which (according to the *Triad*), clubbed together 'to defray Mr A.H. O'Keefe's expenses to Paris for the purpose of allowing him to study his beloved art.'[18]

Two weeks after the launch of the *Triad*, Charles departed by steamer for Christchurch and Wellington. The circulation figures for the first edition had been a terrible disappointment. Confronted with the sobering realities of trying to break into a market that was rather more competitive than he had realised, Charles lost no time in planning a trip that would put the *Triad* on a national footing. It was still early days, but with the birth of another baby in February, a little girl named Estelle, he now had a wife and three children to support and he could not afford to fail.

In Christchurch Charles spent his time hunting around for advertisers and visiting the studio of Petrus van der Velden who, like Nerli, had recently settled in New Zealand. When van der Velden emigrated from Holland in 1890, at the age of fifty-three, he already had a distinguished artistic career behind him and his work displayed much of the technical perfection that Charles most prized in art and music. His dramatic painting of the Otira Gorge, which was purchased by the Otago Art Society in 1893, was universally admired, but as a later comment in the *Triad* shows, Charles found his study *Old Jack* equally impressive:

> *No work has been exhibited in the colony with the force and truth of this piece of brush work. Note the wonderful handling of the grey beard – so solid in its impasto, but so aerial in effect … It is to be hoped one of our citizens will prevent this picture leaving the town.**,[19]

In Wellington, Charles had a busy programme starting at the Opera House with Audran's comic opera, *La Mascotte,* staged by the touring Liliputian Opera Company† and its cast of children. The following evening he enjoyed a 'Popular Concert' from the seclusion of a private box provided by the musical director, Wellington's premier musician Robert Parker. With an eye,

---

* *Old Jack* was purchased by the Otago Art Society shortly afterwards and is now part of the Dunedin Art Gallery's collection.

† The Liliputian Opera Company was founded in Tasmania by James Pollard in the early 1880s and originally included his numerous children. By 1893 it was under the management of his son-in-law, Tom Pollard, who was an outstanding producer of comic opera and had adopted the Pollard name. In the late 1890s, Tom Pollard moved from Australia and settled in Christchurch where he spent the rest of his life.

perhaps, on the need to increase circulation in the Empire City, he made a note, which he included in the next edition of the *Triad*, that 'the audience in Wellington was far more attentive and appreciative, or perhaps, more properly, discriminating, than the usual concert audience in Dunedin.'[20]

The rest of his time was fully occupied with the vital business of finding advertisers, but he still managed to accept an invitation from the Scottish artist, James Nairn, to visit the Wellington School of Design. With Nerli and van der Velden, Nairn belonged to the trio of European artists who were breathing new life into New Zealand's art scene. Before his arrival in 1890, Nairn had been an established member of a modern art group in Scotland known as the Glasgow Boys, and in 1892 he had ruffled a few feathers at Wellington's conservative Academy of Fine Arts by forming the breakaway Art Club, where he encouraged artists to sketch directly from nature and experiment with Impressionism. But Charles was all in favour of the Art Club and in the June *Triad* he reproved the Wellington public for their 'ignorance of what is good in art' and urged the Art Club to 'let people see that New Zealand can show some talent.'[21]

Charles returned to Dunedin just in time to complete the second issue of the *Triad*. Its assured tone gave no hint of the frantic calculations that had taken place since the first edition and its pages were full of instructive criticism and interesting musical information. On the last page readers were suavely informed that 'in future editions ... the Musical and Art Notes relating to Christchurch and Wellington will bulk as largely as those of Dunedin' and that 'a leading artist and musician in each of these cities' had been engaged to provide the coverage.[22]

But the dramatic drop in price from sixpence to threepence, and the inclusion of a free musical supplement, betrayed just how worried he was. In an attempt to make light of his troubles, he printed a wry anecdote about a dying editor who, on being told by the doctor that his circulation was very poor, replied 'with an emotion which no one but a *paper* man can experience ... "thank God, the *ads* (advertisements) are coming in".'[23] The news that two thirds of the stock of his book, *Voice Culture*, had been lost in a warehouse fire could hardly have come at a worse time.

Although the *Triad* was the only magazine of its kind in the country, it faced competition on several fronts – not least from the stream of well-funded journals that poured into both Australia and New Zealand from the British press. Locally, its most serious local rivals were the weekly newspapers such as the *Witness* in Dunedin, the *New Zealand Mail* in Wellington and the *Weekly News* in Auckland, which had developed a cultural role that went far beyond their original purpose of providing a summary of news for isolated rural communities. The *Witness*, for example, in addition to comprehensive coverage of everything from angling to wool sales, listed amongst its contents 'Art and Artists', 'Literary Notes', 'Poetry', 'Theatrical and Musical Notes' and the invariably entertaining 'Passing Notes' of 'Civis'. Furthermore, most of these weekly publications had been in existence for decades and enjoyed the affection and loyalty of their readers. Charles, however, had some trump cards up his sleeve, of which his acerbic wit and the frankness of his criticisms were the most telling. In addition, by lowering his price to threepence, he had undercut the weeklies by half.

Over the following months, Charles continued to woo subscribers with free musical supplements and a continuous stream of amusing articles and reviews. Local performers and audiences were encouraged and chastised in equal measure. Signor Squarise's *Barber of Seville* was declared to be 'one of the best essays at opera by amateurs that we have ever heard',[24] but the Dunedin public was roundly berated for its lack of support. In contrast, the capacity audience that attended a concert in Auckland that featured the visiting tenor, Philip Newbury, was praised for its good taste.

On the international front, readers were kept abreast of the latest musical and artistic developments with articles and clippings, such as the quote from the *Westminster Gazette* on the recent controversy raging over Dégas's celebrated painting, *L'Absinthe*,* which described it as 'a powerful piece of work, showing two persons, a middle-aged Parisian larrikin seated at a *café* table, by his side a fourth-rate and exceedingly plain *cocotte*'.[25]

Charles was particularly attentive to his female readers and in September he hailed 'the advent at the polling booth of our mothers, our sisters, and our wives' as a step that would 'ennoble'[26] politics, science and art. Later, however, he used a provocative quote from Byron – 'they ought to mind home, and be well fed and clothed, but not mixed in society'[27] – to rebuke women who talked in the theatre. Similarly, he commented witheringly on 'the young lady' who in her entry for the *Triad*'s 'six greatest living novelists' competition preferred Charlotte Brontë and Mrs Henry Wood to George Meredith and George Moore. The tone was humorous, but the crusading zeal was never far below the surface.

The regular broadsides in his 'Editor's Note Book' or the 'Answers to Correspondents' column only increased the *Triad*'s popularity. In July, a reader who had sent him a musical composition was told: 'Publish it? No! "Poison yourself first: you'll be glad of it after".'[28],† In a later issue, an aspiring poet was put in his place with equal firmness:

---

*   *L'Absinthe* was exhibited at London's New Grafton Gallery in 1893.
†   Charles is quoting the British humorist, Jerome K. Jerome.

Declined with thanks. We never print poetry *in our columns, especially Spring poetry. 'Ode to Spring', forsooth! ... Write us some humorous verses if you will; but leave poetry to such poor unfortunates as Tennyson [and] Shakespeare ...*[29]

Not even the clergy were spared. Readers who had endured the Rev. Ready's rambling sermon at the Garrison Hall would have relished Charles's comment that he 'added nothing new to our ignorance of God'.[30]

Although he was still taking pupils at home, Charles soon found that the *Triad* was consuming all his time. By day, as Editor and sole contributor, he was fully occupied with writing and collecting material. In the evenings, he became a familiar and increasingly feared presence at musical and theatrical performances, as he sat listening intently and making copious notes in the little black book on his knee. In his late twenties, Charles cut an impressive figure. He stood fully six foot tall with broad shoulders and a fairish beard trimmed to a neat point. He always dressed formally and for evening occasions he often wore white tie and tails, which further added to his air of authority. Only the unruliness of his thick, wavy hair and the gleam of amusement in his eyes as he penned some particularly mischievous squib betrayed his youth and his humour.

Every month, on the evening before publication day, Charles would set out from home with his arms full of *Triad*s, stuffing pillar box after pillar box full to the brim until the protests of other users obliged him to adopt a more professional method of distribution. In the brief lull between each issue, he travelled continually by coach, train or steamer to the smaller centres, appointing agents and scouring the pages of *Wise's Post Office Directory* for likely advertisers. His evenings were spent in provincial theatres and concert halls, or writing up his notes in the dingy bedroom of some local boarding house.

By now the *Triad* had a Wellington edition and an agent in most of the sizeable towns in the South Island, but the circulation figures were still very modest and at the end of April 1894 the Dresden Piano Company ceased its sponsorship. Charles, however, was far too committed to his self-appointed role as the cultural conscience of New Zealand to abandon the venture – especially as he was discovering that the musical life of New Zealand's many small townships was far livelier than he had ever imagined. The programme for Wellington's long-awaited Musical Festival, with Dvořák's 'Spectre's Bride' and two soloists from Melbourne, may have been more adventurous, but in Gore local enthusiasts had produced *HMS Pinafore* and in Oamaru the indomitable local musical society was struggling through Mendelssohn's *Elijah*. A year later Charles recorded his impressions of Hawera:

One cannot help being impressed in travelling through New Zealand with the enormous amount of crude musical talent to be met with in most of the small towns. Hawera is a town with a population of about 3000, and yet it boasts an Orchestral Society and an Operatic Society. The latter body has produced the 'Gondoliers' and the 'Mikado'. I did not have the pleasure of hearing either of these performances. They may have been good, bad or indifferent: but for a town of 3000 inhabitants to stage the 'Gondoliers' at all is sufficiently remarkable.[31]

By mid-1894 Charles was in serious financial difficulties and was forced to move his family to cheaper lodgings. After a brief sojourn in the seaside suburb of St Clair, they settled in a modest house on a steep, narrow street in the low-income area of North East Valley. It was a dramatic comedown from London Street; and for Bella, the challenging gradient of Leith Walk,* combined with its distance from the city centre, must have made housekeeping a nightmare. Charles was far too preoccupied to give her much support, and her only helper was a sixteen-year-old servant girl called Mary Ferguson, whose shaky signature suggests that she had received only the minimum of education.

Five days before Christmas, while six-year-old Carl and his sister, Maida, were picking currants in the garden, little Estelle strayed into the kitchen. Mary had just uncovered the well to draw water, which Charles had cautioned her about doing when the children were in the kitchen. He hated her using the well, but the pump in the yard had been broken for weeks and he had been too busy to get it repaired. As she prepared to lower the bucket into the narrow shaft, Mary pushed the baby into the next door room and closed the door. She was in sole charge. Charles was out and Bella, who was pregnant again, was busy in her room. But as the children seemed happy enough, she slipped across the garden to chat with the neighbours.

In her deposition, Mary claimed that she returned five minutes later and searched everywhere for the baby. Bella could not bring herself to look in the well and sent Mary to fetch Charles. He peered into the darkness and saw, many metres down, the crumpled shape of his little daughter lying at the bottom of the shaft, face down in the water. He stared helplessly at the body, unable to think of any way of recovering it until a neighbour arrived with a long pole and hooked Estelle up by her clothes. They laid her out on the kitchen table and attempted to resuscitate her. When the doctor came, he tried for another hour, but the body remained limp and lifeless. In the end, all the doctor could do was inform Charles and Bella that, in his opinion, their child had drowned instantly.

---

* Now Tay Street.

In March 1895, Charles celebrated the completion of the *Triad*'s second year. In his 'Editor's Note Book' he outlined an ambitious plan to distribute 50,000 free music albums nationwide, and informed readers that he intended to make the *Triad* 'a paper for the family throughout the whole of New Zealand'.[32] But within the family, the mood was less upbeat. They were still desperately short of money and the loss of Estelle had left Bella inconsolable.

Chapter 6

The Fighting Editor

A few weeks after Estelle's death, Charles set out on the first of a series of business trips that frequently kept him on the road for months at a time. By now New Zealand had nearly two thousand miles of rail track, but travel within the country was still arduous and involved an awkward combination of land and sea transport. The four main centres were linked by coastal steamers, which called in regularly at the ports along their route. It was also possible to travel by train between Dunedin and Christchurch, but seventy miles beyond Christchurch, the railway came to an abrupt halt and the only form of transport northwards was by horse-drawn coach.

In the North Island, Auckland and Wellington had yet to be linked by rail. A line ran from Wellington to Napier (with a twenty-mile gap in the middle), but from there the only way to reach Auckland was by rugged coach road across the central plateau or by steamer around East Cape. Another line ran up the west coast from Wellington as far as New Plymouth and Waitara, but beyond this lay the King Country, much of which was still inaccessible by rail, and travellers had to continue north by sea.

On this occasion, Charles's destination was Auckland. As he traversed the country from end to end, he spent many hours on trains and steamers whose timetables were as capricious as the frequent storms that lashed the coastline and regularly washed out the tracks. In the March issue of the *Triad*, he gave an account of the 'roughish' night he spent aboard the *Mararoa* on his homeward journey from Auckland to Napier. Everyone was seasick and by 3 a.m. conditions in his four-man cabin had become so intolerable that he and his fellow passengers 'fled the dismal scene' to spend the rest of the night pacing the deck.

Despite the discomforts of the *Mararoa*, Charles was delighted with Napier, declaring it to be 'a splendid little place' with 'the finest esplanade … and one of the best hotels in New Zealand.' He was equally impressed by the Napier City Band, and advised them to compete in the next band contest where he was sure that they would give 'a good account of themselves'.[1]

The second leg of the voyage was rather more enjoyable:

> *From Napier to Dunedin we sailed in the* Monowai *– one of the best sea boats afloat. Although a gale of almost hurricane force was met with in the straits, and a heavy head sea between Lyttelton and the Dunedin Heads, there was scarcely a roll in the gallant boat; and each night the 'beauty and the chivalry' was present at the concerts promoted by the energetic and enthusiastic Mr S. Jacobs of Dunedin.*[2]

On his return home, Charles flung himself into a frenzy of promotional activity. A short-lived sponsorship had foundered after only five issues and he found himself, once again, liable for the entire cost of the *Triad*. With the additional expenses of an office in the Octagon (close to his new printer, Mills, Dick and Co.), and a sub-editor to oversee publication during his lengthy absences, he urgently needed to increase circulation.

As part of his aggressive marketing strategy, he followed up on his earlier distribution of free music albums by producing a handsome pictorial supplement containing photographic engravings of eight of Dunedin's most prominent musicians. He also offered generous cash bonuses to readers who recruited new subscribers. Advertising was similarly encouraged by requiring competitors in the *Triad*'s monthly competitions to accompany each entry with a receipt from a *Triad* advertiser. Thanks to substantial cash prizes, the *Triad*'s competitions were soon attracting thousands of entries, while their didactic nature served the secondary purpose of furthering Charles's cultural mission.

In March, for example, competitors were asked to choose the six best compositions from a list of songs and pieces that had appeared in the monthly music supplements. The winning entry would be the one that came closest to Charles's choice – which was naturally the correct one. In the next competition, his educational purposes were even more apparent:

> *Write down on paper the names of those whom you consider the six greatest composers, in order of merit, in the following list of living musicians: Cowen, Sullivan, Grieg, Mascagni, Dvorák, Verdi, Leoncavallo, Brahms, Hamish McCunn, Ebenezer Prout, Strauss, Gung'l, Dr. Mackenzie, Joseph Barnby, Reinecke, Tosti, Tschaikowski,* Massenet and Guillmant.*[3]

Although nearly four thousand lists were received, none of them matched up with Charles's version in which he placed Verdi first ('because of his great age' and 'his splendid latter-day compositions'),[4] followed by Brahms, Dvorák, Grieg, Tchaikovsky and Sullivan. The prize money, however, was divided equally between the six runners-up.

---

* Charles noted that Tchaikovsky had died in 1893.

In his monthly 'Editor's Note Book' – now re-named 'Obiter Dicta'* – Charles continued to paint a glowing picture of the *Triad*'s popularity. In April, readers were told that 'it may reasonably be predicted that, before many months, the *Triad* will have a larger circulation than any other paper in New Zealand.'[5] In June they were informed that 'the *Triad* should soon have several thousand subscribers in Wellington.'[6] By August, Charles was able to announce that the *Triad* had an agent and canvasser in nearly every important town in New Zealand, and claimed that the number of subscribers had doubled. The increase in advertisers would have pleased him even more. On the home front, the outlook had improved too, for on 5 May Bella had given birth to a boy whom they christened Rudolph.

Charles barely had time to admire his new son before he once again set off on his travels. This time he was heading for Wellington and then up the west coast to Wanganui, which had a flourishing musical community and where, according to Charles, there was 'a larger proportion of intellectual folk … than in any other town in the colony.'[7] But he found the onward journey frustrating:

> *I think the train from Wanganui to New Plymouth is absolutely the slowest in the world … We leave Wanganui at 8.30 o'clock in the morning and arrive in New Plymouth at 6 in the evening – 102 miles in 10 hours. I think that is the record.*[8]

Transport was not his only problem. The food at the railway refreshment rooms was terrible: stale sandwiches, undrinkable soup and meat so overcooked that it was impossible to tell whether it was beef or mutton. The service also left much to be desired: 'The waitress is doubtless paid to wait, and she certainly waited a long time before she waited on me; in fact, I did most of the waiting myself … .'[9]

By August, Charles was back in Dunedin with a sheaf of new agents and yet more advertisers. Throughout his travels, he had been mailing and telegraphing copy to his office and in August his 'Obiter Dicta' column extended over nearly four pages. It opened, with characteristic braggadocio, by stating that the *Triad* was 'the first musical monthly in the world to give its readers regularly the latest news relating to Art, Literature, and Science, as well as Music', and then roamed over the 'relativity of pleasure', the nature of socialism and the misspelling of French, German and Italian words in English magazines. There was also a long article on H.G. Wells's 'powerful, imaginative romance',[10] *The Time Machine,* a piece on Thomas Hardy and two columns on 'The Wit and Wisdom of Dr Jowett'.[11] An article on Mars

---

* Meaning 'Notes in Passing'.

occupied the science section and the local music coverage consisted of reports on musical activities in Auckland, Napier, Wanganui, Wellington, Dunedin and Invercargill. Under 'Zealandian Art', the work of James Nairn was singled out for special praise.

In the *Triad*, Charles made a point of encouraging local artistic endeavours. One of these was the Otago Art Academy, which was founded in February 1894 by Nerli in partnership with two Dunedin-based artists, John Perrett and Laurence Wilson. The instruction was shared between them, with Perrett teaching landscape and Wilson watercolours, but the main attraction was Nerli's modelling and figure class for which, according to an announcement in the *Otago Daily Times*, he had engaged a Professional Lady Model. By April the new art school was 'so numerously attended'[12] that the *Triad* was calling for more classes to meet the demand.

Meanwhile the impact of Nerli's earlier teaching on the work of Frances Hodgkins was already becoming apparent. In October 1893, the *Triad* included her in a list of artists 'who are really doing something to further art in New Zealand'.[13] Shortly afterwards, she painted a luminous portrait of a girl with flaxen hair which was light years ahead of the awkward 'Goose Girl' that she exhibited at the Art Society's November exhibition. Over the next few years, the *Triad* commented regularly on her progress: 'Miss Hodgkins, of Dunedin, is another young artist who is coming rapidly to the front';[14] 'Miss Hodgkins was also in evidence with a number of clever and bright pictures, though I cannot say I admire her figure study which took the Society's Silver medal';[15] 'Miss F.M. Hodgkins' ... "In Maiden Meditation Fancy Free" is a delightful study of colour successfully carried out.'[16]

During 1894 the Otago Art Academy's rooms in the Octagon became the favourite haunt of Dunedin's more adventurous spirits, dominated by the colourful figure of Nerli with his strong Italian accent and his exotic history of vagabond wanderings in the South Pacific. In September, he and Perrett took off on a painting holiday to Fiji where, like Paul Gauguin (who stopped off in Auckland the following August on his way back to Tahiti),* they were captivated by the colours and the people of the Pacific. When they returned, their comments on 'the picturesqueness of the natives' and the 'charming shades in colour'[17] appeared in the *Triad*.

In the meantime another promising young painter, Grace Joel, whose father owned the Red Lion Brewery, had just reappeared in Dunedin after several years of study at the National Gallery School in Melbourne. She was

---

* Gauguin visited the Auckland Museum where he saw the gateway figure, Pukaki, which later became the central image of his painting *The Idol*. As the carving of Pukaki originally came from the Ohinemutu pa, it has now been returned to Rotorua and stands in the Galleria of the Council Administration Building.

five years older than Frances Hodgkins and, after her sojourn in Melbourne, doubtless less innocent. Before long, rumours began to circulate that she was having an affair with Nerli, but such tittle-tattle never found its way into the pages of the *Triad*, which merely noted her 'remarkable progress' and offered 'unstinted praise'[18] for her study of a nude female figure.

When O'Keeffe came back from Paris in mid 1895, he rejoined his old circle and the first meeting of Dunedin's latest art group, the Easel Club, took place in his studio. Nerli and Grace Joel were both founder members of the club, which soon acquired a Bohemian reputation that was a far cry from the sedate drawing parties of the Otago Art Society. But Frances Hodgkins kept her distance, wary perhaps of the faint aura of impropriety that surrounded the club's activities – although this did not deter her from enrolling at the Dunedin School of Art where Nerli had been headhunted to teach painting.

Apart from the contributions of his small band of art and music correspondents, Charles wrote most of the *Triad* himself. But keeping abreast of local and international developments in music, art, literature and science presented a daunting task. For much of his international coverage, he relied heavily on clippings from other magazines. One of his favourite quarrying grounds was the Australian edition of the monthly *Review of Reviews,* which contained well-chosen extracts from all the leading British, European and American journals. In early issues he quoted from it so copiously that, at the end of the *Triad*'s first year, he felt compelled 'to confess and acknowledge our manifold indebtedness to our admirable and useful contemporary the *Review of Reviews.*'[19] In July 1895, however, his enthusiasm for the *Review* was somewhat dampened by a seven-page article on 'Musicians and Musical Taste in New Zealand' which angered him so much that his response in the August *Triad* was barely coherent. After a furious splutter, he set off for Nelson and left the writing of a more measured reply until September.

This was Charles's first visit to Nelson and his reactions to its location were ecstatic: 'Nelson is a splendid place in which to live, or even to die. If the magnificence of the climate were only thoroughly known in New Zealand and Australia, this gorgeous sunshine would become a most substantial asset.'[20] The weather was not Nelson's only attraction. Since 1893, its long-established Harmonic Society had been conducted by a gifted German musician named Michael Balling who had opened a school of music. Balling's musical motives were irreproachable:

> *As a foreigner I am singularly struck by the prominence given to 'sport' of all kinds ... With so much time and money for sport, we may resolve to reserve a little for higher things such as music ... and even with a city of 7000*

> *inhabitants surely 3000 could find 1s. 0d. each for a year, which would yield the sum of £150, sufficient to provide and maintain instruments and music, a modest 'school of music' for which I am prepared to undertake the direction and upon which I would expend great pains.*[21]

But Charles, ever business-like, was worried about his maths:

> *The fees are much too low ... it would be all right if things had turned out as Herr Balling in his innocence, supposed they would. His idea was that the poor people would learn from him at the Academy for 30s, and the rich would continue to pay him the usual fees for private tuition ... [but] people in New Zealand (and small blame to them) like to buy in the cheapest market ...*[22]

Balling left New Zealand a few months later and went on to a brilliant musical career, which culminated in the conductorship of the world famous Hallé Orchestra. In the meantime, despite Charles's concerns, his school in Nelson continued to flourish (in the following year, the *Triad* was able to report that it had a hundred and thirteen pupils).

By the weekend, the novelty of Nelson's sunshine had worn off. Charles was tired and irritable. He attended a Sunday service at the Cathedral, where he noted tetchily that the bells were out of tune and that the congregation said '"rorth", "cuvernunt", "heavun", "trinurty" and "glowry" ... and yet they say there is no accent in New Zealand.'[23]

Charles's views on pronunciation often make him sound like an Australasian version of Henry Higgins, the irascible elocutionist in Bernard Shaw's brilliant satire on the British class system, *Pygmalion*.* In *Pygmalion*, Shaw's socialist sympathies are clearly with his cockney heroine, Eliza Doolittle. Nevertheless in his preface he makes the observation that 'the English have no respect for their language, and will not teach their children to speak it'[24] – a charge which Charles also levels at Australians and New Zealanders.

Charles's insistence on correct pronunciation, however, had little to do with snobbery, for his father's early death and his mother's dramatic change of faith had left him in a social limbo with few class affiliations. In Dunedin he was often accused of being a foreigner and in Canterbury, the heartland of New Zealand's landed gentry, many people would have agreed heartily with the *Tapanui Courier*, which labelled him 'a regular bounder'.[25] The group with whom he felt most at home, and who shared his passion for music and language, were performing artists and musicians.

---

* In 1956 *Pygmalion* was produced as the stage musical, *My Fair Lady*, which was followed by a film version in 1964 starring Rex Harrison and Audrey Hepburn.

His repeated tirades against bad diction and mispronunciation, therefore, were seldom made in a social context. Sometimes his concerns were educational: 'To speak bad English is to brand yourself an illiterate.'[26] Similarly, his statement that 'anything approaching a prevalence of bad English was dangerously bad, and must in the end be morally bad, for an English community'[27] smacks strongly of his own particular brand of cultural evangelism. But more frequently his criticisms were made from the perspective of a professional critic of vocal performances in which the correct pronunciation of the words is as important as singing in tune.

On his way home from Nelson, Charles travelled to Picton on the box seat of a coach and four. Shortly after the horses had been changed, a stray heifer tumbled down the embankment beside the road and fell under one of the leader's hooves:

The horse's indignation knew no bounds and he lost all traces of self control ... After the driver had tried to restrain the enthusiasm of his steeds for some time, it was proposed by myself, seconded by the driver ... that I should take one set of reins, while he retained the other, and in the course of time, the coach, or rather the horses were stopped.[28]

The driver was lucky that Charles was an enthusiastic follower of the bodybuilder, Charles Sandow (who later appeared in the *Triad* as Hercules, in a pair of leopard skin-briefs), and he would have pitted considerable muscle against the bolting horses.

In September, Charles's stinging reply to the article which had so incensed him in the *Review* appeared in the *Triad*. It was addressed to the Very Rev. Alfred Fitchett, the Dean of Dunedin's Anglican Cathedral and, ironically, the elder brother of his earlier foe, 'Civis'. The offending item in the Dean's otherwise innocuous article was his damning comment that 'there is no music in New Zealand'. Although Fitchett went on to qualify this statement, for Charles – who probably thought that he should have been invited to write the article himself – it was like a red rag to a bull. The fact that the *Review*'s Australasian editor was another brother of the Dean's had also not escaped him. He was spoiling for a fight:

Save his kinship with the editor of the above-mentioned journal, the Dean of Dunedin can put forward no claim we know of to be chosen as the mouthpiece of music in New Zealand. He is not a musician; we cannot even concede his claim to be regarded as an amateur. If we had to define his status, we should put him down as a 'dabbler in music'.

The Dean was one of Dunedin's most revered figures, a man of outstanding ability and an eloquent preacher, but Charles could not have cared less. Like 'Civis', the Dean had trespassed on his patch and, moreover, Charles knew that he could prove him wrong. Over the past two years, he had travelled to almost every town in New Zealand and had attended dozens of musical occasions at which challenging instrumental and vocal works had been performed by gifted amateurs. How dare the Dean suggest that in New Zealand 'taste is low and knowledge scanty' or that 'the cometary passage of foreign artists leaves no trace'. In a tone of righteous indignation, and conveniently forgetting that his own comments on provincial performers were not invariably complimentary, Charles leapt into the fray:

> *Most certainly we will not stand by idly and allow the many good musicians and the thousands of intelligent amateurs, who have lovingly tended our beautiful art, to be insulted for their pains to please the inordinate vanity of the Dean of Dunedin. The Dean deserves grave censure for an article which is neither more nor less than a slander upon our nation.*

Warming to his task, he moved on to an impassioned defence of 'the small, hard-working and scattered population, straining every nerve over the exhausting struggle involved in building up this fair land', and concluded with a stirring evocation of New Zealand's musical destiny:

> *Yet withal, music in New Zealand flourishes and grows apace, certain of a brilliant future. Our people love it. Every town, large or small, harbours an enthusiastic body of workers and followers of the noble art ... Our musical societies, where well conducted, turn out some capital works ... and there are growing up amongst us many ardent students of music, evincing the keenest delight in their work, and carrying their appreciation of the works of the great masters into a thousand happy homes ... He who cares to listen can readily discern the throb of musical life and progress throughout New Zealand. For the Dean, these pregnant facts are but signs that 'There is no music in New Zealand!'*[29]

It was, of course, a public relations triumph and Charles's reputation as the fearless champion of the musical community soared – together with the *Triad*'s circulation. Meanwhile the Dean, who had given the *Triad* a generous mention in his article, must have found his Christian charity strained to the utmost.

Charles's professional credentials had also taken on an added lustre with the sudden appearance, in August, of the letters L.Mus., L.C.M. after his name on the masthead. These stood for a Licentiate in Music from the British-based London College of Music which, like the Trinity College of Music, offered professional musical qualifications to candidates throughout the English-speaking world. Charles never reveals how he acquired this qualification, but since he was listed as the L.C.M.'s official representative in New Zealand from 1894 – and arranged for the College's local examinations to be inaugurated in 1895 – he could hardly have laid false claim to one of its diplomas. The Licentiate examination could be sat at home; it would have been typical of him to have tossed off a paper, just for fun, some time after he was first appointed. Authorising it would have presented no problems either, for, as he quaintly reassured his readers in the *Triad*, 'It does not matter in what town you reside in New Zealand, arrangements can be made to send examination papers to your clergyman, who will certify that you did the work unaided.'[30]

The Diploma of Licentiate in Music was the most prestigious of the College's qualifications in musical theory and required a high level of musical competence. According to the Annual Register for 1894, potential candidates had to submit 'an exercise of original Composition for four voices with Organ or Stringed Accompaniment'. Only those whose exercises were approved were permitted to sit the examination. The questions ranged from harmonisation to musical history and in a sample paper, which reflects the romantic tastes of the period, candidates were asked to write (in five parts) 'a Cadence in B minor, introducing the Neapolitan Sixth'.[31]

From mid 1895 onwards, the L.C.M.'s examinations were promoted in the *Triad* with a vigour which suggests that Charles was well rewarded for his pains. Organising the exams and appointing local agents also gave him a perfect pretext for calling on musicians and music teachers all over the country and extending his musical network. The elementary and intermediate examinations were soon widely patronised, but for many years Charles remained the L.C.M.'s only Licentiate in New Zealand.

After his successful demolition of the Dean, Charles abandoned all pretence of circumspection in the *Triad*. His unbridled opinions began to dominate its pages and his devastating criticisms, which in early editions had usually been aimed at long-winded clergymen or the hapless correspondents, spared no one. In Timaru local apathy to a lecture by Mark Twain* left him apoplectic:

> *The great American humorist has been, been heard and seems to have conquered about ten per cent of his hearers. It says very little for our appreciation of good humour, subtle satire, and wonderful descriptive power, that nine out of every ten who heard Mark Twain were hugely disappointed ... I am simply amazed. One gentleman remarked that Mark Twain would make a good second cook on a station ... Most Maorilanders haven't a particle of reverence for anything or anybody*

---

* Mark Twain (pseudonym of Samuel Langhorne Clemens), author of the American classic *The Adventures of Huckleberry Finn*, went bankrupt in the 1890s and embarked on a world lecture tour to recoup his losses.

outside their own little admiration clique. If the arch-angel Gabriel were to play a trumpet solo, they would say it wasn't a patch on Bill Smith 'on the cornet'.[32]

Charles's remarks were never without foundation, but their bluntness often offended. In New Plymouth he caused an uproar admitting that he had little enthusiasm for the local women's choir – and made it worse by quoting a provocative verse about a 'shrieking sisterhood'.[33] In Auckland his comments that 'Aucklanders seem to read less',[34] and that 'the general level of culture is lower there than in any of the other centres of Maoriland',[35] prompted the *Observer* to make a spiteful attack on his 'easily won distinction of L.Mus., L.C.M.'[36]

Aspiring contributors also continued to receive frank advice:

J.H.S. (Wellington) I am sorry that 'your pathway is dreary,' but I don't think the fact is of sufficient interest to my readers to allow you a column and a quarter in the Triad *to tell them about it. Write to Mr Marshall, Dunedin, for some of the 'liver and lights mixture' which he makes up for Mr Fish.*[37]

Some of his most memorable outbursts were in defence of music and musicians and when Government policy encroached on musical matters, not even Seddon was exempt:

The Old Age Pension Scheme, propounded by the Hon. the Premier, includes the not quite original suggestion of a tax on concert tickets … As the musical organ of the colony, however, we beg to protest emphatically against a proposal that is simply disgraceful …

Our legislators may not be aware that concert-giving is probably the most precarious form of enterprise existing … concerts of artistic merit, promoted by the musical societies, by musicians of reputation residing in the colony, and at intervals by travelling celebrities … rarely yield any profit at all … the proposed tax would affect and bleed to death the best type of music which we should be eager to foster.

A country like ours, spending hundreds of thousands on education, stultifies itself by imposing a tax on music … Nothing has ever been done for music by any New Zealand Government … and now the Ministry propose to tax music as if it were like truffles – a luxury.[38]

His arguments were unanswerable, and in the following issue he reported that the Government had 'somewhat narrowed their views. The pensions are to be paid by persons who drink beer, go to the theatre, post letters or indulge in the luxury of mortgaging their property.' A capitalist at heart, Charles never really approved of the Liberals' socialist agenda and he concluded by noting that the political writer, Goldwin Smith, 'has just – with excessive rudeness – termed Australia "a skittish young democracy". But he has no idea how skittish New Zealand can be.'[39]

Such lively jousting created plenty of amusement, but readers were also attracted by Charles's authoritative music criticism. From the *Triad* they could learn that there was 'a very noticeable difference in quality between the different registers'[40] in the voice of visiting French soprano, Antoinette Trebelli, and that the local singers who supported her were 'quite as good as any of the companies which usually accompany a great artiste.'[41] Similarly, admirers of the Dunedin singer, Mabel Manson, could discover that Charles considered her to have 'one of the purest and sweetest soprano voices in New Zealand'.* They could chuckle too, at the remark he overheard from a member of the audience who was laboriously following an English translation of the aria that was being sung in Italian: 'That's the worst of Mrs Manson, when she sings anything operatic, you can never hear a word she says.'[42]

Charles excelled at evaluating vocalists, but he also subjected instrumentalists to rigorous scrutiny:

> *I could write pages of the* Triad *in criticism of the fine movement from Beethoven's Third Symphony ... It opened broadly and in tune, the 'cellos playing well, but soon became most chaotic and discordant. The second violins did not take up their leads together, wrong notes were noticeable almost throughout the orchestra and the intonation was very faulty ... The best item of the evening was the clarionet solo 'The Heaven is smiling o'er us', from Meyerbeer's* L'Etoile du Nord, *which was uncommonly well-played. In the same selection, the euphonium solo was in marked contrast, being badly phrased and out of tune.*[43]

Although the Dunedin Orchestral Society may not have appreciated Charles's comments, his grasp of his subject was undeniable.

Musically, the city to which Charles 'gave the palm' was Wellington: 'Wellington has in many respects reached a higher stage of civilisation than the other Maoriland towns. There is more music in the Empire city. There is a really effective technical school; there are good clubs; and there is a fine restaurant – the Trocadero – where meals can be obtained till 12 at night.'[44] In September 1896 he told a Dunedin correspondent that 'we are leagues behind Wellington in music, and also in genuine musical enthusiasm.'[45]

---

* Mabel Manson went on to a distinguished singing career in England, where she became a great favourite at concerts for the New Zealand troops during WWI.

Much of Wellington's musical pre-eminence was due to the talents of the organist and choirmaster, Robert Parker, who had taken over the Choral Society in 1878 and still led the city's musical life. But Thomas Trimnell and Maughan Barnett (whose musical backgrounds were similar to Parker's) and the violinist, Alfred Hill, were equally highly regarded. By late 1896, Wellington's musical community was feverishly preparing for the opening of the Industrial Exhibition in November, for which each of the leading musicians had been asked to write an original composition. Hill had embarked on a cantata based on the Maori legend of Hinemoa and in October the *Triad*'s Wellington music correspondent, 'Diapason', revealed that 'the young composer has sought the seclusion of Island Bay for the purpose of completing his orchestration by the sad sea waves.[46]

By November, however, Hill had thrown musical Wellington into an uproar by resigning his post as conductor of the Orchestral Society and joining forces with the visiting Belgian violinist, Ovid Musin. The cause of Hill's resignation was an eighty-year-old pianist, the self-styled Chevalier de Kontski, who was touring New Zealand in a blaze of publicity and claimed, amongst other things, to be 'the only surviving pupil of the immortal Beethoven'. More showman than musician, his star turn was playing a couple of works with his hands under a blanket. Hill suspected some trickery and when he heard that the Orchestral Society had agreed to play for the Chevalier's concert in Wellington, he refused to conduct and walked out in disgust.

The Chevalier continued with his programme undismayed and, according to 'Diapason', played to huge audiences with 'brilliancy' and 'rhythmic power'. In Christchurch the *Triad*'s music correspondent, 'Allegro', was less enthusiastic and found his interpretation of the 'Moonlight Sonata', supposedly 'gathered at the feet of its profound composer', distinctly unsatisfactory:

> *Beethoven must indeed have been a revengeful man if he did hammer these two first movements so cruelly into the head of the infant prodigy now before us. 'Never,' exclaims enthusiastically the responsible critic of a contemporary, 'never have we heard such an interpretation of the work.' Wonderfully true; and let me add, I fervently trust that we shall never, never, hear it thus interpreted again!*[47]

In Wellington, the storm blew over as quickly as one of the capital's notorious 'southerlies'. The opening of the Exhibition was a triumph; at the afternoon ceremony, the Governor was greeted by a perfectly trained choir of 350 children from the city's schools. At the evening concert, the high point of the programme was *Hinemoa*, which Hill had returned to conduct. 'Diapason' pronounced it a 'distinct success',[48] but it was left to 'Allegro' to point out that this was 'the first musical work ... that is worthy to be regarded as a work of art and written by a native born* N.Z. composer.'[49]

In April 1898, on the *Triad*'s fifth birthday, Charles indulged in his annual display of 'puffing'. On this occasion, his claims to thousands of new subscribers were rather more justified, for the *Triad* was making money and had grown to forty pages. Moreover, his intrepid editorial stance and trenchant opinions on everything from Tolstoy to the railway tea-rooms at Waipukurau were gaining him a devoted following.

In August a parody of Longfellow's 'Village Blacksmith', appeared in the *Triad* composed by an anonymous contributor:

Ode to the Fighting Editor

Under a spreading roof, you see,
The Triad's office stands.
The Fighting Editor is there,
With huge and knotty hands;
....
His brow is wet with honest sweat,
He fights whoe'er he can,
And looks the whole world in the face,
For he fears not any man.[50]

Charles had fought every inch of the way, but the battle for survival had been won.

---

* Hill was born in Australia, but moved to New Zealand at the age of two.

'The "Triad" – "I am The Man".' Cartoon by 'Blo', New Zealand Observer, *1906*. Papers of Dr John Baeyertz.

Chapter 7

The Critic in Maoriland

Once the *Triad* was firmly established, Charles lost no time in moving his family away from Tay Street. Initially they lived on the busy commercial thoroughfare of George Street, but by 1899 they had moved to Mornington, a modest suburb to the west of the city which was linked to the centre by tramway. Charles was still constantly on the road, but during his intermittent periods at home his family found him far less stern than his editorial persona would suggest, and his enthusiasm for new gadgets and theories provided them with endless entertainment. At one stage, he persuaded the whole household to exercise daily with Sandow's dumbbells. Later, he recommended that they make regular use of a muscle vibrator which had been given to him by an advertiser. In August 1897, at the peak of the cycling craze, he managed to win a free bicycle from Guinea Gold Cigarettes by buying 450 packets and selling them on to friends. By 1901, he had bought himself a camera and taken up ping pong.

Charles's willingness to experiment with anything new was typical of his generation, which had benefited more than any other from the many inventions of the nineteenth century. In a book review for the *Triad*, he noted that 'the century has revolutionised thought' and listed 'thirteen first-class inventions and practical applications of science',[1] ranging from electric lighting and steam ships to anaesthetics and X-rays. His fascination with the latest scientific discoveries spilt over into the *Triad*'s science section, where articles on the new 'telegraphy without wires' invented by 'the Italian electrician, Signor Marconi'[2] rub shoulders with discussions on atomic theory. He was also a convinced evolutionist and the names of Charles Darwin, Thomas Huxley and Herbert Spencer cropped up constantly, beside clippings from *The Lancet* or *Science Siftings* on such hotly debated subjects as whether boys should be birched and the perils of vegetarianism.

Closer to home, Charles viewed the cosmic theories of Canterbury College's first professor in Chemistry, Alexander Bickerton, with a certain scepticism:

His argument in favour of the immortality of the cosmos is at least ingenious. I should like to become a convert ... His theory may possibly account for the revivifying of dead stars ... but his effort to prove that 'partial impact' is answerable for more than this is frothy and unsatisfying.[3]

Bickerton's eccentric ideas received little support from the scientific community and he would have ended his days in penury if one of his physics students from Canterbury, Ernest Rutherford, had not later secured him an annuity from the Royal Society of London.

Much of the *Triad*'s scientific coverage was less serious. An article headed 'Women Who Should Shave'[4] and the claim that a 'foreign savant' had discovered that 'the most prevalent cause for hysteria in women is high-heeled shoes'[5] were clearly intended to amuse. Other topics like 'Murderous Plants' and 'The Decline of the Big Toe'[6] were aimed at children. Charles loved children, and most of them responded to his sense of fun. A photograph taken around this time shows him sitting with Carl and Rudolph on the narrow porch of the house in Mornington. He looks a picture of benevolence, with his arms around his sons, both of whom are sitting on his knee. Within the family, however, the apple of his eye was Maida and in 1899 he included in the *Triad* a poem she had written. Only her initials were given, but Charles noted with paternal pride that 'this little child has evidently an intuitive feeling for rhythm and her rimes [sic] are perfect.'[7]

In his reminiscences of his father, Rudolph Baeyertz describes him sitting down to his favourite meal of rare beef followed by apple pie, after which he would invariably declare that his wife was 'noted for her piety'.[8] Despite his geniality at home, for his younger son Charles remained a rather overpowering figure, whose puns were excruciating and who became embarrassingly moist-eyed as he read aloud to his children from the short stories of O. Henry and the plays of Oscar Wilde.

Outside the family circle, young people found him surprisingly approachable. In Wanganui, he spent an afternoon playing rounders with a group of Maori children. They enjoyed it so much that one of the girls sent him a note in Maori inviting him to return the next day. Charles's reply to his nine-year-old correspondent was reproduced in the *Triad*:[9]

Kia Rouie,

E hoa tena koe. Kai nui taku aroha atu ki a koe. Kai te pai to tuhituhi he kotero aroha koe. To kupu e tika. K[a] tai[ma] i to kainga i ten Ra mo te patua pora, taku kupu ki te homai tete aroha ki a koe taku mohio he mai paipai mo taku.

[Hoa aroha]
To hoa nui,
Nga Pereti.*

Even allowing for the typos of his Dunedin printer, Charles's note suggests that he was more at home with spoken than written Maori, but his acceptance of the invitation reveals how much he enjoyed the company of children.

Ever since his arrival in New Zealand, Charles had been interested in learning Maori, prompted by his love of languages. Dunedin had few Maori speakers, but in 1894 he recorded that he was 'making frantic efforts to learn Maori' and that he was looking forward to practising it in Wellington. There, his first attempt ended in farce when the fishermen he accosted with his carefully prepared 'Tena Koe; He aha o koutou ika?'† turned out to be Italian.[10]

Later contacts were more successful and by the time he travelled up the Wanganui River in 1896 his Maori was fairly fluent. On his return to Wanganui, he was invited to play the hymns at one of the Maori churches where he met several colourful local figures, including the eighty-year-old Taki Taki whose photograph appeared in the December *Triad*. The same issue also contains a striking photograph of Haimona Hiroti, a hero of the 1864 battle of Moutoa,‡ who according to Charles was 'in receipt of a Government pension for his valorous deeds'.[11] The many Maori photographs that Charles collected on this trip were destined for the *Triad*'s souvenir Christmas Supplement, which he hoped his readers would send to friends in England. His accompanying text is blatantly pitched at potential tourists, with titillating references to Maori ferocity and their earlier practice of cannibalism.

Like everyone of his generation, Charles believed that Maori were facing extinction and that their cultural legacy was in danger of becoming little more than a tourist attraction. Yet his adoption, in common with many others in the 1890s, of the term 'Maoriland' for New Zealand also implies a tacit acknowledgement that New Zealand's defining characteristic was its Maori heritage.§ Furthermore, while Charles undoubtedly shared in his

---

* A very rough translation is: 'My friend, greetings. I have a lot of respect for you. Thank you for your note. You are quite right. I will be at your house, at that time, on the day, to play the ball game. My thanks to you. I think it will do me good. With love from your great friend, Baeyertz (Pereti).

† 'Good day. What sort of fish have you got?'

‡ The Battle of Moutoa took place on an island in the Wanganui River. After fierce fighting, a group of Wanganui Maori fought off a war party of marauding Hau Hau and saved the town from attack.

§ In the introduction to their recent book, *Maoriland*, Jane Stafford and Mark Williams make the important point that the adoption of the term 'Maoriland' by Pakeha New Zealanders when Maori were 'conveniently figured as a dying race' was a typical act of appropriation by a settler society which 'lacks a past so it takes over that of those displaced'. *Maoriland: New Zealand Literature 1872–1914.* Wellington: Victoria University Press, 2006, pp. 11, 20.

contemporaries' underestimation of Maori resilience, he differed from many of them in his respect for their language. The incorrect pronunciation of Maori irritated him quite as much as the mispronunciation of English: in July 1899 he dedicated nearly two pages of the *Triad* to a succinct guide to Maori pronunciation with a strong recommendation to 'mix with the Maoris themselves'.[12]

One positive outcome of the mistaken belief that the Maori race was doomed was the formation of the Polynesian Society. The Society was co-founded in 1892 by the amateur ethnologist, Stephenson Percy Smith, and the Polynesian scholar, Edward Tregear, who amongst his many other achievements had compiled a widely acclaimed Maori-Polynesian dictionary. Although the Society's charter embraced much of the Pacific and its patron was the Queen of Hawaii, the preservation of traditional Maori knowledge before it was lost to posterity was one of its prime objectives. As an energetic champion of Maori language, Charles would have approved of the scholarly articles in the Society's quarterly *Journal*, but he was well aware that such earnest deliberations would not appeal to the *Triad*'s broad range of readers who, despite his flattering references to them as 'the intelligent and thinking minority',[13] were more middlebrow than highbrow. On the other hand, he warmly recommended the first two parts of a magnificently illustrated series on Maori art by Augustus Hamilton, who was a founding member of the Society.

At a more popular level, Maori subjects had been a feature of New Zealand literature ever since the advent of Sir George Grey's *Polynesian Mythology* in 1855. Grey's book made Maui and Hinemoa household names and, after its publication, there was scarcely an aspiring writer or poet in the country who did not pen a few lines on Maori. The politician and writer Alfred Domett quite excelled himself with a 488-page Miltonian epic set in Rotorua called *Ranolf and Amohia,* which he later expanded to 611 pages to ensure that nothing was left unsaid. In 1890 Thomas Bracken's collection of poetry, *Musings in Maoriland*, contained well over 400 lines on 'The March of Te Rauparaha', which further enhanced his status as national poet.*

Not surprisingly, therefore, one of the *Triad*'s earliest literary contributors also wrote prolifically on Maori. But unlike Domett and his generation, who tended to regard Maori mythology as a local substitute for European classical traditions, Alfred Grace portrayed his characters as uniquely Maori. Grace had strong Maori links through his missionary father and through two of his brothers, who had married high-born Ngati Tuwharetoa women.

---

* Bracken's greatest claim to fame is as the author of 'God Defend New Zealand', which he wrote in 1875.

His own wife was Pakeha, but his short stories are peopled by powerful, uninhibited Maori women, such as the passionate and importunate Hinerau, the vengeful Hira who 'made love ... without exchanging many words',[14] and Reta who drank the blood of a leper to repulse an unwanted suitor. All these figures appeared in Grace's first collection, *Maoriland Stories*, where their frank sexuality must have raised a few eyebrows. But in his first contribution to the family-orientated *Triad*, he prudently eschewed sex and violence and settled for a tongue-in-cheek sketch called 'The Translation of Poppinfex'.

In the first part of the story, a group of young Pakeha men hiccup their way drunkenly to oblivion, while calling on New Zealanders to liberate themselves from 'the pap and coddling of the British matron'. 'If we believe in ourselves ... conquer the world ... separation ... independence ... Cheers and more whiskey. Silence.' In the second part, Grace conjures up the imperial fury that such aspirations would arouse in London and concludes sadly 'they could crush us like flies.'[15] These sentiments, expressed not long before several thousand New Zealand volunteers rushed to fight in the Transvaal* to demonstrate their loyalty to the Empire, were distinctly subversive. But Grace typically adopts a mocking stance towards his characters and leaves it to those who cared to read between the lines to infer his own position.

Charles commended the story's cleverness and, despite its stylistic shortcomings, awarded it first prize in the *Triad*'s 1897 short story competition. Grace's originality and quirkiness must also have caught the eye of the *Bulletin*'s literary editor, A.G. Stephens, for a couple of months later Charles noted 'with pleasure' that the *Bulletin* had accepted several of his stories.[16]

Grace's second contribution to the *Triad*, 'Rawiri and the Four Evangelists', is written in his characteristic folk-tale manner and would have appealed to those who still believed that early New Zealand was inhabited by paternalistic Pakehas and forelock-touching 'natives'. In his next story, 'Patopato and the Water-Nymphs', he lingers over a group of shapely bathers and slyly pokes fun at both Maori ('when a Maori is pouri† he takes it lying down') and Pakeha ('he was sick with that love ... of which the cultivated, artificial, unnatural pakeha knows nothing').[17]

In 1902, Charles wrote a flattering review of Grace's latest collection, *Tales of a Dying Race*, and complimented him on 'an immense improvement in style':

---

* New Zealand sent ten contingents of volunteers to the Boer War (1899–1902) totalling nearly 6500 men.
† Dejected.

> *Mr Grace ... is the only writer, with whose stories I am familiar, who gives us a true picture of the subtle and illusive Maori character. Moreover, there is atmosphere in these tales, and only those who really know the inner workings of the Maori mind, with its curiously bizarre medley of chivalry, dignity, and dalliance, can thoroughly appreciate these tales at their true worth.*[18]

Grace's stories were rare local offerings in the *Triad* and appeared amongst a welter of literary clippings from international journals that ranged from the notebooks of Alphonse Daudet to a few choice verses by 'a discharged literary prisoner'* on his recent experiences in Reading Gaol.[19] Although the *Triad*'s literary content was increasing, Charles still saw the primary role of his magazine as instructive and critical. Local musicians, artists and writers were to be encouraged and admonished, but apart from printing prize-winning essays and stories, he had no ambitions to create a forum for New Zealand authors. Hopeful contributors were often cruelly rebuffed: 'I regret that I cannot print your story. I know the great public is very long-suffering, but even the worm will turn.'[20]

In October 1899, however, a fresh outlet for New Zealand writers emerged in the form of a prestigious new literary journal which was launched in Auckland with an opening manifesto that was quite as spirited as *Zealandia*'s:

> *There comes a time in the history of every colony – at least every colony of British origin – when the new country ceases to be a mere appanage of the old ... Signs of the coming of literary power in New Zealand are not wanting ... New Zealand has shown through her sons that the power of the pen is also hers. But as yet the literary instinct has been content to express itself through the forms of the Old World to appeal to a distant public ...*
>
> *The New Zealand Illustrated Magazine, if it be true to its name, if it be truly New Zealand in matter and in manner, if it serve to focus all that there is of literary power in this colony, is the first step upon the road. There is before such a Magazine a mission and a responsibility. It goes forth with good omens of success. May these omens be fulfilled!*

Below this effusion the editor, Thomas Cottle, stated the magazine's business more bluntly:

> *As our desire is to encourage Colonial Literature and Art, we shall be pleased to give a most earnest and careful consideration to signed contributions which in any way are likely to be of general interest to our readers.*[21]

---

*   Oscar Wilde.

At one shilling, the *Illustrated Magazine* was tastefully laid out and could hardly have presented a more striking visual contrast to the disorderly pages of the *Triad*. Some of its early illustrations were done by Frances Hodgkins and the list of contributors reads like a roll call of New Zealand's leading writers and poets of the period – together with half the members of the Polynesian Society. Among those who flocked to publish in its pages were Jessie Mackay, Arthur Adams, Edith Grossman, Alice Kenny, G.B. Lancaster, Dora Wilcox, James Cowan, Elsdon Best, Johannes Andersen, Augustus Hamilton and Alexander Bickerton. With the strong support of New Zealand's intelligentsia, the *Illustrated Magazine* posed a considerable threat to Charles's hard-won foothold in the cultural market-place, which may explain why he never once mentioned it in the *Triad*. Apart from a back-handed reference to the *Triad*'s 'Art Notes', the *Illustrated Magazine* was equally reticent.

Within a few months Thomas Cottle was trumpeting the magazine's success from his discreetly placed 'Publisher's Desk' on the back page. But the anticipated turf war between New Zealand's two cultural journals never materialised, for the *Triad*'s musical subscribers were far too devoted to the cut and thrust of Charles's music reviews – and the free monthly supplements of songs and piano pieces – to forsake them for a decorous literary publication which took care to offend no one. The two magazines simply ignored each other and once the *Illustrated Magazine* abandoned its early attempts at music criticism, their paths seldom crossed. The *Illustrated Magazine* stuck to its role of publishing the work of New Zealand writers and poets, with courteous monthly reviews of local drama, while the *Triad* continued to hold forth on every conceivable cultural subject with a blithe disregard for persons.

On the rare occasions that their coverage overlapped, their approaches were conspicuously different. In his review of a novel by Harry Vogel, the son of Julius Vogel, Charles shot straight from the hip:

> *The style of this story is so staccato that in the middle of dozing over the pages we wake up every now and then with a start, convinced that something must be happening ... This is the only distinguishing mark of a story which records the evil things that happened because John Anderson took up with a beautiful Maori, when he had already a legal wife.*[22]

The respectful tone of the *Illustrated Magazine* was in marked contrast:

> *'A Maori Maid' by H.B. Vogel ... should appeal strongly to the colonial public by its fresh and vivid description of back-country life and scenes. It has much genuine human interest too and though there is some attempt at*

a treatment of the sex problem, the moral of the tale is distinctly healthy ... and one is left with a pleasurable expectation of Mr Vogel's next novel.[23]

Young Harry may have been the son of a former premier, but his *Maori Maid* was even worse than his father's *Anno Domini 2000*, which at least had the merit of foreseeing the prominence of women in New Zealand's political life.

On the other hand, the differences between Charles's harsh review of Arthur Adams's first book of poetry and the more measured comments of the *Illustrated Magazine* were stylistic rather than substantive. Both reviews, which appeared within a few weeks of each other, agreed that at twenty-eight Adams was 'a writer whom time will ripen'[24] and commended many of the same poems. But while the *Illustrated Magazine* couched its reservations in tactful euphemisms, Charles launched straight into the attack, criticising Adams's rhymes and finding fault with his grammar. After citing a particularly clumsy line, he exploded: 'What in the name of common sense does this mean? ... rubbish, also bunkum and bosh!'[25]

Such treatment of the nation's golden boy of poetry, whose libretto for Hill's *Hinemoa* had been widely acclaimed (although not by the *Triad*), not only ruffled New Zealand's literary establishment but also provoked an angry response from A.G. Stephens, who was responsible for the book's publication by the *Bulletin*. Stephens was a brilliant critic and, since his appointment in 1894, the *Bulletin*'s literary 'Red Page' had become the most influential literary column in Australasia. Elated at having stung the celebrated Stephens into action (and getting a mention in the 'Red Page'), Charles reprinted his comments in the *Triad*:

> *Arthur Adams's 'Maoriland and Other Verses' [sic] receives minute verbal criticism from the energetic and rather pedantic person who edits* The Triad *[sic]. It seems there are still people more concerned with the letter which killeth than with the spirit which giveth life.*[26]

The correspondence rumbled on for months. In May, Johannes Andersen,* whose own verses appeared regularly in *Illustrated Magazine*, rallied to Adams's support. His letter to the *Triad*, which was sprinkled with references to Petrarchan sonnets and 'truncated trochaic measures', concluded: 'Finally, of New Zealand poets that are, or have been – so far as I have seen – Mr Adams holds first rank in my estimation.'[27] By June, Stephens was getting sick of the whole affair and accused Charles of bypassing 'the poetical value

---

* Danish-born Andersen arrived in New Zealand at the age of one and is best known as the first librarian of the Alexander Turnbull Library, a post which he occupied from 1919–37.

of a verse in order to pick imaginary holes in the syntax.' But Charles, as usual, insisted on having the last word: 'I go back to my original contention that there is no poetic quality, no original thought, or brilliant epigram to justify a clumsy construction.'[28]

Charles's views on poetry were based on a typically nineteenth-century veneration for metre and rhyme. For him the rules of poetry were as clear-cut as the rules of musical harmony. Earlier in the year he had published a series on 'Versification' in the *Triad*, adapted from an essay by Thomas Hood, in which he discussed the merits of iambic and anapaestic measures and the mysteries of the octosyllabic tetrameter. His primary objective was to initiate his readers into what he perceived as the essential disciplines of poetry, but he may also have hoped that Hood's daunting guidelines might stem the flow of unpublishable poems that poured monthly over his desk. Characteristically, Charles held strong opinions on poetry, but his critical touch was at its surest with music.

Throughout the 1890s, the musical taste of the New Zealand public was dictated by a nationwide passion for the operettas of Gilbert and Sullivan. In 1879, *HMS Pinafore* was performed in New Zealand for the first time by the locally-formed Riccardi Company. It was an instant success and for the next two decades audiences were provided with a steady stream of Gilbert and Sullivan performed by touring operatic companies. Most of these were under the management of J.C. Williamson,* who was based in Australia and had acquired the Australasian rights to the works of Gilbert and Sullivan. In 1882, his Royal Opera Company arrived in Dunedin from Melbourne for the start of a blockbuster tour of the four main centres with a repertoire of *HMS Pinafore*, *The Pirates of Penzance* and the recently launched *Patience*. On later tours he leavened his fare with English versions of fashionable French operettas, such as Audran's *La Mascotte* and Planquette's *Les Cloches de Corneville*. Within a few years, operetta had completely supplanted any other form of musical entertainment in the affections of the New Zealand public; by 1892, Williamson's stylish productions included a line-up of high-kicking dancing girls whose version of the musical hall song, 'Ta-ra-ra-boom-de-ay', became the popular hit of the decade.

With his broad readership, Charles could not afford to ignore contemporary musical tastes – or his faithful Dunedin subscribers, who relied on his guidance to get good value for money. Thus, his comments on *The French Maid* and *La Poupée* were written with the same thoroughness as

---

*   J.C. Williamson's partnership with George Musgrove began just after his 1882 tour of New Zealand and lasted until 1890. In 1892, the partnership was resumed for a further seven years, after which both parties operated independently.

his reviews of classical concerts and the 'refined and artistic'[29] performances of Wellington's Glee and Madrigal Society. Similarly, the *Triad*'s illustrations feature the curvaceous chorus of Tom Pollard's Liliputian Opera Company quite as frequently as the worthy members of the Dunedin Liedertafel.

Tom Pollard, with his juvenile opera company, was New Zealand's second main purveyor of operetta. During the 1890s, the members of his troupe toured the country so frequently that the *Triad* described them as 'almost fixtures'.[30] Many of the children had been recruited in New Zealand and the company enjoyed loyal support all over the country. In 1895, the Pollards lost most of their scenery and costumes in a fire at the Theatre Royal in Palmerston North, but the local community raised enough money to replace their losses, and in a little over two weeks the company was back in action.

By 1896, most of the performers were no longer children and the troupe was re-launched as an adult company. In the June *Triad*, a photograph of Wellington-born Marion Mitchell, fetchingly attired as a boy, shows a striking brunette with a smouldering gaze and a pair of well-shaped legs in thigh-length stockings. The nineteen-year-old soprano enjoyed a considerable following and not even Charles, in his critic's hat, was entirely impervious to her charms: 'Miss Marion Mitchell is another strong member of Mr Pollard's company … This young lady possesses the somewhat rare quality known as archness in England and what our French friends would describe as *piquante* … we hope to see this excellent actress again and before long.'[31] So did many others. In 1899, after two years of ardent pursuit, she was captured by a wealthy young brewer, Ernest Davis, and in the best traditions of musical comedy went on to become Lady Davis and a gracious mayoress of Auckland.

During the period that operetta ruled supreme, grand opera virtually disappeared from the New Zealand scene. Few touring companies were willing to take the financial risk of crossing the Tasman, with all the paraphernalia of grand opera, to be faced by half-empty houses. Such considerations, however, did not deter George Musgrove from embarking in 1900 on a tour of Australia and New Zealand with a grand opera company. Musgrove, who had just made a fortune in London with the American musical comedy, *The Belle of New York,* lavished money on the production. The sets and the costumes were made in Europe and many of the soloists and the conductor, Gustav Slapoffski, were recruited from the celebrated Carl Rosa Company in London.

The scale and the sumptuousness of the staging far surpassed anything that had previously been seen in Australasia and, when Musgrove's Grand Opera Company arrived in Auckland in July 1901, it created a sensation. The company's repertoire consisted of Wagner's *Lohengrin, Flying Dutchman* and *Tannhäuser*, Bizet's *Carmen*, Gounod's *Faust*, Verdi's *Il Trovatore*, Balfe's

Bohemian Girl and Wallace's *Maritana*. But the greatest excitement was caused by Wagner's operas, which except for *Lohengrin*, had never been performed in New Zealand. In Wellington, Charles attended the opening night of *Tannhäuser* and wrote a review for the *Triad* in which he could barely contain the intensity of his passion for Wagner:

> *Wagner is a supreme master of instrumentation and colour. His orchestration is different in the quality of tone to that of any other composer. No other writer has achieved the richness of effect, and no other composer has treated the inner part of the string quartets as he has. No one has ever equalled him in the skill with which he subdivides the violins, violas, and 'cellos. No one has approached Wagner in writing for wood-wind and brass.*

Wagner's music appealed to an emotional side of Charles that few people outside his immediate family knew existed. Despite his excitement, he still managed to make a careful analysis of the performance, but the block capitals in the last sentence reveal the strength of his feelings:

> *I recommend all my readers ... NOT TO MISS ONE OF THE OPERAS ... IT WILL BE THE GREATEST TREAT THEY HAVE HAD FOR VERY MANY YEARS.*[32]

In October, photographs of Musgrove's leading soloists appeared in the *Triad* and Charles once again urged his readers to attend. A few weeks later, when the *Dunedin Star* dared to suggest that Wagner's music was 'over-praised', Charles dismissed the writer as not knowing 'the A B C of the language of music' and appropriated Wagner for the musically literate:

> *To fully understand Wagner, it is necessary to have some knowledge of the language in which Wagner writes – orchestration, counterpoint and harmony. The critic must understand leit-motif, the canto fermo, chromatic and enharmonic progressions, and such like ... all students of Wagner are agreed as to Wagner's place in music.*[33]

On 14 October, Musgrove's company left Dunedin aboard the 'gallant' *Monowai*, which had so often carried Charles through the storms of Cook Strait. Nearly two weeks later, amidst growing concerns about its non-arrival in Melbourne, the ship reappeared in Dunedin under tow. Two of the propeller blades had sheared at sea and before it had been found by another ship, the *Monowai*, complete with the opera company, had spent ten days adrift.

While Musgrove was raising the curtain on grand opera in New Zealand, on the imperial stage another – far grander – curtain had fallen. On 22 January 1901, Queen Victoria died, after a sixty-four-year reign during which she had presided over an epoch of unprecedented British influence and prosperity. Throughout the Empire, fulsome eulogies to the late Sovereign poured from her loyal subjects – including those in New Zealand. The *Illustrated Magazine* devoted two pages, framed in black, to the Queen's death. Charles, however, managed to squeeze his tribute into a few lines, concluding briskly: 'Well, our Queen has gone to her rest, and Edward VII rules in her stead … Long may he reign. God save the King!'[34] He did not mourn the passing of the Victorian age, despite subscribing to many of its views on art and poetry. In both his personal and business outlook, he was far closer to the liberal and cosmopolitan Edwardians.

A few months later, when the spate of patriotic poems from his grieving readers had eased off, Charles published some irreverent comments on Queen Victoria's musical preferences, gleaned from the *Quarterly Review*:

> *The queen's tastes do not seem to have been of a very high order … she had a great liking for the hopelessly effete 'Norma' and found Sullivan's comic operas an 'endless delight'. She confessed her dislike of Handel's oratorio texts, declaring his music to be dry and formal … Wagner and Brahms were quite incomprehensible …*[35]

Such sly titbits were typical of the *Triad* which, according to Charles, now had the second highest circulation of any magazine in the country. Its controversial editor was also becoming something of a celebrity and appeared, with a group of other well-known Dunedin personalities, in Fred Rayner's popular *Sketcher* competition.

Rayner's brilliant caricatures were unnamed and the object of the competition was to identify the subjects. There is no mistaking Charles. In addition to his bearded profile, complete with Homburg hat and an expensive-looking cigar, a copy of the *Triad* has been tucked under his arm. His expression is haughty and the caption reads 'The Modest One'. This gibe would not have worried him in the least. Rayner's sketch was valuable publicity and Charles was revelling in his growing reputation as a critic to be reckoned with. But like his crusading mother, he also imbued his role with a higher moral purpose:

> *The critic who ever expresses outright satisfaction with anything but the best in art fails in his duty to himself, to the artist and the art concerned, and to the public … The highest standards are the only true criteria of intelligent and honest criticism. The critic should judge always as though he heard the artist for the first time in his life, in some city in which he was a stranger. It is not for him to inquire who Mr Noodle's relatives are, or who taught Miss Shrill to make such offensive noises. He is to judge the artist, as a craftsman judges a machine, by comparison with the best of its kind.*[36]

'The Modest One', by Fred Rayner, Sketcher, *Dunedin, 1 Jun 1898.*
Hocken Periodicals Collection, Uare Taoka o Hakena, University of Otago, Dunedin.

Until now, Charles's critical appraisals had been largely confined to local performers or middle-ranking touring musicians. This was partly because, in the aftermath of the long depression of the 1880s and early 1890s, leading artists who visited Australia had often omitted New Zealand from their itineraries, believing that it would prove unprofitable. By the onset of the Edwardian period, however, the country's economy was booming. New Zealanders had money in their pockets and a stream of visits from international stars enabled Charles to exercise his critical skills on some of the greatest performing artists in the world.

Chapter 8

Walking with the Stars

In September 1901, Jean Gerardy was the first world-class European musician to perform in New Zealand for nearly a decade. The Belgian-born cellist was an acclaimed international soloist, who had made his first appearance in London at the age of twelve and had later been commanded by Queen Victoria to play at Windsor. Charles, however, in a fit of pique over a failure by the theatre management to send him his customary free 'press' pass, declined to review him – although he still attended his concert in Dunedin and declared himself 'immensely pleased'[1] with it. But nothing so trivial prevented him from commenting on New Zealand's next visiting celebrity, who was not only one of the greatest operatic stars of her generation, but also hailed from his home town of Melbourne.

Since her début in Brussels in 1887, Nellie Melba had become one of the world's leading sopranos. In London, where she had a permanent dressing room at Covent Garden, her popularity was so great that in 1893 the Savoy Hotel's famous chef, Auguste Escoffier, created his classic recipe of peaches with raspberries and ice cream in her honour. When she returned to Australia in 1902, her homecoming was more like a royal progress than a concert tour. Triumphal arches were erected along her route and rapturous crowds, bursting with local pride, greeted her wherever she went. In New Zealand, which had recently declined to become part of the newly formed Commonwealth of Australia, regional solidarity still prevailed and she was welcomed with wild enthusiasm as a local girl who had made good.

The *New Zealand Herald*'s review of Melba's first concert in Auckland in March 1903 captures the euphoria:

> She presented a dazzling picture of comely womanhood, garbed in an exquisite evening dress – a gem of the dressmaker's art – of light gray satin, lavishly embroidered with pale pink roses ... There was the gleam of many a diamond from her faultlessly-cut bodice, and a magnificent necklace formed of the same sparkling jewels encircled her throat ...
>
> 'What of Melba's voice?' it will be asked ... It is the loveliest voice that has ever been heard in New Zealand, a voice of such rare beautiful quality that

> *it has no peer in Europe, and one that for flawless perfection may never have an equal ... the impression made upon her audience was electrifying ... her performance was a revelation ... delivered in liquid cadences, which flowed as easily from her lips as rippling waters flow in stone-strewn brooks ...* [2]

Charles did not hear Melba until she reached Christchurch, but since the coverage of the Wellington press had been equally hyperbolic, his expectations were high. Throughout the performance, as he sat listening intently and making notes in his little black book, Charles must have been well aware that he was facing one of the greatest challenges of his critical career. Although Melba's voice was magnificent, something vital was missing. Later, when he interviewed Melba, they enjoyed a delicious musical gossip in which the notoriously territorial prima donna rubbished both Ada Crossley and Amy Castles, who were two of Australia's most popular singers and considerably younger than she was. She also took a swipe at the British contralto, Clara Butt, declaring that she had 'a God-given voice, but no brains.'[3]

Charles's carefully written review of Melba appeared in the March *Triad*:

> *Granted that she has a voice of great compass and wonderful flexibility, a voice of rare quality and magnificent cultivation, the greatest voice that has ever been heard in Maoriland, the conviction still remains that she is not by any means the greatest artist who has sung in the colonies. The tears in her songs are not reproduced in her voice; her singing is not passionate intuition, but is rather the result of indomitable energy and perseverance. A superb voice is like a perfect piano, or a magnificent Strad; each should be the vehicle of emotion and thought. It is the mind and spirit behind the voice, the piano, the violin, that is of supreme importance ... Madame is a great artiste, and doubtless one of the greatest* coloratura *singers living ... but while giving the voice and the stage presence, she withheld the temperament.*[4]

For Charles, a singer without temperament was little more than a 'mechanical nightingale'. Predictably, his suggestion that Melba was less than perfect aroused widespread indignation. Much of his review, however, was reprinted in the *Bulletin*, where A.G. Stephens noted that 'some of the best musical criticism in Australasia comes in *The Triad*.'[5] In New Zealand, as the outrage at his remarks grew, Charles remained defiant. A few months later, he seized upon a critical article on Melba in the British *Saturday Review* to point out, with his customary modesty, that the influential English music critic, John Runciman, was in complete agreement with him.

Melba was not a concert singer and Charles judged her less harshly after he had heard her in opera, but the comparison he draws between her and the French soprano, Emma Calvé, reveals his preferences:

> *Calvé has emotion, warmth, glow, personality, enthralling verve, soul … call it what you will. The heart of a breathing woman tumultuously alive is in her every note … Calvé sings for herself, and is the exultant thrall mistress of her art … Melba has no temperament. Calvé is temperament incarnate.*[6]

It was temperament, too, that first attracted his attention to a young New Zealand soprano named Rosina Buckmann, who had been forced by ill health to abandon a promising career in England. Within a few weeks of her return home in March 1904, Charles heard her singing in Wellington and immediately realised her potential: 'Miss Buckmann is decidedly an artist … and above all she has temperament.'[7] A year later, when the leading soprano in Alfred Hill's new opera, *A Moorish Maid*, fell ill, Charles gave Rosina her first professional break by persuading Hill to give her the part of La Zara in which she became an overnight success.

A Moorish Maid toured the country and when the cast arrived in Dunedin, Charles invited Rosina to stay at the family's new home in the prosperous suburb of St Clair.* She was an easy-going guest who drew a pig in Rudolph's 'pig book' and made friends with the whole household. In his reminiscences, Rudolph recalls her practising (and forgetting) her lines as she dressed for the performance. He also remembers Alfred Hill coming to the house to teach her his famous song, 'Waiata Poi', which immediately became a popular hit and was later a best-selling record.

After his triumphant début with *Hinemoa*, Hill had spent five years in Sydney where he conducted the Sydney Liedertafel and composed a series of light romantic operas. In 1902 he returned to New Zealand for the première of his comic opera, *Tapu*, which like *Hinemoa* played to his unique gift for setting Maori themes within the context of western music. Charles held him in high regard. After hearing the initial production of *A Moorish Maid* in Auckland, he wrote an enthusiastic review for the *Triad* in which he describes Hill's musicianship as being 'of an altogether rare order'.[8] A few months later he wrote another glowing review for the *New Zealand Times*, praising the opera's 'masterly scoring' and repeating his claim that 'Mr Hill has never been appreciated at his true worth as a creative artist.'[9]

---

*   Charles had rented a house in an attractive, tree-lined street then known as Arthur Street, but now re-named Hobson Street.

For a local musician, such words of support from the hard-hitting editor of the *Triad* carried considerable weight, but by now visiting artists were also beginning to realise that Charles's approval was the key to a successful tour. The German pianist, Albert Friedenthal, courted him shamelessly and was rewarded with a series of flattering reviews and a full-page interview. Charles entertained him at home where they spoke German together, and when Friedenthal returned to Berlin they kept up a regular correspondence which Charles quoted (in German) in the *Triad*. Between 1899 and 1905, Friedenthal visited New Zealand three times, and while Charles genuinely admired his playing, Friedenthal's little attentions undoubtedly helped to oil the wheels.

The British bass, Watkin Mills, was another regular visitor who made sure that he was on the best of terms with New Zealand's most influential critic. He and Charles played each other at billiards and became such good friends that Charles even composed a humorous 'Owed' to him, which appeared in the *Triad*. For Mills, the friendship paid handsome dividends and produced copious publicity and a lengthy interview. Despite the personal relationship, however, Charles had no qualms about rebuking Mills for his 'doubtful taste'[10] in glaring angrily at an erring instrumentalist. Nor did he balk at publishing a mixed review of his performance as Mephistopheles in Gounod's *Faust*.

Even a world star like the Russian pianist, Mark Hambourg, who made his first visit to New Zealand in mid 1903, went out of his way to be charming. At twenty-four, Hambourg already had a towering musical reputation which, combined with his pouting lips and shoulder-length hair, had won him thousands of fans, including a rebellious New Zealand schoolgirl in London who later changed her name to Katherine Mansfield. Given Hambourg's megastar status, Charles was only too happy to give him all the publicity he wanted. In the July *Triad*, he published a full-page photograph of him, signed for his fans, accompanied by a two-page interview. Such exclusive coverage must have sent the *Triad*'s sales through the roof, but Charles was also genuinely impressed by Hambourg's artistry. After hearing him perform in Dunedin, he described the young Russian as an 'astounding virtuoso' and 'one of the greatest living interpretative musical geniuses'.[11]

At a personal level, Charles found Hambourg to be 'a man of wide general culture and sympathy'[12] whom he invited home to meet the family. Now that the *Triad* was making money, Charles could afford to entertain his overseas guests in style, and there was nothing he enjoyed more than escorting them around his private 'cabinet' which, in the best traditions of European intellectuals, he had furnished with scientific curiosities and a small collection of pictures by his favourite artists such as van der Velden and the landscape painter, C.N. Worsley. He also had an excellent piano, and musical evenings around the Bechstein grand later became a standard feature of his hospitality. Although Charles and Hambourg both had professional agendas, their relationship blossomed into a lasting friendship, but it was left to another pianist, whose international reputation was even greater than Hambourg's, to give Charles one of the most remarkable scoops of his career.

Ignacy Jan Paderewski arrived in New Zealand in August 1904 with a grand piano, thirty-seven trunks and an Australian parrot. Paderewski was a charismatic and romantic figure who, like Hambourg, possessed many of the attributes of a modern pop star, including a huge mane of tousled hair. He enjoyed a world-wide following and his effect upon women was so legendary that cartoonists regularly depicted him surrounded by swooning females – or protected from their attentions by policemen. At this stage in his career, however, his concert tours were little more than moneymaking exercises to cover his lavish lifestyle* and he shunned all unnecessary publicity. But he had not reckoned on Charles, who through a mixture of guile and diplomacy managed to coax his way into a coveted personal interview:

> *Knowing how cordially Paderewski detests being interviewed, I made my plea for an interview as forcible as possible ... I emphasised the fact that the Triad was the only magazine in Australasia devoted to music and art [and] assured him that he would be conferring a very great favour on all music teachers in this country, if he would consent to give them his ideas on the technique of pianoforte playing. I further disclaimed any desire to know how many trunks of wardrobe and general luggage he carried, what he had for breakfast, or whether his parrot used Pears' soap.*[13]

Disarmed, Paderewski invited Charles to his hotel room where they had a long conversation about music which, thanks to his powers of recall, Charles was able to reproduce in full in the *Triad*. At close quarters, Charles was dazzled by Paderewski's charm:

> *No man, to say nothing of woman, could possibly be brought into contact with Paderewski without falling under the spell of his powerful and alluring personality ... I am firmly convinced he is a hypnotist ... [and] I am perfectly satisfied that his wonderful triumphs are in no small measure due to his personal magnetism.*[14]

---

* An ardent patriot, Paderewski also donated generously to political causes in his native Poland. After World War 1, he became the first Prime Minister of the newly independent Poland.

According to Rudolph, Paderewski also visited the family home, but from the safe distance of his seat in the Wellington Opera House, Charles's assessment of the great pianist was typically clear-eyed:

> *An infinite deal of nonsense has been written by most of the Australasian dailies about Paderewski's playing ... [B]oth the 'Waldstein' and the C sharp Minor Sonatas just stopped short of being great ... I was most disappointed with the Beethoven Sonatas which seemed to lack both depth and breadth, and the first movement of the Sonata in C sharp minor was cold and colourless ... I am quite certain that I have not heard Paderewski at his best.*[15]

Charles's suspicions were well founded. Paderewski was exhausted by his hectic touring schedule and was later forced to take a two-year break from performing to recover.

Despite these heady contacts with international celebrities, Charles never lost sight of his cultural mission to New Zealand. While he dined with the stars (too well, on one occasion, by his own admission), he still found time to ensure that his readers developed suitable literary tastes through regular competitions in the *Triad*. His Twelve Best Novels competition elicited between ten and eleven thousand replies, although he complained that 'the vast majority of the competitors display an appaling [sic] ignorance of the classic English Novel.'[16] His own list started with Fielding's *Tom Jones* and ended with Meredith's *Ordeal of Richard Feveril*. He also carried on a running battle with the Dunedin Liedertafel over their 'uncertain' attack and 'slip-shod' enunciation,[17] and devoted three columns of the *Triad* to a blistering review of James Izett's recently published *Maori Lore*, which he called a 'travesty on Maori mythology' and condemned as 'the most shockingly crude, inartistic, unreliable publication dealing with Maori traditions and history that I have ever seen'[18] – a view that many modern readers would share.

Other sallies were even more brutal:

> *Miss Lilian Irvine looks about seventeen years of age, and is the more or less happy possessor of a voice which in the middle register is hard, strident, and entirely lacking in colour or tone. Her style of singing is vulgar in the extreme, and she mispronounced every word that was by any chance mispronouncable ...*
>
> *If it is intended to do anything with Miss Irvine's voice in the future, it is absolutely imperative that she cease singing at once. She must be educated, not only vocally, but as regards the native tongue of some of us.*[19]

This particular onslaught spawned a furious correspondence with the *Canterbury Times*, which had earlier published a hostile article on the *Triad* suggesting that Charles's professed aim of raising the general standard of music would be better served if he tempered his remarks 'with consideration for a performer's sense of feeling.'[20] In a subsequent letter, his anonymous critic also claimed that his 'objectionable methods'[21] would only discourage young singers.

Although he wrote a spirited defence ('I decline to be tortured for anybody's sake'),[22] Charles was cut to the quick. The cultivation of youthful talent was one of his greatest passions and he prided himself on the guidance he gave to promising amateurs. Moreover, wherever he saw real potential, he was generous in his praise – as the tone of an earlier review shows:

> *Miss Marion Watson has a light mezzo-soprano voice, which is both sweet and true. This young lady is evidently exceedingly nervous and sensitive, and I am quite sure was by no means heard at her best on this occasion. Nevertheless, her phrasing was intelligent throughout, in spite of her obvious attack of stage fright. Miss Watson must persevere, and accustom herself to appearing in public. She has the temperament without which nothing can be done in any art.*[23]

For local performers who measured up to his standards, Charles went out of his way to promote their careers. The attractive (and gifted) Amy Murphy of Dunedin, whose mother Charles had long admired, was a case in point. From the time of her début in 1899, she received constant encouragement and advice in the *Triad*, and in October 1904 her prospects were given a further boost by a flattering article and a full-page photograph, strategically placed just after one of Paderewski. Rosina Buckmann was similarly nurtured and in 1906 a picture of her in a long white dress, with a determined tilt to her chin, appeared in the August *Triad* above the caption: 'The artistic and temperamental soprano.'[24]

Despite his reputation for severity, Charles's amicable relations with young performers are eloquently demonstrated in a series of photographs which appeared in the *Triad* in late 1906. The first shows Charles on his knees, surrounded by a bevy of young men and women who are apparently attacking him with umbrellas and brooms and even a large screwdriver. He is dressed in white tie and tails, but his shirt, with its four-inch collar, hangs open at the neck and his chest is pierced by several 'arrows'. One of his assailants is pulling his hair. The caption reads 'Judging at the Dunedin Competitions' followed by '"Strike if you must, this old grey head, but spare – my one dress suit!" he said'.[25,*] Another photograph shows him once again on his knees, equally dishevelled and pleading for mercy.

---

* A parody of Whittier's 'Barbara Frietchie' which had featured in the programme.

The Dunedin Competitions began in 1902, inspired by a similar scheme in Ballarat, and were aimed at encouraging the study of music, art and literature through contests and prizes. From the outset, Charles gave the project his fullest support. By its second year, he had been invited to join the panel of judges with responsibility for the section devoted to recitation (then known as 'elocution'). The scheme caught on like wildfire, soon attracting

SKETCHES AT THE COMPETITIONS.

BAEYERTZ'S DREAM.

Oh! I have passed a miserable time,
So full of fearful sights, of ugly sounds,
That by the conscience of a Christian critic
I would not pass another such a week.
Not for a wilderness of umpire's bays,
So full of dismal horror was the time.

O Lord! Methought what fell cacophonies
Assailed the battered porches of mine ears;
Methought I saw our mother speech un-
limbed,
And flung in bleeding fragments at my feet.

Dissevered aitches, suffocated pauses
Bestrewed the oozy pavement of my chamber,
Like putrefying offal of a shambles.
Behold me when returned to my bosomed family—
A battered wreck, a son of prodigal.—(*Boris*).

Cartoon by Fred Rayner in the Sketcher, *Dunedin, 1 Nov 1903.*
Hocken Periodicals Collection, Uare Taoka o Hakena, University of Otago, Dunedin.

hundreds of competitors as well as large audiences who were quite willing to pay the guinea subscription ticket to enjoy the spectacle of their family and friends performing. From 1902 onwards, the impressive programme for Dunedin's 'Grand Annual Musical & Elocutionary Festival' was prominently displayed in the *Triad* with a daunting list of competitions ranging from a Humorous Dialogue ('not to exceed 20 minutes'), to a Song for Ladies ('without music and accompanied by self'),[26] and a Grand Choir Contest.

Charles took to his role of adjudicator like a duck to water. It was a perfect outlet for his didactic gifts and for his sense of humour. After the 1903 Competitions, his methods were discussed in the *Otago Daily Times*:

> *It has appeared to many people that Mr Baeyertz's frequently rather humorous way of exaggerating the defects of competitors amounted to burlesque; but if so, he had good authority for what he did. Any feeling of resentment, however, was probably dispelled as far as the competitors were concerned, when Mr Baeyertz met them in conference and pointed out not only their defects but also how to overcome them.*[27]

By 1906, Charles had become one of the stars of the show whose performance as a judge provided quite as much entertainment as the competitors. But, as the *Otago Daily Times* pointed out, his abilities as a teacher and his commitment to his task were unquestionable:

> *Mr C.N. Baeyertz has made no enemies this year. There remains no excuse for doubt of Mr Baeyertz's high qualities as a judge of elocution. He is fastidiously careful, and he adds to his virtues, knowledge. Also he takes infinite pains with competitors, going through their work with them, instructing, advising, suggesting. No man could do more, and competitors fully realise that few men would do as much.*[28]

Such dedication, however, combined with the effort of covering so many different cultural activities, took its toll on even Charles's boundless energies and probably accounts for his frequent recourse to clippings from overseas publications to fill the pages of the *Triad*. At the same time, he was also busily collating a mass of facts and figures for inclusion in his forthcoming guidebook, which was published in June 1902. This additional pressure may explain a regrettable lapse in cultural standards in the March issue when, 'taking advantage of the presence in our midst of Mr Holn of the firm Weingarten Bros., New York',[29] he published a series on corsets. Such blatant connivance with a manufacturer does Charles little credit, but in an age when a well-made corset could contribute to a woman's figure quite as dramatically as the modern wonderbra, the series would certainly have interested his readers. It also gained him a faithful advertiser: for the next decade, the *Triad*'s pages were graced by an astonishing hourglass-shaped woman encased in a 'W.B. Erect Form Corset'.

Charles's *Guide to New Zealand: The Scenic Paradise of the World* was the first New Zealand guidebook to be published in New Zealand and came with the blessing of the Government Tourist Department. In his introduction, Charles alerted his target audience of overseas tourists to the unsurpassed beauties that awaited them:

> *The compiler of this Guide has journeyed through our marvellous Maoriland from the far North even to its farthest South. He has seen and felt some of 'the might – the majesty of loveliness' of our glorious lakes girt about with bush-clad hills, of snow-capped mountains frowning through the clouds, of our sublimely noble fjords, in all their solitary grandeur.*

Several paragraphs follow, laden with references to the 'awe inspiring evidences' of 'our Good Mother Nature'[30] and sprinkled with poetic quotations. Much of the main text is in a similar vein, and includes the claim that the celebrated coach road through the Otira Gorge is of such 'a dizzy boldness' that those in the Alps, the Carpathians, the Balkans and the Himalayas appear 'tame and prosaic'[31] in comparison. Charles, who had never been outside Australasia, was quoting the widely travelled war correspondent, Archibald Forbes, but his statement gains some credibility from the accompanying photograph which shows a spectacular road, barely the width of a vehicle, clinging to the side of the Gorge above a raging torrent. Nevertheless, even by the standards of the day, such high-flown language was slightly over the top, and in later editions the introduction at least is rather more restrained.

Apart from its promotional overload, the *Guide* contains a wealth of practical information and gives detailed descriptions of recommended excursions. Foremost amongst these is a visit to Mahinapua Creek to admire 'some of the most wonderful reflections to be seen anywhere in the world'[32] and a boat trip from Wanganui to Pipiriki on one of Mr Hatrick's 'well-appointed river steamers'[33] – a journey that took seven and a half hours and included winching the boat over numerous rapids with steel cables.

It was typical of Charles to have turned the necessity of constant travel into a money-making venture. The books sold for a shilling and went into several editions, which must have produced some useful additional income. Yet there was nothing feigned about his admiration for the New Zealand landscape. Throughout its first decade, the *Triad* was full of scenic photographs, some taken by Charles himself, and in his 'Obiter Dicta' column he regularly extolled the charms of the West Coast and bewailed its neglect by tourists.

In January 1902, while his guidebook was still in preparation, Charles dedicated the first two pages of the *Triad* to an account of his first visit to Rotorua and the surrounding thermal district. Here tourism was already well established and Charles took a steam launch across the lake to inspect Hinemoa's famous bath for himself. There, he persuaded a local chief to dictate his own version of the legend to him in Maori, which he included in the guidebook. After years of battling around the countryside on business, he revelled in being part of an organised tour:

> *After viewing the sights of Waiotapu, we passed on to that most delectable spot, Wairakei. Our party included a doctor, a Canadian settler; a Cambridge 'varsity man and some ladies ... we had a capital time at the Geyser House Hotel. We saw geysers, champagne pools, lightning pools, mud volcanoes, rapids, falls, and last but not least an amazing blow-hole ... When not sight-seeing we were bathing, shooting, or playing croquet. There are few better places in which to spend a holiday than in Wairakei.*[34]

Although Charles made a point of never mentioning his family in the *Triad*, the suspicion remains that, as usual, he undertook this jaunt alone.

With the success of the *Triad*, his absences from home seem only to have increased. For example, in September 1905, he brushed off a gibe in Wellington's weekly *Free Lance*, which had pounced on a grammatical slip in the *Triad*, by claiming that since he had only just returned to Dunedin after an absence of six months, the mistake must have been a printer's error.

Despite his incessant travels and an increasing number of musical performances to review, Charles's coverage of science, literature and art remained surprisingly consistent. In the 'Science Jottings', he ranged over subjects as diverse as the use of substitutes in the food industry and the 'demoralising intoxication'[35] of cocaine. Literary commentary* and reviews also continued to feature prominently – although most of New Zealand's poets received short shrift. In the case of Hubert Church, who worked as a clerk at the Treasury, Charles concluded a review of his first book of verse† with the stinging comment that 'reason stands aghast to see such turgid verbiage committed to print.'[36]

Like much New Zealand writing at this time, Church's poems were published by the *Bulletin*'s publishing house in Sydney, which sent Charles a stream of books to review – including a volume of poetry by A.G. Stephens.‡ Stephens was a far better critic than he was a poet, but mindful perhaps of the need to mend his fences after their dispute over Arthur Adams, Charles

---

* Literature was not mentioned on the cover until 1903 when Charles altered the *Triad*'s masthead and adopted a new and more elegant cover design.
† Hubert Church, *West Wind*. Sydney: Bulletin Newspaper Co., 1902.
‡ A.G. Stephens & Norman Lindsay, *Oblation*. Sydney: A.G. Stephens & N. Lindsay, 1902.

wrote a tactful review and vented most of his disapproval on Norman Lindsay's erotic illustrations, which he described as 'occasionally coarse to the verge of nastiness.'[37]

In the meantime, a series of departures and deaths had robbed New Zealand's art scene of much of its vitality. In February 1898, Dunedin's artists (who were still lamenting Nerli's sudden move to Auckland in late 1896) were devastated by the death of William Hodgkins. Hodgkins had been the leading light of the city's cultural life for over two decades and after his death Dunedin never fully recovered its artistic pre-eminence. At the opening of the Otago Art Society's annual exhibition in November 1899, the new president deplored the general decline in standards: 'Our local artists are not doing anything great ... for all lovers of art must admit that Dunedin is one of the worst places in New Zealand as far as any encouragement to art and artists is concerned ... Not many years ago things were different.'[38]

Even Frances Hodgkins got little praise and her sketches were deemed to be below her usual standard. By now Frances was desperately trying to save money through teaching and magazine illustration to pay for further study in Europe and the news, only a few weeks after her father's death, that her erstwhile mentor, Nerli, had eloped with an Auckland girl and departed for Australia can only have strengthened her resolve to pursue her career overseas. Barely a month later, in April 1898, New Zealand lost yet another important artistic figure when van der Velden also left for Australia, lured by the mistaken belief that his prospects would be better in Sydney.

By the end of 1898, James Nairn was the only remaining member of the group of European painters who had brought so much vigour and inspiration to New Zealand art in the 1890s. Over the years, through his teaching and his all-male painting parties at a ramshackle bach called Pumpkin Cottage in the rural settlement of Silverstream, Nairn had inculcated a whole generation of young painters with the 'plein-air' principles of Impressionism. For most of this time, his work received favourable coverage in the *Triad*, and in September 1897, two of his paintings were among the first New Zealand works to be reproduced in its pages. But by 1903, the *Triad*'s Wellington art correspondent, 'Criticus', had sided with the city's conservative art establishment, referring darkly to Nairn's 'shockingly bad influence' and accusing him of spreading the teaching of 'slovenly blots and smudges ... nothing short of the most disgraceful rubbish'[39] from Nelson to Wanganui.

Within a year Nairn was dead, aged only forty-four, and the mantle of New Zealand's best-known painter had fallen on the Aucklander, Charles Goldie, who had returned home in 1898 after studying for four and a half years at the Académie Julian in Paris. Much of his training took place in the studio of the leading 'Salon' painter, William-Adolphe Bouguereau, from whom he acquired a devotion to realism that lent an almost photographic quality to the melancholy Maori portraits that were gaining him a nation-wide reputation.

In December 1902, after seeing some of Goldie's paintings at the Otago Art Society's annual exhibition, Charles wrote a cautious review: 'They are very equal in merit, beautifully drawn, and most carefully painted; and although the treatment might have been a little more sympathetic, still they are much the best studies from the Maori that have yet been painted in New Zealand.'[40] A few months later, the *Triad*'s Auckland art correspondent was rather more specific:

> *There is a certain monotony in these pictures of Maori life, supreme though they are in this style of subject. The observer is struck at once by the splendid academic qualities of Goldie's pictures, but those attributes alone do not make the great artist ...*[41]

But Goldie was a huge success with the general public and at the end of 1903, in a concession to popular taste, Charles published a fulsome article on his work written by the Auckland lawyer, Richard Singer, who was an occasional contributor. Amongst the illustrations is a photograph of Goldie's famous Shortland Street studio, where Hill gained much of his knowledge of Maori music from Goldie's models and where he reputedly composed 'Waiata Poi'. The studio is elaborately arranged in the best Parisian manner, with oriental hangings and classical sculptures. Maori portraits adorn the walls and in centre stage Patara te Tuhi, one of four chiefs who accompanied the Maori king on his visit to Queen Victoria, sits in a fringed korowai cloak sipping gingerly from a dainty teacup and eyeing a plate of biscuits.

Later, Charles complained that Goldie 'never leaves anything to one's imagination',[42] but his popularity was unstoppable: in 1905, five pages of the *Triad*'s art supplement were dedicated to his portraits. Meanwhile, a bevy of promising younger artists, which included Grace Joel and Frances Hodgkins, had long since headed for Europe where Charles kept a watching brief on their activities, reporting proudly on their achievements in London and Paris and welcoming the few who returned.

In April 1905, Charles celebrated the *Triad*'s twelfth anniversary. His tone, as usual, was humorous: 'The *Triad* has made many staunch friends, and some enemies, and I believe that I have been as fortunate in the one as in the other.'[43] He could well afford to be jocular for the *Triad* was fast becoming a national institution. Meanwhile, Thomas Cottle, the editor of the *Illustrated Magazine,* had resigned, and the *Triad*'s closest rival was entering its death throes. Neither Cottle nor his successor had Charles's wit or his sense of business, and in September 1905 the only response to the *Illustrated Magazine*'s final demise was a faint yawn from suburbia.

Chapter 9

New York

Early in 1905, Charles embarked on a series of overseas trips that began with a visit to Melbourne. Australia's musical life left him unimpressed: 'I heard no singer in Australia at all comparable with Mr Hamilton Hodges, Miss Amy Murphy, Mrs Burns, Miss Jeanne Ramsay or many other New Zealand vocalists.' Sydney's city organist was also a disappointment: 'We have many organists in New Zealand with whom he could study for several years with advantage.' But it was the 'colonial accent' of the schoolchildren, 'much more marked in Australia than New Zealand', that aroused his greatest ire. Moreover it could spread to New Zealand: 'If vigorous measures are not adopted to check it, we shall develop an accent in God's own country compared with which the Downeaster in America would be a thing of beauty.'[1] From his point of view, probably the most enjoyable part of the trip was the afternoon he spent watching a cricket match at his old school in Adelaide, at which Prince Alfred Collegians notched up a record 700 runs.

Less than a year later, Charles travelled to Tasmania, accompanied by his family, for a reunion with his mother in Hobart. At sixty-four, Emilia was showing no signs of slowing down. Since 1892 she had been living in England, where she had travelled the length and breadth of the country and preached to thousands. In mid 1904 she returned to Australia with Charles's sister Marion and her husband and family, who planned to settle in Perth. Within a few weeks of her arrival, Emilia had booked a hall seating 1500 for a meeting and by May 1905 she was conducting missions in Melbourne, which were piously reported in religious publications like *The Southern Cross* and *The Christian*. The 'Ladies Page' of Melbourne's *Table Talk*, however, took a more frivolous approach:

> *Slight and petite, her dark eyes glowing with enthusiasm, as she talks of her mission it is difficult to believe that Mrs Baeyertz has already accomplished no less than thirty years' work since her conversion from Judaism. Her face shows little sign of age, her dark hair is still unflecked with grey, and her figure quite of youthful contour. It really seems that work and enthusiasm have kept her young.*[2]

In Sydney Watson's biography, Emilia's first meeting for fifteen years with 'her only and dearly loved son and family' in February 1906 gets only a brief mention before 'God's messenger faced the perils of the sea again' and returned to Western Australia. But Emilia's sojourn in Perth was short-lived: by December 1906 she was back in London, declaring that her mission to Western Australia had been 'a foretaste of heaven'[3] and presiding over yet further scenes of conversion.

When Charles got back to New Zealand, he found that the chief topic of conversation was the forthcoming international exhibition in Christchurch, which was due to open in November. The exhibition was intended to mark New Zealand's elevation from Colony to Dominion* and was being planned on a grand scale, driven by Seddon's desire to celebrate the achievements of the Liberals and show the world 'that New Zealand was a great country'.[4] His Government was underwriting the project and a horde of politicians, civil servants and businessmen had been engaged to orchestrate the various displays. These covered every aspect of New Zealand life, ranging from an exhibition of agricultural machinery to a court full of models and graphs trumpeting the success of New Zealand's labour laws.

As well as the magnificent 'palace of white and gold'[5] that was being built in Hagley Park to house the exhibits, a twelve-acre area known as 'Wonderland' had been designated for outside amusements. These included such novelties as camel rides and a water chute, which were intended to attract the thousands of ordinary citizens whom the organisers hoped would attend. As at earlier exhibitions, there was also a picture gallery and a concert hall offering a daily programme of popular and classical music.

Tom Pollard, who had recently disbanded his troupe after a disastrous South African tour, was appointed as director of entertainments and, after some bungling by the committee, Hill was chosen to conduct the orchestra. Pollard and Hill had already enjoyed a successful collaboration on the production of *Tapu*, which had been played against dramatic backdrops of the famous Pink and White Terraces and included a show-stopping haka. According to the *Triad*, however, their partnership at the Christchurch exhibition was less happy, and Pollard's belief 'in the mission and power of attraction of music-hall music'[6] was often at odds with Hill's determination to provide a high-class classical programme.

From the outset, Hill had an uphill struggle. The Government had only agreed to pay the costs of a small ensemble of thirty players, which he considered quite inadequate for the performance of orchestral music. Charles sided with Hill, and in a letter to the *New Zealand Times* went in to bat for him:

---

*   New Zealand became a self-governing Dominion on 26 September 1907.

> *An orchestra of thirty players is wholly unworthy of any International Exhibition, and only fit to play at such functions as a fancy fair for the benefit of decayed muffin men ... No conductor in the world can achieve a satisfactory result with a band of thirty players ... The credit of the colony is at stake in this matter ... The playing of an orchestra of thirty would be as dull as an alderman at church.*[7]

He also made a convincing case for the financial viability of engaging a full orchestra. Many people shared Charles's view. In September, Sir Joseph Ward, who had become Premier on Seddon's sudden death in June, was won over to the cause, authorising the employment of fifty-six performers.

Charles was jubilant and hailed 'the music-loving Premier's' decision as the first step towards the creation of a publicly funded orchestra:

> *It really amounted to an event of national importance, promising an advance of musical art affecting the whole colony. Personally, I had hoped that the great success of the experiment in Christchurch might be the means of establishing a great and permanent band in New Zealand, periodically appearing in every centre, and maintained either by a system of joint municipal aid or by a State subvention.*[8]

But when the exhibition closed in May 1907, the orchestra was disbanded and New Zealanders had to wait until the creation of the New Zealand Symphony Orchestra in 1946 for Charles's vision to be realised.

The evening before the exhibition opened, Ward hosted a dinner for the numerous representatives of the press, which was accompanied by 'an uninterrupted flow of – good spirits'.[9] Charles was among the guests. Mellowed by such hospitality, he wrote an uncharacteristically mild review of the opening ceremony. Even Johannes Andersen's 'Exhibition Ode', which Hill 'not quite at his best'[10] had set to music, escaped any serious criticism. The *Bulletin*, however, published a letter in its 'Melbourne Chatter' column that described it as 'the most awful ode ever written'[11] – a comment that Charles quoted with a great show of indignation in the *Triad*. Andersen was also wickedly lampooned in Fred Rayner's *Exhibition Sketcher*:*

> *[A] picturesquely romantic figure was seen stalking down the centre of the Grand Hall. It was clad in Cavalier costume of opulent purple, with exquisite ruffles and gold-buckled shoes and a rich profusion of fine, raven-*

---

* Rayner, who produced the *Exhibition Sketcher* for the duration of the exhibition, was about to engage a brilliant sixteen-year old cartoonist from Christchurch named David Low. Low later joined the *Bulletin* and went on to work for the *Evening Standard* in London, where he gained world fame as the creator of 'Colonel Blimp'.

> *black curls drooped low on the shoulders. This was Johannes Andersen carrying his Immortal Ode in his lily white uplifted hand. A reverential hush fell on the people as the Poet gathered the orchestra around him.*[12]

A contemporary photograph shows Andersen as an arresting-looking young man with a fine head of hair, but in other respects this description appears to be fictitious.

Both the orchestra, 'undoubtedly the best we have ever had in New Zealand', and the 'magnitude and attractiveness of the Exhibition' impressed Charles greatly. He also had warm praise for the Director of Wellington's Colonial Museum, Augustus Hamilton, who had overseen the construction of a model Maori pa and 'deserves much kudos for his efforts on behalf of the real and the true in Maori art.'[13] But while he admired the exhibition, it did little to mitigate his dislike of Christchurch.

Ever since his early struggles with the *Triad*, Charles had never felt welcome there. In December 1895, he complained that Christchurch businessmen were 'very different from those in Wellington and Dunedin'[14] and in the following April, he described Christchurch, New Plymouth and Greymouth as 'the three most unfriendly towns in New Zealand.'[15] A few months later, after a three-week visit, he accused Christchurch of being a 'city of cliques – musical, artistic, and social.'[16]

Yet in many ways Christchurch was New Zealand's most lively cultural centre, with a distinguished tradition of choral music fostered by the Anglican origins of the Canterbury Settlement. Its cultural community, however, was blighted by what the musicologist, John Mansfield Thomson, aptly calls 'a capacity to form rival societies in similar fields, which waged internecine war against each other.'[17] In this most English of New Zealand's cities, Charles's antipathies were fully reciprocated, and his boisterous showmanship and outspoken criticisms of amateurs were viewed by the educated élite of Christchurch as 'very bad taste and very bad judgement'[18] and – of course – very unBritish.

After a slow start, the orchestra became one of the star attractions of the exhibition, but in May, when Charles gave his verdict on its performance, he could not resist reminding his readers of how long the Christchurch public had taken to appreciate its merits:

> *The greatest achievement of the orchestra was the conversion of the public; it was a veritable triumph for instrumental music of the highest type. Christchurch had been held up to scorn after the opening of the Exhibition; it has done much to regain its reputation as a musical city. Small and unsympathetic in the early months, the audiences increased in numbers, intelligent appreciation and genuine enthusiasm.*

Charles, who had just returned from the greatest musical experience of his life, had resumed his missionary role with vigour. He concluded his remarks with a homily on the 'sacred duty' of all musicians to 'gain the ear of the people.'[19]

Six months earlier, on 22 December 1906, Charles had sailed from Auckland on the *SS Ventura*, bound for San Francisco, accompanied by Maida, who had just celebrated her seventeenth birthday. This was by no means their first journey together: as a small girl Maida had frequently joined her father on business trips, travelling with him as far afield as Wanganui, where her intelligence and poise were widely admired. Such experiences must have contributed to her sophistication and, judging from the article that she wrote on 'Poets and Women' for the *Triad* as a fifteen-year-old, she was also remarkably well read. Two photographs have survived of her as a young woman. In the first, dated 1909, she looks like a music hall star in a rose-trimmed bonnet with a basket of fruit on her lap. In the second, of similar date, she is part of a family group, perched on the arm of her father's chair in a lace gown that accentuates her perfect figure.

Although Charles never spoke of Maida's role in his epic visit to North America, years later it emerged that she was largely responsible for it. According to family sources, one of the many exotic visitors whom Charles invited to the house – reputedly a Russian count – fell in love with her and offered to pay for her to travel with him to America. The couple were not even engaged and, mindful of his teenage daughter's reputation (and doubtless excited by the prospect of seeing America for himself), Charles decided to act as a chaperone. The identity of Maida's admirer remains a mystery. No one fitting the description of a Russian nobleman is listed among the first-class passengers on the *Ventura*, although the businessman Ernst Schaefer – whose family were Russian-born Germans from the Lower Volga – might just have been wealthy enough to pay for the party's lengthy stay at New York's Hotel Astor. But, irrespective of who was footing the bill (and it seems that the Russian paid for most of it), Charles called the tune.

Their first stop was Pago Pago in American Samoa, which Charles described as 'something like ... the Garden of Eden'.[20] They were anchored for only a few hours, but there was still time to go ashore for a performance of local dancing and singing. At Honolulu they disembarked for a lavish breakfast at the Moana Hotel on Waikiki beach. Charles was amazed by the food, and in the *Triad* he listed the menu of poi, papaya, grapes, guava jam, bananas in cream, fillet of ulu ulua, crab salad, fried bananas and bacon, and frogs' legs, with all the delight of a greedy schoolboy. After breakfast, he called on the Director of Hawaii's fledgling Department of Tourism who, on discovering that Charles ran a magazine, immediately placed a car at his disposal for the rest of the day.

The arrangement suited both parties admirably and later Charles published an enthusiastic account of his visit to Hawaii in which he strongly advised New Zealand tourists to spend some time there.

San Francisco offered a stark contrast. Only eight months previously, a devastating earthquake, followed by a fire, had destroyed eighty per cent of the city. Charles found it such a 'saddening sight' that he preferred not 'to dwell upon its manifold miseries.' The population was still in a state of shock and one of the few tourist attractions that remained was a grubby Japanese village where Charles and his party were served 'abominable' green tea.[21] They could not wait to leave and, after spending an afternoon riding the trams, they caught a train to Los Angeles.

There things went better and, from the luxury of his room at the Hotel de Coronada, Charles cast a more cheerful eye on his surroundings: 'I suppose there is no more interesting spot on this globe of ours than Southern California.' Many of his fellow guests were avoiding the east coast winter and Charles immediately grasped their potential as tourists: 'If our Mr Donne* were only allowed a free hand, thousands of people who spend their winters regularly in Southern California could be induced to cross the water to New Zealand.'[22] Meanwhile the most frequent response to any mention of his homeland was 'Noo Zealand ... Noo Zealand! Why I should know the name. What state is it in?'[23]

During Charles's absence, the *Triad* scarcely missed a beat. Most of the January edition must have been prepared before he left, and in February his 'Obiter Dicta' column was written, quite competently, by Richard Singer. In March there was no editorial column at all, but this shortfall was redressed by a lively article on education in which the American philosopher and writer, Elbert Hubbard, looked forward to the day 'when no school teacher will have more than twenty pupils' and 'all the bugaboo of exams will be consigned to limbo.'[24]

Hubbard was the founder and editor of what Charles called 'that brilliant little periodical of protest – the *Philistine*',[25] who in 1899 had shot to overnight fame with an essay celebrating self-reliance entitled 'A Message to Garcia'.† His magazine was primarily a vehicle for his personal philosophy, and one of his salty maxims – 'To escape criticism. Do nothing. Say nothing. Be nothing',[26] or 'Never explain: your friends don't require it, and your enemies won't believe you, anyway'[27] – was emblazoned on the cover of each edition. With its trenchant stance, the *Philistine* was a publication very much after

---

* Thomas Edward Donne, Secretary of New Zealand's Department of Tourist and Health Resorts from 1901–1909.

† 'A Message to Garcia' became a motivational text for America's businesses and armed forces and was given to every US Marine and naval enlistee in both world wars.

Charles's heart and on his way to New York, he planned to visit Hubbard at his Roycroft Press in East Aurora.

By April, Charles's familiar voice had returned to the *Triad* in the form of a travelogue in which he aired his views on every aspect of American life, from the 'magnificent tram service' and 'the really effective telephone system' to the en suite bathrooms. But his enthusiasm for modern amenities did not impair his critical faculties. In the first instalment he complained that, so far, he had not seen 'anything worthy either musically or dramatically in this country', and treated his readers to a diatribe on the American press: 'It is simply astounding to me that an intelligent nation will tolerate such hopeless imbecility in its daily papers. Although the circulation of the leading paper is over 50,000, it is in every respect far below the standard of the leading dailies in New Zealand.'[28]

After leaving Los Angeles, Charles and his party travelled by train to New York, stopping for a day in Chicago, followed by a few hours at Niagara. The surrounding countryside was blanketed in snow; although he considered the Falls 'one of the few superlatively praised things that I have seen where realisation actually exceeded expectation',[29] he was infuriated at being charged a dollar to see the famous whirlpool, only to find it covered by ice. Later in the day, they changed trains at Buffalo and headed for East Aurora where the Roycroft Press was producing beautifully bound, handmade books inspired by William Morris's Kelmscott Press. By 1907 Hubbard's handicrafts community, the 'Roycrofters', was attracting thousands of visitors and Charles and his party were able to spend the night in the hotel that had been specially built to house them. As editors and businessmen, Charles and Hubbard had much in common. Both were flamboyant individualists: although there is no evidence that they met, the two men would have got on together famously. The following morning, Charles and his party rose before dawn and continued to New York.

Whether by chance or by design, Charles's two-month stay in New York coincided with one of the most remarkable seasons of opera that the city had ever seen. Prompted by the challenge of Oscar Hammerstein's recently opened Manhattan Opera House, the Director of the Metropolitan Opera, Heinrich Conried, presented a dazzling programme of twenty-nine operas with a total of 102 performances. Humperdinck's *Hänsel und Gretel* was performed eight times and the works of Puccini, who came to New York in January to witness four of his operas in person, also featured prominently. *La Bohème* was performed seven times, *Tosca* six and *Madame Butterfly* five. In addition, there were six performances of Verdi's *Aïda* and five apiece of Gounod's *Roméo et Juliette*, Wagner's *Tannhäuser* and *Lohengrin*, and Berlioz's *La Damnation de Faust*.

The Metropolitan's bill was dominated by Caruso and, according to Charles, throughout the winter 'there was practically not an unoccupied seat in the house.'[30] By far the most sensational incident of the season, however, was the presentation on 22 January – and prompt withdrawal – of Richard Strauss's new opera, *Salome*. Charles arrived just after the event, but he was well acquainted with the worldwide controversy that had surrounded the opera's premier in Dresden in 1905, and had reported it extensively in the *Triad*. *Salome*, which was based on a text 'of the most dangerous decadence' by Oscar Wilde, had been banned by the Viennese censors and condemned by the Emperor of Germany. In Munich, critics had branded the subject matter as 'vicious' and 'rotten to its very roots.'[31] A year later, when it was performed in New York, audiences were so shocked that the opera was not heard again for twenty-six years.

The rival programme at the Manhattan was equally lavish and consisted of twenty-two operas, seventeen of which were Italian and five French. Melba was one of the reigning stars and during his first week in New York, Charles heard her in Verdi's *La Traviata*:

> *Needless to say, her acting was quite unconvincing, but to sit with one's eyes shut and listen to the pure stream of melody flowing from the diva's throat in 'Ah, Fors' E Lui' and 'Sempre Libera' was an unqualified delight ... Her voice is very much sweeter, purer and more elastic than it was when I heard her last in New Zealand ... It is a thousand pities that emotion and feeling have been denied her.*[32]

Earlier in the week, at a performance of Donizetti's *Don Pasquale* at the Metropolitan, he had found Marcella Sembrich far more exciting: 'I can imagine nothing finer than her interpretation of the part of Norina. I wanted to jump on my seat, waive [sic] my hat and yell "Hurrah!"'[33]

Charles was having the time of his life: 'Probably more operas are produced in a week in New York during the season than in any other city in the world. Last week, for example, fifteen operas were heard, including matinées – a veritable musical feast.'[34] Nor was the feast limited to opera. During the weeks that followed, Charles saw Elgar conducting his *Apostles* and *The Kingdom* at Carnegie Hall ('and a very un-magnetic and uninspiriting [sic] conductor he is'),[35] and heard the peerless Boston Symphony Orchestra playing Strauss's *Symphonia Domestica*. The orchestra's performance was magnificent, but Strauss's composition struck him as 'a tone poem of ugliness ... a drying up of the sources from which flowed the real beauties of his earlier work ... a valley of dead bones.'[36]

Meanwhile the city was casting its spell. As Charles dashed from the Statue of Liberty to the top of the recently completed Flat Iron Building, and visited the Bowery and the Chinese and Yiddish theatres, its brutal contrasts made a lasting impression:

> *New York is a fearful and wonderful place. A very thin line divides the magnificence from the squalor. Here the rich are the richest; the poor are the poorest; the good are the best and the bad are the worst.*[37]

Not least among its wonders was the Hotel Astor:

> *At the Hotel Astor, where our party is staying, one has a bedroom with a bathroom and two lavatories attached; each room has a heating apparatus which can be regulated by an inconspicuous little dial on the wall ... every room has its telephone, and with this telephone ... you can procure almost any luxury that man could desire.*[38]

Photographs of its four sumptuous dining rooms and its prime location in Times Square later appeared in the *Triad*.

Before long Charles felt completely at home. In cosmopolitan New York, he fitted in perfectly, and furthermore he had been made an honorary member of one of the city's most exclusive clubs. The New York Lambs' Club was named after the nineteenth-century essayist Charles Lamb and his sister Mary and inspired by their famous salon. Membership was restricted to actors and literati, but as the editor of a cultural magazine, Charles was welcomed as a peer. In New York (unlike Christchurch), no one sneered at his German-sounding name – or his Jewish ancestry. Many of America's most brilliant men came of similar stock.

Charles owed much of his success at the Lambs' Club to the story of Pelorus Jack:

> *Amongst many very remarkable things in 'God's Own Country' is a cetacean, known to the learned as the Grampus griseus, and to the rest of mankind in New Zealand as Pelorus Jack. The habitat of this remarkable creature is a stretch of water a few miles on the Picton side of what is known as the French Pass. This fish meets almost every boat that comes through the French Pass to or from Nelson! (Smiles). He always appears at about the same spot, plays about the bows of the steamer for a few miles and then waves his tail pour prendre conge. (Loud laughter). But I assure you, gentlemen, this is a perfectly true story. Indeed, Pelorus Jack has the honour of being the only fish in the world which is protected by an act of parliament. (Uproar).*[39]

The dolphin's gambollings with passing steamers had delighted New Zealanders for years. He was regarded as a national treasure: in 1904, fearing that he might be hooked or harpooned by unscrupulous fishermen, the New Zealand Government had passed a special order for his protection. But at the Lambs' Club no one believed a word of the tale until Mark Twain, who had seen Pelorus Jack for himself, stepped in to confirm its veracity. Thereafter Charles was lionised. For the rest of his stay, whenever a newcomer arrived at the club there were cries of 'Say, tell him that fish story. Why it's the prettiest fish story you ever heard.'[40]

He was lavishly entertained ('I have never enjoyed such splendid hospitality anywhere'),[41] but between sightseeing, socialising and concerts, he also managed to make some professional contacts. One of these was with the sub-editor of Joseph Pulitzer's famous daily, the *New York World*, who took him to the Chinese theatre and reputedly offered him the position of music critic. His duties as a chaperone do not appear to have occupied much of his time. Nor could Maida have accompanied him to an all-male enclave such as the Lambs' Club. But any risks to her virtue were receding fast. By the time she arrived back in Dunedin, her romance had run out of steam and she never became a countess.

Charles and his party returned to New Zealand through Canada where he surprised the venerable founder of the Salvation Army on a train to Vancouver. The opportunity to interview 78-year-old General Booth, who was well-known in New Zealand, was too good to miss, but when Charles asked him if he had any special message for New Zealanders, his response was crushing:

> *Yes; you may tell them not to go ahead too fast with their socialistic legislation, and also to cultivate modesty, and restrain the somewhat marked tendency to boastfulness.*[42]

The voyage home aboard the *SS Aorangi* was sped by favourable winds and enlivened with shipboard entertainments. In Sydney, Charles called on A.G. Stephens, who had recently been replaced by Arthur Adams as editor of the *Bulletin*'s 'Red Page' and was fighting a losing battle for the survival of his literary journal, the *Bookfellow*. In his expensive new shirts from New York, Charles must have looked maddeningly smug and Stephens could not resist taking a swipe at him:

> *Interviewed as to musical impressions received on his American trip, Mr Baeyertz was understood to say that he would have enjoyed himself extremely if he had not met so many examples of defective musical education … Caruso, for example … has a fine natural voice, but his articulation – especially of Italian words – is most distressing. The great prima donna Sembrich pronounces 'tune' as 'choon' and has an unfortunate habit*

of running all her words together as if they were a continuous stream of treacle. Melba, Mr Baeyertz has already criticised unfavourably. Plançon is in some respects the most cultivated singer whom he heard, and if he would take a few simple exercises to get rid of his nasal quality of tone he would be well worth listening to.[43]

When he arrived in New Zealand, the Dunedin *Evening Star* welcomed him home in a similar vein:

It is a relief to know that Mr C.N. Baeyertz has returned safely from his American trip. No doubt, as Pronouncer-in-chief to the English-speaking races, he is duty bound to bestow a portion of his care upon the euphonious welfare of regions beyond 'this small island off the coast of Australia' ... There is some consolation ... in reflecting that the plight of the Americans is worse than ours. Mr Baeyertz assures us that he could 'fill five or six columns' with the record of their blunders.[44]

To the *Southland Daily News* it seemed 'quite like old times to have Pooh-Bah* Baeyertz back again, telling New Zealanders of every degree how woefully ignorant they are.'[45]

Still basking in the glow of New York, Charles responded magnanimously. His recent experiences had only served to affirm his faith in his own critical abilities and, for once, he saw no need to hit back. For years he had been subjected to constant attacks in the New Zealand press over the exacting standards that he applied to both professional and amateur performers and the severity of his comments. One local wit even suggested that *Triad* was simply a misspelling of 'Tirade'. But in New York, he had at last been able to put his critical standards to the test in a wider arena. Moreover, when he measured his judgements at first hand against those of the great New York music critics, such as W.J. Henderson, Henry Finck, Henry Krehbiel and James Huneker, whose hard-hitting reviews were followed by the music-loving public 'as if they were reading sports scores',[46] he discovered that his standards of excellence were no different from theirs.

In New Zealand, however, where society was small and close-knit, objective criticism was virtually unknown and many performers were amateurs. When last night's soprano might well be your neighbour's wife, comments were necessarily tactful. As a result, Charles's outspoken reviews were often misinterpreted and he regularly used his 'Obiter Dicta' column to make statements in defence of his judgements:

---

* A reference to Pooh-Bah, Lord-High-Everything-Else, a character in Gilbert and Sullivan's *Mikado*.

> *There is only one standard for the professional and the amateur – and that is the highest. A singer either sings in tune or out of tune, and there is no amateur scale …*
>
> *The common retort that you must not expect an amateur to be as good as a professional … has nothing to do with the case. The most important aim of true criticism should be to check technical error and to mould talent … Another, and hardly less important aim of true criticism, is to provide criteria of taste …*
>
> *Believe me, our amateur singers will never improve until they pocket their crumpled vanity and welcome honest and unflinching criticism of their artistic merits and their inartistic defects.*[47]

He made no allowances for people or places – 'the critic has not to deal with persons', 'true criticism is never local: it must justify itself to the infinite' – and those who challenged his views did so at their peril. His riposte to a suggestion that he had treated a Christchurch amateur unfairly at a charity concert was typical: 'I was simply carrying on the charitable work … What greater kindness is there than that of enabling a public performer to rectify his glaring faults.'[48]

On his return home, Charles became far more conscious of his position as New Zealand's most serious music critic. Increasingly he aligned himself with figures like Henderson (whom he considered the world's greatest music critic) and Finck. Under fire his favourite tactic was to reprint one of their articles in the *Triad* and point out the similarities between their views and his. The British critics, whose approach was usually more measured, suited his ends less frequently. Nevertheless, he was intensely gratified when an ingenuous article in the *Southland Daily News* suggested that there was 'more than a little analogy' between his methods and those of Bernard Shaw.[49]

At the end of the 1880s, long before he became a successful dramatist, Shaw had turned British music criticism on its head with his biting and witty reviews for the radical newspaper, the *Star*, under the pseudonym of 'Corno di Bassetto'. Later, from 1890–4, he wrote an equally provocative music column for the *World*. Like Charles, Shaw knew a great deal about music – his mother earned her living as a music teacher – but as a critic he always adopted the stance of an artless amateur, whereas Charles never failed to trumpet his professional authority. Yet the observation that Charles had 'a fellow feeling for the brilliant but eccentric Bernard Shaw'[50] was not entirely wide of the mark. Echoes of such Shavian sallies as his observation that Hubert Parry's new oratorio, *Job*, was 'the most utter failure ever achieved by a thoroughly respectworthy musician'[51] are often heard in the *Triad*. The similarity of tone was certainly intentional and, after the article in the *Southland Daily News*, Charles frequently referred to Shaw to ensure that the comparison between them was not forgotten.*

Despite his constant battles with affronted performers – and the local press – by 1907 Charles seems finally to have secured his position as New Zealand's reigning critic. In September, a full-page caricature of him in the *New Zealand Mail* appears to acknowledge this. Standing with sternly crossed arms beside a treble clef and the caption 'Cynic and Critic', he looks every inch the part. Below him some verses parodying the 'old one hundredth'† poke a little harmless fun. But only a few weeks earlier, the same publication had launched a far more damaging attack in which Charles was depicted as an unprincipled businessman whose criticism was simply 'the peg on which he had chosen to hang his enterprise'.[52] The author of this outburst (and of the verses) was a brilliant newcomer to New Zealand's literary scene named Frank Morton, in whom Charles had already detected 'the beginnings of a splendid enemy'.[53]

'C.N. Baeyertz, Cynic and Critic', cartoon by Fred Booty in the New Zealand Mail, *reproduced in the* Triad *1 Oct 1907, p. 21.*

C. N. BAEYERTZ,
Cynic and Critic.

---

* In 1943 the *New Zealand Listener* published a three-page article on the perils of criticism, citing Charles as an example of a critic who was taken to court, and praising the dexterity of Shaw who 'in six years as a music critic of a most outspoken sort … never gave rise to a libel case.' *Listener*, 22 Oct 1943, 'Artists and Critics', p. 5.

† 'All People who on Earth do dwell'

CHAPTER 10

A Splendid Enemy

When Frank Morton arrived in New Zealand in 1905 to join the staff of the *Otago Daily Times*, his stylish prose was an instant success with readers. It was the first time in years that he had earned a regular income and he could hardly believe his luck. A letter to A.G. Stephens reflects his delight: 'I like Dunedin more than ever, and I like New Zealand. The people … have been very kind to me and strangely cordial in their appreciation of my little splurges. For a Puritan community – remembering that I am Me – I'm almost making a record.'[1] A few months later, after an unexpected pay rise, he told Stephens that he was getting 'a thousand times finer and better and more generous treatment from a puritan paper in stuffy Dunedin than I ever got from any paper in Australia.'[2]

Morton was a gifted and prolific writer who, at a moment's notice, could toss off a few thousand words on almost anything. But he also had a drinking problem and, since 1900, had been struggling to survive as a freelance journalist in Hobart. Before then he had spent six years eking out a living with various Australian newspapers and writing poetry. If he had put his mind to it, Morton could have had a brilliant career as a journalist. At heart, however, he was a free spirit and a Bohemian, who disliked working in an office. Only the urgent need to provide for his family had persuaded him to accept a full-time position in Dunedin.

Morton was not an Australian. He was born in England and had emigrated to Sydney with his family at the age of sixteen. Within four years he was aboard an American windjammer working his passage to Hong Kong as a seaman. From there he embarked on a series of jobs that included teaching at a Methodist mission school in Singapore and a stint as a newspaper reporter with the long-established *Straits Times*. Later he moved to Calcutta where, as a special correspondent, he escorted Annie Besant* on her first lecture tour of

---

* The British activist and feminist, Annie Besant, rejected Christianity in favour of the religious movement theosophy, which embraced many of the concepts of Hinduism. In 1893 Besant made her first visit to India and subsequently became a leading figure in the campaign for India's independence.

India and accompanied the Foreign Secretary of the British Government in India, Sir Mortimer Durand, on his mission to Afghanistan. He also became sub-editor of *The Englishman*, which in 1883 had been the first newspaper to publish Kipling's poetry.

Before settling down with his half-Malay wife to produce a family, Morton had savoured the delights of Asia to the full. As a sensualist and an epicure, he revelled in the exotic flavours of the East, thus his return to Sydney in 1894 was probably motivated more by the desire to raise his children in a healthier climate than Calcutta than by any disenchantment with India.

In Australia, however, Morton had proved a misfit. Australia's literary world was in the thrall of the '*Bulletin* school' – rugged writers like Henry Lawson and Banjo Paterson – whose verse glorified the simple life and Australia's pioneering past. Morton, on the other hand, with his passion for graceful French verse forms such as the villanelle and the triolet, saw himself as an aesthete. One of his favourite authors was the sixteenth-century French poet, Olivier de Magny, and his own verse was similarly peopled with nymphs and shepherds – interspersed with references to Rabelais. Although Morton could turn his hand to almost anything, the gulf between the Renaissance court of François I and 'The Man from Snowy River' proved too great even for him to bridge. Moreover, as he explained to Stephens, 'I *cannot* get up any enthusiasm for ... local colour; and I cannot exuberate about Horse.'[3]

In New Zealand, Morton found that Australia's nationalist poetry aroused less fervour ('People here feel, as I have always felt, that local colour (in itself) is not of necessity admirable'),[4] and he was determined to make the most of his unexpected popularity. He stopped drinking and crafted his early articles for the *Otago Daily Times* with all the wit and winsomeness of which he was capable. For many his writing, with its combination of lightly worn erudition and mildly risqué playfulness, was a new experience. Women readers in particular loved it.

Charles, too, was dazzled by Morton's versatility and also enjoyed his company. This may explain his surprisingly mild reaction to Morton's disparaging article in the *New Zealand Mail*, which he shrugged off as something that 'no doubt will amuse my readers.' Apart from its insults, however, the article contained some salutary home truths. In particular, the observation that 'the *Triad* ... does not pretend to pay for contributions' and 'rarely or never publishes original matter of any striking or special quality'[5] may well have given Charles food for thought and speeded the sea changes that were soon to overtake the *Triad*.

Ever since his return from America, Charles had been restless. He had resumed his monthly routine of compiling and editing the *Triad* with mixed feelings. Even writing the music criticism seemed to have become less fun, and at the Dunedin Orchestral Society's first concert of the season in May, for once he felt at a complete loss:

> *As for the playing of the orchestra, I am wholly unable to say whether it was better or worse than usual. I have not heard an amateur orchestra for seven months, and everything seemed out of focus. At this concert, for instance, the finale of Tschaikowsky's Fifth Symphony was played. Two months ago I heard the whole symphony performed in New York by the Russian Symphony Orchestra of ninety-six performers; each man was soloist on his instrument. The Conductor was Altschuler, a pupil and friend of Tschaikowsky. There are about fifty-six players in the Dunedin Orchestral Society, and probably not more than ten of these have sufficient virtuosity on their instruments to enable them to do more than merely play the notes.*[6]

Usually, Charles was supportive of Dunedin's two main orchestras, especially the new Philharmonic Society, conducted with such 'splendid control'[7] by Squarise. But in such a comparison the Orchestral Society and its long-standing conductor James Coombs were, as Charles observed, 'at a hopeless disadvantage.'[8] Later he frankly admitted to having lost his sense of perspective.

Within a couple of months, Charles's spirits were temporarily revived by the arrival in New Zealand of the world-famous Venezuelan pianist, Teresa Carreño. At fifty-four, the 'Valkyrie of the piano'[9] had lost none of her legendary power. Charles considered her 'far and away the greatest pianist that has ever visited New Zealand':[10]

> *Carreno's playing intoxicated me. What an equipment is hers! The mind and fingers of a man dominated by the emotion and sentiment of a woman. What a prodigious technic! What power, breadth, vitality, delicacy and vividness!*[11]

Carreño was one of the earliest female pianists on the world stage. Charles urged New Zealand women to attend her concerts, taking with them 'some mere man' to 'show him what a woman *can* do.' Towards the end of his review, aware perhaps that he had let his emotions run away with him, Charles remarked wryly: 'No doubt it will be urged against me that the foregoing is not a criticism, but a eulogium.'[12] To his disgust, his recommendations fell on deaf ears. Few people had heard of Carreño, and for much of her New Zealand tour she played to half-empty houses.

His response to a return tour by Musgrove's Grand Opera Company was less enthusiastic. He found the orchestra 'immeasurably inferior' to its predecessor in 1901, observing that its conductor, Gustav Slapoffski, 'conducted like a man who had abandoned hope.' Musgrove's efforts to assemble a company that could perform Wagner in German had landed him with a quarrelsome German cast, whom Charles dismissed as 'inept'. For him 'the one star of first magnitude' was Hans Mohwinkel, who possessed 'a glorious baritone voice of over 2 ½ octaves, powerful, round, mellow, rich in emotion ... a really great artist whose splendid gifts would be appreciated in any opera company in the world.'[13]

In September, a spell in hospital with a suspected duodenal ulcer did nothing to improve Charles's mood, but by October he was sufficiently recovered to attend the annual Dunedin Competitions where he had been appointed sole adjudicator for both vocal and elocutionary sections. He had 467 different items to judge and, although he noted 'an immense improvement in pronunciation', he found the standard of singing 'disappointing'.[14] A little later, he lashed out angrily at the Fullers, a father-and-son team who ran New Zealand's most successful vaudeville company, accusing them of living 'to provide the fool public with the cheapest and nastiest vaudeville that the fool public will continue to pay for.'[15]

But he had not completely lost his sense of humour. In the same issue he repeated a 'compliment' that he received from a lady in Hokitika 'who in a room full of people remarked "Oh, yes I have subscribed to the *Triad* for fourteen years, and every six months I make up a bundle of them and send them to the Lunatic Asylum, where they are very much appreciated." I should think so!'[16] His enthusiasm for New Zealand's scenery was also undiminished, despite 'having so recently seen the Canadian Rockies, the Grand Canyon of Arizona, Niagara Falls, and the other wonders of the American Continent'. After travelling through the Otira Gorge to Hokitika, he found the gorge 'more wonderful than ever'.[17] Nevertheless, his glimpse of America's boundless possibilities and the experience of living in New York had altered his outlook. His existence in Dunedin now felt very circumscribed and he longed to broaden his own – and the *Triad*'s – horizons.

Against this background, Morton's taunts about the *Triad*'s dearth of original literary material may have been more timely than he realised. For some months, Charles's business instincts had been telling him that this was a propitious moment to expand the *Triad*'s literary coverage. With the passing of the *Illustrated Magazine* – and little to fear from the Union Steam Ship Company's bland new literary publication, the *Red Funnel* – there was a gap in the market. However, after fourteen years of running a magazine virtually single-handedly, the last thing he wanted was an increase in his editorial workload. As he cast around for someone to share the task of writing and editing, his eye fell on Morton, who would not only bring a wealth of literary and creative skills to the *Triad*, but was also desperately looking for work.

After barely eighteen months, Morton had left Dunedin in disgrace. Some time during 1906, he had met a Christchurch girl and, as he delicately puts it to Stephens, 'got into a hole'[18] with her. As was customary, the girl had gone to have the baby in Australia, but the story had leaked out. Morton was thirty-seven and the girl was nineteen; although his wife ('the best little woman in the world')[19] had learnt to tolerate his infidelities, his employers at the *Otago Daily Times* were scandalised. In Dunedin his reputation was ruined. Late in 1906 he tendered his resignation and moved to Wellington, where he worked as a freelancer, selling his wares wherever he could – including to the *Triad*. But work was scarce and before long he was reduced to living on spasmodic payments from Australian publications, such as the *Bulletin*'s new literary offshoot, the *Lone Hand*, which occasionally published his writing. In the meantime, some of the newspaper articles that he was churning out had taken on the reckless tone that always surfaced when he was drinking.

Insulting the editor of the *Triad*, for the sake of selling a few lines of copy, was typical of Morton's tendency to self-destruct when he was under pressure. But fortunately for him, Charles had taken his remarks in good part and was still prepared to offer him the position of Assistant Editor. By February 1908, their negotiations were complete and Charles was able to announce that 'apart from his own publications' Morton's literary work in New Zealand 'will appear henceforth exclusively in the Triad.'[20] In July, a short article by Charles entitled 'Enemies spoiled in the Making' appeared in the *New York World* in which he humorously lamented the loss of 'a splendid enemy ... because invariably when an enemy has promised to be worthwhile, we have met somehow and become friends and co-workers.'[21] Although no names are mentioned, the reference can only have been to Morton.

With the advent of Morton, the character of the *Triad* began to change. Science had been dropped in 1906 and in recent months the art coverage had dwindled to little more than clippings from popular English art magazines, such as the *Studio*, with occasional reviews of local art exhibitions. The main focus was now on music, drama and literature which, combined with Morton's original contributions of prose and poetry, were giving the *Triad* a new literary lustre. Soon references to Morton's preferred authors – 'decadents' like Arthur Symons, Richard Le Gallienne and Oscar Wilde – were rubbing shoulders with Charles's favourite short stories by O. Henry, together with his own translations of the 'contes' of the French writer, Catulle Mendès (who had been imprisoned for the impropriety of his early writing), and snippets of Renaissance poetry in sixteenth-century French.

In February 1908, Morton celebrated his new status as the *Triad*'s only

'Frank Morton – Man about Town'. Cartoon by Tom Glover, 1914, from Pat Lawlor's More Wellington Days, *Whitcombe & Tombs Ltd, 1962, p. 156.*

paid contributor with a masterly* short story called 'The Man in Red'. The action, which is set in Dunedin, revolves around a mysterious couple named the Verdons, who appear like 'unclassed exotics … amid the hodden greys of that city of sad souls.' Even their maid has an aura of strangeness. She is 'swarthy', 'goodlooking' and 'fashionably dressed', and no one remembers having seen her before. More sinister still is 'The Man in Red', who emerges from the shadows at the Verdons' masked ball and engages the narrator in a disturbing, metaphysical conversation. The climax of the story comes with the discovery of a number of 'perfect virgin bodies'[22] lying dead in the garden and the disappearance without trace of the Verdons.

The narrative, with its sensual overtones and references to the occult, reflects Morton's fascination with decadence. But it was hardly the family reading that Charles had always claimed to provide and with its publication – and the rumours of Morton's misdemeanours – the *Triad* began to acquire a new reputation for 'naughtiness'. The following month, Morton launched his 'Things Visible' column with a gibe at the lack of cultural discernment in Wellington, calling it 'the City of the Adoration

---

* Morton's unpublished 'The Luck of Harris Temple' would not look out of place in a collection of stories by Guy de Maupassant. (ATL MS-0962-1).

of the Obvious, the high place of giggle and squeak'[23] and signing himself 'Epistemon' after a Rabelaisian character who treated his chronic cough by continual drinking.

Charles and Morton were perfect foils for each other. They worked together seamlessly, with Morton's 'Things Visible' acting as an irreverent adjunct to Charles's 'Obiter Dicta'. They also became good friends. In July, the two men met up in Wanganui where Charles hauled Morton out of bed at 10.15 a.m. to scale the 3471 steps to the local high point. They set off together in high spirits, Charles labouring under the weight of his camera while Morton admired the view. Later in the *Triad*, they published a jaunty account of the expedition, writing alternate paragraphs.

After so many years of working alone, Charles found the presence of his new colleague invigorating. Echoes of Morton's audacity began to creep into his own writing. His challenge, for example, to the ageing Edward Tregear to better him in a contest to translate a passage of English into idiomatic Maori, and his claim that the Maori deity, Rongomatane, had sprung 'fullborn and grinning ... out of the flaccid body of Mr. E. Tregear's picturesque and discursive tollerie',[24] have more than a trace of Morton. Such flourishes made amusing copy, but they did not endear the *Triad* to New Zealand's intellectual and literary establishment, which included many members of Tregear's Polynesian Society.

Ever since Charles's savaging of Arthur Adams, local poets and writers had been wary of the *Triad*. Despite all efforts by the *Triad* editor to attract original literary material, they still preferred to send their work to better paid and more prestigious publications in Australia. Charles's unwillingness to pay for contributions was not the only explanation – many writers had after all given their services free of charge to the *Illustrated Magazine*. There was also a concern that the *Triad* was not sufficiently literary and a suspicion that it was far too popular with middlebrow New Zealand to be a vehicle for 'serious' literature. Morton's presence on the staff should have allayed these fears, but shortly before his editorial appointment was announced, he had compounded the problem by making an unwarranted attack in the *Triad* on one of the doyennes of New Zealand poetry, Jessie Mackay.

By early 1908, Jessie Mackay had published three volumes of poetry and established herself not only as a gifted poet, but also as an accomplished journalist and champion of women's rights. Her powerful ballads address many fundamental social and political issues of the period, ranging from the oppression of the Maori by Europeans to women's suffrage. Morton, however, had no time for worthy causes – or middle-aged females – and he regarded the unmarried Mackay as fair game. Her 'immoderate praise'[25] in the preface to a book of bad poetry gave him just the opening he needed:

> *The publication of the verses in book form seems to be due in some part to Miss Jessie Mackay. Miss Mackay writes verses herself. She is the Greatest New Zealand Poetess … You would never discover these things for yourself; so once again you have opportunity to thank God for the newspapers …*
>
> *Miss Mackay has written some good and charming verse, some harmless tripe, and some irreparable rubbish. Wherefore, she has now become a critic and is (I pray you men tread softly!) literary adviser to the firm of Whitcombe and Tombs.*
>
> *I, who love and honour that sweet creature Woman, and am her meekest slave and tiniest poetaster in these seas, I imagine Miss Mackay with a certain joyous glow. I imagine her pouring the vials of her maidenly contempt on the work of all virile and wicked creatures like myself; I imagine her portentous, shrilling instructions into the red and tremulous ears of W. and T., their dignities obsequious. I imagine her exalting (so to speak) her own chignon and having no end of a good time.*
>
> *But speaking strictly between ourselves, the actual spectacle of Miss Jessie Mackay enthroned as a critic yields me nothing but a vast amusement.*[26]

The tone of Morton's remarks and his views on women writers in general incensed Mackay's friends and one of them* fired back:

> *It is hardly worth while, either, I suppose giving more than a passing remark to your half-contemptuous application of the word 'maidenly' to a woman as mature in her way as you in yours; or to your cheap sneer at 'writing women' (I suppose you forgot for the moment that you were speaking of a sex of which George Eliot was one).*

The writer's evident outrage delighted Morton, who fanned the flames yet further by describing Eliot as 'very uneven and erratic' and claiming that few women had ever shown 'distinctive merit'[27] in either literature or painting. Much of the *Triad*'s readership was female and in the May edition, Charles prudently included a witty two-page article entitled 'Women Writers in New Zealand: By One of Them'. In it the author neatly turns the tables on Morton by pointing out that male editors, who forced women journalists to fill their 'Ladies Pages' with trash, were largely responsible for the low standard of women's writing. The article is unsigned, but it sounds not unlike the voice of the poet and short story writer, Alice Kenny, whom Charles later recruited as a regular contributor.

---

* The writer, who reveals herself as a woman, is anonymous, but may have been Mackay's close friend, Blanche Baughan.

Morton was unrepentant. In October, he took another pot shot at New Zealand's women writers in a withering review of *Current Thought*, a new 'prettily printed and pathetically nice monthly' from Christchurch: 'Miss B.E. Baughan is hailed as a genius ... which must be very annoying to Miss Jessie Mackay and Miss "G.B. Lancaster"* whom we had reverenced as the only two.'[28] Later Morton made a half-hearted attempt to mend his fences by noting that Blanche Baughan 'writes some undeniably good poetry that lapses on occasion into rather bad verse; and Miss Mackay has given us, among a mass of stuff of no value whatever, a few good lyrical pieces.'[29] For him, the finest poet in the country was the Canterbury University professor, Arnold Wall.

Not all of Morton's writing alienated women authors. At the end of 1906 Katherine Mansfield had returned to New Zealand from her school in London as a devoted disciple of decadence, imbibed at the feet of her good-looking German teacher, Walter Rippmann, who was an exact contemporary of Morton. Her greatest literary idol was Oscar Wilde and, in open revolt against the sedateness of life in Wellington, she copied some of his more provocative statements into her journal, matching them with ones of her own. Such Wildean maxims as 'the only way to get rid of temptation is to yield to it' and 'push everything as far as it will go'[30] not only suited her defiant mood, but also accorded perfectly with Morton's self-appointed role as 'missionary to the heathen of respectability.'[31]

In April 1908, while Mansfield was fuming at her mother's tea parties and trying to persuade her father to allow her to return to London, a light-hearted article of Morton's called 'The Kingdom of Bohemia' appeared in the *Triad*. In it Morton laments the decline of Bohemianism and leads his readers on a literary romp from Paris to Australia where Bohemians, beset by 'outrageous Puritanism ... have to meet in secret and worship their gods in caves and cellars and many chance holes in the wall.' His call for the 'true Bohemian' to become 'the arbiter of his own destinies' would have been music to Mansfield's ears, while his claim that New Zealand's few Bohemians were 'like wrecked mariners on a desolate coast'[32] closely reflected her own views.

Shortly afterwards Mansfield wrote a letter to her sister in Sydney:

> *I am ashamed of young New Zealand, but what is to be done. All the firm fat framework of their brains must be demolished before they can begin to learn. They want a purifying influence ... We want two or three persons*

---

* G.B. Lancaster was the pseudonym of Edith Lyttleton (1873–1945), a prolific novelist and short story writer, who enjoyed greater literary success overseas than any other New Zealand writer of her generation.

> *gathered together to discuss line and form and atmosphere ... people who would quote William Morris and Catulle Mendès, George Meredith and Maurice Maeterlinck, Ruskin and Rodenbach, Le Gallienne and Symons, D'Annunzio and Shaw, Granville Barker and Sebastian Melmouth, Whitman, Tolstoi, Carpenter, Lamb, Hazlitt, Hawthorne and the Brontës. These people have not learned their alphabet yet.*[33]

Her list of authors precisely mirrors Morton's favourite reading, echoing much of the literary coverage of the *Triad*. On 6 July, Mansfield set sail for London, but before she left she penned a decadent little piece entitled 'The Death of a Rose'. Unlike previous work in the same vein, however, she did not post it off to Australia. She sent it to the *Triad*.

While Morton was busy making his mark on New Zealand's literary scene, Charles had become embroiled in a major controversy over his music criticism. For several months, New Zealanders had been bombarded by a stream of pre-publicity on the forthcoming visit of the massive contralto Clara Butt, who stood six foot two in her stockinged feet and was one of England's most successful singers. In December, the *Triad* jumped on the bandwagon with a full-page photograph of the diva and a gushing article by Charles's aunt from Sydney, Mrs Frederick Aronson, in which she described the singer as 'divinely tall'[34] and, as the wife of a prosperous jeweller, gave a professional rundown on her diamonds. Unusually for the period, Butt's private life also played a major role in the campaign and the public was bombarded with photographs of her with her three small children and her dashing husband, the baritone Kennerly Rumford. By the time the Butt-Rumford duo reached New Zealand, Charles – who was scrupulous about shielding his own family from publicity – was sickened by their commercialism:

> *The masses, the philistine, the satiated bourgeois were prepared: and for them everything was arranged. No feeling of disgust was awakened by this display of home and family life, exhibited as a draw for the populace, not even when the latest baby was put on the placards.*

The choice of songs at their opening night in Dunedin left him even more convinced of their vulgarity:

> *The whole programme was a concession to the bourgeois. A snack of Schumann, a* gout *of Gluck, and happy handful of Händel – just the formal proportions – and then having paid tribute to cant and tolerated the 'classic' music, the joy-filled audience paddled in the shallow water of English drawing-room songs.*

His comments on Butt's voice were predictably crushing:

> *Mrs Rumford owns a big voice, organ-like in quality, but inferiorly played. There is a bad break in the voice. Her notes are coarse and lack polish and roundness. There is no continuous flow of sound ... she makes mincemeat of a song.*

Further on, he likened her efforts to sing 'dainty ditties' and 'other songs about larks, roses, and babies'[35] to playing Schubert's 'Haidenröslein' on a trombone.

A huge uproar ensued. The public, who were flocking to Butt's concerts in droves, were as insulted as she was. In March, Charles reproduced the following paragraph from the *Tapanui Courier* on the opening page of the *Triad*.

> *There is a journal in Dunedin and circulated in the centres of population, devoted to music and art, called the* Triad. *The editor is a German – one Bayertz, a regular bounder – who does most of the criticising; and if a British artist comes along, he gets a rough time in the* Triad. *Of course, German artists get most fulsome flattery ... if Mr Kennerly Rumford gets hold of this alien editor, he should give him a good old-fashioned hiding.*[36]

Predictably, Charles demolished the *Tapanui Courier* in a few lines. In his 'Things Visible' column, Morton added his touch by noting that he had 'heartily enjoyed Mrs Rumford's singing' and that he liked 'the novelty of a much advertised singer who oddly convinces one that she would make an admirable cook.'[37],* The *Bulletin* went one better: 'The Butt phenomenon is a Voice attached to one who is just an ordinary good family woman, and who sans voice would have aroused no abiding interest outside the weighing room of the physical culture establishment of her suburb.'[38]

On the back of the Butt-Rumford scandal, the *Triad*'s sales were booming. In the April issue, Charles celebrated its fifteenth birthday with the claim that there was 'no other magazine ... in the Dominion with anything like our circulation'. But in the face of a torrent of personal abuse, he was also feeling the heat and most of his birthday message was devoted to a defiant 'confession of faith':

---

* Morton's response to Clara Butt's complaint that a Wellington hotel had refused to accommodate her party 'because we were "play acting" people', was equally scathing: 'Good Old Sam Gilmer! He won't have play actors at his little inn [the Royal Oak in Cuba Street], and he seems to have mistaken our dear Madame for an artist.' (*Triad*, vol. 16, no. 5, Aug 1908, 8).

> *The critic who dares to tell the truth impartially in New Zealand is not doomed to profligate popularity among the deliberately 'genteel' and 'cultured' classes. This pinchbeck gentility is one of the greatest curses in the path of artistic progress ...*
>
> *But at least I've tried to be straight. I've never sold myself for an advertisement or an invitation to dinner. Sometimes, often even, by dint of being honest and outspoken, true to my own light, I have given offence to many; and I'm glad of it.*
>
> *A recent notable instance was furnished by the visit of Miss Clara Butt. She had an extraordinary voice, but I found that she did some things execrably and I said so ...*[39]

In June, he enlisted further support in the form of a personal letter from W.J. Henderson in which he reassured Charles that, if the *Triad* did not make enemies, 'it would be of no value at all'.[40]

The controversy rumbled on for months. In September Charles made yet another attempt to define his role:

> *The critic must be discreet. You see it is not enough to tell the truth merely: you must tell it luminously and wisely, not too much at a time. I don't think that I have ever yet been so unkind as to tell the whole truth about any performer who has pained me ...*
>
> *It is urged against me, even by some of my best friends, that I am given to making fun of performers ... but a singer gently ridiculed and advised may go away and in the fullness of time learn to make a less disconcerting noise ... When I hint that a thing is wrong, I always says how and why it is wrong, and I always strive to point the way to a better performance. It seems to me that this is the chief purpose and end of criticism.*[41]

Meanwhile, the task of covering New Zealand's busy musical life continued unabated. In May, a brilliant performance by his protégée, Rosina Buckmann, came as a welcome diversion from the Rumfords. Rosina was fast developing the attributes of a world star, and after seeing her in an amateur production of Jacobowski's comic opera, *Erminie*, Charles observed that 'with a year or two of study Miss Buckmann would make her mark anywhere in opera or oratorio.'[42]

The flow of international performers continued too. In July, the Czech violinist, Jan Kubelik, was received with rapturous enthusiasm – although Charles ranked him as 'a great technician' rather than 'a great interpretative artist'[43] – and later on Mark Hambourg returned for a second tour, shorn of his shoulder-length hair but showing greater mastery of the keyboard than ever. A photograph in the December *Triad* shows him standing on the steps of Christchurch's Catholic Cathedral, surrounded by local dignitaries and dwarfed by several statuesque women in large hats. A little apart from the group stands Charles, smartly turned out in his pin-stripe suit, looking at the camera with a steady gaze. The party was about to be entertained 'with much cordiality and sumptuousness'[44] by the Rev. Father Price, and in Charles's faint smile, there is a suggestion of hopeful anticipation. Only the dark rings under his eyes give any indication of the stresses that were starting to build up in both his professional and private life.

On the professional front, the appointment of Morton was certainly paying handsome dividends: since his arrival, the *Triad*'s circulation had soared. At his prompting, contributions from the smattering of local writers who did not regard the *Triad* askance, such as A.A. Grace and the Christchurch journalist, Godfrey Turner,* were becoming more frequent. In addition, some of his literary flair was rubbing off on Charles, whose style was gaining a new elegance and polish. But Morton's talents came at a price and before long Charles found himself implicated in the inevitable fallout from Morton's perilous practice of mixing professional criticism with personal abuse.

In early 1909, a long-standing feud between Morton and a fellow journalist spilled over into the *Triad* and prompted a spate of spiteful attacks on Charles in both the recently established *Dominion* and a short-lived Wellington fortnightly called the *Citizen*. Charles leapt to his own – and Morton's – defence with a hard-hitting article which bore the strong imprint of Morton and strayed dangerously close to libel. Later in the year, after pages of the *Triad* had been squandered on the squabble, Charles was obliged to publish a fourteen-line formal apology to Morton's antagonist in order to avoid a court case.

Morton's pervasive influence is also clearly visible in a lengthy diatribe, ostensibly written by Charles, against Australasia's leading impresario, J.C. Williamson. Charles's grievance, not without foundation, was that Williamson's touring companies frequently featured second-rate actors whom Williamson regarded as 'good enough for New Zealand.' But such gratuitous comments as 'had Mr Williamson cared more for dramatic art and less for personal gain, he night have done more for the theatre'[45] provoked an outraged response from Williamson and, coupled with a cutting review by Morton, landed the *Triad* in yet another dispute.

---

* Hector Bolitho describes his first meeting with Godfrey Turner on a troop train as being 'like a glass of champagne at a YMCA dinner.' (Lawlor, P., *Confessions of a Journalist*, p. 255)

By December 1909 Richard Singer, a practising barrister who by now had become a regular contributor to the *Triad*, was sufficiently alarmed by Morton's antics to voice his concerns in a letter to Charles:

There are a couple of things I want to speak to you about. Firstly, I want to warn you against such articles as 'Things Visible' in the December Triad. I cannot warn you seriously enough against that style of article ... I really consider the article libellous. You'll be mulcted in a 1000 pounds damages before you can turn the pages on your paper if you are not very careful ... For heaven's sake stop this irresponsible and dangerous lighting of fires which believe me, will lead to some serious disaster if not checked.[46]

But Charles took little notice. He was well aware that Morton sailed close to the wind — that was part of his charm — and he was captivated by his virtuosity. Furthermore, he may well have suspected that Singer's letter was not as disinterested as it appeared: ever since his recent marriage, Singer's friendly regard for Morton had been replaced by a deadly loathing.

At their first meeting in November 1908, Singer and Morton had immediately warmed to each other and afterwards they both wrote humorous sketches of their first impressions of one another for the *Triad*. But early in 1909, their relationship deteriorated dramatically when Singer, now aged thirty-one, fell passionately in love with a young woman named Violet Bird whom he had recently met in Sydney. Ardent in pursuit, he invited her to visit him in Auckland where he promptly proposed to her. Only then did she reveal that she was the girl whom Morton had seduced in Christchurch and that the child at her mother's house in Sydney was hers and Morton's.* Singer married her all the same, but he never forgave Morton. Years later, long after his marriage had foundered, he accused Morton of being 'as jealous as a cat' and, in a malicious reference to his unusually full lips, dubbed him 'the white nigger'.[47] From Charles's point of view, the discovery that his two principal contributors were now at loggerheads must have been almost the last straw, for quite apart from coping with Morton's ongoing indiscretions, over the past few months his personal life had been hell.

In March Charles and his family had moved to Wellington, where he had rented a handsome townhouse at 13 Austin Street on the slopes of Mount Victoria. But within days of their arrival, their enjoyment of

---

* After Singer divorced her in 1918, Violet Bird had an affair with the Australian poet, Christopher Brennan. As 'Vie' she features in several of his later poems and her death in a tram accident in 1925 left him distraught.

their new surroundings was brutally interrupted when thirteen-year-old Rudolph suffered an appalling accident. The first hint that something had gone wrong came when he failed to return home from cycling. As darkness fell, Charles and Bella became increasingly anxious and finally called the hospital, which confirmed that a boy had been picked up from the road at nearby Oriental Bay with critical head injuries. They rushed to the hospital where their worst fears were realised. The front of Rudolph's skull had been shattered, with fragments of bone pressing on the brain, and he was not expected to live. Bella, who was still haunted by the memory of Estelle's drowning, was distraught. At the doctor's bidding, Charles dropped everything and for several days, he and Bella waited in agonised suspense as Rudolph's life hung on a thread. To the astonishment of the doctor, he pulled through and by the end of April, was well on the way to recovery and complaining of nothing more serious than a headache.

Despite Charles's fears that his son would be hideously disfigured, Rudolph's scars soon healed. For Bella, however, the shock of nearly losing another child not only re-opened old wounds, but also brought to a head a host of festering problems in her marriage. The relationship between her and Charles, already strained to the utmost by his continual absences, had reached breaking point. When he left for Auckland in July, she wrote him a bitter little note which plunged him into the worst personal crisis of his life.

His abject reply offers a rare glimpse of the humbler, more vulnerable man concealed behind the all-knowing, editorial facade:

My Darling Bella,

Your little note made me feel very sad. I realize what a stupendous failure I am as a father and a husband. I don't know why it is. It certainly is not for want of love for you and the children. I don't want to make excuses for myself, but I have not been well during the past few years & I have been very much worried in business. My daily life is a veritable crucifixion … I am working very hard. It is the only anodyne for the incessant pain of separation. God help us and lead us out of this country. I have written to the Van Norden Magazine that if they will double their offer, I will go.

Your humble worshipper as ever & always,

Charlie.[48]

Clockwise from top left: *A poised Frances Hodgkins in 1905 during one of her brief periods back in New Zealand.* (Alexander Turnbull Library, F-10660-1/2) *Maida, aged twenty, at the height of her charms.* (Private collection) *A good-looking family: Charles and Bella with their children, c. 1910–11. From left: Rudolph, Bella, Carl, Maida, Charles.* (Private collection)

Top: *The renowned Russian pianist, Mark Hambourg. He and Charles became personal friends.* (Lady Viola Tait Collection, National Library of Australia)
Above, left: *Australasia's 'Queen of Song', Nellie Melba, complete with tiara, c. 1903.* (Alexander Turnbull Library B-K 8181-55)
Above, right: *The legendary Paderewski. He had thousands of fans and even Charles fell under his spell.* (Alexander Turnbull Library 98859-1/2)

Top: *The high-minded Jessie Mackay was one of New Zealand's outstanding poets, but this did not deter Frank Morton from teasing her mercilessly.* (Alexander Turnbull Library F-17416-1/4)

Above, left: *Frank Morton in 1908. His promiscuous writing won the* Triad *thousands of readers and a reputation for 'naughtiness'.* (Alexander Turnbull Library, G-14454-1/1)

Above, right: *The novelist and devoted* Triad *subscriber, Jane Mander, enjoying a biscuit.* (Whangarei Museum)

Right: A.G. Stephens, one of Australia's most influential literary critics and founder of the Bulletin's *'Red Page'.*
(Australian Literary Society photograph collection, National Library of Australia)
***Below:** A publicity photograph for the English contralto, Clara Butt, taken in 1908. Charle described her programme as 'a concession to the bourgeois'.* (Triad, 2 Dec 1907, p. 21, Alexander Turnbull Library S-S 806-21)

Left: Mildred Carey-Wallace, c. 1911. The demure beauty who became the great love of Charles's life. *(Private collection)*

Below: Charles and Mildred canoeing on the Avon in Christchurch, c. 1913, with Mildred's best friend, Lillian Price (centre), acting as chaperone. *(Private collection)*

Clockwise from top: Charles, c. 1915 looking surprisingly youthful without his beard. *(Private collection)* Mildred, c. 1918, in perfect health and a picture of elegance. *(Private collection)* An early photograph of Lillian Price which only hints at her 'wonderful Titian hair'. *(Private collection)*

Clockwise from top left: *The novelist and poet, Robin Hyde, who read the* Triad *avidly and sent it some of her early verses.* (Alexander Turnbull Library F-43599-1/2) *The American poet, Ezra Pound. Despite Morton's rantings against his 'perverted drivellings', Pound paid the* Triad *a handsome compliment.* (Alexander Turnbull Library B-K 819-370) *Rosina Buckmann in the title role of Madame Butterfly. Charles claimed her as his 'discovery'.* (Alexander Turnbull Library 56272-1/2)

Left: A hesitant smile from Charles Brian Butler Baeyertz. He never recovered from four years in a Japanese prisoner-of-war camp.
(Private collection)

Below: The end of the road: Charles and Lillian taken by a street photographer in 1942, when Charles was already terminally ill.
(Private collection)

Chapter 11

Empire City

Of course, Charles had no real intention of abandoning the *Triad*. The recent offer of an editorial position from the American periodical, *Van Norden's Magazine*, had been flattering, but he was far too firmly entrenched in Australasia to want to start again elsewhere. Similarly, his slightly theatrical appeal to God to 'lead us out of this country'[1] was probably little more than an attempt to console Bella with a show of solidarity.

One of the contributing factors to Bella's unhappiness may have been the move to Wellington. For Charles, as editor of a national magazine, the transfer to the capital made perfect sense – not least because of its convenient location midway between the country's four main centres. But for Bella, after eighteen years in Dunedin, leaving her circle of friends must have been a wrench. Moreover, apart from its magnificent harbour, early twentieth-century Wellington was a far less attractive city than either of its southern counterparts.

Unlike Christchurch and Dunedin, Wellington had enjoyed few of the benefits of town planning. In 1865, when it had been elevated to the nation's capital and assumed the grandiose title of the 'Empire City', it was little more than a straggling settlement. Many of its buildings were hastily erected to meet the needs of government and the rapidly expanding population. By 1899, the capital's appearance was still so unprepossessing that even a dispassionate observer like André Siegfried* felt obliged to note that it was 'a characterless and inelegant town.'[2] The Christchurch journalist, Oscar Alpers,† was far less restrained. In 1902 he described Wellington's architecture as 'the ugliest in the world', claiming that its square wooden houses with their corrugated iron roofs resembled 'nothing so much as a collection of derelict kerosene tins.'[3]

Despite the dearth of fine buildings, however, life in Wellington had its compensations. Its music was the best in New Zealand, and during the last

---

* The young Frenchman, André Siegfried, visited New Zealand in 1899 and published his classic commentary on New Zealand politics and society, *Democracy in New Zealand*, in 1904.
† Alpers later became a successful barrister and Supreme Court Judge.

days of the Liberal era the capital also boasted a lively band of journalists and writers. This included the legendary A.G. Stephens who, after his second attempt at publishing the *Bookfellow* had failed in 1907, moved to Wellington to work as a leader writer for the *Evening Post*.* In a nostalgic overview of the period leading up to World War 1, the journalist, Pat Lawlor, describes it as a fleeting renaissance: 'Something must have told us that our years of peace and contentment could not last forever. It was our Indian summer and we all made the most of it.'[4]

At the time, seventeen-year-old Lawlor was too humbly employed at the *Evening Post* even to be called a cub reporter, but his developing journalistic antennae sensed the vitality of Wellington's windswept streets: 'There never was such colour of personality and new eccentrics came into being like daisies in spring ... tall well-groomed fellows with orchids in their button holes ... Also there were exotic blooms such as C.N. Baeyertz and Frank Morton.'[5]

When the Baeyertz family moved to Wellington in 1909, the city had a population of nearly 64,000. But because of the earthquake risk, most of the buildings were made of wood; for someone long accustomed to the reassuring masonry of Dunedin's many public buildings, Wellington's air of impermanence could have been unsettling. Bella's most serious grievance, however, does not appear to have been her new home – or the depressing prospect of the year-long convalescence that the doctors had prescribed for Rudolph – but rather her husband's neglect of his family.

Over the years, Charles's business trips, with lengthy sojourns in hotels, had become a way of life. In April, when Rudolph was barely out of danger, he took off to Christchurch to hear Melba who was on a return tour. There he wrote a hard-hitting review of her concert in which he memorably described her tone as 'liquid as a crystal snow-fed brook – and as cold'.[6,†] But since she was performing at sixteen different venues throughout the country, he could surely have attended a concert closer to home. During the same period, he also lavished attention on the British songwriter, Albert Mallinson, whom he regarded as 'the finest song-composer England possesses.'[7] His skilful interviewing of Mallinson and his warm correspondence with his Danish wife highlight the ease with which he mixed with international celebrities – and the distance that he had moved from the circumscribed world of vicarage tea parties and music lessons from which he had plucked his bride.

---

* In 1909, when Stephens resigned his post to return to Australia, Charles commented: 'Of course he was wasted on the *Post* staff. The *Post* don't seem to have had the remotest idea of what to do with a man like that.' (*Triad*, vol. 16, no. 10, p. 9.)

† In the same review, however, he conceded that her 'mad scene' from *Lucia di Lammermoor* was both 'brilliant and moving.'

Charles had always been open-minded, and since his marriage at the age of twenty, his horizons had expanded and his tastes had become more worldly. Bella, on the other hand, who excelled at pie-making and still restricted her children's Sunday reading to *Pilgrim's Progress* and the improving *History of the Fairchild Family*, had remained as homely and devout as ever. As their differences grew, Charles seems to have compensated for the limitations of his marriage by spending far more time travelling than was necessary. Judging from the accounts of his activities in the *Triad* (and a little note in French from Antonia Dolores* inviting him to join her for dinner), 'the incessant pain of separation'[8] seldom troubled him. Moreover, his close association with Morton – whose views on sex were extremely advanced – can only have widened the rift with Bella.

In June 1910, several years before Freud's psychoanalytical theories had gained currency in the English-speaking world, Morton provoked a furious debate in the *Triad* on the role of sex in love poetry by claiming that 'all sentient life on this planet responds most surely and immediately to the thunderous appeal of the sexual instinct.'[9] Similarly, his contention that the work of the great classical poets was 'intensely and magnificently sexual'[10] and that 'sex underlies all human activity'[11] was, by contemporary standards, daring in the extreme.

Predictably, Morton's own poetry fully endorsed his theories, although his most explicit 'phantasy in verse',[12] *The Secret Spring*, was prudently issued for private circulation only. Its forthcoming publication† was advertised in the *Triad* and from Charles's caveat that it was 'not for the Young Person',[13] it is clear that he was familiar with its contents. His critical reactions to Morton's fervid tributes to the 'enthralling splendour of the sexual union'[14] and coy allusions to the 'sobs of joy'[15] of Sapphic lovers are not recorded, but after his Wesleyan upbringing he must have found Morton's uninhibited approach to life quite an eye-opener. Shortly afterwards he told Bella that Morton's erotic verse was 'below par'[16] and that he could not print it in the *Triad*.‡

Perhaps the most appealing manifestation of Morton's sensuality was his series of articles on food, 'The Compleat Gastronomer', which from a culinary point of view were as far ahead of their time as his views on sex. In an era when Katherine Mansfield's favourite recipes included curried

---

* The French soprano Antoinette Trebelli, who toured New Zealand on several occasions, changed her name to Antonia Dolores after the death of her mother.

† Despite several announcements in the *Triad*, *The Secret Spring* was not published until 1919 in Sydney, but it may have been circulated in typescript.

‡ Morton also wrote a very questionable political novella called *The Angel of the Earthquake*. Melbourne: The Atlas Press, 1909, which Dennis McEldowney describes in *The Dictionary of New Zealand Biography*, as 'proto fascist'. ('Frank Morton', vol. 3, 1901–1920, Auckland University Press; Wellington, NZ: Dept of Internal Affairs, 1996, p. 351).

vegetables (with a thick white sauce), cornish pasties (with a thick brown gravy), and baked rice pudding (served with custard),[17] Morton's clarion call for oil and garlic as 'two of the primary essentials of good cookery'[18] seems to come from another planet. Similarly, his instructions for a Hungarian goulash ('you can look into Her face while the pan chuckles, and whisper Hungarian rhapsodies heart to heart')[19] – served with Veuve Clicquot – and his three-page dissertation on mushrooms and truffles would do credit to any modern cookery book.

As a good cook, Bella may well have found Morton's culinary tips illuminating, but with her strait-laced Protestant background, she can only have viewed the growing complicity between him and her husband with profound misgiving. Although her note to Charles has not survived, the tone of his reply indicates that it voiced some serious concerns. But he did little to curtail his travels and in October 1909 he set out again for Australia for what was to be one of the professional highlights of his career.

When Charles accepted an invitation to judge the speech section at the 'Grand National Eisteddfod' in Ballarat, he had already judged there on two earlier occasions. But from his account in the *Triad*, it is clear that the 1909 Eisteddfod was particularly memorable. By New Zealand standards, the annual Dunedin Competitions were now a major cultural event at which Charles often had to judge as many as six or seven hundred performances. But at Ballarat, where the Competitions had been running since 1891, participants flocked from all over Australia and performed in a purpose-built hall that accommodated 8000.

The opening ceremony was attended by an immense audience. 'There was a sea of faces, and amid that vastness, the rostrum on which we, the talkers, stood, seemed to be a pitiably little thing.' With no form of amplification, even Charles was daunted. When the first speeches were delivered, he noted with concern that they were almost inaudible. As a platform speaker, however, Charles had inherited his mother's skills: when his turn came, he 'took all sorts of care that I should be heard' and soon had the audience eating out of his hand. The theme of his speech was, as usual, the pursuit of excellence – 'the prizes are not for the man who is satisfied with the grey average' – and it evoked thunderous applause. The next speaker was Alfred Deakin, the Prime Minister of Australia, who flatteringly suggested that the spectacular 'Aurora Australis' that had illuminated the southern skies on the eve of the opening was 'partly as a compliment to Mr Baeyertz, who comes from the south.'[20]

After such an introduction, Charles enjoyed the status of a celebrity, basking in the attentions of the Australian press. His triumphal progress continued to Melbourne, where a dinner party for journalists and literati was

'Mr C.N. Baeyertz, The Judge, The Whole Judge and Nothing But the Judge, of the Competitions.' Cartoon attributed to David Low, Spectator, Christchurch. reproduced in the Triad, *11 July 1910, p. 7.* ATL

given in his honour. Amongst the guests were the literary columnist Walter Murdoch, who wrote for the Melbourne *Argus* as 'Elzevir', the scholar and essayist, Archibald Strong, and Henry Champion, the founder and editor of the literary journal, *Book Lover,* with whom Charles had some spirited exchanges. By now the *Triad* had a considerable following in Australia and throughout his trip Charles was constantly asked why he did not publish an Australian edition. Later he visited Sydney and in the November *Triad* waxed eloquent on its charms.

On his return home, Charles flung himself into his editorial tasks with renewed enthusiasm. The *Triad*'s evident popularity in Australia had raised not only his spirits, but also the exciting prospect of expanding his activities across the Tasman. In the meantime, he was acquiring a small stable of local writers and the volume of original literary material in the *Triad* was increasing. The main contributors were still Morton and Singer, supported by A.A. Grace and Godfrey Turner,* but recently they had been joined by a pensive young Wellingtonian named Dick Harris, whom Charles considered one of the best poets in Australasia.

At twenty-two, Dick Harris, who was one of New Zealand's few home-grown 'decadents', had a disturbing preoccupation with death. Morton called him 'the oldest young man I ever met'.[21] Unlike some others, however,

---

* Grace also wrote as 'Fantastika', while Turner took the pseudonym of 'Pan Optes'.

Harris's world-weary stance was not just a fashionable pose. For weeks on end, he would retreat to his tiny book-lined room in the Wellington suburb of Brooklyn to wrestle with depression. His melancholy temperament emerges in such pieces as 'Some Forgotten Things' – in which he flees with his 'familiar', Pierrot, to 'the Valley of Ten Thousand Dreams'[22] – and his retelling of a child's brief life in 'My Best Beloved Babe'. Both are imbued with a wistful charm that brought a new and more reflective voice to the *Triad*.

Harris was also the first to comment on 'the kinship' between the verse of the *Triad*'s first regular woman contributor, Alice Kenny, and 'the modern Irish writers.'[23] Although Harris did not mention any names, he was probably alluding to W.B. Yeats, the leader of Ireland's literary renaissance, whose poem, 'Father Gilligan', duly appeared in the *Triad* shortly afterwards. The Irish qualities of Kenny's poetry were soon widely recognised and are the most plausible explanation for the attention that her work attracted, two years later, from one of Yeats's greatest admirers, the young American poet Ezra Pound.

By the time Kenny joined the *Triad*'s growing band of writers in 1910, she had been contributing to newspapers and periodicals for over a decade, including to the *Illustrated Magazine*. Much of her gentle, lyrical verse touches on loneliness and lost love, whereas her short stories tend to be ironic and humorous with a focus on Maori subjects. Like many other women of her era, Kenny's marital prospects had been sacrificed to the demands of her family. At thirty-five, she kept house for her siblings and was firmly 'on the shelf'. But her single state never appears to have rankled with her, and in her delightful article on 'Women and Other Women', she maintains that a life which contains 'a cat, a garden, a book, and a good friend'[24] is always sweet.

Charles's second female contributor, Gladys Kernot, was a less happy choice. Doubtless her pert, provincial voice was intended to supply the *Triad* with the 'Ladies Page' element that had been so successfully exploited by the *Bulletin*. Charles's favourite epithet for her slight verse was 'dainty', but Singer, who could never resist passing on gossip, later suggested that Charles only accepted her work because, as the wife of the wealthy local agent for Johnny Walker whisky, she did not expect payment.

Another new recruit, who probably also gave his services free, was the Chief Librarian of the Parliamentary Library, Charles Wilson. In March 1910, he contributed a scholarly four-page article on Aubrey Beardsley, accompanied by reproductions of his suggestive drawings for the *Yellow Book* and his equally controversial illustrations for Oscar Wilde's *Salome*. Beardsley's artistic career began in 1892 – just before Charles founded the *Triad*. Six years later, at the age of twenty-six, he was dead of tuberculosis, but long after his death the decadent and erotic undertones of his art continued to send shock waves through the public. The illustrations to Wilson's later article on book-plates were less risqué, except for Morton's languid Messalina, who was drawn by the *Bulletin* artist, David Souter, in response to a complaint by Morton that all his women were fully dressed.

In April a humorous sketch appeared over the initials of New Zealand's preacher-turned-poet, David McKee Wright, a colourful and unconventional figure who had recently lost all his possessions in a bankruptcy case. His marriage, like Charles's, was in trouble and shortly afterwards he moved to Sydney where fellow New Zealander, Arthur Adams, now occupied the heights of Australia's literary establishment.

Despite his growing market in Australia, Charles (like Morton) remained strongly opposed to the nationalism that still dominated Australia's literary life. His belief that art had 'no limits of locality'[25] is vividly expressed in a review of a newly founded Australian publication, *Lilley's Magazine*, in which he fumes at 'the cheap Australian idea that there is any special virtue in being Australian ... [A] man is born wherever his mother happens to be staying at the time ... If it is insisted that the work must be "Australian", the magazine is surely damned from the beginning.'[26] The days when the *Triad* congratulated itself on every passing mention in the 'Red Page' were long past; by this time, its pages resounded with irreverent criticism of the 'cheap Australianism'[27] of the *Bulletin* and 'the glaring and inexplicable faults'[28] of the *Lone Hand*.

The *Lone Hand* was the realisation of the *Bulletin* founder Archibald's long-held dream of extending his empire to include an upmarket literary monthly, but its appearance had been postponed by his deteriorating mental health. In 1906 he had gone so 'spectacularly and beautifully mad'[29] that he was forcibly removed to an asylum from which he was discharged only in 1910. Meanwhile, the launching of the *Lone Hand* had gone ahead in 1907. When Adams was appointed as Editor in 1909, the *Triad* monitored his performance in a series of waspish reviews by Charles:

> *Mr Adams, as editor, has yet to win his spurs. On the editorial staff of the* New Zealand Times *he was not a success ... Neither can it be said that Mr Adams has done great things with the Red Page of the* Bulletin.[30]

His comments on Adams's decision to publish 'the alleged memoirs of Melba' were withering. When they appeared in the *Lone Hand*, he dismissed them as 'such astounding and nauseating piffle that one can only decide that they have been written on bilious Sundays by the diva's maid.'[31] Later he took another swipe at Adams's editorship: 'The *Lone Hand* ought to have been a great magazine; but, to the irritating squawk of one small tin trumpet, it has fallen flatter than the walls of Jericho.'[32] Adams's stewardship only lasted until 1911, when he became Editor of the *Sydney Sun*, but with the wealth and prestige of the *Bulletin* behind it, the *Lone Hand* survived until 1921. Its declining literary merit, however, supports the *Triad*'s view that it was a 'shocking disappointment'.[33]

Nevertheless, apart from some intermittent sniping, the well-informed debate on literary developments in Australia that regularly appeared in the *Triad* suggests that many New Zealanders took a close interest in Australian literature, not least because much of the material that was published in Australian journals was written by New Zealanders. By now almost every issue of the *Triad* featured some discussion of Australian writers and poets, with Morton airing his views knowledgeably on such iconic figures as Henry Lawson ('sombre, strenuous, ungraceful, sometimes vague'), Victor Daly ('brilliant and satisfactory'),[34] and lesser authors like Randolph Bedford ('a big bull-necked man, who dresses roughly and talks like a heavy gale').[35]

As the *Triad* blossomed into a lively literary forum, even the *Lone Hand* deigned to pay tribute:

> *The* Triad *is certainly an astonishing production for a young civilisation; and of it Editor Baeyertz has reason to be proud. It is a musical, critical, literary publication of the highest quality ... that to a great extent disproves the charge sometimes made against Maoriland of a narrow mental outlook.*[36]

Years later, Lawlor captured the flavour of the *Triad*'s heyday rather less pompously:

> *Ah, those were great days! We had few distractions then so that the monthly appearance of 'The Triad' issue would be excitedly scanned for the latest shattering dramatic or musical criticism by Baeyertz, for the latest audacity of Frank Morton, for the most recent and utterly candid book review. Had Baeyertz just overstepped himself in his critiques or was that terrible Morton just too naughty?*[37]

The awe that Charles inspired in the youthful Lawlor was echoed by the more seasoned Alan Mulgan, who in June 1910 was awarded a second prize by Charles in a speaking competition. In his reminiscences of New Zealand's literary past, Mulgan portrays Charles as walking the streets 'with the standing and authority of an institution' and notes that 'his combination of intellectual power and physical presence' made him 'the most forceful and picturesque personality of the kind in our annals.' Further on, Mulgan describes his appearance:

The physical man was known all over the country. He was big, deep chested, and fine-looking; held himself well, and kept in good trim. He had a strong aquiline countenance, which with his red beard and impressive confident bearing, gave him a rather fierce Mephisthophelean touch.[38]

Contemporary photographs bear out this portrayal. In one, Charles sits in profile, pipe in hand, wearing a well-cut tweed jacket and discoursing with evident enjoyment on the large oil painting in front of him. Beside him, the artist C.N. Worsley watches his patron's reactions with some trepidation while at his elbow Worsley's talkative wife hovers ready to chip in at the first opportunity. Another photograph shows him looking straight at the camera with an expression of complete self-assurance, albeit tinged with a hint of weariness.

Charles's professional self-esteem was not unjustified. The *Triad* was fast becoming the leading critical organ in Australasia and under his guidance it was spreading his cultural gospel far and wide. By January 1910, he could state with confidence that it was going 'all over Australasia and has many European and American subscribers'.[39] A year later, he reproduced a postcard from a reader living in a remote town in Southern Siberia, followed by a light-hearted letter from another reader claiming that so many Russians were enjoying the *Triad* that Charles should produce a Russian edition.

In December 1909, he printed further convincing evidence of the cultural lifeline that the *Triad* constituted for those who lived in isolated areas of New Zealand:

Where is my October Triad? *Where is my Art Supplement? What have I ever done to the* Triad *but seize it from the post, and, deserting all else, rejoice in it alone? Why, the only thing that keeps me from preaching temperance … or marrying a Sunday School teacher in this brain-benumbing, stimulus-stifling, sense-stultifying, soul-searing silence is the invasion of the* Triad.

The author of this plea was the novelist, Jane Mander who, together with Edith Searle Grossmann,* became one of New Zealand's most powerful voices in the ongoing struggle for women's rights. Her most famous novel, *The Story of a New Zealand River*, was not published until 1920 when it was deemed so immoral that in her home town of Whangarei it was placed on the discretionary shelf at the local library. When she wrote to the *Triad* in 1909, her career as a writer had barely started and she was deeply frustrated, but the throw-away line towards the end of her letter conveys something of

---

* The *Triad* reviewed Grossmann's 1910 novel, *The Heart of the Bush*, as follows: 'We all know Mrs Grossmann as a brainy woman with a courageous point of view. She has written a good deal that is worth preserving, but this book is proof enough that she can never be successful as a novelist.' (*Triad*, vol. 18, no. 11, p. 10).

her free spirit: 'Please take great care of Frank Morton. There's a man I could live with and love, especially if he did the cooking.'[40] Furthermore, Mander's clamouring for her Art Supplement confirms that the illustrations in the *Triad* – for which it has been so roundly berated by later critics – appealed to some of its most intelligent and educated readers.

Over the years, the *Triad*'s visual content had evolved from a scattering of photographs of scenery and musical performers, together with the ubiquitous 'pretty children' and 'Maori belles', to a monthly six-page insert containing photo-engravings of popular paintings and photographs of groups or individuals. Charles's interest in the new process of photo-engraving dated from 1897 when he visited the magnificent gallery that the art dealer, McGregor Wright, had recently built in Wellington. In the following issue of the *Triad*, he published reproductions of several works by New Zealand artists, including a brooding landscape by James Nairn and accomplished portraits by Mollie Richardson* and George E. Butler. This promising development, however, was short lived and by 1899, when Charles was finding himself increasingly busy, he revisited McGregor Wright's gallery and found what seemed to him the perfect solution to his art coverage:

> *This firm also has a magnificent assortment of photogravures in their Art Gallery. These works are reproductions of the best paintings of almost all the well-known artists of the present day in England, France, and Germany ... Amongst the pictures on the walls are reproductions of Mary Dicksee's 'The Child Handel'; Marcus Stone's 'A Sailor's Sweetheart' and 'In Love'; Rosetti's famous 'Blessed Demozel'; Henry Moore's 'The Clearness after rain'; Millais' 'Speak! Speak!'; Leighton's 'Perseus and Andromeda'; Alma Tadema's 'The Coliseum.' All the reproductions are exquisitely done, and must be seen to be appreciated.*[41]

Charles's enthusiasm sprang from his eagerness to educate. In the 'photogravure' he saw a means of enabling ordinary New Zealanders to enjoy some of the world's most famous paintings. According to Colin Mitchell's informative thesis,[42] popular pictures from the *Triad* were so treasured by poorer families that they often put them up on their walls as the only form of art they could afford. But apart from a supplement on Goldie and occasional works by local artists, Charles's admiration for nineteenth-century European paintings spelt the death knell for any serious visual coverage of New Zealand art in the *Triad*.

The random nature of his selections also suggests that he was obliged to publish whatever local galleries had to hand. Thus much-loved devotional

---

*   Later Mary Elizabeth Tripe.

classics such as Holman Hunt's *Light of the World* and Feruzzi's touching peasant Madonna could be found rubbing shoulders with A.J. Elsley's syrupy compositions of dogs and children, Bouguereau's fleshy damsels and the frothy cover girls of Edouard Bisson. The popular nature of most of the *Triad*'s illustrations was in such striking contrast to its discerning standards of musical and literary criticism that in October 1909, Charles felt obliged to justify his policy:

> *Some critics have averred that the* Triad *supplements might contain pictures of a generally higher art value ... The highest art – the art expressive or representative of some of the latest movements in the great centres – is not generally known or esteemed in this country. Rodin and Carrière, with many other of the greater moderns, only appeal to an advanced minority ... So the pictures published in the* Triad, *while being good pictures, are the pictures that will make the surest appeal to intelligent families ... families that feel and think.*[43]

The *Triad*'s Art Supplements formed part of Charles's astute balancing act between commercial and cultural considerations and he was well aware that they helped to sell the magazine. Moreover, as the sentimentality of some of the child photos and his championship of C.N. Worsley's conventional landscapes indicate, he probably shared the typically Victorian tastes of his readers. Nevertheless, the appearance in 1909 of a series on the world's leading cartoonists, entitled 'Black and White', succeeded by monthly articles on painting by Worsley, was probably an attempt by Charles to raise the standard of his art coverage. Whether he had any idea at this stage that the innovations of the French sculptor, Auguste Rodin, and the symbolist painter, Eugène Carrière, were already being superseded by a new movement in art, so radical that its adherents were dubbed the 'wild beasts' or 'les fauves', is open to question.

One display of savagery that did not escape the *Triad* was the 1909 manifesto of Futurism, the brainchild of the anarchic Italian poet, Filippo Marinetti, and a precursor of the approaching revolution in art and poetry:

> *The essential elements of our poetry will be courage, audacity and revolt ... we will destroy museums, libraries and fight against moralism, feminism and all utilitarian cowardice ... to admire an old picture is to pour our sentiment into a funeral urn ... will you thus consume your best strength in this useless admiration of the past ... ?*

Charles and Morton thought it was hilarious: 'Futurism is terrific ... and M. Marinetti's own translation is ... a truly delicious shriek.'[44]

Throughout this period, visiting musical performers continued to keep Charles busy. In his review of the Cherniavski brothers, he described the 'mature musicianly feeling' of the trio's youngest member, Mischel, as 'little short of miraculous.'[45] A photograph of the young Russians shows three delicate-looking boys whose pallor suggests that, after months on tour, they were in the last stages of exhaustion. Charles invited them home for a meal, where twelve-year-old Mischel innocently told Bella that he enjoyed coming to see her because he liked her food.

In August 1910, the 'empty benches' that once again greeted Carreño on her second tour of New Zealand left Charles fuming for months: 'New Zealand's shocking neglect of Carreño ... a woman who ranks with the greatest pianists of the world ... is worse than disappointing: it is indecent.'[46] J.C. Williamson's Grand Opera Company was also touring the country with a repertoire of Puccini and Bizet and two well-known sopranos, Amy Castles and Bel Sorel. As a local artist, Rosina Buckmann was engaged to sing some of the lesser roles and although she was unwell when Charles heard her in *Madame Butterfly*,* in the part of the maid, Suzuki, he still considered her performance 'a genuine artistic success'.[47]

The prospect of Emma Calvé's arrival in September sent Charles into ecstasies: 'Calvé is unique. She is palpitating, she is intense, she is irresistible.'[48] In New York, Calvé's magnificent performance as Carmen had aroused Charles's intense admiration and he published a full-page photograph of her in the *Triad* displaying an impressive bust line that was doubtless well shored up by the rust-proof corsets of the period. Meanwhile, in London there had been a glorious sequel to the Butt-Rumford controversy when Rumford (taking his cue from the *Tapanui Courier*) had assaulted the *Times* critic for an unfavourable review of his wife. Charles was jubilant and immediately claimed that his criticisms had swayed international opinion: 'No English critic worth notice ever pretends now that Miss Clara Butt is a great artist.'[49]

Much of Charles's energy was also channelled into judging at the Competitions, which by now were being held all over New Zealand.† In October 1910, he was invited once again to judge speech and singing at Ballarat, where he crossed swords with a redoubtable local priest named Father Flynn, who had taken exception to his earlier comments on 'the dreadful prevalence of the Australian accent'.[50] Charles's complaints that

---

* The presentation of Puccini's *Madame Butterfly*, which was performed at New York's Metropolitan Opera for the first time in 1907, demonstrates the speed at which new operatic works reached New Zealand.
† Musical and vocal competitions continue to flourish in New Zealand operating under the New Zealand Federation of Competitions Societies.

Australian English was 'truly awful' and full of 'gross mispronunciations ... false inflections, slurred and gobbled consonants, vowels flattened and horribly misused' were rendered all the more insulting by his assertion that 'the English spoken in New Zealand is very far ahead of the English spoken in Australia.'[51] Worse still, as Charles had predicted, the coveted first prize at the Ballarat band contest was scooped by the Wanganui Garrison Band. Father Flynn accused Charles of being a bounder and dubbed him 'Brayertz',[52] but he was certainly not alone in taking Charles to task over his harsh views on pronunciation. Morton called him 'pernickety' and even his personal friends told him that he did 'diction to death'.[53]

The following year, the Australians did not invite Charles back and he had to console himself by judging the Competitions in Invercargill. At this gently paced event, during which a competitor was accompanied on stage by 'a sympathetic dog',[54] Charles was relaxed and at his most attractive. At the opening ceremony, he regaled the audience with a nostalgic account of his first glimpse of New Zealand from the pitching deck of the *Hauroto* as she battled her way to Bluff. Between events, he passed the time chatting with a local teacher, a young girl with a commendable devotion to enunciation, whom he had known as a competitor since childhood. Now aged twenty, she had suddenly grown up and her long dark hair, which Charles remembered streaming over her shoulders and down her back, had been gathered becomingly under a hat. After the snub from Ballarat, her youthful deference was balm to the soul and Charles spent hours advising her on her pupils. In the next issue of the *Triad*, he broke all his own rules on the promotion of individual teachers* and outlined the qualities of his ideal 'elocutionist' in what amounted to a glowing account of her gifts: 'Intelligent, sympathetic, speaks elegant but not pedantic English ... must love children.'[55]

Charles followed her to the Competitions in Dunedin, where he had also been dropped as a judge, and endured the ignominy of watching the speech sections from the sidelines in order to see her compete. His account of Miss Carey-Wallace's performance in the *Triad* speaks volumes:

> *Her entire sensibility was given to her work, she invested her lines with quiet tenderness ... from a technical point of view Miss Carey-Wallace never mispronounced a word ... her work was full of variety, colour, genuine emotion, delicacy of appeal, and insight.*[56]

---

*   Charles claimed that he preserved the *Triad*'s critical independence by refusing to advertise individual teachers and performers, or to accept free tickets from visiting musical and dramatic companies. But in practice he did not always adhere to this.

When the judge who had replaced him dared to relegate this elocutionary paragon to second place, Charles championed her cause with all the ardour of an unhappily married man who had fallen passionately in love.

Morton was vastly amused by his editor's condition and for the November *Triad* he dashed off a piece called 'The Song of the Lady Elocutionist'. His allusions to her perfect diction and discreetly rounded curves were typical of the private jokes that he and Charles often enjoyed in the *Triad*, but their full significance would have completely eluded the readers – including the unsuspecting Bella.

Chapter 12

A Leap of Passion

The physical attractions of Mildred Carey-Wallace are confirmed by a contemporary photograph which shows a demure Edwardian beauty wearing a hat trimmed with ostrich feathers. In another more casual shot, she perches on the arm of a deck chair in an old cardigan and smiles shyly at the camera. The perfect oval of her face is framed by her dark hair, which is parted in the middle and hangs well below her waist in a single, glossy plait. But Mildred was more than just a pretty face. She was also highly talented and had some distinguished musical connections.

Her uncle was the Irish composer, O'Brien Butler,* who wrote *Muirgheis* – the first opera to be written to a Gaelic libretto – and from an early age Mildred had displayed similar musical gifts. As a twelve-year-old at Dunedin's Dominican Priory, she gained junior grade honours in the Royal Academy of Music's pianoforte examinations. She went on to become an accomplished pianist. Years later, Charles described her playing of Beethoven and Chopin in almost the same terms as those he used for Carreño and spoke of her 'rare interpretative gift'. He also praised her compositions – 'art songs' and 'musical monologues' – which she performed with 'personal magnetism' and 'a beautiful speaking and singing voice.'[1] Charles was hardly an unbiased observer, but others were equally impressed. In 1920, when several of her songs were published in Australia, they received flattering reviews in such leading newspapers as the *Sydney Morning Herald* and the *Sydney Sun*.

After the Dunedin Competitions in October 1911, Charles did not see Mildred perform again until December when she took part in the Competitions in Auckland. In the January *Triad*, he second-guessed the judges at every turn, launching into a furious attack on the vocal judge, Professor Ives, for failing to recall Mildred for the 'Irish Song' and the 'Contralto Sacred'. Sorely smitten, he continued to complain about her mistreatment in the next issue, despite the fact that Ives had awarded her first place in both the mezzo-soprano and contralto solos and in the musical monologue. A few weeks later, however, when she came to perform at a

---

* Butler's real name was Whitwell.

recital in Wellington, he made a half-hearted attempt to stand back from his personal feelings, noting that she 'sang sharp twice on the upper D'.[2] After this, except as a composer in the music supplement, Mildred's name was never mentioned again in the *Triad* which suggests, given Charles's practice of shielding those closest to him from publicity, that their liaison may have started at this time.

At home Charles tried to keep up an appearance of normality. He and Bella continued to entertain as usual and early in 1912 a report of a musical evening at their house in Austin Street (fancifully named 'Carlsruhe') appeared in the local papers. The Bechstein grand was played by 'the brilliant pianist'[3] Baxter Buckley, who was another of Charles's protégés. Among the guests was the influential editor of the *New Zealand Times*, P.C. Freeth, with whom Charles had become good friends.

But below the surface all was far from well. By July Bella had retreated to Rotorua, pleading ill health and leaving Maida to organise a farewell party for Rosina Buckmann. Rosina had recently completed a successful tour with the celebrated Irish tenor, John McCormack, who together with Melba had finally persuaded her to return to Britain. Charles, too, had been urging her to go to Europe 'before it is too late'.[4] Over the years, she had been a frequent guest of the family, and on 7 July, she wrote to Bella expressing her disappointment at not seeing her and giving her the following assurance: 'I am going to work hard Mrs Baeyertz and I hope that some day New Zealand will be proud of me.'[5]

Charles was not Bella's only concern. Carl, who had been living a bachelor existence in Dunedin, was also a worry. Since his return from Wesley College in Melbourne, where he had been sent to complete his education, Carl had been working at the *Triad*'s Dunedin office and only rejoined the family when the *Triad*'s head office was transferred to Wellington in April 1912. By then, however, he had got a Dunedin girl 'into trouble', who was already four months pregnant when the young couple were bustled up the aisle of the Presbyterian Church in Wellington. Under normal circumstances Charles would certainly have attended his eldest son's wedding, yet on the marriage certificate the witnesses are given as Bella and Maida, which strongly suggests that he was absent.

Initially, no such clouds appeared to overshadow Maida's forthcoming marriage in December, which was being planned as a full-scale society occasion at Wellington's St John's Church with the city organist, Maughan Barnett, in attendance. But just as the final arrangements were being made, Charles's affair with Mildred was revealed to his family by an apparently innocent telephone call (presumably from a hotel at which Mildred and Charles had been staying), enquiring 'where Mr Baeyertz and Miss Wallace would like their possessions to be sent?'[6]

Somehow Charles and Bella managed to get through the wedding. According to the newspapers, Maida wore a 'delicately charming' dress 'festooned with the palest pink roses'[7] and sported a diamond ring given to her by the bridegroom, Heron Wyinks. Bella put on a brave show, in a suit of blue shot silk with a feather waving gallantly from her hat, but the reception afterwards at Austin Street must have been a painful affair, for Charles had already told her that he was leaving. Although his abrupt departure shocked the family, for someone whose trademark had always been honesty – to a fault – the subterfuges of the preceding months would have been a degrading experience. The emergence of the truth can only have come as a relief. Later, however, he was to pay a terrible price for what Morton aptly termed his 'leap of passion'.[8]

For the next two years, Charles lived without fixed abode, moving from town to town as his professional commitments dictated, and staying at hotels and boarding houses. Whenever possible he saw Mildred, but in a society which still regarded mixed bathing as an affront to common decency, there was no question of their living together until Charles could obtain a divorce. Moreover, at the risk of being drummed out of town – as Morton had been from Dunedin – in public they were obliged to keep up a pretence of propriety.

In this context, Mildred's enslavement of an older, female friend, who could act as a chaperone, proved to be a priceless asset. At thirty Lillian Price was an independent-minded and amusing woman whose humorous pieces occasionally appeared in the *Triad*. According to Richard Singer, her only claim to beauty was her 'wonderful titian hair',[9] but a photograph suggests otherwise, revealing a jaunty figure with an appealing and lively face. Lillian, who worshipped the ground that Mildred walked on, did all she could to help the lovers; in a picture of the trio canoeing on the Avon, she acts out her role of chaperone to prefection by sitting primly between them in her canoe. They all appear remarkably sedate and Charles, who is puffing on his pipe, looks far more like an indulgent uncle entertaining two pretty nieces than the male lead in a passionate affair.

Throughout this time, Charles's musical coverage remained as professional as ever, but a sudden upsurge in the number of articles dealing with marriage and divorce – which were hardly part of the *Triad*'s cultural agenda – hinted at some of the personal problems that were preoccupying him. Amongst the *Triad*'s modern and enfranchised female readers, divorce was a hot topic. Thus when Charles began using Morton's book reviews as a means of venting his frustration at Bella's refusal, on religious grounds, to consider a divorce, he was assured of an attentive audience. In December 1912, Morton's comments on Bertrand Russell's new book, *Divorce*, were so apposite that it is hard to believe that they were not written at Charles's behest:

> *We do not pretend to believe that the union of a man and a woman who live in antagonism and a common misery can ever be a marriage blessed and ordained by God and by God's authority proved inviolate.*[10]

Even more pointed was the appearance in the *Triad* of a long extract from a book by the free-thinking social activist, Edward Carpenter, calling for reforms to the legislation which forced couples to remain legally married, 'however hateful the alliance may turn out to be for both parties, and however obvious its failure to the whole world.'[11] According to the law at the time, as Morton helpfully pointed out to the *Triad*'s readers, a divorce could only be obtained 'if one or other party is prepared to go into the open as a sexual sinner.'[12] It also required the agreement of both parties, and in a later review some of Morton's comments sound suspiciously like a suggestion that Bella's stance was motivated by the desire for vengeance rather than by her religious convictions:

> *It is the virtuous woman whose husband has dared to love another and leave the furnace or the refrigerator of his lawful home – that is the woman who is willing to throw decency to the winds and go to any lengths to overthrow her adversary.*[13]

The *Triad*'s forays into social issues were not restricted to divorce. Charles and Morton had also started voicing their opinions on a whole range of other subjects of topical interest. Prominent amongst these was the British suffragette movement, whose members had recently resorted to violence after years of fruitless lobbying for women's enfranchisement. In April 1913, just two months before Emily Davison horrified the world by flinging herself to her death beneath the hoofs of the King's horse at the Derby, Charles devoted most of his 'Obiter Dicta' column to the folly of Britain's leading suffragette, Mrs Pankhurst, with a few digs at Lady Stout,* who was her ardent supporter. The 'wiser and more consistent Feminists', on the other hand, gained his full support: 'The *Triad* has always stood for the woman's cause in all matters ... every woman must have as full right to live her life and achieve her destiny as any man has.'[14]

Closer to home, where women's enfranchisement was no longer an issue, the *Triad* participated vigorously in the furious debate sparked off by the suggestion that New Zealand's theatres should dim their lights. Before

---

* Anna Stout was a foundation member of the Women's Christian Temperance Movement in 1885, and as one of the early vice-presidents of the National Council of Women, stood shoulder to shoulder with New Zealand's most celebrated suffragette, Kate Sheppard. From 1909 to 1912 she was in England, where she became friendly with Emmeline Pankhurst and joined her Women's Social and Political Union.

the advent of the cinema, all auditoriums had been fully lit and many people believed that watching films in a darkened theatre would lead to an outbreak of immorality. But Charles poured scorn on them and called on theatre managers to resist 'the whip of prigs and numbskulls whose religion and morality consist mostly in the discovery of evil'.[15] His views on film censorship were equally sane:

> *When any picture or any public entertainment is positively indecent or obscene, it can be prohibited. The machinery is already in existence ... Outside that limit, church people have no more warrant to interfere with what they call worldly amusements than theatre managers have to interfere with the order of church service ... if men have not equal rights as to their amusements ... democracy is a farce.*[16]

Even a subject as taboo as homosexuality was briefly aired by Morton. In a review of two more books by Edward Carpenter, he declared that 'the question of sex-inversion is a delicate one, but it should on no account be avoided by just and thoughtful people'.[17] He went on to claim, breezily, that women were more inclined to it than men. Morton's tolerant approach to what, for men, was a criminal offence may have been linked to his admiration for Lord Alfred Douglas, whose homosexual relationship with Oscar Wilde had led to Wilde's celebrated trial and imprisonment in 1895. Charles disliked Douglas and considered him a poseur, but Morton wrote a fulsome piece on his 'bold and courageous' editorship of the literary magazine, *The Academy*, and praised him as 'the only English poet alive that can write sonnets aglow with that indescribable something that is significant of greatness.'[18]

According to a correspondent, Morton's attentions were reciprocated by *The Academy* a few months later when Douglas's assistant editor, Thomas Crosland, arrived at a Bohemian gathering at Piccadilly's Café Royal brandishing a copy of the *Triad*. The object of Crosland's admiration, however, was not Morton's triolets or his villanelles, but rather his lethal recipe for an absinthe and coconut milk cocktail that had appeared in the 'Compleat Gastronomer'. Since the Café Royal had no coconuts, the entire party headed off in the small hours of the morning to purchase them at the market in Covent Garden, where the cocktail was sampled with disastrous consequences.

Despite Charles's assertion that the *Triad* did not 'bother itself overmuch with politics',[19] political commentary was beginning to intrude on its coverage. After years of political stability, the death of Richard Seddon in 1906 had signalled the onset of the Liberal decline. While Charles lauded the more urbane Joseph Ward for his support of the Exhibition Orchestra,

New Zealand's workers felt they had lost a champion. An early sign of their disenchantment came in 1908, when West Coast miners shunned the Liberal Government's much vaunted arbitration process and succeeded in extending their lunch break from fifteen to thirty minutes by going on strike. This led, a year later, to the foundation of the Federation of Labour, known as the 'Red Feds', which represented the interests of several unions (including the watersiders and shearers) and marked a significant advance for the Labour movement.

Meanwhile, in July 1912, over twenty years after the Liberals had first taken office, the political tide had turned. The opposition (now renamed the Reform Party) finally gained enough support in Parliament to defeat the Government. In his August 'Obiter Dicta' column, Charles hastened to give his views on the new Prime Minister, William Massey, dubbing him a 'predestined blunderer ... a man of slow thought and erratic impulses, and all his impulses are unsafe.'[20] Massey's handling of both the Waihi Strike in November 1912, where a striker was clubbed to death, and the Wellington watersiders dispute in October 1913, where the brutality of the mounted specials earned them the title of 'Massey's Cossacks', seems to bear out his views. But although Charles intensely disliked Massey, he equally had no time for the strikers. In May 1914, he made his position abundantly clear by stating bluntly that the *Triad* was 'flatly opposed to Revolutionary Socialism.'[21]

Like many others, he suspected the leaders of the newly formed United Federation of Labour of being imported agitators, describing them as 'a foreign association of men pledged to calculated disturbance.'[22] He regarded the labouring majority as a band of innocent dupes who were being 'huddled down a drive by clever fellows who are by quaint paradox styled its leaders.'[23] Amongst the 'clever fellows' whom Massey arrested to break the general strike that had been called by the UFL were future Labour Prime Minister, Peter Fraser, future Labour Cabinet Minister, Bob Semple, and Harry Holland who in 1918 became leader of the Labour party. One of those who escaped arrest was Michael Savage, who was later New Zealand's first Labour Prime Minister.

Yet another reflection of the *Triad*'s increasing involvement with politics was the introduction to its pages of political caricatures. Since the services of David Low – now emerging as New Zealand's most brilliant cartoonist – had already been commandeered by the *Bulletin*, Charles contented himself with the Wellington artist, Fred Hiscocks.* But Low's talents had not escaped

---

* Fred Hiscocks was one of several gifted New Zealand cartoonists who later worked for major British newspapers. In 1925 Hiscocks became the cartoonist for the London *Daily News*.

'We chuckle in this office, chortling "Why, it's C.N.B.!/ We know those hyacinthine locks. We know that gamboge beard./ We know the calm terrific gaze those squealing maids have feared!"/So gaze on the Creation, and be glad along o' we!' Cartoon by Fred Hiscocks, Triad *11 May 1914, p. 270.* ATL.

him. In April 1912 he observed that his work was far superior to that of the *Bulletin*'s long-established staff artist, Alf Vincent: 'There is more pulse of humanity in it, more unforced genial humour, a more effective fluency of line.'[24]

Amongst the politicians and public figures depicted in the *Triad*, Hiscocks included both Charles and Morton. Charles looks splendidly comic, with hair askew and an impressive paunch. Morton, who fancied himself as a dandy, looks funnier still dressed in an extraordinary check suit and flaunting an outsize cravat pin. For a correspondent from the Wellington suburb of Khandallah, the realities of Morton's ample girth and balding pate came as rather a shock:

> *Woman-like, I have pictured the man – tall, slender attenuated even, dark dreamy-eyed, ethereal, something between Sir Galahad and Colonel Lovelace. One day lately on the Quay, my attention was directed by a friend to a man passing. 'Look that is Frank Morton of the* Triad.*' Palpitating, I turned and gazed. Dear, dear, dear!!!* [25]

In the following issue, a lady from Napier who had attended one of Morton's lectures rushed to his defence, declaring him 'very mild and benevolent, though not so beautiful as Mr Baeyertz.'[26]

After five turbulent years, the partnership between Charles and Morton was beginning to show signs of strain. Morton had long since disregarded their agreement and was writing for any publication that would pay. But as his workload increased, so did his capacity to offend. In 1911 a review that he wrote on Amy Castles,* in his fluctuating position as music and drama critic for the *New Zealand Times*, so infuriated her manager that he refused Morton admission to the theatre. On occasion, Charles could be equally imprudent: a few months later, after writing a stinging review of the Canterbury Art Society's annual exhibition, he was once again obliged to publish a public apology in the *Triad* (and pay the costs) in order to dissuade an insulted artist from suing him for libel. The most frequent culprit, however, was Morton and in March 1913 Charles referred openly to their differences – including Morton's perilous habit of taking 'the coach too near the edge of the cliff'.[27] But he could no longer survive without him: as his ambitious business plans for the expansion of the *Triad* began to occupy more and more of his time, he gave Morton an increasingly free rein.

Several of Morton's initiatives, such as his monthly book reviews, were very successful and kept readers up to date with the latest literary trends, ranging from the works of the Bengali poet, Rabindranath Tagore, whose poetry had recently been acclaimed by Yeats, to a new publication called *Poetry*:

> *Some of the matter published may not be quite so fine and compelling as the Editor thinks it; but all is poetry ... and printed with such assured good taste and finely cultivated reticence that it is a truly marvellous thing to come out of America.*[28]

The editor in question was Harriet Monroe who, with Ezra Pound as her foreign correspondent, had founded a journal in Chicago that was at the cutting edge of poetic developments in the English-speaking world. Since Marinetti's 'delicious shriek'[29] in 1909, a new poetic movement, known as 'Imagism', had emerged under the leadership of Ezra Pound, which embraced a view of poetry that was light years away from Tennyson's sonorous stanzas and the thumping rhythms of Kipling. For the Imagists, poetry should be succinct, hard and clear, and its poetic statements should be made by an exact visual image – preferably in 'free verse'. Within a few months, Morton

---

* Morton, who knew little about music, may have taken his cue from Charles's remarks on a 'truly shocking performance' by Amy Castles in 1909 (*Triad*, vol. 17, no. 8, p. 11), and his critical review in the preceding *Triad* which concluded: 'Miss Castles will never be a great singer.'(Ibid., vol. 18, no. 11, p. 10).

had begun to suspect that the Imagists were not to his taste and complained that he was 'becoming a little disappointed with *Poetry*'. Nevertheless, he published a lengthy extract from Yeats's memorable speech to the Chicago poets,[30] in which the Irish poet voiced his support for a style that was 'as simple as the simplest prose, like a cry of the heart.'*

Morton's book reviews, in which he typically described *Zuleika Dobson* as 'the sort of ecstatic fooling that would inevitably drive Dunedin to lunacy',[31] showed him at his best, but much of the weak verse that he and his imitators wrote for the *Triad* expressed the sort of vague generalities that the Imagists most despised. In December 1913, Stephens, who by now had revived the *Bookfellow*, neatly summed up New Zealand's poets:

> Mr Morton writes ingenious journalists verses. Mr Adams wrote a little poetry a long time ago. Mrs Kernot writes pleasant sentimental verse ... Miss Baughan has written vigorously, vividly, beautifully, sympathetically, poetically. Miss Mackay is a poet.[32]

In his struggle to support a wife and five children by his pen, Morton churned out thousands of words a month on an old typewriter whose worn keys had long ago lost their letters. He often spread his talents too thin and some of his contributions to the *Triad* were little more than space fillers. Even more frequently, as Charles himself noted, he wrote whatever came 'into his head'.[33]

Until Morton made his unfortunate remarks in March 1913, John Fuller's name had only been mentioned in the *Triad* in connection with his vaudeville company. Fuller owned a string of theatres at which he also performed, but as his repertoire consisted of such songs as 'Sally in our Alley' and 'Geraldine', Charles considered him vocally beyond the pale and never took him seriously as a singer. Thus, when Morton responded facetiously to a Sydney journal which had 'fulsomely beslobbered' Fuller's singing, he may have thought that he was in line with editorial policy. But his fatal quip 'while John had a shrill and tuneful enough little pipe years ago, it is now not much more musical than a pig's whistle' – compounded by his comments on Fuller's 'managerial meanness'[34] – created an uproar and provoked the most celebrated court case in the annals of the *Triad*.

Within days Charles received a letter from Fuller's lawyer demanding a public apology. When Charles refused, claiming that no 'personal sting'[35] had been intended, Fuller brought a libel action against the *Triad* and demanded £10,000 in damages. Charles tried to defuse the situation by inviting Fuller

---

* Morton adds: 'This is all very interesting and it is all very true ... Mr Yeats is unquestionably a very fine and a very true poet; but to pretend he is one of the greatest living poets is a little absurd.' (*Triad*, vol. 22, no. 22, p. 264).

for a drink. But by now Fuller was baying for blood. While he accepted the drink, his considerable vanity had been dented and he rejected any efforts at peacemaking. Later, at the bar of Wellington's Thistle Hotel, he announced his intention of ruining Charles and taking over the *Triad*. He also approached the committee of the New Zealand Competitions Society in Wellington and told them that Charles was unfit to act as a judge.

Despite his regular tiffs with the societies in Christchurch and Dunedin, Charles held the Competitions in high regard and prized his position as a judge. In 1911, he had been a prime mover in the first Competitions to be held in Wellington, which proved to be the largest and most successful event of its kind in New Zealand. Since then he had been invited back to Ballarat and had also judged at many of the local societies that were springing up throughout New Zealand. For Charles, who believed passionately in the importance of educating the public and nurturing young talent, the Competitions embodied some of his most cherished ideals. Fuller's clumsy attempts to damage his reputation with the powerful Wellington committee must therefore have caused him considerable anxiety.

The quality of his defence is an indication of how seriously he took the case. For his counsel, he hired one of the top K.C.s in the country, Sir John Findlay,* and he also engaged Richard Singer, who was an effective barrister. This heavyweight team must have persuaded Fuller to rethink his position, for by the time the case was heard at the Supreme Court in Auckland, he had reduced his claim to £501† and the whole affair had taken on an air of farce. Fuller himself, in the best music hall traditions, played up to his part by entering the witness-box with a roll of music protruding from his back pocket and a tuning fork. A huge crowd was in attendance, including most of the cast of the touring 'Pink Dandies'. For the next three hours, according to the *Triad*, 'the courthouse rocked with laughter'.[36]

The defence ran rings around the plaintiff and even made him sing a scale. But the humorous high point came when, in response to Fuller's furious complaint that 'it was degrading to compare my voice to any part of a pig', Findlay solemnly assured him that 'in the Oxford Dictionary and the Encyclopaedia Britannica a pig's whistle was defined as meaning a low whisper – a low, weak voice – and nothing more.'[37] The *Triad* won hands down and Fuller paid the costs. The 'Pig's Whistle' case was widely reported in the press and gave the *Triad* some of its best publicity in years, but Fuller had the last laugh, for he recouped his losses by putting on a one-man show about the case which played to packed houses for a week.

---

*   Findlay had been Attorney-General in the Ward Government.
†   A claim for less than £500 would not go before a jury of twelve.

Inside the Courtroom: The Pig's Whistle Case. Cartoon by Fred Hiscocks,
Triad, 10 November 1913, p. 271. ATL

Meanwhile, with his music and drama criticisms, Charles had been making plenty of waves himself. His first victim was John McCormack, who at the age of twenty-eight already had a global fan club, thanks to the recordings of the Victor Talking Machine Company. Early in 1912, Charles heard him at the Wellington Town Hall, and while he acknowledged that he had 'a very pretty tenor voice', considered him greatly inferior to Caruso. He was also disappointed by McCormack's lack of temperament:

> *One expects from a Celt more fire, magnetism, personality, but the big dramatic pulse never throbs. At his best ... he charms by a delicate sensibility, and a poetic imagination, but he always woos the sense, rather than the intellect.*[38]

McCormack got off lightly.* Charles's next review of a visiting celebrity was a four-page massacre.

As a performer, H.B. Irving had the disadvantage of being the son of Henry Irving, who was considered one of the greatest Shakespearean actors of all time. His famous name, however, assured him and his company a rapturous welcome in New Zealand. Young Alan Mulgan wrote a respectful notice of his *Hamlet* for the Christchurch *Press* in which he politely refrained from more than passing comment on his curious mannerisms of diction. Charles had no such reticence. Under the heading of 'IN SHAKSPERE'S NAME: Mr H.B. Irving's Deplorable Hamlet', he blasted Irving's performance to oblivion:

> *Irving has a certain staggering audacity; he virtually tells Shakespeare that he was an arrant fool, to write in verse at all ... Irving speaks hundreds of lines with no caesura, botching and mutilating and mangling both the sense and the music ... He rants, mouths and snarls by turns, and ... gave us no suggestion of the idealism, the subtlety, and the dignity of Hamlet's mind ... Mr Irving makes him a paltroon and a coward, devoid of sensibility and thought ... I never saw a more completely unsatisfactory Hamlet.*[39]

Irving's acting had left Bernard Shaw equally unimpressed and, shortly after his Australasian tour, he left the stage. Over half a century later, the playwright and critic, Bruce Mason, whose own reviews were said to 'fill – or empty – a theatre',[40] cited Charles on Irving, noting that, for the next fifty years, 'no more magisterial piece of Shakespeare criticism was, to my knowledge, written in New Zealand.'[41]

Others, such as the musical comedy star, Ethel Irving,† were more gently handled. Morton described her performance as 'delightful and striking'[42] and his review of the legendary actress, Ellen Terry, who was well into her sixties by the time she visited New Zealand on a lecture tour in 1914, was equally favourable. He also wrote lyrically on the Danish dancer, Adeline Genée and when the Canadian dancer, Maud Allen, toured a few months later with

---

* When McCormack returned to New Zealand two years later, Charles accused him of trying to emulate Caruso's dramatic tenor by adopting 'the "big tone" habit' and sacrificing his 'pretty little lyric voice' to mere noise. (*Triad*, vol. 21, no. 10, p. 57).
† She was unrelated to H.B. Irving, whose father had taken Irving as a stage name.

her 'Vision of Salome',* both Charles and Morton agreed that her exquisite dancing was 'inviolably chaste' and 'cries to the mind and to the soul'.[43]

The *Triad* was equally enthusiastic about the heroic members of the Sheffield Choir who, after battling through a cyclone to reach New Zealand, still managed to 'sing like larks' on the night of their arrival in Auckland. Despite being 'worked and driven to death' by their inept management, in Charles's estimation 'the singers' work was superb'. He claimed that he had rarely heard such 'amazing and impeccable appreciation of note value'. But even they did not get away scot-free: 'These good folk are of Sheffield' and Charles's acute elocutionary antennae detected a noticeable North Country accent. Nor was their diction perfect: 'We had "Angels an' dark angels" for instance: but when the singing was so fine I have a feeling that the archangels wouldn't mind.'[44]

In the meantime, New Zealanders were continuing to enjoy a succession of visits by acclaimed international soloists. Among these was the English contralto, Louise Kirkby-Lunn, whom Charles had heard singing with Caruso in New York. He urged his readers to attend her concert: 'My children do not miss her.'[45] Her performance did not disappoint him but, not for the first time, he was infuriated by 'the debased idea that entrepreneurs seem to have of the musical taste of New Zealand' and complained that Kirkby-Lunn's programme included pieces 'which she would never dream of singing in England or America'.[46]

One of the most unexpected developments of this hectic musical period was Charles's unprecedented capitulation over Clara Butt, who had returned to New Zealand on tour in December 1913. His declaration that she had made 'a notable advance in the art of singing since her last visit to New Zealand'[47] was greeted with derision and although he claimed that his change of heart had nothing to do with the Butt-Rumford charm offensive, no one believed him. He had met the couple in the Grand Hotel in Auckland, where Rumford had not only admired Charles's specially made pipe, but had also – the soul of tact – insisted on spending a morning with him as he judged at the Auckland Competitions.

The last notable musician to arrive before World War I brought New Zealand's golden age of visiting stars to a close was the Ukrainian violinist, Mischa Elman. Elman's manager had decided that his Australasian tour should start in Wellington, having made the discovery (as Charles put it) 'that nothing fails in Australia if it has first succeeded in New Zealand.'[48] This bold statement, made in May 1914, was a clear reflection of Charles's strong conviction that, having conquered New Zealand, the *Triad* was more than ready to take on Australia.

---

*   Inspired by Oscar Wilde's play.

Chapter 13

The Australasian *Triad*

Three months earlier, after months of careful planning, Charles had taken the first step towards establishing the expanded Australasian edition that he had been dreaming of ever since his triumphant visit to Ballarat in 1909. In his February 'Obiter Dicta' column, he announced that the *Triad* had become a public company and that, once sufficient advertising support had been found in Australia, it would be printed, edited and published in Sydney, with separate editions for New Zealand, Victoria and New South Wales.

Despite the strictly businesslike tone of his 'little talk, as 't were, within the family', Charles's excitement is palpable. In a scheme very reminiscent of the *Triad*'s early days in Dunedin, he outlined his plan to send 30,000 free copies monthly for the first year to householders in every state in Australia, followed up by door-to-door canvassers. With a third of the company's shares now on sale, he also reassured his potential shareholders that the New Zealand edition would remain 'a *Triad* for New Zealanders' and stressed the commercial wisdom of the move: 'The population of Australia is five times ours* ... In Australia today there is no magazine on the lines of the *Triad*.' Furthermore, in Sydney the printing costs were lower and as an Australasian publication, the *Triad* would command 'an immense amount of English and European and American advertising'.[1] Brimming with self-confidence, he even guaranteed his shareholders a ten per cent dividend for the first three years.

Charles's sales pitch must have impressed his readers. By March he was able to report that all 6000 of the £1 shares that had been made available to the public had been sold. The *Triad* was valued at £18,000 and of the remaining 12,000 shares, 6000 were held by Charles, amounting to a third of the capital, while his two co-directors† took 3000 each. Investors were probably encouraged by the news that Charles had agreed to act as the

---

*   Charles was exaggerating. In fact, Australia's population was only four times that of New Zealand.

†   The three original directors of The Triad Magazine Ltd were Charles, an accountant named Arthur Whyte and the barrister and occasional *Triad* contributor, David Findlay.

'managing editor' for another ten years. In keeping the *Triad* solvent – and profitable – for over twenty-one years (during which the price had risen from a modest threepence to an equally modest sixpence), he had more than proved his business credentials and his ability to give value for money.

But his assurances that the *Triad* would not lose its New Zealand character were less convincing. In May 1914 a thoughtful article by A.A. Grace voiced the concerns of many:

> *The* Triad *is in its way a unique publication. Making no appeal with the sensational, eschewing politics … [I]t has treated of the artistic in Literature, in Music, and to a lesser degree, in pictorial Art – and has been able to prove that a publication devoted to these subjects can not merely exist, but flourish in New Zealand … Will it be so in the future?*
>
> …
>
> *In Australia, the goal of all clever writers is the office of the* Bulletin *… it has certainly created a literary style of its own … [I]t is peculiar, distinctly of Australia, extremely modern, effective – to be avoided as the very devil … The danger of extending the scope of the* Triad *to Australia is that it may possibly be swamped by* Bulletin *writers … The* Triad *as the* Triad *is unique and a publication for which intellectual New Zealanders are grateful; for it to become merely a little* Bulletin *would make the soul of its readers sick.*[2]

Since the *Triad* was now commenting regularly on political issues – and owed much of its popularity to Charles's notoriously outspoken reviews and Morton's 'naughty' writing – Grace's remarks were not entirely accurate. Nevertheless, his anxiety that the *Triad* would be subsumed by Australia's powerful culture reflected the widespread fear that a long-standing feature of New Zealand's cultural landscape was about to be appropriated by Australia.

In his response to Grace's article, Charles insisted that the individuality of the *Triad* would be 'jealously preserved'. But mindful of the need to coexist peacefully with his new neighbour in Sydney, he also expressed his 'cordial respect' for the *Bulletin*, noting that it had published 'most of the best work of the most original Australian writers for a quarter of a century.'[3] Despite these soothing statements, however, the *Triad* was inundated with letters deploring the move to Sydney which, according to one reader, would dispossess New Zealand of 'a great educational asset, and one of its prominent institutions.'[4]

Inflated as these claims may seem, they contained more than a grain of truth. By 1914 the *Triad* had expanded its role far beyond 'disseminating a small modicum of musical, artistic and scientific information throughout

New Zealand',[5] and with Morton producing some of the best literary coverage in the region, it had become a significant player in the nation's cultural life. But music still remained its strongest suit: after over two decades of publication, the flow of encouragement and advice to local singers and musicians continued unabated.

From the outset Charles had applauded the musical endeavours of small communities – such as the efforts of the Hawera Operatic Society and the formation of the Huntly Orchestral Society with eleven members, including a first violin aged eight and two second violins aged nine and ten respectively. Later, he was equally supportive of the Feilding Choir, which he singled out for special praise at the Competitions in Napier in 1912, declaring that, 'with the sole exception of the Sheffield Choir, I have heard no choral singing in New Zealand in any way comparable.'[6] Similarly at Greymouth, where he had long since revised his initial impression of unfriendliness, he described the annual Competitions as 'inspiring' and noted: 'The Coast makes no pother of culture, but the Coast has brains.'[7]

In the larger centres, he also gave unstinting praise where it was due, with complimentary reviews of such bodies as the chorus of the Auckland Amateur Operatic Society, which was improving steadily under the tutelage of Tom Pollard. In Wellington, too, he used his considerable clout to try and persuade the City Council to fund the impoverished Municipal Orchestra: 'The Council would at all times rather endow a dustbin than an orchestra.' Despairing of the Councillors' ability to understand 'that good music really does matter', he appealed to their business instincts:

> *A good orchestra is a commercial proposition. There is no reason why the musicians composing it should not be paid and every reason why they should be. Amazing as the thing may seem, there is money in good music. Orchestral concerts of the right sort could easily be made to pay.*[8]

Such championing of local causes was typical of Charles. Indeed, there was hardly an aspect of New Zealand's performing arts on which he did not voice an opinion – or try to exert his influence. Consequently, he must have been highly gratified when, shortly after he had advised J.F. Montague's 'Shakspere Society' to read Ibsen and Shaw, the Society gave a public reading of Shaw's *Captain Brassbound's Conversion* in Wellington and invited him to take the part of the judge. On another occasion when the New Zealand actor, Harry Plimmer, formed his own Plimmer-Denniston Company, he pronounced it 'a remarkable company to have been formed by two young managers in so short a time' – but added: 'Mr Plimmer can't act much.'[9] The *Triad* also had a keen eye for emerging talent, like young Marie Fix, who later gained fame and fortune as the actress, Marie Ney. In December 1913, her performance

Charles on his perilous pedestal. Cartoon by W. Macbeth, 1917. From Pat Lawlor's Old Wellington Days, *Whitcombe & Tombs, 1959, p. 132.*

as Molly Seamore in an amateur production of *The Geisha* was described as 'the surprise of the evening ... She looked uncommon well in the part' with 'a pretty little trickle of a singing voice, but it got well over the footlights.'[10]

Occasionally Charles shamelessly embellished the *Triad*'s track record. For example, there is no evidence to support his claim, made just after Michael Balling had been appointed conductor of the Hallé Orchestra, that the *Triad* had long ago foreseen the day when 'musical people would be making pilgrimages to Nelson to worship at the shrine where Balling had lived and taught.'[11] Nor could he resist needling his readers with references to 'the New Zealand twang' which he predicted was 'coming surely' and would be 'very vile'.[12]

In an attempt to reverse the trend, he published a lengthy address given by a Mr E.W. Andrews of Napier Boys High School on 'the curious local dialect' that was 'gradually evolving in New Zealand'. Andrews, who feared that 'the harsh voice noticeable in many of our children' could lead to 'many minor throat and chest disorders', had made a detailed analysis of his pupils' unhealthy speaking habits: 'Lazy' consonants, the failure to trill the 'r' and 'eccentric' vowel sounds – 'especially dipthongal ones'. The only sop of comfort was the 'h' 'so commonly misplaced in England ... I have never come across a boy, born and educated in New Zealand, who had any great difficulty with this refractory letter.'[13] Charles undoubtedly sympathised with Andrews, but he was far more irritated by what he called 'distressful Papanui* affectations':

> *Recently a lady rang me up on the 'phone. I asked for her number and she told me 'Nayne, fayve, fayve.' ... I think such affectations as these are worse and viler than what we are beginning to execrate as the Australian accent. 'May' for my, 'bay' for by, 'cray' for cry – the revolting idiocy of it all! ... These foolish folk seem to think that a disfiguring of English by the simple process of talking with the tongue against the teeth is a sort of accomplishment or mark of breeding ... Refined people throughout the Empire speak accurate English. The other sort is only spoken by the snobbish daughters of tradesmen and the unclassed of little Pedlington.*[14]

Not everyone was prepared to take Charles's comments lying down. Over the years, the protests of incensed readers – and the *Triad*'s devastating replies – became a regular feature of the letter page. Some correspondents, like 'Pavona',† hit back hard:

---

* A suburb of Christchurch.
† 'Pavona', whom Morton condescendingly describes as 'a cleverish little girl' was possibly the prolific novelist, Isabel Peacocke, whose first children's novel, *My Friend Phil*, was published in 1914 and was favourably reviewed in the *Triad*.

Sir, do you ever condescend to meet your critics on the intellectual plane you consider yourself to occupy? ... I do not doubt your erudition ... but your readers are not all illiterate boors, to be instructed from superior heights where you sit, Jove-like, forging editorial thunderbolts.[15]

The Christchurch magazine, *Tatler*, expressed a similar exasperation:

If we are to judge a man by his writings, we must conclude that Mr Baeyertz poses not only as a critic whose conclusions are necessarily correct, but as one who challenges any view to the contrary.[16]

In April 1911, another disgruntled reader decided to 'get things of his chest' before cancelling his subscription:

When I first read your paper some two years ago, I thought that it contained interesting and good reading and I liked it immensely ... [N]ow it seems to contain nothing but a lot of tiresome and weary poems Etc by the Immortal Frank Morton and pages of hard criticism by you on everything and everybody. Have you ever felt pleased with anything in your life? You give no credit for a thing, and if anyone tries to stand up for himself, you just publish his letter and sit on him in that very self-opinionated way of yours.[17]

Charles's practice of publishing angry correspondence provided him with plenty of free copy, but it was also an essential part of his strategy for stirring up debate. His chief objective had always been to arouse a greater interest in the arts; even when he was licking his wounds after a serious attack on his critical methods by the *Canterbury Times*, he consoled himself with the thought that at least he was creating 'a desire for truth in art'.[18] Moreover, despite the howls of protest, the honesty of his reviews and his fearless tilting at pretensions won him quite as many admirers as enemies. A reader from Christchurch, which was home to some of Charles's greatest detractors, called him 'the best hated man I know of' and congratulated him on 'doing a noble job' in destroying the 'beastly, narrow, grey and horrid little prejudices' of the 'smuggest city in New Zealand'.[19]

In the meantime, apart from his spasmodic tirades against Australian nationalism and the Australian accent, Charles was busily wooing his trans-Tasman subscribers. After his return from Ballarat in 1910, he had devoted much of his 'Obiter Dicta' column to a paean of praise for Australia, which he described as 'a great, glad, friendly, joyous, hearty, hospitable island.'[20] His friendship with the editor of Ballarat *Echo*, Charles King, was also proving useful. In October 1911, King gave the *Triad* just the sort of publicity Charles loved:

> *There are some people in Ballarat who are guilty of reading the 'Triad' ... 'Mr Baeyertz is a very nice man,' pronounced a society dame recently 'but what a shocking paper the "Triad" is. It is positively pagan.'*[21]

Like many others, Charles was unable to resist the lure of the greater profits that could be made in Australia, but a further attraction of the move to Sydney was that it offered a perfect solution to the problem of his personal life. In New Zealand, where he was a well-known figure, his relationship with Mildred (who was facing constant criticism from her devoutly Roman Catholic family and friends) was severely curtailed. In a city like Sydney, however, with its population of over half a million, they could live together in anonymity – and peace.

On 26 June 1914, Charles sailed from Wellington on the *SS Ulimaroa*. The name that appears next to his on the passenger list is Miss Carew, which is close enough to Miss Carey to suggest that, even aboard ship, Mildred's virtue needed a fig leaf. Charles describes the day as 'bleak and lowering', but within a few hours they were steaming cheerily 'through a clear night of stars' and reached Sydney in glorious sunshine, little guessing that the assassination on 28 June of an Austrian Archduke in Sarajevo was about to plunge the world into a European war.

Charles was ecstatic:

> *Writing from this cordial clime ... I am in no mood to mince matters. Sydney is absolutely delightful. I have nested in a waterside suburb. I have a room quite near to heaven – probably as near to heaven as I am ever likely to get ... From this aerie, I look over the harbour. Cold night and dewy morning, there lies the harbour spread below my windows: a picture that makes my room exquisite at all hours and in all weathers.*

He and Mildred had 'nested' in a furnished flat in Cremorne, where they revelled in their escape from moral censure:

> *Here there is literally no puritanical pose at all. People don't get up in the morning and pray to their God that they may be shocked during the day as often and as much as possible.*[22]

Charles shaved off his beard, perhaps to disguise his identity, but more probably to please Mildred because it made him look ten years younger.

Charles's rosy view of Sydney was only partially coloured by his new domestic arrangements and his hopes of business success. He was also captivated by the city. After his visit in 1909, he wrote lyrically of Sydney's 'deep skies of gleaming blue' and 'the joyous beauty of the Sydney sea'.[23] After a further visit in 1910, he described it as 'the city of my love' and claimed that, while Melbourne displayed 'all the marks of modern progress', Sydney bore 'the footprints of the gods'.[24] As Australia's largest city, Sydney exuded an atmosphere of glamour and vitality which not even Melbourne could rival. Since the disastrous crash of 1891, Melbourne had recovered much of its former prosperity so that, when Australia became a federation in 1901, its two greatest cities had vied for the title of capital. As a compromise, this honour was eventually bestowed on Canberra, and while the new purpose-built capital was under construction, Melbourne became the seat of government. But although this may have added to what Charles termed its 'admirable poise and dignity',[25] for him no other Australian city could match Sydney.

Charles wasted no time settling in. Within a few days of his arrival, he had posted off an authoritative overview of Sydney's cultural life for inclusion in the July *Triad*. Music was 'at a pretty low ebb' and the selection of music at an organ recital at the Town Hall had been lamentable. The Wellington organist, Bernard Page, 'would laugh in the face of any man who asked him to play such a programme on the Wellington organ.' On the other hand, the choice of theatrical entertainment was breathtaking: Charles included an impressive list of current shows to demonstrate that 'in Sydney one need never go short of entertainment.'[26]

With his personal life more settled than it had been for years, Charles was flourishing. To add to his happiness, Sydney was proving 'the cheapest place on earth to live'.[27] Business seemed to be going well too. Advertisers were on the increase and the new Australian office was scheduled to open in December. In the meantime, Morton would edit the *Triad* in Wellington, with Charles contributing a substantial monthly column from Australia. But this was the lull before the storm. By the time Morton penned his first 'Obiter Dicta' column in August, war had been declared and both Australia and New Zealand were gripped by a patriotic fervour that was laced with jingoism and virulently anti-German.

In New Zealand, anti-German sentiments were nothing new. During the Boer War, when the German press had sided with the Boers, there had been a vicious backlash against German nationals and products, which Charles had severely rebuked in the *Triad*. But in 1914 Germany was the aggressor; as a New Zealand force sailed proudly off to liberate Western Samoa, reports of German atrocities in Belgium unleashed a wave of anti-German feeling that bordered on hysteria. In Wellington, the long-established Liedertafel became the 'Wellington Male Choir', and for several nights the harbour was plunged into darkness to confuse suspected German cruisers. The Auckland Liedertafel also transformed itself into a 'male choir', while in Dunedin the *Triad*'s first sponsor, the Dresden Piano Company, nervously adopted the name of Bristol – although this did not prevent an angry crowd from staging a riot outside its offices in Wanganui.

Another target of the hate campaign was German music. Charles was incandescent. After reading a letter in the Australian press that called for a boycott of German songs, he exploded: 'Crass bigotry and twaddling insensate jingoism ... the arts, literature, music, painting, sculpture – what have they to do with international war?'[28] Far more sinister, however, were the attacks on individuals and groups. Anyone who sounded foreign was suspect. In Hamilton the Dutch conductor and music teacher, Johannes Wielaert, was mistaken for a German and assaulted. In Northland there were calls to intern the Dalmatian gum-diggers who, as Charles pointed out, were all Slavs who hated their Austrian overlords. Those with German names or of German descent were publicly hounded. In Wellington, the prominent academic, George von Zedlitz, was accused of being a German agent and in response to public pressure, the Government passed the Alien Enemy Teachers Act to drive him from his professorial post at Victoria University College. Even the British royal family decided to change its name from Saxe-Coburg-Gotha to Windsor, and in Australia, where a similar mood prevailed, it was only a question of time before someone picked on Charles.

The attack came within a few weeks of the outbreak of war when a Sydney rag named the *Theatre Magazine*, with whom Morton had been trading insults for some time, slyly referred to Charles as 'Herr Baeyertz'. Over the years, his German-sounding name had often given rise to speculation that he was German. For publications like the *Tapanui Courier*, his criticisms of English singers and his well-known preference for German composers fully justified their gibes about the 'Faderland' and snide references to sauerkraut and beer. At the time Charles laughed these off, but in the witch-hunting atmosphere of 1914, to be fingered as a German was far more damaging. From a business point of view, the timing could hardly have been worse. After retorting that he did not have 'a drop of German blood',[29] Charles decided to postpone the launching of the Australasian *Triad* and sue the *Theatre* for libel.

As acting editor of the *Triad*, Morton confronted the outbreak of war in his usual inimitable style. Well aware that war was the only subject that would interest his readers, he devoted the first two pages of the August edition to it: 'I am not going to pretend to glory in the fact of war. War is, in fact, an abomination.'[30] Morton knew what he was talking about:

> *I once marched through jungle country that a little war had harried. Here and there we came across dead women and children – the bodies grotesquely bloated and dehumanised ... I was cured forever of any idea I may have*

had of the glamour and glory of war ... But such horrors are likely to prove merely trivial by comparison with the horrors of a great European war under modern conditions.[31]

A few editions later, when the general public still had no concept of the approaching carnage of Gallipoli or the protracted nightmare of the Western Front, his words were chillingly prophetic:

The element of death is one that we do not adequately consider when we talk of war ... [T]he sum of human pain that this war has already cost is enormous. Men in the trenches, amid foul waters and fouler odours, cold, half mad (maybe) from want of sleep, suffering pain. Men dying, with thoughts of their dearest left behind. Men grim and dogged among leaping terrors – men with only the dimmest idea of what it is all about.[32]

Few people shared his pessimism; indeed, throughout the country men of military age were flocking to volunteer. Among them was the *Triad*'s cartoonist, Fred Hiscocks, who sailed from Wellington with the New Zealand Expeditionary Force in October 1914 and promptly established an onboard magazine called *The Gunner*. Meanwhile, the patriotic frenzy continued and Morton's lecture tour of the North Island, during which he tried to promote a greater sense of realism, met with limited success:

I should have done far better if I had talked on 'Women and Wine' or 'Why Women Love Love' ... When I told them that our New Zealanders and Australians were already fighting in the Dardanelles, and that the deaths and casualties would probably make a heavy list, they judged me to be an alarmist with a taste for fiction.[33]

In stark contrast to his sober reflections on war, Morton's violent outbursts against the Germans would have satisfied the most patriotic audience. His comments on the Belgian atrocities were racist in the extreme, and his jingoistic calls for all Germans in New Zealand to be 'put away in a safe place as soon as possible' were equally inflammatory. From Sydney, Charles had little control over what Morton wrote. As he tried to counter the *Theatre*'s smear by insisting that his family was Belgian, Morton's rantings against 'the many Germans busily representing that they are really of some other origin'[34] can only have increased his discomfiture. Morton also tried to enlist his readers' anti-German sentiments to justify a literary quarrel of his own by claiming that Futurism and Vorticism were 'queer mad growths that sprang from the mental and moral degeneracy of moonstruck fools in Berlin and Vienna.'[35] Later on he repeated the charge: 'As to all this Vorticist humbug, we need be in no doubt whatever. It originated in Germany.'[36]

The new artistic movement, Vorticism, was Ezra Pound's latest intellectual adventure and Morton's salvo was yet another round in a long-running dispute between Pound and the *Triad*. In October 1914, Morton had written a savage review of the Vorticists' magazine, *Blast*, whose pages featured the bewildering abstractions of Wyndham Lewis and the equally perplexing poetry of Pound. As far as Morton was concerned, the Vorticists were fit only to be 'the inmates of asylums ... As for this Mr Ezra Pound, he becomes a public nuisance. To pretend that he is a poet in any sense of the word is preposterously silly.'[37]

Despite the strength of his feelings, however, Morton was not the originator of the *Triad*'s celebrated attack on Pound. The culprit was Alice Kenny. The saga had begun two years earlier when Pound, in his capacity as foreign correspondent for *Poetry*, wrote to Kenny and invited her to submit some verse to him. In his search for foreign talent, he must have noticed her work in the *Triad* – perhaps because of its Irish affinities. Not long afterwards, on Pound's advice, Harriet Monroe exchanged subscriptions with the *Triad*, but she never published anything by Kenny. Over a year later – possibly piqued that the most prestigious poetry magazine of the era had failed to recognise her gifts – Kenny lashed out with a tongue-in-cheek article entitled 'Whitman Out-Walted: Words in Appreciation of *Poetry*'.[38]

Whenever she emerged from the Celtic twilight, Kenny wielded a feisty pen. Doubtless egged on by Morton, she laid into *Poetry*'s Modernist poets with gusto, aping the Imagist style of Amy Lowell and referring to Pound as Mr Isaiah Ounce – a tribute to *Punch* which had dubbed him Ezekiel Ton. Pound treated Kenny's punning with lofty disdain – if he ever bothered to read it. But three months later, Morton's six-page tirade against *Blast* was more serious and merited a response.

Pound's letter to the *Triad* of 21 December 1914 is a model of restraint. In it he gently chides Morton for his folly of trying to measure 'non-representative art by the footrule of representational art' and dismisses his outrageous personal insults with wry humour. He concludes graciously:

I suppose Mr Morton is to be pardoned. It is too much to expect that a man of one generation, living in one corner of the world, should know or even be able to see clearly just what men of another generation are rebelling against in the opposite corner.[39]

Pound was right about the generation gap. As a man of the 1890s, Morton was baffled by the Modernists and he found their rejection of traditional poetic conventions little short of blasphemous. From his editorial chair, Charles would have sympathised with this view, for it was only in publications like Edward Marsh's *Georgian Poetry*, which contained the more conservative work of such figures as Rupert Brooke and John Masefield, that he and Morton could find contemporary poetry that they could respect and understand.

Meanwhile the exchanges between Morton and Pound continued, with Pound boasting that he was '"boring his little hole in the adamantine stupidity" of New Zealand', while Morton insisted that New Zealand had made 'a little hole in the adamantine stupidity of Mr Ezra Pound'.[40] Over the next four years, Morton continued to snipe at Pound, although he had a growing respect for Monroe, whom he considered to have been duped into publishing Pound's 'perverted drivellings'.[41] But to his lasting credit, Pound never held any grudge against the *Triad*, and in 1918 he paid it a handsome compliment in the introduction to the February number of the New York, *Little Review*:

> *It is something in the nature of a national disgrace that a New Zealand paper,* The Triad, *should be more alert to, and have better regular criticism of, contemporary French publications than any American periodical has yet had.*[42]

Morton's dislike of Pound eventually mellowed into a warm admiration, but his initial failure to recognise Pound's genius has been held against the *Triad* ever since.

In terms of the *Triad*'s critical reputation, it was also singularly unfortunate that its first view of Post-Impressionism should have been filtered through the unschooled eye of Gladys Kernot, who in December 1912 visited the second of Roger Fry's ground-breaking exhibitions in London: 'I entered the Grafton Galleries and found them full of estimable Londoners who were absolutely rocking with laughter.' Later she struggled to describe a canvas by Matisse, observing that if 'the master signwriter at Kaiwarra ... put such a thing on a hoarding he would be executed.' Cézanne and Van Dongen fared slightly better, but 'of the Cubists, I refuse to speak; and indeed I cannot, for they speedily reduce me to a state of aphasia.'[43]

Today Kernot's reactions seem unpardonable, but at the time the Post-Impressionists shocked many more discerning viewers. The poet and traveller, Wilfred Blunt, described the same exhibition as 'either an extremely bad joke or a swindle' and the art as 'nothing but that gross puerility which scrawls indecencies on the walls of a privy.'[44] At least Kernot had the grace to suggest that perhaps 'we are judging the Post-Impressionists by the wrong criteria.'[45] The *Triad* did not discuss Cubism and Post-Impressionism again until 1917, when an article entitled 'Art in Paris since the War' informed readers that 'the shrieking lunatics of the artistic cosmos flourish unblushing and unashamed.'[46]

Back in Sydney, as he waited for his action against the *Theatre* to come to court, Charles was scratching around for cultural news: 'There is not much to write about ... entertainments – save patriotic concerts – have languished since the outbreak of war.' But Melba had found a new vocation and Charles's sardonic review of her first fundraising concert in Sydney aptly captures the emotionally charged atmosphere of the early days of the war:

> *Every person present had been presented with a flag and when the national hymn ceased there was a vast amount of flag-waving and a tremendous outburst of enthusiasm ... When the flag-waving was over, the wave of patriotic fervour had reached such a height that the whole audience rose and sang (more or less) the Old Hundredth. For her opening, Melba brought out her old and trusted 'cheval de bataille', the Mad Scene from Lucia ... As a final encore, she accompanied herself on the piano and sang 'Home Sweet Home'.*

According to Charles, her diction was 'flagrantly faulty',[47] but the crowd loved her and a total of £1900 was raised for the Patriotic Fund. In response to the prevailing mood, even the *Triad*'s picture supplement took a break from its customary fleshy damsels and featured a full-page portrait of Lord Kitchener, together with a photograph taken in a Belgian town that the Germans had reduced to the rubble.

To pass the time, Charles busied himself with canvassing for the *Triad* and on the warm summer evenings, he joined a small group of music-lovers who met on a veranda where they discussed Wagner and played his music at 'the maximum of resonance'[48] on a gramophone. Over Christmas he and Mildred stayed at a guest house in the picturesque seaside resort of Avoca. But his nerves were on edge and on the return journey, in a display of misplaced gallantry, he knocked down a man for jostling a female passenger at the railway station in Woy Woy. When his libel case was finally heard, it had many of the elements of farce that seemed to accompany all his appearances in court, with both sides claiming the victory. In fact, the jury gave the verdict in favour of Charles, but their token award of one shilling for damages caused widespread amusement. Melbourne *Table Talk* reported the case:

> *The matter appears to have entertained everybody connected with it, and probably Mr Baeyertz himself – who is of Belgian descent – has hung the shilling on his watch-chain and had many a chuckle over it since the case closed. But precedents are tricky things and it isn't safe to assume that you can call anybody a German for a bob.*[49]

Charles was not amused: 'There can be no more scandalous libel than to accuse a man of being of German origin ... Germans are cordially detested ... and will be ... by all civilised people (unless the world goes mad) for many years to come.'[50] With the mounting casualty figures of Gallipoli, his attitude to the Germans was hardening and he was appalled by the torpedoing of the passenger liner, *Lusitania*, on which Mildred's uncle, O'Brien Butler, had died. Once the court case was safely behind him, Charles's calls for the internment of Germans were often quite as extreme as those of Morton.*

Meanwhile the countdown to the launch of the new Australasian edition was about to begin and in April Charles made a flying visit to New Zealand to oversee the closing down of the Wellington office. Despite his infatuation with Sydney, he was looking forward to a visit home: 'I have enjoyed every minute of my sojourn in this gladsome city, but my pulse beats a trifle faster at the thought that very soon I shall be once more in God's own country.'[51] A trip to Dunedin prompted a wave of nostalgia:

> *Seriously speaking, Dunedin is one of the loveliest of Australasia's little cities. It has glorious effects of light and shade. The hills that stand round and lean over it are superb of contour. The climate between blizzards is delicious. And the people, even at their narrowest, are honest and sincere.*[52]

By the time Charles returned to Sydney in May, Morton had already arrived from New Zealand to co-edit the Australasian edition, together with Carl who was to run the new head office at No. 7 O'Connell Street. All that remained in Wellington was a mail box. Shortly before the launch, Charles received some frank advice from an Australian contributor: 'If you begin telling us that Mrs Tomkins of Boggabri makes all her v's into b's, or that Mrs Jenkins of Murwillumbah has too much frontal tone – well then, goodbye.' But her most damning remarks were directed at the *Triad*'s appearance: 'That Supplement stuck in the middle is a terrible thing as a rule. You need illustrations and you need them badly. But you don't need illustrations of that sort.' Worse still were the advertisements: 'Most of your pages are so loaded with advertising matter that it would be difficult to include illustrations on a general scheme.'[53]

New Zealand subscribers had also complained that the *Triad* was in danger of becoming an advertising medium. Their objections were not without foundation, for by 1914 about fifty per cent of the available space in the *Triad*'s sixty-odd pages was occupied by advertising. But in a country with insufficient population to support a cultural magazine by subscriptions alone, advertising was the only means of survival. Having witnessed the demise of so many other New Zealand journals, Charles was well aware that advertisements were the life blood of the *Triad*.

Later critics have often derided the *Triad*'s high volume of advertising.

---

* Morton's ability to imitate his editor's style sometimes makes it difficult to know which of them was writing the 'Obiter Dicta' column.

From the pages of the elegant literary quarterly, *Landfall*, K.K. Ruthven* scoffs at its unsophisticated typography. What he fails to take into account is that Charles Baeyertz, unlike Charles Brasch (the founder of *Landfall*), had no personal fortune with which to embellish his magazine. Moreover, despite the remarks of Charles's candid contributor, in an era when the front page of the London *Times* was devoted to Personal Columns, contemporary readers were well used to picking their way to the serious reading matter through a mass of extraneous material.

In October 1915, therefore, amidst an abundance of new advertising, the Australasian *Triad* made its long awaited debut. It had a different cover design, an upbeat editorial by Charles and copious contributions from Morton as 'Epistemon', 'Selwyn Rider' and 'T.F. Monk-Orran'. It also included a letter from Hiscocks in Gallipoli, a review by A.G. Stephens and a two-page interview with the newly-appointed Director of the Sydney Conservatorium of Music, Henri Verbrugghen. But apart from a few extra pages, and the reintroduction of the monthly music supplement, the new edition barely differed from its predecessor. For Charles, on the other hand, the onset of war had changed the situation dramatically and the glorious business success that he had anticipated was turning into something very different.

---

* K.K. Ruthven's comments appear in his memorable article 'Ezra Pound, Alice Kenny & the "Triad"', *Landfall*, vol. 23, no. 1 (Mar 1969), 73–84.

Chapter 14

THE ABOMINATION OF WAR

Shortly before the launch of the Australasian *Triad*, Charles was party to another event with which he was even more intimately involved. On 22 August 1915, Mildred gave birth to a son whom they christened Charles,* with Brian Butler as his middle names in memory of Mildred's composer uncle. The decision to have a child out of wedlock is an indication of Charles and Mildred's commitment to each other, but the baby's illegitimacy must have rankled with them and can only have increased their bitterness towards Bella.

By this time, Bella had moved to Auckland, where she was living in modest circumstances with Rudolph, who was studying for a law degree. In a letter written many years later, Richard Singer refers darkly to Charles's neglect of his New Zealand family and accuses him of leaving them destitute. Yet in Rudolph's affectionate reminiscences of his father there is no hint of resentment – or any suggestion that he mistreated his family.

Charles, meanwhile, was living in a convenient ménage à trois in a handsome house in Double Bay,† where the devoted Lillian supervised the housekeeping, while Mildred cared for the baby and worked on her musical compositions. In the *Triad*'s music supplement for February 1916, Charles published one of her 'monologues', whose wistful text (written by one of the co-directors of the *Triad*, David Findlay) tactfully suggests that the joy of love does not survive in matrimony.

Ironically, the same issue also contains a spirited article on the ideal husband by the unmarried Lillian in which she claims to 'yearn for a comradely, human, not too immaculate, ridiculous, cuddlesome male … something I can humbug and coax'. Later she observes that the average man 'has to handle the most complicated and fragile instrument in the world and he generally marries before he has learned anything whatever about the machinery.' Originally, Charles had asked her to write something more

---

*   As Carl was also christened Charles, this meant that Charles's first and third sons had the same name.
†   The electoral rolls list him as living at 'Caston', Pearce Street, Double Bay from 1916–1920.

serious and the piece echoes with the lively banter that evidently took place between them: 'How can I be serious in these stockings … I feel as gay as a lark and as twitchy as a tickled frog.' Further on, she refers to his 'tired but unvacillating eye'[1] and his constant preoccupation with business.

Straddling the interests of both New Zealand and Australian readers was not proving as straightforward as Charles had imagined and he frankly admitted to being 'worked half to death.'[2] In April, his response to the flood of criticisms from both sides of the Tasman betrays his weariness, to which the demands of a six-month-old baby can only have added:

We know as well as anybody knows it, that we can't please everybody … when, on good and sound warrant, we praise New Zealand, some valorous Australians are bound to get sore: just as when, in some comparison with Australia, New Zealand seems to suffer, a few good friends in the Dominion are sad about it. But … an Australasian magazine written and edited solely for the satisfaction of Dunedin would not live a month.[3]

He was also discovering that Australians did not take kindly to his blunt reviews and was once again obliged to spell out many of the same arguments that he had so frequently hammered home in New Zealand:

I am not concerned with what people think about me or the Triad *… If I go to a theatre, I go to enjoy myself, just as any other fellow does. If I do enjoy myself I try to make it clear why: that is honest criticism. If I do not enjoy myself, or there are serious flaws on my enjoyment, I again try to show why … If I praise a show I don't enjoy, merely because the mob around me is praising it, I am not a critic at all. I am a prostitute of the mob.*[4]

Charles continued to be disappointed by Sydney's musical life. In January 1916, he stirred up a storm with a devastating review of a recital from which he 'silently stole away, marvelling that in a city of three quarters of a million people such things could be.'[5] His disgust at the poor standard of the Anzac Commemoration Concert on 25 April was even greater: 'We rode home musing sadly on this organised effort to honour the memory of our matchless heroes. What a prodigy of ineptitude and fearful taste – the whole affair!' Almost the only redeeming feature of the evening was Henri Verbrugghen's 'perfect artistry in the sombre romance of Wieniawski's "Legende".'[6]

For Charles, the recent arrival in Sydney of the brilliant Belgian violinist and conductor, Verbrugghen, was the one bright spot in an otherwise lacklustre musical scene. Such was Verbrugghen's charm that he had persuaded the Government to pay for the members of his own string quartet to join him in Sydney, where they performed both as the Verbrugghen Quartet and as part of the new symphony orchestra that he had established.

In May 1916, Charles wrote a well-balanced review of the first of a series of concerts by the orchestra and urged 'those who profess a love of music'[7] not to miss any of them. In less than a year, Verbrugghen's outstanding musical leadership had made its mark; in a second article, devoted to the newly-founded Conservatorium, Charles praised his 'luminous mind' and depicted him as 'a strong man in a glorious young country'.[8]

Throughout 1916 Charles coaxed and cajoled his new Australian readers with a blend of provocation and flattery. In June, the *Triad* sported a full-page advertisement headed 'To our Readers and Others of the Best People', in which he suggested that those who purchased the *Triad* were 'stepping into line'[9] with the most intelligent and open-minded people in the country. By November, the *Triad's* self-promotion had assumed global dimensions:

> *The* Triad *makes a far more catholic appeal than any other Australasian monthly ... on its postal-list are people all over Australasia and people in places as widely sundered as New York and Vladivostock, Glasgow and Callao ... No other magazine in the South reaches such a big and various public ... The Triad is an institution.*[10]

During this period of transition, the *Triad's* New Zealand coverage was often patchy, but it still evokes much of the flavour of wartime life. Throughout the country fundraising 'Queen Carnivals' were all the rage, with fierce competition between the four main centres. In Auckland, the whole of Queen Street was converted into a bazaar that raised £250,000 for the wounded. This left Dunedin trailing with a mere £125,000, while Wellington and Christchurch only managed to produce £70,000 and £50,000 respectively. Christchurch, however, which had been a prime mover in organising the carnivals, later inaugurated successful 'Violet' and 'Daffodil' days during which 'white clad damsels'[11] sold bunches of flowers and did a flourishing trade in buttonholes.

Musical life too inevitably revolved around the war. In December 1915, the Royal Wellington Choral Society performed *Elijah* before a large crowd which had gathered to welcome home the soldiers from Gallipoli. With close to 8000 New Zealand casualties,* the patriotic euphoria had given way to a more sombre mood. As the stream of visits from international stars and touring theatre companies dwindled to a trickle, New Zealanders had to fall back on home-grown talent, including local amateurs, for their musical and dramatic entertainment. In Dunedin, the *Triad's* correspondent described the only amusements as 'vaudeville, pictures,† recruiting rallies, arrivals of

---

* Of this number, 2701 were fatalities.
† Films

hospital ships and departures of transports. What more does any city want in war-time?'[12]

The *Triad*'s literary coverage also reflects the universal preoccupation with military themes. Amongst the poetry reviewed was a slim volume called *Soldier Songs from Anzac*, written by a signaller, Tom Skeyhill, who had been blinded at Gallipoli and was reciting his verses night after night on stage. Although his poetic gifts were modest, his message was unequivocal:

> *Well, I've picked up me old Lee-Enfield,*
> *And buckled me Webb about;*
> *I'm only a bloomin' private,*
> *An' I've got to see it out:*
> *An' though 'e shames 'is man'ood,*
> *An' stains 'is pedigree,*
> *Thank God, we are still in the trenches,*
> *An' we'll fight until we're free.*
> *But if I do get shrapnelled,*
> *Though I die without a groan,*
> *Well, the one who's really killed me*
> *Is Me Brother Wot Stayed at 'Ome.*[13]

The spectacle of poor, blind Tom, however, did little to encourage recruitment. By mid 1916, when two thirds of the New Zealanders who were eligible for military service had yet to join up, conscription had become the country's most hotly debated topic. At the same time, young men who declined to volunteer were being publicly humiliated by dispensers of white feathers.

Within Charles's immediate family, the question of active service did not arise. At fifty, he was above military age and Carl, with a rapidly expanding family to support, was not under any pressure to enlist. Only Rudolph, who was a conscientious objector, remained and he later served as a stretcher bearer with the New Zealand Medical Corps in France, where he was wounded. But Morton's case was very different. Both his elder sons had volunteered immediately – the younger one at only eighteen – and his fury against 'shirkers' knew no bounds. His arguments in favour of conscription, shored up by some questionable demographic theories, became a constant theme in the *Triad*:

> *If any more of the best go, we shall have none but the scrubs and wasters left ... That is why a lot of thoughtful girls are beginning to believe in conscription. Under a scheme of that sort we should lose at least as many wasters as we lose good men ...*

Every good man killed on the battle-front means so many good babies lost ... There will be babies begotten by the wasters and malingerers; but those are not the sort of babies that Australia would prefer. New Zealand's plight is every bit as bad. Much of the finest young blood in the country has been spilled ... It would be a good thing if every young man going to the front could be married a week or two before he left.[14]

Morton's concerns about the impoverishment of the gene pool were shared by Charles. As the casualty figures mounted, he sanctioned the publication of a controversial story about a young woman who seduces a handsome stranger on the eve of his departure for the front in order to have a child by him. At the end of the story, Charles appended an explanatory note:

We hesitated some time over Mr Jeffries's story; but after all ... the subject matter is serious and merits consideration ... It is certainly a serious thing for any country that tens or hundreds of thousands of its best and most stalwart young men should die suddenly and without issue ... [I]t is better that they should be succeeded by a baby son of their own quality than that their race should die.[15]

The fine appearance of the departing New Zealand Expeditionary Force in October 1914 had made a lasting impression on Morton: 'I never saw uniforms set better on any men, and I never saw men look more sprightly and keen and fit.'[16] Two and a half years later, when the legendary good looks of the ANZACs had become part of history, the *Triad* printed copious extracts from John Masefield's recently published *Gallipoli*, in which he describes them as 'the finest body of young men ever brought together in modern times':

For physical beauty and nobility of bearing they surpassed any men I have ever seen; they walked and looked like the kings in old poems, and reminded me of the line in Shakespeare: – 'Baited like eagles having lately bathed.' As their officers put it, 'they were in the pink of condition and didn't care a damn for anybody.'[17]

The following month, the *Triad* published another tribute to the ANZACs, written by the ill-fated commander-in-chief of the campaign, Sir Ian Hamilton, portraying them as 'a new race of heroes born and bred under the sign of the Southern Cross' and concluding: 'Before the War who had ever heard of Anzac? Hereafter who will forget it?'[18]

In August 1916, New Zealand adopted conscription and from then on Morton's ire was largely directed against Australia, where conscription was rejected twice by public referendum. When his younger son was shot through the lung, his responses to suspected 'shirkers' became even more savage: 'Who and what are you, Mr Smirk, that my sons and the sons of other men should fight and die for you?'[19]

By now many of the Australian and New Zealand servicemen who had survived the Dardanelles were fighting in France, their numbers bolstered by fresh recruits from home. Despite the appalling conditions, a postal service was in operation, and in May 1917 Charles published the following letter from the trenches:

> *Dear Triad,*
> *It may interest you to know that the* Triad *penetrates to our very front lines over here and is greatly appreciated. Since I landed in France, it has been forwarded to me regularly each month ... To the best of my knowledge it has not yet been sent over to Fritz, but we are contemplating enlarging your sphere of influence by presenting one of your leading articles to him.*[20],*

Several soldiers became regular contributors and the horrors of the Western Front live on in their verse:

> *So, now the fury of the fight is spent,*
> *I hang upon a wire entanglement*
> *A prey to all the odours of the dead*
> *The flies keep consort on my grim-set jaws.*
> *High in the sky I hear the mocking 'caws'*
> *Of black-fledged carrion circling overhead*
> *With cruel patience and with thirsty beaks.*
> *Far overhead I hear the vengeful shrieks*
> *Of angry shells on which Death rides to meet*
> *Cruel Destiny at the appointed spot.*
> *The blood around my wounds begins to clot*
> *And a great calmness holds me. It seems sweet*
> *To hang and care for no one, friend or foe.*

In the final stanza, the stretcher bearers come to retrieve the body:

> *What's that he said? 'Poor bloke clean through the brain;*
> *It must 'ave fixed him quick, 'ed feel no pain.'*
> *Ah, yes! Of course, Three bullets in my head*

---

* The *Triad*'s presence in the trenches may have been a result of Charles's offer to send 500 free copies to the Front, with subscribers paying the 4d postage. Later a New Zealand ex-serviceman confirmed its popularity. 'Throughout the campaign in Ypres and the Somme, there was generally a copy of the *Triad* in my battle equipment ... which was regularly handed around among the intelligentsia of my Company.' (*Triad*, vol. 30, no. 12, pp. 47–8.)

I recollect it now again, I'm shot.
I got picked in the charge. I clean forgot
For quite a time that I was hooked there, dead.[21]

Little over a year later, the same poet wrote of his exile to 'a darkened world' and dreamed of an antipodean Grantchester in a 'land of my own where the sun is strong'. Underneath, readers were informed that the author of the poem, George Hambidge, 'made his last sacrifice'[22] two days after he wrote it.

After a few shaky issues, the *Triad*'s New Zealand content began to regain its equilibrium, partly due to the regular contributions of the Australian poet, Will Lawson, who had just taken a job with the *New Zealand Herald*. Like many other talented writers, Lawson was obliged to make a living from journalism, but his first love was poetry, much of which was about New Zealand. In his review of Lawson's *Three Kings and Other Verses*, Morton styled him a New Zealander by adoption and applauded his work, although he picked holes in his rollicking 'Ngahauranga Road', claiming that the road was a sea of mud and far less steep than the poem suggested. Lawson's robust tone was well suited to the spirit of the times and his admiration for adventurous pursuits, coupled with his love of the sea, are both reflected in his article on the arrival of Ernest Shackleton's *Aurora* in Wellington and his homage to the 'Great Sea-Road'[23] between Wellington and Sydney. But his most common point of reference was the war and he linked a thoughtful article on the Treaty of Waitangi (entitled 'A Scrap of Paper') to a description of the Maori contingent marching off to fight from their camp at Narrow Neck outside Auckland.

For Maori, enlistment had been a bone of contention, especially in the Waikato where tribal leaders questioned the wisdom of allowing their young men to join up. But in other parts of the country they had been eager to enlist and quickly established a fearsome reputation. In October 1916, the *Triad* reprinted a flattering article on 'The Fighting Maoris' from the London *Times*, which depicts them as 'a race of chivalrous warriors' and includes a vivid account of their exploits at Gallipoli. The author also describes coming across the Maori contingent in France, 'swinging along between the high poplars to the tune of "Tipperary" sung sweetly in their soft voices and with the perfect time that all Polynesian races are able to put into their music.'[24]

At home, where Maori communities were fundraising for their wounded, the poignancy of a poorly attended Christmas entertainment organised by the East Coast Maori did not escape the *Triad*'s reviewer. Like everyone else, he believed that Maori were facing extinction.

> *The pathos of this race, which knows itself to be dying ... was never more affecting than when, after long debate, its chiefs ... called the fighting men*

of their several tribes to die side by side with the Pakeha on the far-off fields of Turkey and Flanders.[25]

Many others were celebrated in the *Triad*. In January 1917, Lawson hailed 'Lieutenant-Colonel Bernard Freyberg, V.C., of the New Zealand Forces' as 'one of the greatest heroes of the war', noting that 'The Dominion is a remote and sparsely peopled country, but its war record is made splendid by the heroism of its fighters.'[26] In 'Irish Girls' he saluted Auckland's Irish community:

They've sent their men to battle,
Their husbands and their sons,
Their sweethearts and their brothers,
Their best-belovèd ones.
Oh! something makes you swallow
And brush your moistened eyes –
Your heart is full of sorrow
And all your laughter dies,
When splendid Nora Daly,
That broke men's hearts for fun,
Leads home her stalwart Anzac,
Her blinded soldier son.[27]

As the war dragged on, the shortage of men became all too apparent. In August 1917, the indomitable Lady Stout pointed out to the Council of Education that a compulsory certificate in Domestic Science for girls had limited value in a country where 431 out of every 1000 women would never find a husband. Lady Stout's figures were exaggerated, but the depleted ranks of the Auckland Choral Society, whose fifty-five sopranos and thirty-nine contraltos were gallantly supported by eight tenors and twelve basses, amply demonstrated the point she was trying to make. Nevertheless, cultural activities continued, but amidst the antics of the 'Charley's Aunt' Club and Wellington's 'Cercle Français' – at which an enthusiastic amateur draped herself in the French tricolour and sang the 'Marseillaise' – the rare visits of overseas artists were warmly welcomed.

In September 1914, the Scottish entertainer, Harry Lauder, had just managed to squeeze in a New Zealand tour before rushing back to England to raise huge sums for war charities.* Over two years later, the Gonsalez Italian Grand Opera Company, which had been travelling continually since

---

* Early in 1919, the *Triad* reprinted an account of Harry Lauder singing about 'the boys coming home' just after he had lost his own son. 'He sang it to the end without faltering, and left the stage amid the sympathetic silence of the audience.' (*Triad*, vol. 26, no. 12, p. 10).

it had found itself stranded in Vladivostock in August 1914, gave New Zealanders their first taste of professional grand opera since the start of the war and was accorded a rapturous reception. The visit of the celebrated British actress, Marie Tempest, aroused even greater excitement. Feisty and flirtatious, the middle-aged Tempest arrived in December 1917 with 'the best supporting company that New Zealanders have ever seen.'[28] For a small nation, reeling under its losses, Tempest's genius for comedy temporarily banished the spectre of death. As the *Triad*'s drama critic watched the 'gay, rustling, chattering, throng'[29] that had gathered to see her perform in Somerset Maugham's 'Penelope' and 'Mrs Dot', he found it hard to believe in the reality of war.

Meanwhile in Australia, Charles's noisy assertions that the *Triad* was 'doing quite famously'[30] sound suspiciously like salesmanship. The true picture was rather less rosy. Financially the *Triad* was still struggling to establish itself and in April 1916 The Triad Magazine Ltd was obliged to replenish its coffers by issuing four £500 debentures, which were purchased by the Directors. Rumours of Charles's supposedly German origins were also refusing to die down: on several occasions, Morton lashed out on his behalf at the 'wretchedly and unscrupulously dishonest' fools who 'still pretend that the Editor of the *Triad* has German blood'.[31] In musical circles, Charles's forthright criticisms had further increased his unpopularity, and in October 1916 he was the target of an anonymous pamphlet:

> *The Musicians and Musical Public of Sydney would like to know when THE EDITOR OF THE TRIAD will give a PIANOFORTE AND VIOLIN RECITAL in Aid of various Patriotic Funds. This gentleman has taken nearly all our best Artists to task. It is now up to him to show in a practical manner how the Great Masters should be interpreted.*[32]

Of course, Charles declined. But this incident, combined with wartime paper shortages and the business challenges of producing a ten per cent dividend for his shareholders, may well have influenced his decision to hand over the *Triad*'s music and drama criticism to a less controversial figure. He had already delegated much of the Melbourne reviewing. In Sydney he found an admirable successor in A.L. Kelly, whose gentler tone was less discomfiting to local egos.

Dealing with the disgruntled musicians of Sydney, however, was the least of Charles's problems. He was also having serious editorial differences with Morton, whose political tirades were becoming increasingly unbalanced. In April 1916, the comments in his 'Things Visible' column were so offensive that Charles took the perilous step of defending the Germans:

> *We don't think it does any good at all to call the German people Huns and swine. There are in Germany many millions of sincere, industrious God-fearing, philanthropic folk; folks who have been led by the nose into this hellish and unpardonable war.*[33]

But one glance at the *Bulletin* reveals where some of Morton's virulently anti-German views were coming from. Throughout the war, Norman Lindsay's hideous 'Hun Ape' prowled the title pages of the *Bulletin*, inciting a fear and hatred of the enemy that was further inflamed by his gruesome images of ravished women and bayoneted babies. Morton's ravings may have been a reflection of his well-publicised admiration for Lindsay; but as the tone of his outbursts grew more irrational, it became apparent to Charles that, quite apart from his drinking, he was heading for a breakdown.

Ever since the launch of the Australasian edition, Morton had been writing half the material for the *Triad* under his various pseudonyms. To Charles, his prolific output was a source of wonder: 'Just put him in a bare room with a typewriter and he will write on anything.'[34] But in addition to coping with his heavy workload, Morton was also playing hard in Sydney's literary and theatrical Bohemia, which was peopled with former colleagues and friends.

As the home of the *Bulletin*, Sydney had long acted as a magnet to writers and poets. Within a few weeks of his arrival, Morton commented on the large number of New Zealanders that were among them. Later he noted that 'the profession of journalism in this continent is full of men who once served the *New Zealand Times*' and described 'the Bohemian writers and painters of Sydney town' as 'a happy family'.[35]

Amongst the most illustrious members of the family were figures like Arthur Adams, with whom both Charles and Morton continued to have an uneasy relationship. Adams was often the butt of Morton's humour. In his mischievous 'Cyclopaedia' for 'The Blushing Beginner' he listed him as 'an Australian poet trying to live down a New Zealand past.'[36] On the other hand, Morton was on excellent terms with David McKee Wright, who had recently become editor of the 'Red Page'. Although Wright still looked like the Congregational parson he had once been, he led a turbulent private life. By 1913 he had separated from his wife and was living with another woman, whom he later abandoned for the poet and actress, Zora Cross. In November 1917, the *Triad* described Cross's *Songs of Love and Life* as 'hot and palpitating from the human furnace of sensuous passion'. But the reviewer also observed that it seemed a pity that 'she should devote so much of her powers to the one theme'.[37]

Morton embraced Sydney's greater moral freedom joyfully, teaming up with the notorious womaniser and entrepreneur, Hugh McIntosh, who had just acquired a controlling interest in the Sydney *Sunday Times*. In his photograph in the *Triad*, McIntosh looks like a cross between Clark Gable and Douglas Fairbanks junior; according to Singer, he and Morton went 'hunting females together'.[38] Singer also accused Morton of refusing to take any contribution from a woman 'unless she consented to sleep with him.'[39]

Given his punishing lifestyle, the quality of Morton's literary contributions remained surprisingly high. Even his slight column on the delights of Manly, which by his own admission was often written lying on the beach (probably nursing a blinding hangover), possesses a certain whimsical charm. In July 1916, *Triad* readers voted it their favourite feature and showered Morton with love letters. But by December 1916, his nerves had reached breaking point. Tormented by insomnia, he resorted to passing his nights walking the streets and when he finally turned up, many miles from home, at Norman Lindsay's country retreat in Springwood, his condition was such that Lindsay's wife* drove him to a doctor, who promptly admitted him to hospital. In the meantime he had left nothing prepared for the forthcoming issues and Charles was close to despair.

On Christmas day 1916, Charles rushed down to the wharf to meet Singer, who had just arrived from Auckland. According to Singer, he cut a woeful figure and implored him to compile the next issue. Singer graciously agreed, and until Morton 'crawled back'[40] into Charles's good books, he helped to edit the *Triad*. In the meantime, Morton spent four months drying out in a hospital for 'nervous cases' where, as a compulsive scribbler, he wrote an account of his breakdown for the *Triad*.

Morton emerged unrepentant and continued to poke his nose into every imaginable fray – from the treachery of the Roman Catholic Archbishop of Melbourne, Dr Mannix (who opposed conscription), to the crimes of the anti-war IWW.† But by this time he and Charles had resolved their differences. Moreover, on many editorial issues, such as the content of the monthly Art Supplement, they were partners in crime.

After the move to Australia, despite mounting criticism, Charles continued to pitch the *Triad*'s illustrations at the least discerning sector of its readership. In May 1916, he responded defensively to the protests of the Australian poet, Edward Dyson, claiming that 'scores of other folk, especially folks who seldom get a chance of going near an art gallery, are very grateful for these reproductions.'[41] Two months later Arthur Adams declared that Morton deserved to go to Hell 'where, for his sins, he and his co-editor will be compelled for all eternity to pore over the Art Supplement of the *Triad*.'

---

* His former model, Rose Soady.
† The union of the Industrial Workers of the World.

Frank Morton's writing dominated the wartime Triad. *Cartoon by Fred Hiscocks,* Triad, *10 November, 1913, p. 272.* ATL

Further on, he called Charles and Morton 'two delightful damned souls' and accused them of attempting 'to bind Art in the chains of an enormous circulation.'[42] Looking at some of the *Triad*'s illustrations during the war years, it is hard not to agree with Adams. But the Art Supplement did not reach its nadir until the war was nearly over when Morton and Charles contrived the publication of a series of pictures of a naked girl, which purported to be photographic representations of the work of a French painter.

As the two editors had undoubtedly foreseen, the virginal, snow white body of 'Mélisande' was an overnight sensation. For the final months of the war, the *Triad*'s letter page became a battlefield of conflicting opinions on nudity. Views ranged from the incensed reader who could no longer defile his home with the *Triad*, to the hopeful subscriber who asked for the model's address – and was told that she had joined up as a nurse and was serving in France. Charles and Morton naturally took the higher moral ground, citing the sculpture of ancient Greece and claiming that 'there was in the picture no hint or taint of any impurity.'[43] The photographs are indeed discreet and the girl's nudity is far less titillating than the suggestive drapery that usually graced the heroines of the Art Supplement. Yet the editors' arguments have a hollow ring. Uncomfortably perched on her rocky outcrop, 'Mélisande' was lifting the circulation figures to new heights. In his reply to a reader who called for 'more of the contemplative spirit', Charles tacitly acknowledged that money-making was high on his agenda: 'Our correspondent is right, mostly; but a magazine is, must be, what the Americans call a business proposition.'[44]

Charles's preoccupation with money was understandable, for although the *Triad* had weathered its earlier start-up problems (no doubt helped by an issue of 5000 preference shares in 1917), it was still not sufficiently profitable to sustain his considerable lifestyle. With an establishment in Double Bay and an elegant Talbot car, Charles was living beyond his means and during the war years he sold off over half of his shares in the *Triad* just to supplement his income. By the end of the war, however, Charles was confident that business success was finally within his grasp and, more enamoured than ever, he set about organising an extended overseas trip during which he planned to launch Mildred on a dazzling international career.

Chapter 15

The Wages of Sin

Early in 1919, Charles made a visit to New Zealand where he had a meeting with Rudolph, who had just been invalided home from France. In his reminiscences, Rudolph refers to the occasion and comments admiringly on Charles's 'massive forehead' and his 'keen, intelligent' eyes which, to his adoring gaze, revealed 'the intellectual giant'[1] that he believed his father to be. But Rudolph's touching hero-worship does not seem to have aroused any particular warmth in Charles, for he never bothered to see him again. Years later, when Rudolph wrote to him suggesting that they play chess by correspondence, he brushed off the invitation by claiming that he had 'scant time for such dissipations'.[2]

At this stage, all Charles's affections were focused on Mildred who, according to a newspaper report, accompanied him to New Zealand where she gave a 'delightful reading'[3] of Teresa del Riego's* songs in Dunedin. Urged on by Charles, she had been working hard on her compositions, most of which took the form of musical monologues. This now outmoded art form consisted of a recitation with a piano accompaniment and was ideally suited to her talents as a pianist and elocutionist. Moreover, with her winning smile and shapely figure, she must have had an alluring stage presence. Charles had high hopes for her future as a performer: during their forthcoming overseas trip he had arranged for her to give a series of recitals in London and New York.

A contemporary photograph shows Mildred in a dainty Edwardian costume, complete with parasol. Such romantic styles had long since gone out of fashion but Mildred, who loved dressing up, had probably donned the outfit for fun. Poised and self-confident, she looks a picture of elegance and every inch the consort of a moneyed man. In another photograph, taken at the beach, she sits on the sand holding Charles's dog on her lap. Slightly dishevelled, with her feather boa askew, she glows with health and vitality. On this occasion, however, the scene is stolen by little Charlie, who sits sturdily beside his mother with golden curls escaping from under his sun hat.

---

* Teresa del Riego was an English composer of Spanish parentage and is best known for her songs which became popular during WWI.

In the January issue of the *Triad*, Charles's trip to New Zealand was not mentioned, but there was plenty about the deadly influenza epidemic, which had been raging all over the country for weeks. The first outbreak had occurred in Auckland at the end of October 1918. By January, the epidemic had run its course and the death toll had reached eight and a half thousand, which was more than half the number of New Zealanders killed in World War I.*

Although influenza had been around for decades, the origins of this particularly virulent strain, which claimed thousands of victims worldwide, are still unclear. Some recent studies link its emergence to the use of mustard gas on the Western Front, where the most lethal wave of the pandemic started, and attribute its rapid spread to the massive troop movements of World War I. But at the time, all that people knew was that the strain was highly contagious. In New Zealand, rumours were rife about how it had entered the country. By November, these rumours had crossed the Tasman and were reported by Charles in the December *Triad*:

> *As this note is written – November 10 – there is a disquieting rumour current in Australia. It is to the effect that Sir Joseph Ward and Mr Massey of New Zealand arrived in Auckland by the* Niagara*, and flatly refused to be quarantined; and as a result all sorts of people were landed from the infected ship.*[4]

Prime Minister Massey and Finance Minister Ward, who had formed a joint wartime administration, had returned from England in mid October on the *Niagara* which berthed, without quarantine, with 101 influenza patients aboard. Within two weeks, the epidemic was raging in Auckland and local doctors were almost unanimous in their view that the *Niagara* was to blame. Even today opinions remain divided, but the commission which later investigated the causes of the epidemic completely exonerated Massey and Ward of using their position to flout the regulations.

In Australia, the health authorities had responded far more promptly than in New Zealand and initially the strict quarantine regulations appeared to be keeping the epidemic at bay. But in January influenza broke out in Victoria, and by the end of the month four cases had been reported in Sydney. In February, the *Triad*'s 'Obiter Dicta' column opened ominously: 'Pneumonic-influenza has got loose in Australia, and as this edition of the *Triad* goes to press no man can predict what havoc the pest will cause.'[5] The March issue reported widespread outbreaks in Melbourne where the hospitals were said to be so short-staffed that 'a distress-call'[7] for extra nurses had been sent to New Zealand. During the following weeks, the epidemic

---

* New Zealand's official death toll for WWI was 16,697.

continued on its deadly path. In his May editorial, Charles noted that in New South Wales the 'pneumonic pest ... is now plainly running its course more rapidly than in Victoria' and added: 'Sydney is certainly very dull. No theatres, no picture shows, no public gatherings of any sort, no races. But the gloom is well worth while, if the pest is beaten.'[7]

On 4 June 1919, Charles and Mildred steamed away from Sydney aboard the *Sonoma*, which plied the route between Sydney and San Francisco, with stops at Pago Pago and Honolulu. It was a voyage that Charles had immensely enjoyed twelve and a half years earlier and doubtless he wanted to share the experience with Mildred. They would have been in high spirits: with little Charlie left behind in Sydney, the whole trip was beginning to resemble an extended honeymoon. Their feelings, however, are not recorded. Instead, all that remains is a terse entry in Charles's diary in which he noted, without comment, the sequence of devastating events that followed:

4. 6. 1919   *Left for America. Sonoma.*
9. 6. 1919   *Mildred died. 11.45 p.m.*
10. 6. 1919   *Mildred buried. Pango Pango.*[8]

The suddenness of Mildred's illness and death was typical of the influenza, which had an incubation period of less than forty-eight hours and in more serious cases turned rapidly to pneumonia. Another of its trademarks was the high percentage of fatalities amongst the young and healthy. In New Zealand, those worst affected were European males aged between thirty and thirty-four. The most vulnerable age group for women was between twenty-five and twenty-nine, closely followed by those aged thirty to thirty-four. Mildred, who had celebrated her thirtieth birthday on 29 January, fell precisely within this group. For Charles, these must have been the worst days of his life; as he went ashore to bury the body in the American naval cemetery at Pago Pago, the Samoan paradise which he had once likened to the Garden of Eden must have seemed closer to a living hell.

Mildred had died at sea and in a tribute written several months later, Charles drew some parallels between her death and that of her uncle:

Early in the war her uncle, O'Brien Butler, perhaps the finest and most sincere of modern Irish composers, went to New York. He arranged with Frohman* to produce his Irish opera 'Murgheis' in America. He and Frohman journeyed together in the ill-fated 'Lusitania' and both were drowned. Thus uncle and niece, both richly gifted, died at sea – each cut off just when fame and fortune were about to smile upon them.[9]

---

*   Charles Frohman was a Broadway producer and theatrical impresario.

The *Sonoma*'s brief stop at Pago Pago left Charles with little time for graveside mourning. Within a few hours of the burial, he was once again aboard ship, leaving Mildred lying in a lonely grave, many thousands of miles from her Otago homeland. As he reflected on her solitary exile, however, he consoled himself with the thought that Robert Louis Stevenson, whose verse she had so often sung in musical settings, was buried in the same group of islands.

Despite Mildred's death, Charles carried on doggedly with his programme, but his wretchedness permeates his writing. In San Francisco and Chicago the 'amusements' were 'for the most part, wretchedly bad'. The women were 'plain', the acting was 'feeble' and the singing was 'beneath contempt'. He found Chicago 'the rudest place I have ever been in' and described the American papers as 'poisonous'.[10] As in 1907, he crossed the continent by train. This time, however, he did not loiter in New York and on 1 July, barely a week after he had arrived in San Francisco, he left for England.

In the circumstances, Charles's first experience of the legendary British homeland, whose cultural influence was still all-pervasive in New Zealand and Australia, can hardly have been the joyful experience he had anticipated. His accounts of his dutiful pilgrimages to such cultural shrines as Oxford, Cambridge and Winchester are studiously impersonal and often sound like a guidebook. Laden with historical detail, the only clues that they give to his state of mind are in the occasional asides: the outrageous price of grapes in Dorking; the 'pert and insolent red-headed hussy'[11] in Winchester who refused to serve him morning tea; and the difficulty of having a bath in an English hotel. But despite these irritations, there were some moments of genuine pleasure. He saw Oxford 'at its best in the late summer months when all the rich meadow-lands were most tranquil, green and mellow, and seemed to reflect the peace of the ancient city'.[12] He also enthused about the car that he had been lent by his brother-in-law, James Kirkland, for which he employed a chauffeur.

No mention is made of Emilia, but she can only have disapproved of his unlawful relationship with Mildred. Charles was a sinner and Emilia may even have regarded Mildred's untimely death as an act of divine judgement. On the other hand, she could not have forgotten her own passion when she eloped with his father – or her anguish when she too lost the great love of her life in the flower of his youth.

Despite his sorrows – or perhaps because of them – Charles devoted much of his time to business. During his four-month visit, he called on dozens of publicists to promote the *Triad*. In the September issue, Morton announced loftily that 'the Managing Director ... is going around the world on business for the magazine.'[13] His greatest media coup was an article in the mass-circulation *Daily Mail*, entitled 'A Critic from "Down Under"', in which he successfully concealed the rawness of his wounds with well-practised bonhomie:

> *One of the most interesting men in Dominions journalism is at present on a visit to London – Mr C.N. Baeyertz, editor of the* Triad, *a monthly critical magazine devoted primarily to the arts and published simultaneously in Australia and New Zealand. When I first knew the* Triad *and marvelled at it, it was published only in New Zealand ... Today the* Triad *is loved – and* feared *– not only over the whole of Australasia but also in the islands of the South Seas ... A little conversation only is needed with Mr Baeyertz to understand how this has been done. Big, blond, with eyes a-dance with merriment, he is a personality that impresses. And you find the impress of that personality on every page of his entertaining magazine.*[14]

The *Daily Mail* was part of the newspaper empire presided over by Lord Northcliffe, whom Charles regarded as 'the greatest and ablest newspaper man in the world.'[15] Northcliffe was also the proprietor of the London *Times* and in another deft commercial move, Charles managed to acquire a testimonial, signed by the great man, which he subsequently paraded in the *Triad*:

> *The Times*
>
> *With some knowledge of the Australasian press ... I would say, that if I had only one medium to choose for the advertising of a high-class article, I should most certainly select 'The Triad'. My agents inform me that it is found in every club, hotel and reading-room throughout Australasia.*
>
> *Northcliffe*
> *16 October, 1919.*[16]

Later, he even sent a copy of the *Triad* to Buckingham Palace and received a gracious letter of thanks from the King's private secretary.

In his spare moments, Charles investigated the book shops: 'There is not a single bookseller's shop in the whole city to equal Angus and Robertson's in Sydney, S & W Mackay's in Wellington, or Whitcombe & Tombs.' Outside London, the selection of 'belles lettres' was lamentable: 'When our country towns (especially in New Zealand) are compared with towns of twice or thrice the size in England, the disparity in this regard is even more startlingly in our favour.' His comments on the locals were equally scathing and he claimed that the average intelligence in England was far lower than 'down under'.[17]

Drained by its wartime losses, Britain was at a low ebb and Charles similarly found little to applaud in London's post-war music. He described Sir

Henry Wood's concerts at Queen's Hall as the 'greatest disappointment' and the famous conductor himself as 'devoid of everything that matters most'. His warmest remarks were reserved for Rosina Buckmann: 'I rejoice at her success, partly, because, in some sort, Miss Buckmann was a discovery of mine.'[18]

Since leaving New Zealand in 1912, Buckmann's hopes had been realised beyond her wildest dreams. Shortly after her arrival in London, she had performed under the baton of the brilliant conductor, Thomas Beecham, and when he formed his own opera company in 1915 she had become his principal soprano. By the time Charles reached London in 1919, the unknown New Zealander, whom Williamson had relegated to play the part of the maid, was being hailed as the greatest Madame Butterfly on the operatic stage and was alternating the leading role of *La Bohème* with Melba at Covent Garden.

On his return journey, Charles spent over a month in New York, where a magnificent season of music helped to revive his spirits. The city's wealth was continuing to attract many of the world's greatest musicians and singers. Charles's music notes abound in famous names: Caruso's voice was 'as fine as ever'; Rachmaninov, playing his own compositions, was 'very interesting, though it would not have been so interesting if the player had not been Rachmaninov.' The eighteen-year-old Polish violinist, Jascha Heifetz, was 'a perfect miracle' and the celebrated pianist, Leopold Godowsky, was 'charming'. But he found that the American soprano, Geraldine Farrar, 'had gone off very considerably since I heard her twelve years earlier.'[19]

He also heard many of the great orchestras, including 'a thrilling and astounding performance' of Rimsky-Korsakov's 'Scheherazade' suite by the Philadelphia Orchestra: 'I don't think I ever had an hour and-a-quarter of keener enjoyment'. On 16 November, he attended a 'vastly entertaining'[20] 'gambol' at the Lambs' Club and shortly afterwards set out on his homeward journey, reaching Sydney in early January – once again aboard the *Sonoma*.

During Charles's absence, Morton had edited the *Triad* on his own, producing much of the copy himself. The appeal of his writing to younger women was as strong as ever and the *Triad* now claimed to have more women subscribers than any other magazine in the Southern Hemisphere, 'with the exception of one or two magazines devoted solely to bibs, frocks, cakes and cackle'.[21] The large number of advertisements for luxury goods, ranging from expensive underwear to a full page advertisement for a Rolls Royce at £1750 reflected the tastes – and the affluence – of the latest generation of readers. The survivors of World War I were hell-bent on enjoyment: for the fast-living young women whom they escorted, this meant short skirts, bobbed hair and dancing till dawn.

In an attempt to cater for the *Triad*'s more frivolous subscribers – and compensate for its dearth of female contributors* – Morton came up with an ingenious solution. He initiated a monthly column of outrageous gossip, which purported to be written by a society lady named 'Susan Gloomish'. Her identity was never revealed, but she was almost certainly Morton.† Revelling in his new, trans-gender role, he penned pages of frothy 'cackle', interspersed with sisterly advice on such subjects as the need for more openness in the sex education of young women. In the giddy atmosphere of what became known as the 'Roaring Twenties', the column immediately attracted a following – although Northcliffe's statement that 'the most interesting *Triad* writer is Susan Gloomish'[22] was probably not intended as a compliment.

In July 1919, Ms Gloomish proffered some words of wisdom to aspiring women journalists: 'It is a hard life, and if a girl loves peace of mind and ease of body, she will do well to keep out of it.'[23] This counsel – if she read it – would have given food for thought to a young Wellingtonian named Iris Wilkinson, better known under her pseudonym of Robin Hyde, who joined the staff of the *Dominion* at the age of seventeen and was an avid reader of the *Triad*. In 1919 she was still a schoolgirl, but her poems and stories were already appearing in her school magazine. In her book, *Journalese*, she recalls cutting out and keeping the *Triad*'s tactful rejection ('Shows signs of unusual promise') of an early poem. As one of the *Triad*'s more serious readers, Hyde also comments on its literary quality: 'In the 1922 days stuff you remembered was going into Triad pages, some haunting poems, prose that had an edge like a scimitar'. She adds: 'A man called Baeyertz was running the show. He was rather excitingly rude to almost everyone.'[24]

Encouraged by the success of 'Susan Gloomish', Morton invented a second female contributor. Before long, poems by an ardent young woman named 'Rosemary June' started to appear, but her explicit verse on the yearnings of a convent girl – and worse – blew Morton's cover and he had to banish her. He was also doing plenty of writing under his own name. Throughout 1919 and 1920, notices of the forthcoming publication of his *The Secret Spring* featured prominently in the *Triad*, together with references to his *Exultant Bride* ('a rhapsody on love and marriage'), *Naked Notorieties*, which 'will offend some timid souls',[25] and *Widows Wistful*, which was billed as the tale of a war widow who became a chorus girl.

After nearly two years, 'Susan Gloomish' was joined by 'Lalie Seton Cray', whose column similarly covered pages of the *Triad*. But readers soon

---

* Since the *Triad*'s move to Sydney, Alice Kenny and Gladys Kernot had ceased to be regular contributors, although Gladys Kernot later became one of the magazine's directors.

† After Morton's death, Susan Gloomish continued to write for a few months, but this may have been an attempt to perpetuate the myth – or simply unused copy of Morton's.

worked out that her name was an anagram for the New Zealand 'comedienne' Coralie Stanley, who was an old friend of Charles's and also wrote for the *Triad* under her own name. Stanley had recently moved to Sydney and her comments on Australians and New Zealanders were true to the mischievous spirit of the *Triad*:

> *New Zealand men dress better than Australians and generally talk better, but they are stiffer and more self-conscious because they have been taught from the cradle that the proper end of man is to be respectable ... One likes Australian men, though ... they are abominably casual ... they have no manners and what you call no style.*[26]

In 1923 Morton identified another suitable writer for the *Triad*'s women's column, a young Australian named Pamela Travers who contributed regularly to the 'Women's World' section of the Christchurch *Sun*. At only twenty-three Travers, like Stanley, had already enjoyed a lively career as an actress before turning to journalism. Some of her poetry appeared in the *Bulletin* and when the occasion demanded, she could be quite as uninhibited as 'Rosemary June'. Her column for the *Triad*, 'A Woman hits back', was unmemorable, but in her mid-thirties she wrote the children's classic *Mary Poppins*.*

Given his taste in women, it was almost inevitable that Morton would also befriend Dulcie Deamer, who came from the little township of Featherston outside Wellington and was a leading figure in Sydney's artistic underworld. Famed for her leopard-skin outfit and her hula dancing, she was later crowned 'The Queen of Bohemia'. But her original claim to fame – or notoriety – was a prize-winning story about a caveman which she wrote in 1907 at the age of seventeen. In an era when respectable young women walked up the aisle with minds as innocent of carnal knowledge as their bodies, her evident familiarity with the facts of life scandalised New Zealand. Morton saw things differently:

> *We knew Dulcie Deamer first of all as the little daughter of a genial doctor over in New Zealand. The medical man had his own ideas as to the bringing-up of daughters, and Dulcie grew quite simply and naturally into her knowledge of all human relations, including the most intimate ... She was never handicapped by that innocence which consists solely of ignorance.*[27]

Dulcie later wrote a stream of torrid novels and her occasional contributions to the *Triad* were in a similar vein.

Despite its pitch at a younger, more feckless market, the *Triad* also continued to publish some thoughtful articles. The passionate defence of Ettie Rout by the Christchurch journalist, Godfrey Turner, is a good example.

---

* The film version was made by Walt Disney in 1964.

An eccentric, middle-aged New Zealander, Rout was one of the earliest 'safe sex' campaigners – and was vilified for her efforts. During the war, when thousands of servicemen contracted venereal disease, she produced her own prophylactic kit and sold it to soldiers in Christchurch. Later, she went to Paris where she greeted the troops at the Gare du Nord with the address of a hygienically run brothel. The French gave her a medal and dubbed her the guardian angel of the ANZACs, but in New Zealand she was considered so immoral that her name was banned from the newspapers. Turner called her a saint and the *Triad* continued to champion her cause for many months to come. In April 1922, Charles described her as 'one of the staunchest women of the Great War.'[28]

Equally, as Robin Hyde points out, the post-war *Triad* still had some interesting literary coverage, with the Australian columnist, L.L. Woolacott, writing authoritatively on such figures as Tolstoy and Whitman, while Morton kept readers abreast of recent American and European publications with his book reviews. In August 1919, he singled out *Wheels*, the latest anthology to emerge from the Oxford intelligentsia, for special praise, and printed poems by Aldous Huxley, Wilfred Owen and Edith Sitwell. He later also made a complete U-turn on Ezra Pound:

> *We must learn from our mistakes. When Mr Ezra Pound first began to write, he seemed rather silly to some of us ... but since then he has written beautiful poetry in those queer forms of his that are so formless to the conventional eye.*[29]

By July 1922, he was positively gushing:

> *Apart from the Vorticists, his own work is often golden with a singular delight. Some of his versions of small poems from the Chinese are perfect gems in their kind, and often his ripe learning makes us humble.*[30]

Morton had been disarmed by Pound's gracious comments on the *Triad* in *The Little Review*, but his change of heart was probably prompted by the publication of Pound's collection, *Cathay*, whose merit he was enough of an artist himself to recognise.

Since the move to Australia, most of the *Triad*'s drama and music criticism had been focused on Sydney and Melbourne. Surprisingly, however, this did not appear to diminish its popularity in New Zealand – possibly because, apart from this, much of its content continued to have a New Zealand perspective. A.A. Grace's Maori stories featured frequently and Turner, who had just returned home after spending the war years in London, often wrote on subjects that were close to New Zealand hearts:

> *Over there in England the talk turned always to New Zealand and Australia. Even I was loud as the rest ... I wrote of my native land with such love ... that gin-drunken compositors blistered my copy with tears ...*
>
> *Strangely enough, a good deal of it was true ... Down in the steaming alleys and crowded courts of English cities, I swore there could be no life like ours. Nor could there be ...*
>
> *[But] tonight in a hut on a back station ... I feel I had rather be a lamp-post in Piccadilly than a farmer in Canterbury. In Bayswater I have sworn I'd give all the West End for a clean breath of Colonial air.*[31]

Such conflicts of loyalty tormented many writers and artists of the period, but according to the *Triad*'s most recent New Zealand recruit, Hector Bolitho, the allegiances of the author of a new collection of short stories called *The Garden Party* were not in doubt:

> *Some of the English reviewers agree that Miss Katherine Mansfield is the pioneer of a new school of short story writing. Most of them greet her as a genius ...*
>
> *But these grand tributes and marks of success must not overshadow my more parochial attitude towards Miss Katherine Mansfield. Behind the pen-name, hides a New Zealander whose stories are coloured with the impressions which she stole from her country ...*
>
> *Although we have sent many writers abroad, some of them have been submerged in the charm of new countries and new people. But Miss Mansfield has been loyal to Aotaroa [sic]: she has remained true to the unstinted beauty of the country which cradled her.*[32]

Eight months later, Katherine Mansfield was dead of consumption. The front page of the *Triad* carried a black-framed message of condolence to her family which described her as 'the most original and the most elusive of our contemporary adepts of the short-story.'[33]

Reactions to the writing of Jane Mander, who had also left New Zealand, were more mixed. The *Triad*'s only remaining correspondent in New Zealand, 'Oliver Pageant', complained that he could 'never discover any virtue'[34] in her work. But Morton's review of her novel, *The Strange Attraction,* was more encouraging:

> *A few years ago Miss Mander was a young girl stuck away in one of those queer old places north of Auckland, and we used to write to her about her promise, and she used to write to us about her soul. Since then she has got out into the world and learned how to write about men and women: how they sin and what they suffer ... Miss Mander tells her story very well.*[35]

In March 1919, the *Triad* published a rare art review of another New Zealander who was making a name for herself overseas. Although Frances Hodgkins had spent over fifteen years in Europe since her departure from New Zealand in 1901, the *Triad* had kept an eye on her progress. In July 1912, for example, it quoted a letter from the New Zealand landscape painter, Owen Merton, in which he stated that 'her work has long had a very large circle of admirers in Paris' and predicted that 'in another year or so she will make a very big reputation'.[36] Despite this update, neither New Zealand nor the *Triad* were prepared for the influence that Modernism was having on her work. In 1917, when two of 'her excursions into Futurism' were displayed at the annual exhibition of the Academy of Fine Arts in Wellington, they created an uproar:

> *A kind of guessing competition was being conducted in front of her pictures all the time the gallery was open. After wandering to and fro for some time trying to focus the wild welter of coloured smears which represent no. 39 ... I disentangled the voluptuous form of the two washerwomen. Their billowy curves would have delighted the eye of a vorticist, I'm sure ... When people remember the really fine work that Miss Hodgkins has done ... these pitiful examples in our gallery are more a subject for sorrow than laughter.*[37]

In 1919, when her pictures were exhibited at the Fine Art Society in Melbourne, the *Triad* demonstrated a similar lack of comprehension. The reviewer rebuked 'her hilarious palette' and 'riotous shadows' and concluded sadly: 'Miss Hodgkins is too brilliant a draughtswoman, and too solid in the technics of her craft to make a success of ... doleful imposture.'[38]

The *Triad*'s track record on international art criticism is not a glorious one. Modern developments in painting left both Charles and Morton bewildered and the few examples of cutting-edge art that appeared in the *Triad* were usually subjected to ridicule. But in New Zealand, apart from Charles's weakness for the work of C.N. Worsley, the *Triad* showed greater discernment. Throughout the pre-war years the paintings of artists like William Gibb, Dorothy Richmond, Margaret Stoddart, Sydney Thompson, Alfred Walsh, Nugent Welch, Frank and Walter Wright, and many of their contemporaries, were all frequently and intelligently reviewed. Later, Raymond McIntyre's successes in England were proudly reported and in 1915 Mina Arndt, who like Frances Hodgkins had been exposed to contemporary influences in Europe, was given a rave review on her return home: 'Miss Arndt has no peer among the women painters of New Zealand. Her work is superbly personal and in the best sense virile ... [S]he has definitely arrived.'[39] Many years earlier in Dunedin, Charles had pondered over a still life by Arndt, then an untrained schoolgirl of fifteen, and applauded her skill in giving a pile of books 'just the appearance of not being new'.[40]

Although no circulation figures survive for the *Triad*, by February 1920 Charles was claiming a monthly readership of 100,000. His chief occupation still remained the business of procuring advertising, but in an effort to fill the sudden emptiness of his private life, he had begun to re-engage with the critical side of the *Triad* and write articles. Shortly after his return from England, he and Charlie moved with Lillian to a flat in Neutral Bay, where he was maddened 'to the point of murderous fury'[41] by noisy neighbours. Mildred was constantly in his thoughts and in June 1920 he published a collection of her musical monologues prefaced by an emotional tribute. His only consolation was his little son, whose sayings cover pages of his diary:

> *How much do you love me, Daddy? I love you better than everyone else in the world together. Better than Mummy? No darling. We both love Mummy best of all.*

Absorbed in his own grief, he seems to have assumed that Lillian's willingness to remain as his housekeeper and childminder was simply a reflection of her devotion to Mildred. He dismissed Charlie's innocent questioning out of hand.

> *Would you marry Lily,* Daddy? No dear, I wouldn't marry* anyone. *Not Mummy, Daddy? No darling, I can't marry Mummy. But did you marry Mummy, Daddy ... ?* [42]

---

*   Within the family, Lillian was also known as 'Lily' and 'Lilian'.

Chapter 16

The End of an old Adventuress

For Charles, 1920 was a dismal year. Quite apart from his unhappiness over Mildred's death, he was plagued by ill-health. Furthermore, as a flatmate, the emancipated Lillian was proving to be very different from the dutiful Bella – or the compliant Mildred. In his diary entry for 20 April, when Lillian had left him alone all day with a high temperature, the tone of self-pity is unmistakable. On her return home, far from soothing his fevered brow, Lillian promptly telephoned a friend. Charles was incensed:

> After Lily had been talking to that consummate ass, 'Tommy' for over 20 minutes, I called out 'O ring her off'. When the conversation was over Lily came into my room, where I was lying helpless, raging with temper and said: 'You are as bad as Bobby Walder, and his mother says she wishes she had drowned him when he was a baby.'[1]

Others, however, took his ailments more seriously. A few weeks later, when he was struck down with gastric flu in Melbourne, he ended up spending two weeks in hospital.

The flurry of complimentary reviews that followed Charles's publication of Mildred's *Eight Musical Monologues* must have been one of the few bright spots in an otherwise depressing period. In the *Triad*, A.L. Kelly also tried his hardest to please his editor with a laborious article entitled 'A Mistress of the Monologue'. Later in the year, Charles published a further collection entitled *Two Triolets and a Little Song* which he described as being 'for the delight of refined amateurs. Mere suburban bleating is the sort of thing that Mildred Carey-Wallace detested.'[2] But Charles's enjoyment of Mildred's posthumous success was soon marred by another falling-out with Morton.

Morton was drinking as hard as ever and by early September, he and Charles were at such loggerheads that Charles wrote a confidential letter to L.L. Woolacott asking him if he would be prepared 'to take up Mr Morton's work on the "Triad" if we found it necessary to dispense with his services.'[3] When the *Triad*'s company secretary visited Sydney in November, Charles recommended that Morton be dropped from the staff. But as usual, Morton's charm won the day. Bowing reluctantly to the pressure of his co-directors, Charles gave him a last chance. In a further letter to Woolacott, however, he stated ominously 'I am sure that ultimately, Mr Morton will break out once more, & then nothing shall save him.'[4] To add to his troubles, the *Triad* was facing yet another legal action, which had been brought by an irate tenor whom a *Triad* reviewer had described as singing like a trussed turkey.

Philip Newbury, like John Fuller, was an ageing singer. He was raised in Dunedin and over the years had enjoyed some very fair reviews in the *Triad*, starting with Charles's warm comments on his performance at a concert in Auckland in 1894. He and Charles had always been on good terms and later Charles alleged that it was Fuller, in a spirit of vengeance, who had incited Newbury to sue the *Triad*. Still struggling to come to terms with his loss, Charles had no appetite for litigation. Moreover, given the *Triad*'s precarious finances, he was nervous about embarking on an expensive court case. In an attempt to defuse the situation, he published a sympathetic explanation in the November *Triad*, citing Newbury's 'heavy cold and relaxed throat' on the day of the performance and noting that 'we have on many occasions expressed our appreciation of Mr Newbury's gifts and artistry as a singer, and the last thing we should desire would be to do him an injustice.'[5] But the *Triad*'s review had cost Newbury a lucrative engagement in New Zealand and he refused to withdraw his claim.

On 17 December, the hearing took place at the Sydney Supreme Court in a blaze of publicity. But despite its similar echoes of the farmyard, the 'Trussed Turkey' case had none of the vaudeville elements of the 'Pig's Whistle' and was conducted before a judge and jury who had little sympathy for the *Triad*. During the proceedings, the offending passage was cited in full:

> But the heavy artillery of the blame should be reserved for Mr Philip Newbury. He was the first solo voice heard in 'The Beatitude'* at the opening of the prologue. Here a determined and appalling sound suddenly broke upon the affrighted air with the words 'Night brooded then o'er the land.' The peculiar trussed turkey quality of his squawk is somewhat difficult of analysis. At times his throat appeared to possess the real rigor mortis rigidity and yet to be actively engaged in voice production of an excruciating and persistent nature.[6]

Under cross-examination, Charles vainly attempted to defend the author of the review, who was a respected musician in her own right and the wife of the Professor of History at Melbourne University. But the *Triad* lost the

---

* César Franck's oratorio 'The Beatitudes' performed at the Melbourne Town Hall on 21 July 1920.

case. According to the *Otago Daily Times*, the jury's award of £500 and costs to Newbury was greeted with 'obvious delight' by 'the anti-Triadites in the court'.[7] With typical bravado, Charles tried to make light of his loss, reprinting a complete account of the proceedings in the *Triad*. Newbury's original claim had been for £5000 and in some respects, Charles had got off lightly. But for an enterprise that was still as painfully short of cash as the *Triad*, the costs of the case tipped the balance and sent it into a financial decline from which it never recovered.

In later years, Charles openly admitted that the *Triad* had been wrecked 'on a remark that a visiting tenor sang like a trussed turkey'.[8] At the time, however, he gave no hint of his troubles and exploited the mass of free publicity that the case had generated to the hilt. As a result, during 1921 he became increasingly sought after as a musical and elocutionary judge. In June, amongst other engagements, he was invited to be the chief adjudicator at a major choral competition in the Melbourne Town Hall. Later on, he delivered a lecture entitled 'The Reading of Shakespeare's Blank Verse' to the Shakespearean Society of New South Wales. By 1923, his standing was such that he shared the role of music judge at the prestigious Ipswich-Blackstone 'Eisteddfod' with the distinguished musician, Arundel Orchard, who shortly afterwards succeeded Verbrugghen as director of the Sydney Conservatorium of Music.

The high demand for his services must have helped to raise Charles's spirits. In September 1921, in a sure sign that he was feeling more cheerful, he contributed his first humorous verses in years to the *Triad*. Not long afterwards, he berated Sydney audiences for their disgraceful 'concert manners'[9] and wrote a spirited piece on a young Polish pianist named André Skalski, who was temporarily conducting the State Orchestra. But the real reason for improvement in his morale was probably something more personal. In the May issue, his trenchant editorial on the need for a reform of the divorce laws hints at the direction in which his thoughts were moving. A further clue is the bouquet which he gave to Lillian for playing some of Mildred's songs 'with rare insight, and appreciation'[10] at a recent charity concert.

From the entries in Charles's diary, it is clear that his relationship with Lillian was often stormy. However, from his later letters addressed variously to 'my darling', 'my beloved' and 'Lilian mine',[11] there can be little doubt that he fell in love with her. Moreover, according to family sources, she had been secretly in love with him for years. Proximity and pragmatism doubtless played their part. Charles needed a housekeeper and little Charlie, whom Lillian adored, needed a mother. But there had also always been a certain 'frisson' in their relationship and they became a devoted couple – although this did not prevent them from continuing to argue so fiercely that at times they walked home on opposite sides of the street.

Meanwhile, in a concerted effort to improve the *Triad*'s finances, he raised its price from sixpence to a shilling and introduced a new cover which featured paintings by Australian artists, designed to appeal to local readers. But although much of the *Triad*'s coverage was now aimed at Australians, its most loyal subscribers were still in New Zealand. Even Charles's blatant bid for the Australian 'housewife' market with a series of articles on bungalows brought few new subscribers and he later acknowledged that, despite his claims to the contrary, his Australian circulation had never been 'indecently'[12] large. In April 1922, on the *Triad*'s thirtieth birthday, he confronted his Australian readers head on:

> *When I brought the* Triad *to Australia, I got just the sort of hospitable reception that one may confidently expect from Australians ... But I discovered some astonishing things. I found, for instance, that Australia is far more easily offended than New Zealand is, and that in Australia the purely literary sense is not nearly so highly developed as it is in the sister Dominion. More than that ... I found that Australians have not as keen and constant a sense of humour as New Zealanders have.*

These comments were probably an attempt to cajole Australians into subscribing. But middle Australia never embraced the *Triad* as New Zealand had done. Although Morton enjoyed a cult following amongst young women, his promiscuous writing – which Charles claimed 'New Zealand came to like ... as a delicate girl will like the shock of a shower bath' – had alienated many people. With his sights set on the far larger Australian market, Charles made another fruitless attempt to rein Morton in:

> *When Morton talks about our differences of policy he does not fairly state the position ... The difference of policy lay simply in this: that I said to Morton: 'Don't write stuff that must offend decent people ... the timid people who have grown up with certain conventions ...'*

Morton's response was defiant:

> *I am not afraid of the Justice of God, or of Beauty, or of Sex ... The thing I loved about the* Triad *for many years in New Zealand was that month by month I was able to say without subterfuge ... exactly what I felt and thought ...*

> *I know that the effect of the Great War on our nerves has been such that we are greatly disturbed, and liable at any moment to be greatly shocked by any clear statement of truth ... Pretty soon we shall settle down [and] ... I shall be able again to refer to a bee's knee or a cow's digestion without fear of offending some shrinking spinster at Wolga Flat or Pooroogalaboo.*

> *Miss Marie Tempest said to me a little while ago: 'There are occasions when your* Triad *suggests to me a brave old adventuress grown timid and wearing a calico chemise over her other clothes to prove that she is, after all, a very nice pusson.' Hooray!*

In a bid to quell the widespread gossip about their clashes, Charles went on to maintain that, 'in all matters of criticism, the two men responsible for the *Triad* have always lived in the happiest concord.'[13] But his renewed involvement with the *Triad*'s music reviewing was creating tensions with A.L. Kelly, with whom he often disagreed. During 1921 and 1922, his passionate championing of André Skalski,* whom Charles dubbed 'The Most Romantic Pianist Since Paderewski',[14] set them on a collision course. Kelly, like many others in Sydney, had reservations about the young Pole and when 'Susan Gloomish' leapt into the fray in support of Skalski, the whole affair developed into an undignified in-house squabble with Gloomish attacking Kelly, who in return aimed most of his ire at 'the person who writes as Susan Gloomish'. In his final sally, before Charles closed down the correspondence, Kelly's plaintive observation that he did 'not believe for a minute that the Editor was in any way responsible'[15] rather suggests that he suspected otherwise.

In New Zealand, Skalski was given a warm welcome and Charles, who was piqued that his support for the young pianist had been largely ignored in Australia, seized the opportunity to take another shot at Kelly:

> *The gratuitously devoted enemies of Mr André Skalski in Australia will be moved after their manner by the news that he has made a remarkable success in New Zealand ... The* Triad *is not in the least surprised, because in matters of taste and aesthetic perception New Zealand is very far ahead of Australia.*

Still sore about his own treatment during the war, he added: 'nor could New Zealand nourish rancorous spite against the Polish pianist because his name doesn't happen to be Bloggs or Scroggins.'[16]

After seven years of meticulous reviewing for the *Triad*, Kelly certainly deserved better, but beside the far wider dispute that was raging around the figure of Verbrugghen, the *Triad*'s domestic disagreements paled to nothing. By 1922, Verbrugghen had taken leave of his post after months of unseemly wrangling with the New South Wales State Government over their refusal to pay him a conductor's fee. For once in agreement, both Kelly and Charles deplored the Government's meanness. In July 1920, a few months after

---

* Despite his musical gifts, Skalski never fulfilled Charles's expectations by becoming a world star. Around 1927, he left Australia for the richer pickings in the United States and settled in Chicago where he founded the Skalski Orchestra.

Verbrugghen had returned from 'an all-conquering tour of New Zealand',[17] Charles noted tartly that, 'in having such a man in our midst, we are vastly more fortunate than most of us are apt to realise.'[18]

For New Zealand's music lovers, Verbrugghen's two tours with the State Orchestra were the orchestral highlights of the period. The first tour began in January 1920 when Verbrugghen arrived in Auckland with a hundred players, which was the largest group of instrumentalists that the city had ever heard. According to the Auckland *Star*, the orchestra was 'at the top of its form'[19] and played to packed houses all over the country, giving more than thirty concerts. Alfred Hill, who by this time had settled permanently in Australia, accompanied the tour as deputy conductor and as a member of the viola section.

Since leaving New Zealand in 1910, Hill had become a leading light in musical circles in Sydney, where he was often claimed by the Australians. In the *Triad*, however, Charles made a point of calling him 'the New Zealand composer'. He issued a sharp rebuke to Sydney's *Theatre Magazine* for referring to him as an Australian: 'Even the *Theatre Magazine* should know by this time that ... Mr Hill spent a few of his baby days in Victoria, but he is still a New Zealander.'[20]

Despite his intense involvement with the musical life of Australia, Hill continued to draw inspiration from Maori legends and music and on the orchestra's second New Zealand tour in January 1922, his Maori lament, *Tangi,* and Verbrugghen's orchestration of his 'Waiata Poi' were both played at a concert in Wellington. But working so closely with Verbrugghen, whose epic stature overshadowed his deputy, did not help Hill's career. As the years passed, even Charles, who had once hailed him as a possible founder of a New Zealand school of opera, became more muted in his praise and during the Skalski rumpus, 'Susan Gloomish' declared that, if Kelly preferred Hill's conducting to Skalski's, 'I can only pray the good God to help him.'[21] When Verbrugghen finally resigned in late 1922 to take up a salary of $25,000 a year as conductor of the Minneapolis Symphony Orchestra, Hill was passed over for Director of the Conservatorium and Charles's co-adjudicator, Arundel Orchard, was appointed instead.*

In addition to the departure of Verbrugghen, the early 1920s brought numerous deaths that prompted a spate of obituaries in the *Triad*. Amongst the first to be farewelled was Caruso, who died in August 1921 at the age of forty-eight. A few months later, Godfrey Turner finally lost his long-

---

* In 1933, Hill's second bid for the directorship also failed, but he continued to compose prolifically and in later years such achievements as his *Welcome* overture and his *Joy of Life* and *Australia* symphonies earned him the title of Australia's 'Grand Old Man' of music.

running battle with tuberculosis and was widely mourned by his fellow contributors. In September 1922, Charles wrote on the recent death of Northcliffe and in October he paid generous tribute to Tom Pollard and Henry Lawson. The following May, after C.N. Worsley had died unexpectedly on a trip to Italy, he was given an equally handsome eulogy. Even the *Triad*'s old enemy, John Fuller, got half a page, and in November 1923 the New Zealand poet and playwright, Dora Wilcox, wrote movingly on the death of the Christchurch poet, Mary Colborne-Veel. Another lamented figure was A.G. Stephens, who by 1923 was so deeply embittered by the failure of his *Bookfellow* that he had completely withdrawn from 'Sydney's circle of good fellows'.[22]

Amongst the new writers filling the gaps was Pat Lawlor, who had just arrived in Sydney to work. In February 1923, he rushed into print to defend his new Australian colleagues, whom the *Triad* had earlier accused of having a 'fear and hate [of] imported New Zealand journalists' from 'an outlandish country which publishes newspapers still for the most part in English'.[23] In a footnote, Charles dismissed Lawlor's comments as 'all very nice' and insisted that 'very few of the new men in Sydney can write at all.'[24] Nevertheless, some of the points that Lawlor made on the changing face of journalism would not have escaped him. He was all too aware of the need to move with the times and within a few months of Lawlor's article, he announced a massive makeover for the *Triad*, which was 'designed to gain ... another thirty or forty thousand subscribers' and whose success was 'virtually assured.'[25]

But Charles's confident predictions were simply another display of bravado. In reality, the new-look *Triad*, with its pages of fashion notes and serial stories, was a last-ditch effort to keep the show on the road. Unknown to all but its long-suffering shareholders (most of whom were New Zealanders), The Triad Magazine Ltd was already in liquidation. Over a year earlier, on 17 July 1922, a resolution had been passed at an extraordinary general meeting in Wellington to wind up the company. According to the company records, its assets and liabilities were offered for sale to the debenture holders* for the pitiful sum of £1700, but since the debenture holders were already owed £1000,† only £700 of the payment was to be made in cash and the shareholders would have received virtually nothing.

For Charles, the collapse of the business venture in which he had invested so much of himself must have come as a cruel blow. But he was determined to try and save the *Triad* by making a pitch for the booming women's magazine

---

* The four debenture holders were the three original directors, Charles, Findlay and Whyte, plus H.M. Hayward who became a director in 1915.
† In 1918, £1000 had been repaid to the debenture holders leaving an outstanding balance of £1000.

market. In the opening editorial to the new edition in December 1923, he outlined his reasoning with his usual bluntness:

> *With this issue the* Triad *sets out to cut a wider swathe ... and new features of popular appeal will be added ... so that, while keeping faith with readers who like to read criticisms of music, we must consider also the thousands of new subscribers who could hardly be persuaded to read musical criticisms for a fee ...*
>
> *In addition to the smart and accomplished girls who have been our champions and candid friends, there are the other smart girls who think that life is all a rag, and serious reading all a swot. We want to bring all the smart women into the fold.*

Such dumbing down was a risky strategy, but Charles insisted that the magazine would remain 'the old *Triad*' while 'broadening its view and going about more'.[26]

As Associate Editor, Morton would have shouldered much of the workload of preparing the new edition, especially as Charles had been heavily engaged in writing a 75-lesson correspondence course on 'Masterly English', which he launched in April 1923 under the imposing title of 'The C.N. Baeyertz Institute'. With the company in liquidation, this new venture was an attempt by Charles to boost his income. He promoted it shamelessly in the *Triad* with full-page advertisements assuring readers that, after taking C.N. Baeyertz's course, they would be 'LIKE A KEEN SWORDSMAN AMONG AN UNARMED RABBLE'.[27]

In June, Morton wrote an article endorsing the course, but his tongue-in cheek title, 'A Word from the Prison-House',[28] suggests that he was feeling the pressure in the office. Shortly afterwards he took a much-needed holiday in New Zealand, where he still had to produce his quota of copy and wrote a light-hearted piece in praise of 'Restful Wanganui'. Amongst his usual banter, his veiled references to 'those odd little twinges of pain' that 'whisper insistently to me that it would well to go home and keep still'[29] passed unnoticed. He was only fifty-four, and the news of his death from 'acute nephritis'[30] on 15 December, after barely a week of illness, hit Charles like a bolt from the blue. Two days later he was buried at the Baptist cemetery in Rookwood.

While Charles was still reeling from the shock of Morton's death, a further disaster struck:

> *On Christmas Eve the sky over Sydney was illuminated with the January issue of the* Triad. *Our printers' premises were burnt to the ground, and the Editor awoke to the knowledge on Christmas morning that he was without even one block or line of type with which to bring out the issue.*[31]

Faced with this second calamity, Charles cancelled the January edition.

In February, having cobbled together some of the copy that had escaped the fire, Charles produced a special issue dedicated to Morton. For all their editorial tussles, the two men had always made up their quarrels and in Morton's personal correspondence there are some warm testimonies to their friendship. In 1907, for example, he told A.G. Stephens that Charles was 'damn'd decent, really one of the best fellows I have met here'.[32] Later he defended him to Singer: 'I know that he has his little vanities, like the rest of us; but I have found him generally a man staunch to his friends and a good chap in emergencies.'[33] Morton's 'emergencies' tended to be financial, and from similar hints in the *Triad*, it can be inferred that Charles regularly bailed him out: 'Baeyertz has a great heart, and I am his debtor for all sorts of gracious and unobtrusive kindnesses',[34] and still more pointedly 'I owe you so much that I am quite unprepared to talk about it.'[35]

At the back of the 'Frank Morton Memorial Number', in unhappy apposition to the £1000 competition prize blazoned across the front cover, was an appeal for donations for the hapless Louise Morton:

> *With all his amazing talents, Mr Morton never made more than enough to keep himself and his family, and he was unable to save anything. Thus Mrs Morton is quite without resources.*[36]

Despite Charles's efforts to shame people into contributing by publishing a monthly list of donors, by September the fund had only reached a paltry £93. 3s. 6d. Verbal tributes were more forthcoming. In the February issue, the whole editorial page was devoted to a graceful obituary of Morton by one of his drinking mates, a gifted and unruly journalist named Adam McCay. In April, Hector Bolitho painted an endearing picture of the family man:

> *The public had a wrong conception of Frank Morton. Stories were told of him, and most of them were untrue. They never imagined a quiet, homeloving man, who presided over a family dinner table of ten or twelve people ... who played the piano for his daughters to dance.*[37]

Many echoed Bolitho's sentiments with tales of 'a happy Bohemian home ... where every meal was a moveable feast',[38] and fond memories of his house in Wellington where he lived surrounded by friends 'smoking his tobacco (or he theirs) reading his books ... and discussing everything under the sun'.[39] Morton's death also spawned the rumour, voiced by Lawlor in his *Confessions of a Journalist*, that 'it was Morton and not Baeyertz who made "The Triad" and, when Morton died, "The Triad" virtually died.'[40] Later, Lawlor changed his tune, alleging that the real 'master mind' behind the *Triad* was Charles, who 'had the mental and physical weight to carry it all'.[41] But, given the poor standard of the issues directly following Morton's death, his earlier comments are understandable.

Disgusted subscribers bombarded the Editor with letters:

To be perfectly frank, I am annoyed with the latest pranks of the Triad. *Increased circulation should mean increased literary value, not a hotchpotch wherein keen criticism of music and books rubs shoulders with sensational thrillers, hints on women's fashions and highly polished advertisements disguised as original essays ... Don't write for the masses, write at them.*[42]

Bolitho, who by now was editing a magazine in Johannesburg, was equally dismayed:

17 July 1924

This is a sad day. I have received the Triad *– the new* Triad *since Frank Morton is dead ... all is change and decay. The* Triad *... is dead – and a sort of John o'London's Weekly is born in its place.*

Not for the first time in his life, Charles had his back against the wall, but he had always been a survivor. By August, he had pulled the *Triad* back from the brink by appointing L.L. Woolacott as his new Associate Editor and was himself writing accomplished criticisms of Sydney's grand opera season. The fashion pages and the popular features remained, but as Woolacott's crushing reply to Bolitho demonstrates, the *Triad* was also attracting contributions from some prominent figures:

It is true that we suffered an irreparable loss when Hector ceased to contribute. Since Hector's departure we have had to fill our pages with the work of nonentities like John Galsworthy, H.L. Mencken, Frank Harris, Henri Barbusse, A. St. John Adcock, Harold Brighouse, A.A. Milne, Dale Collins, H.A. Vachell, C.N. Baeyertz, ... to mention at random but a few of the misguided people who seem rather pleased to appear in the pages of the dead-and-gone-to-bed New Triad.[43]

On 30 August, everyone at the *Triad*'s offices was feeling sufficiently cheerful to attend the annual Artists' Ball at the Sydney Town Hall. Charles appeared in his usual fancy dress outfit as a cowled monk, while the red-haired office boy went as his cigar. Yet without Morton, the *Triad* was a duller magazine. Although Charles enjoined his new columnists to 'churn out something fresh, something witty, something humorous',[44] 'Epistemon', 'Selwyn Rider' and 'T. Monk-Orran' were irreplaceable.

Apart from a one-page feature entitled 'A voice from New Zealand', coverage of New Zealand had almost ceased. A few articles appeared on

'The Pen is Mightier than the Sword'. Cartoon by Jack Quale, Triad, *1 August, 1926, p. 5. ATL.*

the continuing debate over the need for 'a decent gallery'[45] in Wellington,* and a posthumous exhibition of van der Velden's paintings prompted some melancholy reflections on his reclusive last years in New Zealand. On the whole, however, during these final months Charles neglected his most faithful subscribers and his suggestion that the new *Triad* was 'neither Highbrow nor Low-brow' but 'Broad-brow'[46] did little to allay their fears that the *Triad* was selling its soul to the mass market.

Despite his competent new team, Charles's attempt to transform the *Triad* into a modern magazine, combining cultural and popular features, was a failure. Although the loss of Morton speeded the downhill process, a prime cause for the *Triad*'s decline was the incompatibility between its traditional supporters and the new readers whom Charles was trying to capture. But another fundamental difficulty was the growing divergence of taste on either side of the Tasman. Over the years, Charles and Morton had frequently exploited trans-Tasman rivalries in order to provoke debate, secure in the knowledge that the cultural climate in both countries was strikingly similar. By the post-war years, however, a quarter of a century had passed since the formation of the Australian Commonwealth and the two nations were set on separate courses. In New Zealand, this had brought a new sense of

---

* Despite a government pledge of £100,000 and a generous bequest from Sir Harold Beauchamp (the father of Katherine Mansfield), the new Dominion Museum building, which housed the National Art Gallery, was not opened until 1936.

nationhood, but the common cultural outlook which had once enabled the *Triad* to speak with equal relevance to audiences on both sides of the Tasman had become a thing of the past.

As a relic of a bygone Australasian age, the *Triad*'s days were numbered – and Charles knew it – although this did not prevent him from writing a brilliant and eloquent review of the visiting Italian soprano, Amelita Galli-Curci. A few weeks later, he wrote a piece on the world-famous Austrian violinist, Fritz Kreisler, which Kreisler himself considered to be one of the finest pieces of criticism he had ever read.* It was Charles's last music review for the *Triad*. His ten-year contract as 'managing editor' was nearly over. In October 1925, his name disappeared from the masthead and he left the *Triad* without a word.

The magazine was purchased by Woolacott† who was soon in financial difficulties and sold it on in January 1927 to the hugely successful *Art in Australia*. The new proprietors cut the price to sixpence and reduced the number of pages, but by June it had changed hands again and had been taken over by the poet, Hugh McCrae, and the wealthy patron of the arts, Ernest Watt, who re-launched it as the *New Triad*. The first issue opened stylishly with a striking cover designed by McCrae's talented daughter, Mahdi, and an editorial by McCrae in which he assured his readers that the *New Triad* intended 'to regain the position' that the *Triad* had 'once so proudly occupied'.[47] But despite this spirited start, the venture failed. In June 1928, after only eleven numbers, it ceased publication. The *Triad*'s legacy, however, does not end there. Nearly a decade later, a humble sixteen-page journal in Wellington revived the name:

> *In assuming the title of 'The New Triad' after a long (and we hope) useful career under the name of 'Spilt Ink' our object is twofold. Firstly the new name is less flippant and more dignified, and secondly, it is hoped that those New Zealanders of some years ago who supported the original 'Triad' in its heyday, will be interested in this newest venture.*[48]

Compared with the glossy latter-day *Triad* and McCrae's fashionably presented *New Triad*, this modest cultural offering, quaintly published in quarto by the Handcraft Press in Wellington's Manners Street, was a poor relation. Yet it remained in print until 1942, and with its poems, book reviews and regular column of musical news, it came far closer than any of its Australian predecessors to the original spirit of the *Triad*.

---

*   Galli-Curci and Kreisler also toured New Zealand and, according to the August *Triad*, played to packed houses.
†   A letter from the liquidator states that the *Triad* was taken over by an Australian company in June 1924, which suggests that Woolacott may have waited for Charles to retire to make the announcement.

Chapter 17

The Last Crusade

Charles's initial reaction to leaving the ailing *Triad* may well have been relief, especially as – thanks to his contacts with Hugh McIntosh – he had already lined up a new job. McIntosh was still in control of the *Sunday Times* and, within a few days of leaving the *Triad*, Charles had taken up the position of editor. News of his prestigious appointment soon reached New Zealand, and on 10 November it was reported in the *Otago Witness*. But behind the scenes, the *Times* was in quite as much strife as the *Triad*, for McIntosh was plundering its coffers for his personal use.* By 1927 McIntosh was so deeply in debt that he had to sell the *Times*, which limped on for another three years before finally foundering in 1930. Charles, meanwhile, survived for little more than a year. When McIntosh sold the paper, he and the new owners failed to agree and he tendered his resignation.

At sixty-one, Charles was at an age when many people contemplate a more leisurely lifestyle, but his losses with the *Triad* had left him with few financial resources so that retirement was out of the question. After the *Times* debacle, the full implications of his departure from the *Triad* seem finally to have sunk in. In July 1927, he wrote a nostalgic letter to Hugh McCrae, looking back on his own thirty-two years as Editor and wishing him success as the new proprietor. Despite the absence of an editorial platform, however, Charles could still trade on his formidable reputation: by 1929 he had begun to carve out a place for himself in a new field that was at the forefront of the latest scientific developments.

Given his lifelong fascination with new inventions, it is perhaps hardly surprising that Charles should have taken so readily to radio. In the *Triad*, he had always kept a watching brief on the astonishing advances in 'wireless telegraphy'; in 1924, in response to the widespread interest in amateur radio, he had launched a new feature called 'Wireless Whispers'. Moreover many of his personal attributes, such as clarity of diction and a pleasing and persuasive speaking voice, were ideally suited to this new medium. Like

---

* Among his many extravagances, McIntosh had recently leased Lord Kitchener's former estate in England and re-laid the cricket pitch with soil from New South Wales.

Ourselves

"'Tis better to be brief than tedious."

BEARING in mind this sentiment expressed by the second murderer in "Richard III," we shall not weary our readers with a long preamble, but plunge at once into the midst of things. This magazine, in common with all other magazines, is made to *sell* (this word has a somewhat equivocal meaning, but we scorn to erase it, otherwise we should say to be sold); at the same time we make bold to hope that it may be the means of disseminating a small modicum of musical, artistic, and scientific information throughout New Zealand.

It has often been represented to us that there would be scope for a monthly paper which might give the latest information from the leading English and European journals, and at the same time contain reliable reports of music, &c., in Australasia. It is our intention to give the enterprise twelve months' trial; and to popularize the TRIAD, we have determined to offer a prize, well worth winning, to any of our readers who will obtain four yearly subscribers to the magazine. In addition to this we offer a monthly prize of £1 1s. in accordance with certain conditions contained on page 7. The yearly subscription, postage paid to any part of New Zealand, will be 5s. (payable in advance), and those who have the interest of music, science, or art before them may aid our humble efforts by obtaining subscribers, and, at the same time, gain a handsome prize for themselves.

We should like also to express our indebtedness to *The Musical Magazine*, *The Musical Times*, *The Monthly Musical Record*, *Truth*, *The Strand*, *Nature*, *The Scientific American*, *The Review of Reviews*, *Tit-bits*, *The Menestrel*, *The Revue de deux mondes*,

---

The *Triad* covers in this section range from the first issue in April 1893 to one of the last issues edited by Charles Baeyertz, in June 1925. Copies of the *Triad* are held in the Alexander Turnbull Library and other major archives.

MUSICAL SUPPLEMENT.

Träumerei.

ROBERT SCHUMANN.

FEBRUARY 10, 1910. [REGISTERED AS A NEWSPAPER] WELLINGTON EDITION

The Triad

A Journal Devoted to Literature, Art, Science & Music

Bartlett

Portrait Photographer
(OF AUCKLAND)

10 Willis Street, **Wellington**
(BETWEEN CARROLL'S AND GRAND HOTEL)

W. Littlejohn & Son,

By Appointment to His Excellency the Governor.

Watchmakers, Jewellers, & Opticians,

222, 224 LAMBTON QUAY, **WELLINGTON.**

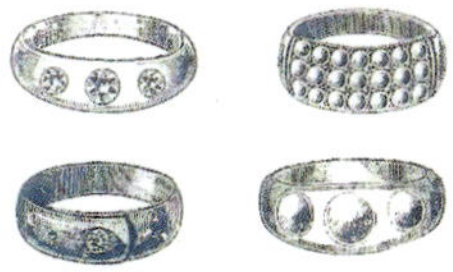

Manufacturers and Importers of Choice Jewellery.

Many REGISTERED and NEW DESIGNS in Finest London-Made BROOCHES.

High Grade PIANOS at Moderate Cost.

Before INVESTING in a PIANO or ORGAN it is advisable to communicate with the —— **D.I.C.** ——

D.I.C. FOR QUALITY

A really First-rate INSTRUMENT can be obtained from the **D.I.C.** on payment of a Small Deposit and on Easy Terms, without disturbing one's Capital.

The D.I.C offers exceptional Value in Pianos and Organs.

All INSTRUMENTS carry the Company's Full Guarantee.

OCTOBER 10, 1915.   WELLINGTON.

THE TRIAD

A JOURNAL DEVOTED TO LITERARY · PICTORIAL · MUSICAL ··· AND · DRAMATIC · ART ···

All communications to be addressed to "Manager, TRIAD, P.O. Box 536, Wellington.

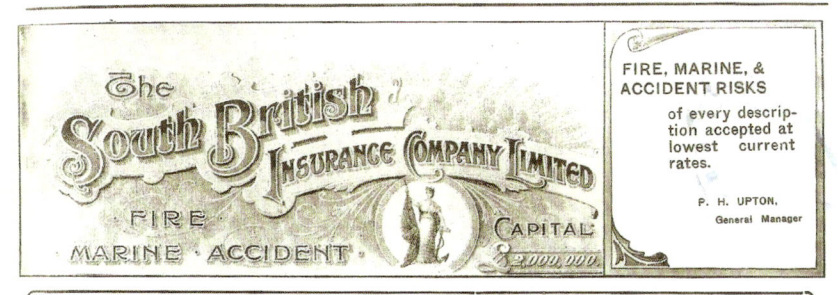

The **South British** INSURANCE COMPANY LIMITED
FIRE · MARINE · ACCIDENT   CAPITAL £2,000,000

FIRE, MARINE, & ACCIDENT RISKS
of every description accepted at lowest current rates.

P. H. UPTON,
General Manager

TRUTH IN PHOTOGRAPHY — BARTLETT PHOTOGRAPHS.

EVERY PORTRAIT from the BARTLETT STUDIO is a faithful and familiar expression of the original; they are True portraits of People as they are. Every Picture portrays a phase of Actual Character. They are not mere hard charts of the obvious.

W. H. BARTLETT - - - 10 Willis Street, Wellington.

BY SPECIAL APPOINTMENT TO H.E. LORD LIVERPOOL

W. LITTLEJOHN & SON,
Jewellers, Silversmiths, and Opticians,
Maintain their reputation for Fine Quality Goods by selling only "the best procurable."
WRITE FOR OUR "T." CATALOGUE.
222-224 Lambton Quay, Wellington.

NEW ZEALAND EDITION.

JANUARY-FEBRUARY DOUBLE NUMBER

February 11, 1924.

THE TRIAD

The National Magazine of Australia & New Zealand

PRICE 1/- Registered at G.P.O. Sydney for transmission by post as a Newspaper

THE TRIAD'S WIDENING APPEAL

FRANK MORTON MEMORIAL NUMBER
(Contains some of the most brilliant of his "TRIAD" work)

ANOTHER CRAIG KENNEDY DETECTIVE STORY

The Fantastic Adventures of Randolph Blow, Airman. By Gilbert Frankau
(FIRST OF FOUR ENTHRALLING STORIES.   SOLE RIGHTS FOR AUSTRALASIA).

LETTERS FROM LONDON, PARIS AND NEW YORK

NEW COMPETITION. First Prize, £1000 CASH

COLOUR PICTURES, DRAWINGS, PHOTOGRAPHS

PICTURES : BOOKS : LIFE : PEOPLE : PLACES

JANUARY 1, 1925.　　　　　　　　　　　NEW ZEALAND EDITION

The TRIAD

The National Journal of Australia and New Zealand

Pictures : Books　　Price 1/-　　People : Places
　　　　　　　　　　　Life

[Registered at G.P.O., Sydney, for transmission by Post as a Newspaper.]

APRIL 1, 1925. SPECIAL EASTER NUMBER NEW ZEALAND EDITION.

The TRIAD

The National Journal of Australia & New Zealand

Price 1/-

GRAND OPERA TO-NIGHT 8 P.M. LA BOHEME

[Registered at G.P.O., Sydney, for transmission by Post as a Newspaper.]

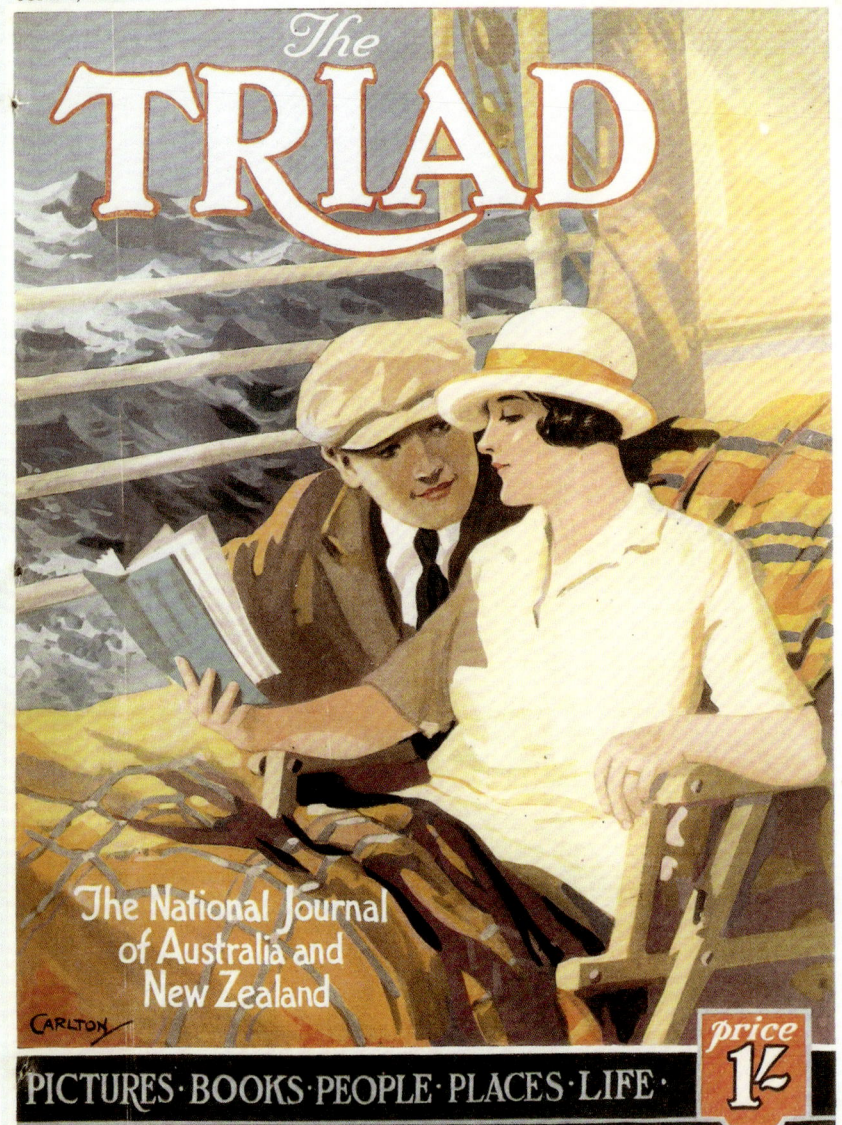

JUNE 1, 1925. NEW ZEALAND EDITION.

The TRIAD

CARLTON

The National Journal of Australia and New Zealand

PICTURES · BOOKS · PEOPLE · PLACES · LIFE

price 1/-

[Registered at G.P.O., Sydney, for transmission by Post as a Newspaper.]

King George V, whose epic first Christmas address was beamed across the Empire from Sandringham on 25 December 1932, Charles was a natural broadcaster and he slipped into his new role effortlessly. In September 1929, he featured in the Sydney radio magazine, *Wireless Weekly*, as the 'Programme Personality' of the week in a lengthy interview which suggests that his well-known severity had already become the stuff of legend:

> We had often heard the name Baeyertz spoken by broadcasting artists, in waiting rooms outside the studios in tones which mingled sorrow, anger, humiliation, and awe. The talk might be of some great artist who had visited Australia, or some great Australian artist; and someone would say, 'Did you ever hear what Baeyertz said about him?' What Baeyertz said about him would follow; then there would be low laughter, paralleling the croaking chuckles of the damned.[1]

Yet when the youthful interviewer finally encountered Charles – after stealing into 2BL's studios in Sydney 'to see what this Baeyertz bloke looked like' – he was completely disarmed. The eyes were piercing, but the handshake was instant and his manner as he talked 'with a slight drawl on all sorts of subjects' was charming. Charles had mellowed and he brushed aside any suggestion that he was still a figure to be feared: 'I am afraid that is all very much exaggerated ... I am not really like that. Not now. It is so easy to destroy – so difficult to create.' Later on in the interview, he spoke eloquently about the *Triad*, describing it as 'my vocation' and 'my enthusiasm, since I was a cub'.[2]

Much as Charles regretted the passing of the *Triad*, at this stage he was quite confident of developing a new career as a freelance cultural commentator. His correspondence school, the C.N. Baeyertz Institute, was still listed in the 1929 *Sands New South Wales Directory*, but it had never been more than a sideline. The rapidly expanding field of broadcasting seemed to offer far greater opportunities. On the home front, the outlook appeared equally bright. He and Lillian had long since moved from their noisy flat in Neutral Bay to a secluded house in the pleasant suburb of Chatswood.*
Moreover, Bella's death in February 1929 meant that they were at last free to marry.† But, as in 1914, at a crucial turning point in his professional life Charles's ambitions were thwarted by world events. On 24 October 1929, later known as Black Thursday, the New York Stock Exchange experienced the worst crash in its history, plunging the US economy into a disastrous tailspin and triggering a global depression from which many countries did not fully recover for over a decade.

---

*   5 West Parade.
†   Charles and Lillian were married in the office of the District Registrar at Chatswood on 4 September 1930.

Throughout the 1930s, both New Zealand and Australia were hard hit by the Great Depression, which brought massive unemployment and endless hardship for those without private means. By mid 1930, unemployment figures in Australia had doubled to twenty-two per cent, and by 1932 thirty-two per cent of Australians were out of work. In Charles's case, this meant that his chosen field of radio suddenly became overrun with out-of-work actors, singers and entertainers who were quite as anxious to find broadcasting work as he was. In the struggle for survival, Charles had little choice but to abandon any high-minded ideas that he may have had of creating a purely cultural role for himself and take any job that was offered. He was also quick to spot the commercial possibilities of broadcasting. By 1930 he had transferred his allegiance from the A-Class station, 2BL – where no advertising was permitted – to one of Sydney's B-Class commercial stations, 2UW.

At 2UW, he soon demonstrated his business skills by persuading firms to sponsor the broadcasting of the 1930 Test Match scores from England, where the legendary Australian batsman, Don Bradman, was demoralising English bowlers with hundreds of runs a day. According to K.S. Inglis's definitive work on the ABC,[3] the original proposal in 1930 to simulate play by using cablegrams came from a commentator on one of the A-Class stations, who passed it on to his commercial colleagues. But even if Charles did not dream up the idea, his execution of the scheme was brilliant, with crowds flocking to listen to the ball-by-ball descriptions at downtown electrical stores which remained tuned to 2UW throughout the night. An anonymous typescript deposited in Dunedin's Hocken Library describes Charles presiding over the broadcasts 'in the wee smaa hours of the morning', filling in the intervals between the cablegrams with 'stories both grave and gay'[4] as well as advertisements – often written by himself – for everything from hats to stockings.

Some of Charles's radio work was more intellectually challenging. Further on in the Hocken typescript, the unnamed author also mentions Charles's talk on public speaking entitled 'The Melody of Speech' and refers to his memorable debates with the feminist and radio commentator, Emma Littlejohn. In May 1931, a correspondent to the *Wireless Weekly* wrote of listening 'with delight' to his lunchtime music sessions, even going so far as to praise the advertising, which was always delivered in 'that calm, sardonic voice, breathing what delicate flattery to the dear ladies beginning with Adam and Eve and ending with face cream.'[5] Later, Charles's Sunday morning programme of classical music, 'Music of the Masters', became a universal favourite on 2UE.* When it was finally taken off the air in 1935, an outraged music lover declared that it

---

*   Another of Sydney's commercial stations.

'was not very complimentary of the B stations to think that the average listener is not above saxophones and crooners.'[6] Undoubtedly many listeners would have supported the *Bulletin*'s verdict that Charles 'did a bit of broadcasting – uncommonly well'.[7] But in conceding to the requests of firms that he both write and deliver their advertising (presumably for a fee), Charles had gone down in the world and he knew it.

Many years later the *Bulletin* journalist, Ronald McCuaig, wrote of descending in a lift with him from the studios of 2UW:

> *As the lift-door opened I made some foolish forced joke about going down in life and quoted Slessor's line 'How should we find, like Lucifer, the abyss?'... Mr Baeyertz took up my remarks in a hollow reverberating voice: 'Fallen! Fallen! No one will ever know how low I have fallen!'*
>
> *How much of this was amateur dramatics, and how much was a cry of the artistic heart, I should not care to say. At first I thought he was joking, and I was about to say something; then looked at him, looked away and said nothing.*[8]

Despite the mask of jocularity behind which he habitually concealed his emotions, Charles felt his descent from editor to advertising hack keenly.

Against this background, the invitation that arrived from the Wellington Competitions Society asking him to judge the public speaking section at their 1931 festival – billed in the *Evening Post* as 'The Greatest Musical, Dancing and Elocutionary Festival ever held in N.Z.'[9] – must have been particularly welcome. Joyfully scenting the battle far off, Charles leapt into action and dashed off a long letter to the *Post*, in which advice for prospective competitors was well-larded with crowd-pleasing statements:

> *I am forced to confess that in good taste, critical appreciation of art, literature, and music; in purity of diction, and love of the beautiful, the New Zealander, on the average, is as superior to his fellow across the Pacific as a Whistler Nocturne is superior to a tea-tray landscape.*

Further on, he got onto his favourite hobby horse of Australian English:

> *I have met so many Australian girls with charming figures, pretty faces ... but when they opened their mouths to speak, ye gods, what a disillusioning was there.*[10]

Charles also made sure that he would occupy much of the limelight by proposing a new 'Champion of Champions' class, at which 'artistic giants' would 'strenuously contend'[11] for elocutionary excellence at a widely publicised evening session judged by himself.

From the newspapers and Charles's own letters, it is evident that, from the moment he set foot in New Zealand, he was feted as a celebrity. On 10 August 1931 – the day his ship docked in Wellington – his photograph appeared in the *Post* together with an interview. From then on, and throughout the two and a half weeks of the festival, his judicial pronouncements were assiduously reported by the press. At the opening ceremony, which took place in front of a packed audience at the Town Hall, he was singled out for attention by the Mayor, who described him as 'a critic of such trenchant abilities that no one could stand before him in the competitions without some feeling of fear'.[12] Charles was one of the great draw cards of the festival: his section alone attracted more than one and a half thousand entries.

Shortly before the competitions started, he gave a broadcast of his talk on the 'Melody of Speech' on 2YA. The following morning, he wrote an ecstatic letter to Lillian: 'I'm having a most wonderful time: people are making tremendous fuss of me. Last night's talk on the Melody of Speech was a hit – a palpable hit.' Complimentary letters and invitations were pouring in:

> *I'm getting that swell-headed there'll be no holding me ... Every day I'm stuck up [sic] in the street by people who tell me that 20, 22, 25, years ago, I wrote a terrible criticism of them, & they all end up – 'and it was quite true & did me a lot of good.' ... My God if you were only here to share the appreciation – that's what I feel every minute of the day.*[13]

Since the onset of their relationship, Charles and Lillian had never been apart for any length of time and from the opening sentence of his next letter, it is clear that he was missing her: 'My precious, love, lorn Lilian, it seems years since I last saw you.' His closing words to her and Charlie are even more telling: 'God bless and keep both of you. You are all I have to love and live for.'[14] Much of the letter revolves around his judicial duties, but it also contains a three-page account of his experiences as the guest of honour at the Wellington Savage Club:

> *The 600 fellows gave me a rousing welcome ... Everyone wanted to capture me ... I've never had such a welcome in my life. They had me on a table conducting choruses ... No, I was perfectly sober. Yes I did have two small whiskies ... We've nothing in Sydney in the same street with the Wellington Savage Club. They sang the Volga Boat song at 2 in the morning, many of them well sozzled, forming a snake-like procession, each clasping the man in front ... I conducted that also, & the effect was prodigious.*[15]

As the night wore on, Charles found himself being handed from group to group amongst cries of 'Here, you've had Baeyertz long enough, pass him on.'[16] The party was riotous, but everyone was genuinely glad to see him.

Like the *Triad*, he belonged to a vanishing world. For many people his presence evoked a happier age when the *Triad* was in its heyday and New Zealand still basked in prosperity. In the meantime, a new and more insular generation, whose cultural outlook would be shaped by New Zealand's desolate social landscape during the 1930s, was already emerging from the wings and speaking with a very different voice.

A decade earlier when the young poet, R.A.K. Mason, talked to his former schoolmate, A.R.D. Fairburn, about founding a monthly arts review, he envisaged 'a sort of cross' between the *London Mercury*, H.L. Mencken's *Smart Set* and the *Triad*, in which they would 'adopt a high-tone, anti-democratic tone – "to uphold fearlessly & without regard to class or creed etc etc etc."'[17] But his plans came to nothing and by the early 1930s, his world-view had changed radically. He had discovered Communism and was contributing to New Zealand's first serious 'little magazine', the *Phoenix*,* often hailed as the earliest evidence of New Zealand's literary awakening. But although the group of Auckland University College students who founded the *Phoenix* shared Charles's objective of 'guiding the public taste',[18] they were determined to distance themselves from their forbears. Their earnest publication had none of the easy cosmopolitanism and irreverent humour of the *Triad*. In his celebrated essay for *Art in New Zealand* in 1934, Fairburn voiced his scorn for the preceding generation quite explicitly: 'There are many older men who still live in the world of the "Triad". But such cases of arrested development must hold no interest for the young writer.'[19]

When the Savage Club party finally broke up in the early hours of the morning, Charles returned to his hotel in the private car which the members had thoughtfully provided for him. It had been an emotional evening during which many people had pressed him to stay in New Zealand. Charles was sorely tempted: 'I'd like to stay here very much. We shall see. Everyone seems to want me to settle, but of course I want something tangible.'[20] With an estimated 70,000 New Zealanders out of work, however, Charles's hopes of finding employment in Wellington were little more than a pipedream. In Sydney he was living from job to job, but at least he had a foothold in radio.

Throughout his visit, the plight of the unemployed was constantly in the press. As he skimmed through the daily papers in search of coverage of his own exploits, he could hardly have missed the frequent references to 'Relief Camps', where men would be provided with 'plain food and simple tent accommodation, and ... approximately 10s per man per week'.[21] On 7

---

* The *Phoenix* modelled itself on the *New Adelphi*, published in London, where small, non profit-making literary magazines had long played an important role in encouraging innovative writing.

September, a 'Communist demonstration' took place in Wellington at which speeches were made urging the unemployed to shun such 'prison camps',[22] but this did little to deter 300 single men from applying for the eighty places at a newly established labour camp in Akatarawa.

When Charles discovered that one of his own children had fallen victim to the Depression, the desperate situation of many New Zealanders must have been brought home to him even more forcefully. On the day of the Savage Club party, he had received a disquieting telegram from Rudolph telling him that Maida was ill and asking him to visit Auckland. Rudolph gave no indication of how ill she was, but later it emerged that she was having a nervous breakdown. Since her marriage, Maida's life had not been easy. Her husband had died tragically young of T.B. and by 1931 the ravages of the Depression had left her in such dire financial straits that she had become homeless. Although Charles never got to Auckland, in 1932 Maida and her son came to live with him in Sydney, where this attractive and cultivated woman, who had once written so knowledgeably on 'Poets and Women' for the *Triad*, took cleaning jobs to survive.

With his household now numbering five and seventeen-year-old Charlie still at a private boarding school, Charles was working harder than ever to make ends meet. His curt reply to Rudolph's suggestion that they play chess by correspondence dates from this period and judging from the number of newspaper articles that he was churning out, his claims to overwork are quite plausible. Between 1933 and 1936, he mined every subject in his repertoire of lectures and reminiscences to keep the wolf from the door. His usual outlet was the popular Sydney newspaper, the *Sunday Sun and Guardian*, in which he wrote copiously on everything from the kings of England and the New York Lambs' Club to misquotations and the correct pronunciation of foreign names on air. When the City of Sydney Eisteddfod was inaugurated in 1934, he was appointed as Chief Elocutionary Adjudicator. He was also invited by the *Australian Women's Weekly* to join the panel of their 'Screen Personality Test', which was timed to coincide with the Eisteddfod. From time to time, he picked up other work, such as examining students in 'the art of speech' for the Conservatorium of Music. In 1936, when he was in his seventieth year, a letter he wrote to Lillian from the little town of Young suggests that he was showing few signs of slowing down. In addition to a heavy schedule of examining, he had been interviewed by the local newspaper and taken a comprehensive tour of the town with the Mayor.

Nevertheless, such jaunts were becoming increasingly rare and many of Charles's days were spent at home. Money was tight – even hiring a deckchair at Manly Beach was a luxury – and his favourite recreation became tuning into concerts from all over the world on the new 'all-wave' radio, which he had recently been given by an appreciative advertiser. Originally, most radio stations had used the long waves favoured by Marconi, but the discovery by radio amateurs that transmissions on short wave could cover far greater distances had transformed international broadcasting. Charles, with his passion for music, found the ability to listen to music being broadcast live from Europe and America little short of miraculous. In a letter to Lillian, dated July 1938, he applauded the quality of a Bach concerto coming from Prague. Some months later, he similarly enthused over 'a superb performance' of *La Traviata* from La Scala in Milan: 'All the voices were good, the interpretation fine, gorgeous orchestra and the reception absolutely flawless.'[23] By then war clouds were gathering over Europe, and two days earlier, with his fluent German, he had listened to one of Goebbels's propaganda broadcasts from Berlin: 'What a swine! What a liar!'[24]

Meanwhile, the special bond that had always existed between Charles and his youngest son remained as strong as ever. When Charlie left home in 1934 to work on a remote farm over a hundred miles from Sydney, Charles worried about him incessantly. He had grown into a good-looking young man with a marked resemblance to his mother, but he was not cut out to be a farmer. Even after he had married his employer's daughter in 1937, Charles continued to fret over him and wonder if he had enough to eat.

Despite their tight budget, Charles and Lillian were not entirely deprived of amusements. They both played excellent bridge and Lillian also enjoyed an occasional flutter on the horses. Domestic help was cheap and plentiful: in Charles's letters there are references to a flighty housemaid named Kathleen, who spent the night out dancing, and an unaccommodating Scottish gardener. But the days when he was a familiar sight at every musical or dramatic performance of note were long since past. Instead he took up the time-honoured pursuit of gardening and spent hours arranging his beloved dahlias in vases around the house. Radio work was still trickling in, as well as occasional requests for advertising copy, but during Lillian's frequent visits to Charlie and his family, time hung heavily on Charles's hands and he filled the empty hours by writing her long, intimate letters full of homely details of his daily life. In them descriptions of his modest meals and his struggles to dye his hair rub shoulders with his views on Aristophanes and declarations of love: 'I want you to understand one thing and that is – with all my faults & thoughtlessness ... I DO LOVE YOU.'[25]

In 1941, after over a decade of helping firms to promote their face creams and digestion pills on air and spasmodic bouts of examining and broadcasting, Charles finally acquired a position with the ABC that was more commensurate with his abilities. By now the ABC had grown from its modest beginnings in 1932 into a complex organisation with nationwide commitments that included news, education and culture. But while Charles's appointment as 'Tutor in Voice Production' to the ABC's announcers was certainly a tribute to his tireless crusade against Australian English, for many listeners the ABC's devotion to BBC English was laughable. A headline quoted by Inglis from the populist weekly, *Truth*, makes the point: 'ECTUELLEH, THE AIR BEER CEER COULD DO BETTAH.' Charles, however, had never belonged to 'the plum-in-the-mouth-Mayfayah-phoney-English school'.[26] By all accounts he had no marked 'English' accent, and he is remembered by the announcer, Bruce Webber, as 'a gentle old man with a slight aspirant in his voice'[27] who did not suffer fools gladly. In Webber's case, Charles's training certainly bore fruit and he went on to occupy one of the ABC's top slots of reading the national news.

But the ABC job came too late. Within a few months of starting work, Charles fell seriously ill on a tutoring tour to Adelaide. On his return to Sydney, he was diagnosed with cancer. A photograph of him and Lillian taken in 1942 plainly shows the ravages of the disease. Staring bleakly at the camera, his face pitifully drawn, he looks like a faint shadow of the ebullient editor of the *Triad*.

During his last illness, Charles finally dropped off the radar screen. He had no savings and his declining days were spent in a cottage provided by the family of his daughter-in-law, Lois, not far from her parents' farm. Later, he and Lillian moved to another cottage in the nearby township of Rylstone. As his condition deteriorated, Maida came to help Lillian and Lois to nurse him. Charlie, however, was already a prisoner of war and Charles never saw him again. On 5 June 1943, at the age of seventy-six, Charles died. The following day he was buried at Rylstone cemetery. The only people to attend his funeral were his wife, his daughter and his daughter-in-law as this flamboyant figure, who had spent so much of his career in a blaze of self-generated publicity, bowed out of life with as little fanfare as he had bowed out of the *Triad*.

Epilogue

Although Charles died in obscurity, the news of his death soon spread and within a few weeks tributes started to appear in the Australian press. On 23 June, the *Bulletin* was one of the first to note his passing with a warm reference to his broadcasting skills; in July, the Melbourne *Herald* described him as 'possibly the greatest authority on the English language that we possessed'.[1] His death was not reported in New Zealand until August, but the perfunctory tone of his obituaries in the *Otago Daily Times* and the *Evening Star* was more than compensated for by Lawlor's two generous articles, which appeared in successive issues of the *New Zealand Magazine*.

The first, entitled 'The Passing of C.N. Baeyertz', depicts him as a man who 'was big both spiritually and mentally' and 'played a tremendous part in the nourishment of culture in New Zealand'. Lawlor's claim that 'he was in his day as great in stature in our art and journalistic world as was Richard John Seddon in politics' is clearly an overstatement, but his observation that Charles's success owed much to 'his own ability, his assurance, his suavity and a modicum of bluff'[2] is a shrewd assessment of his qualities. In his second article, entitled 'In the Days of "The Triad"', Lawlor outlines Charles's 'manifold activities' besides the *Triad* and concludes with a call to abandon Modernism and return to 'the grand old traditions … where the Baeyertzes were the grand revolutionaries'.[3]

Marooned between the era of the *Triad* and the young lions of the *Phoenix* generation, Lawlor felt a strong kinship with 'the old order'[4] and after Charles's death, his popular reminiscences of early Wellington did much to perpetuate the memory of the *Triad*. Both Lawlor and Singer toyed with the idea of writing Charles's biography, but nothing came of it. Another keeper of the flame was Alan Mulgan. He too considered writing a biography, and in 1962 he devoted six pages of his *Great Days in New Zealand Writing* to an appreciative overview of Charles's achievements.

A decade later, when Charles and the *Triad* were all but forgotten, the former editor of the *New Zealand Listener*, Monte Holcroft, wrote a well-balanced article on the *Triad* for the weekly publication, *New Zealand's Heritage*, in which he stressed Charles's significance as a music critic. In

1985 the musicologist, John Mansfield Thomson, made the same point in his book, *The Attentive Ear*, noting that 'apart from the work of Charles N. Baeyertz … there is scarcely a name in the 19th century to which one can attach a recognisable style and a reasonable body of published criticism'.[5]

Another writer who pays tribute to Charles is Hamish Keith. In 1978 he wrote a nostalgic piece for the *Listener* citing the Butt-Rumford scandal and lamenting the days when a critic might write what he thought. Similarly, in his book, *New Zealand Yesterdays*, he not only quotes copiously from the *Triad*, but also devotes an article to it in which he describes the *Triad* as 'one of the country's most successful and popular magazines'.[6]

Other judgements were less favourable. Some criticisms, such as K.K. Ruthven's scholarly article on the *Triad*'s undignified squabble with Ezra Pound ('Morton admired writers who bravely ruffled the flag on top of the Establishment building, but made no attempt to rock the foundations'),[7] are well founded. But Patrick Evans's scathing attack in *The Penguin History of New Zealand Literature*, in which he jeers at the *Triad*'s 'philistinism which allowed every kind of patent medicine to be offered amongst the poems and prose', ignores the fact that the pages of many contemporary publications – including the *Bulletin* – were equally chaotic. Further on he derides 'Bayaertz's [sic] obsessive interest in elocution' and, in a below-the-belt pun on a *Triad* advertisement for a well-known laxative, observes: 'To him, literature properly spoken could be every bit as searching as the Bile Bean. It kept the vowels open.'[8]

The fortunes of Charles's family were equally mixed. By the time Charles died, he and Lily were virtually penniless. He left no will and Lily had to eke out a living by giving piano lessons. Despite being fourteen years his junior, she became increasingly frail and in 1949, she died in Manly hospital during an asthma attack. The fate of Charlie was sadder still. He survived the war, but his four years in a Japanese prisoner-of-war camp had inflicted psychological wounds from which he never recovered. On 11 March 1947, when he failed to return home for lunch, Lois and a group of neighbours rode out into the bush to look for him. They found him hanging from a tree. According to a member of the family, Lois carried his body home on her horse. She never told her two daughters the full story, but sixty years later, Leone still vividly recalls her emotions when, aged nine, she was told that her father had 'gone': 'Something happened to my heart. I think it may have broken.'[9] Charles's heart would have broken too.

His elder children fared rather better. Carl died in his early sixties, but both Maida and Rudolph, who became a well-known Auckland lawyer, lived to a ripe old age. Ironically, as the child by whom Charles had set the least store, Rudolph contributed the most to the preservation of his legacy. In

1957 he sent Charles Brasch, as Editor of *Landfall*, his uncritical 52-page memoir of his father, which he hoped would be published. Brasch replied with exquisite courtesy:

> *I have long hoped that someone would make a proper study of* The Triad *and its place in our social history ... what I hadn't looked for yet was a biography of its founder and editor, and it is a matter for congratulation that you have been able to set down so much material that would otherwise have been lost.*
>
> *While your ms isn't quite suitable for publication in* Landfall, *I would like to suggest, if I may, that you should either deposit it in the Hocken Library in Dunedin, or allow a copy of it to be made and deposited there.*[10]

As a leading member of New Zealand's Modernist élite, whose adherents had little time for the *Triad*, Brasch might well have left matters there. But Charles's commitment to artistic excellence was an ideal that Brasch shared and, far from dismissing the possibility of a biography, he asked Rudolph to supply some further details. Rudolph responded enthusiastically and sent his reminiscences to the Hocken accompanied by a wealth of newspaper cuttings and other papers. This collection, combined with the lively testimony of the 397 issues of the *Triad* in Wellington's Alexander Turnbull Library, not only documents Charles's career, but also represents a unique chronicle of New Zealand's cultural life during the spacious Liberal era and the dark days of World War I.

Today many New Zealanders still subscribe to the popular myth that New Zealand had no independent cultural existence before the 1930s. Large numbers also continue to associate the creative environment of the *Triad* years with 'colonialism and embarrassment'.[11] Yet a closer study of this neglected period reveals a world of large-minded men and women whose knowledge of music, art and letters was matched by their commitment to fostering the arts in New Zealand. For decades their contribution has been ignored, but in the twenty-first century, when our cultural life is more vibrant than ever before, the time has now come to celebrate the vigour and vision of those who helped to lay its foundations – including the redoubtable Charles Baeyertz.

NOTES

CHAPTER 1

1. *Colac Observer*, 10 Mar 1871, cited in Sydney Watson, *From Darkness to Light: The Life and Works of Mrs Baeyertz*. London: 26 Fore St, c. 1900, pp. 42–3.
2. Samuel Curtin Candler, Addenda to Diary 1867–8 (LaT Lib), p. 374, cited in Paul de Servile, *Pounds and Pedigrees*. Australia: Oxford University Press, 1991, p. 105.
3. Watson, *From Darkness to Light*, p. 2.
4. Ibid., p. 14.
5. Isaac Hebb, *The History of Colac and District*. Melbourne: Hawthorn Press, 1970, p. 340.
6. Watson, *From Darkness to Light*, p. 29.
7. *Colac Observer*, 10 Mar 1871, cited by Watson, *From Darkness to Light*, p. 42.
8. *Colac Herald*, 23 Jun 1982, unidentified page.
9. Ibid., 7 Mar 1871, unidentified page.
10. Ibid.
11. Watson, *From Darkness to Light*, p. 45.

CHAPTER 2

1. Watson, *From Darkness to Light*, p. 51.
2. Graham C. Evans, 'Colac and District, 1860–1890', MA Thesis, University of Melbourne, 1968, p. 131.
3. Clipping from an unidentified Christian publication, Los Angeles, 1890. Family papers.
4. Watson, *From Darkness to Light*, p. 53.
5. Ibid., pp. 54–5.
6. Letter from Charles Baeyertz to Hugh McCrae of 11 Jul 1927. Family papers.
7. *Triad*, vol. 30, no. 1 (Apr 1922), 5.
8. Evans, 'Colac and District', p. 129.
9. Rudolph Baeyertz, 'Baeyertz and his "Triad"', Hocken MS-0464-2, p. 5.
10. Watson, *From Darkness to Light*, p. 62.
11. Ibid., p. 70.
12. Prince Alfred College Archives 86/1, Admissions 1881.
13. *Triad*, vol. 19, no.12 (Mar 1912), 3.
14. Ibid.
15. Ibid., 4.
16. *Truth and Progress* (South Australian Baptist Association), 1 Oct 1881, p. 112
17. Ibid., 1 Jan 1883, 4.
18. Ibid., 1 Sep 1883, 97.
19. Ibid., 1 Jun 1882, 70.
20. Ibid., 1 Dec 1883 'Mrs Baeyertz at Gladstone'. Unidentified page.
21. *Otago Witness*, 22 Dec 1891, 8.

CHAPTER 3

1. R.E.N. Twopeny, *Town Life in Australia*. London: Elliot Stock, 1883, pp. 2, 3.
2. C.N. Baeyertz, Dedication, *Voice Culture and Practical Suggestions to Singers*. Dunedin: Stone & Co., 1892.
3. Cited in Horace Wyndham, *The Magnificent Montez*. New York: B. Blom, 1968, p. 218.
4. 'Society News' (unidentified newspaper), Newspaper Cutting Book, Hocken MS-0464-3.
5. *The Southern Cross*, 8 Jun 1888, 455.
6. Cited in Frank S. Greenop, *History of Magazine Publishing in Australia*. Sydney: K.G. Murray Publishing Co., 1947, p. 155.
7. 'Papers relating to the *Triad*', letter from Richard Singer to Pat Lawlor of 29 Apr 1960, ATL 77-067-6/28, p. 1.
8. Rudolph Baeyertz, 'Baeyertz and his "Triad"', Hocken MS-0464-2, p. 12.
9. Ada Cambridge, *Thirty Years in Australia*. London: Methuen & Co., 1903, pp. 187–9.
10. Unidentified Christchurch newspaper, ?Jan 1890, 'Mrs Baeyertz: Her Mission in Christchurch'. Newspaper Cutting

Book, Hocken MS-0464-3.
11 Cited in *Wanganui Chronicle*, 23 Aug 1890, 2. Newspaper Cutting Book, Hocken MS-0464-3.
12 Unidentified Auckland paper, ?Sep 1890. Newspaper Cutting Book, Hocken MS-0464-3.
13 *Otago Daily Times*, 5 Mar 1891, 1.

CHAPTER 4

1 *Specifications of the Steel Screw Steamer 'Hauroto' for the Union Steamship Company of New Zealand, Limited*. London: Waterlow & Sons Ltd., 1881.
2 *Otago Daily Times*, 3 Mar, 1891, 1.
3 *Triad*, vol. 18 no. 6 (Sep 1911), 56.
4 Anthony Trollope, *New Zealand*. London: Chapman & Hall, 1874, p. 41.
5 Ibid., p. 42.
6 *Triad*, vol. 22, no. 10 (Jan 1915), 23.
7 Anthony Trollope, *New Zealand*, p. 57.
8 Ibid. pp. 59–60.
9 *The Strangers' Vade-Mecum or South Land Guide*. Dunedin: C.W. White, 1889, p. 15.
10 Ibid., pp.19, 87.
11 Unidentified newspaper article, 28 Feb–6 Mar 1942, 'Melba called him a Devil: Reminiscences of C.N. Baeyertz.' Family papers.
12 *Triad*, vol. 9, no. 8 (Nov 1901), 4.
13 *Otago Witness*, 22 Oct 1891, 35.
14 Ibid., 5 Nov 1891, 33.
15 Ibid., 12 Nov 1891, 33.
16 *Otago Daily Times*, 23 Jan 1892, 3.
17 C.N. Baeyertz, *Voice Culture*, preface.
18 *Otago Witness*, 7 Jul 1892, 26.
19 Ibid., 14 Jul 1892, 26.
20 Ibid., 21 Jul 1892, 25.
21 *Otago Daily Times*, 24 Sep 1892 (Supplement), 1.
22 Ibid., 1 Oct 1982 (Supplement), 1.
23 *Otago Daily Times*, 4 Oct 1892, 6.
24 *Triad*, vol. 16, no. 1 (Apr 1908), 9.
25 *Otago Daily Times*, 30 Jan 1893, 3.
26 Ibid., 20 Mar 1893, 3.
27 Ibid., 6 Feb 1893, 2.
28 Ibid., 13 Feb 1893, 3.
29 Ibid., 13 Jan 1893. Unidentified page. Newspaper cutting book, Hocken MS-0464-3.
30 Ibid., 18 Feb 1893, 1.
31 Ibid., 11 Mar 1893, 1.
32 Ibid., 20 Mar 1893, 3.

CHAPTER 5

1 Beatrice Webb, *Visit to New Zealand in 1898: Beatrice Webb's Diary with Entries by Sidney Webb*. Wellington: Price Milburn & Co., 1959, pp. 54–5.
2 *Zealandia*, vol. 1, no. 1 (Jul 1889), 2.
3 Ibid., vol. 1, no. 12 (Jun 1890), 730.
4 *Triad*, vol. 1, no. 1 (Apr 1893), 3.
5 Ibid., 4.
6 *New Zealand Musical Monthly*, vol. 1, no. 1 (Jan 1888), 4.
7 Cited in a letter from C.N Baeyertz to Hugh McCrae of 11 Jul 1927. Family papers.
8 *Triad*, vol. 16, no. 1 (Apr 1908), 10.
9 Ibid., vol. 30, no. 1 (Apr 1922), 5.
10 Ibid., vol. 1, no. 1 (Apr 1893), 3, 16, 7.
11 Ibid., , 8, 10.
12 Ibid., 12.
13 Ibid., 15.
14 Ibid.
15 Ibid., vol. 1, no. 2 (May 1893), 16.
16 Linda Gill, ed., *Letters of Frances Hodgkins*. Auckland: Auckland University Press, 1993, pp. 27–8. (Letter to Isabel Field of 9 Jun 1893).
17 Ibid., p. 29. (Letter to Isabel Field of 29 Apr 1894).
18 *Triad*, vol. 1, no. 9 (Dec 1893), 19.
19 Ibid., vol. 1, no. 8 (Nov 1893), 18.
20 Ibid., vol. 1, no. 2 (May 1893), 11.
21 Ibid., vol. 1, no. 3, (Jun 1893) 20.
22 Ibid., vol. 1, no. 2 (May 1893), 16.
23 Ibid., p. 4.
24 Ibid., vol. 1, no. 7 (Oct 1893), 11.
25 Ibid., vol. 1, no. 3 (Jun 1893), 18.
26 Ibid., vol. 1, no. 6 (Sep 1893), 5.
27 Ibid., vol. 2, no. 6 (Sep 1894), 3.
28 Ibid., vol. 1, no. 4, (Jul 1893) 10.
29 Ibid., vol. 2, no. 7 (Oct 1894), 12.
30 Ibid., vol. 1, no. 6 (Sep 1893), 17.
31 Ibid., vol. 3, no. 5 (Jul 1895), 1.
32 Ibid., vol. 3, no. 1 (Mar 1895), 3.

CHAPTER 6

1 *Triad*, vol. 3, no. 1 (Mar 1895), 3, 4.
2 Ibid.
3 Ibid., vol. 3, no. 6 (Aug 1895), 7.
4 Ibid., vol. 3, no. 11 (Jan 1896), 6.
5 Ibid., vol. 3, no. 2 (Apr 1895), 3.
6 Ibid., vol. 3, no. 4 (Jun 1895), 3.
7 Ibid., vol. 4, no. 7 (Oct 1896), 3.
8 Ibid., vol. 3, no. 5 (Jul 1895), 3.
9 Ibid., vol. 4, no. 7 (Oct 1896), 4.

10 Ibid., vol. 3, no. 6 (Aug 1895), 3, 15.
11 Ibid., p. 9.
12 Ibid., vol. 2, no. 1 (Apr 1894), 20.
13 Ibid., vol. 1, no. 6 (Oct 1893), 19.
14 Ibid., vol. 4, no. 3 (Jun 1896), 5.
15 Ibid., vol. 4, no. 9 (Dec 1896), 25.
16 Ibid., vol. 5, no. 7 (Oct 1897), 17.
17 Ibid., vol. 2, no. 7 (Oct 1894), 8.
18 Ibid., vol. 2, no. 5 (Aug 1894), 8.
19 Ibid., vol. 2, no. 1 (Apr 1894), 6.
20 Ibid., vol. 3, no. 7 (Sep 1895), 5.
21 Cited by Shonadh Mann, *F.G. Gibbs: His Influence on the Social History of Nelson, 1890–1950* (Stoke (NZ): Nelson Historical Society, 1977), p. 143. (M.A. Thesis in History, presented to Victoria University College in 1954).
22 *Triad*, vol. 3, no. 7 (Sep 1895), 3.
23 Ibid.
24 George Bernard Shaw, *Pygmalion*, Definitive Text. Harmondsworth: Penguin Books, 1941, p. 5.
25 *Triad*, vol. 15, no. 12 (Mar 1908), 3.
26 C.N. Baeyertz, *C.N. Baeyertz Self-Training Method of Instruction in Correct English, Public Speaking, Elocution, Voice Production*, vol. 1 Sydney: 1924), p. 8.
27 *Triad*, vol. 30, no. 1 (Apr 1922), 5.
28 Ibid., vol. 3, no. 8 (Oct 1895), 3.
29 Ibid., vol. 3, no. 7 (Sep 1895), 6, 7.
30 Ibid., vol. 4, no. 4 (Jul 1896), 4.
31 *The London College of Music Annual Register, 1892*. London: William Reeves, 1892, appendix.
32 *Triad*, vol. 3, no. 9 (Nov 1895), 4–5.
33 Ibid., vol. 6, no. 9 (Dec 1898), 6.
34 Ibid., vol. 4, no. 2 (May 1896), 3.
35 Ibid., vol. 5, no. 2 (May 1897), 4.
36 *NZ Observer and Freelance*, 29 May 1897, 19.
37 *Triad*, vol. 4, no. 6 (Sep 1896), 25.
38 Ibid., vol. 4, no. 5 (Aug 1896), 18.
39 Ibid., vol. 4, no. 6 (Sep 1896), 5.
40 Ibid., vol. 4, no. 3 (Jun 1896), 20.
41 Ibid., vol. 5, no. 1 (Apr 1896), 19.
42 Ibid., vol. 6, no. 7 (Oct 1898), 30.
43 Ibid., vol. 5, no. 1 (Apr 1897), 20.
44 Ibid., vol. 4, no. 6 (Sep 1896), 4.
45 Ibid., p. 25.
46 Ibid., vol. 4, no. 7 (Oct 1896).
47 Ibid., vol. 4, no. 8 (Nov 1896), 23, 30.
48 Ibid., vol. 4, no. 9 (Dec 1896), 28.
49 Ibid., vol. 6, no. 2 (May 1898), 25.
50 Ibid., vol. 6, no. 5 (Aug 1898), 36.

Chapter 7

1 *Triad*, vol. 6, no. 7 (Oct 1898), 25.
2 Ibid., vol. 5, no. 10 (Jan 1898), 21.
3 Ibid., vol. 5, no. 9 (Dec 1897), 10.
4 Ibid., vol. 7, no. 6 (Sep 1899), 27.
5 Ibid., vol. 6, no. 8 (Nov 1898), 20.
6 Ibid., vol. 5, no. 12 (Mar 1898), 20, 21.
7 Ibid., vol. 7, no. 8 (Nov 1899), 4.
8 Rudolph Baeyertz, 'Baeyertz and his "Triad"', Hocken MS-0464-2, p. 4.
9 *Triad*, vol. 4, no. 9 (Dec 1896), 4.
10 Ibid., vol. 2, no. 2 (May 1894), 3.
11 Ibid., vol. 4, no. 9 (Dec 1896), 5.
12 Ibid.., vol. 7, no. 4 (Jul 1899), 12.
13 Ibid., vol. 5, no. 1 (Apr 1897), 3.
14 A.A. Grace, *Maoriland Stories*. Nelson: Alfred G. Betts, 1895, p. 89.
15 *Triad*, vol. 5, no. 4 (Jul 1897), 10, 13.
16 Ibid., vol. 5, no. 6 (Sep 1897), 4.
17 Ibid., vol. 7, no. 4 (Jul 1899), 16, 17.
18 Ibid., vol. 9, no. 12 (Mar 1902), 3.
19 Ibid., vol. 6, no. 5 (Aug 1898), 11.
20 Ibid., vol. 4, no. 4 (Jul 1896), 12.
21 *New Zealand Illustrated Magazine*, vol. 1, no. 1 (Oct 1899), 1–2.
22 *Triad*, vol. 6, no. 9 (Dec 1898), 13.
23 *New Zealand Illustrated Magazine*, vol. 1, no. 3 (Dec 1899), 242.
24 Ibid., p. 241.
25 *Triad*, vol. 7, no. 10 (Jan 1900), 4.
26 Ibid., vol. 7, no. 12 (Mar 1900), 6.
27 Ibid., vol. 8, no. 2 (May 1900), 4.
28 Ibid., vol. 8, no. 3 (Jun 1900), 3, 4.
29 Ibid., vol. 8, no. 2 (May 1900), 3.
30 Ibid., vol. 4, no. 3 (Jun 1896), 18.
31 Ibid.
32 Ibid., vol. 9, no. 6 (Sep 1901), 36.
33 Ibid., vol. 9, no. 8 (Nov 1901), 3.
34 Ibid., vol. 8, no. 11 (Feb 1901), 3.
35 Ibid., vol. 9, no. 8 (Nov 1901), 31.
36 Ibid., vol. 16, no. 1 (Apr 1908), 10.

Chapter 8

1 *Triad*, vol. 9, no. 6 (Sep 1901), 5.
2 *New Zealand Herald*, 4 Mar 1903, p. 8.
3 Cited in the *Bulletin*, vol. 24, no. 1206, 'Red Page', 28 Mar 1903 (Original *Triad* missing).
4 Ibid.
5 Ibid.
6 *Triad*, vol. 18, no. 7 (Oct 1910), 7, 8.
7 Ibid., vol. 12, no. 2 (May 1904), 5.
8 Ibid., vol. 13, no. 4 (Jul 1905), 41.
9 *New Zealand Times*, 9 Sep 1905, p. 9.

10 *Triad*, vol. 12, no. 7 (Oct 1904), 38.
11 Ibid., vol. 11, no. 4 (Jul 1903), 29.
12 Ibid., 30.
13 Ibid., vol. 12, no. 10 (Oct 1904), 9.
14 Ibid., 10.
15 Ibid., 3, 4.
16 Ibid., vol. 10, no. 8 (Nov 1902), 16.
17 Ibid., vol. 11, no. 5 (Aug 1903), 3.
18 Ibid., vol. 12, no. 5 (Aug 1904), 7.
19 Ibid., vol. 14, no. 3 (Jun 1906), 7.
20 *Canterbury Times*, 2 May 1906 (unidentified page), cited in the *Triad*, vol. 14, no. 3 (Jun 1906), 8.
21 Ibid., (unidentified date), cited by Rudolph Baeyertz, 'Baeyertz and his "Triad"', Hocken MS-0464-2, p. 36.
22 *Triad*, vol. 14, no. 3 (Jun 1906), 9.
23 Ibid., vol. 12, no. 5 (Aug 1904), 4.
24 Ibid., vol. 14, no. 5 (Aug 1906), 23.
25 Ibid., vol. 14, no. 8 (Nov 1906), 21.
26 Ibid., vol. 10, no. 5 (Aug 1902), 10.
27 *Otago Daily Times*, 26 Oct 1903, p. 4.
28 Ibid., 13 Oct 1906, p. 6.
29 *Triad*, vol. 9, no. 12 (Mar 1902), 22.
30 C.N. Baeyertz, introduction to *Guide to New Zealand: The Scenic Paradise of the World*. Dunedin: Mills, Dick & Co.,1902.
31 Ibid., p. 77.
32 Ibid., p. 76.
33 Ibid., p. 37.
34 *Triad*, vol. 9, no. 10 (Jan 1902), 4.
35 Ibid., vol. 10, no. 8 (Nov 1902), 13.
36 Ibid., vol. 11, no. 3 (Jun 1903), 7.
37 Ibid., vol. 12, no. 2 (May 1904), 23.
38 Ibid., vol. 7, no. 9 (Dec 1899), 32.
39 Ibid., vol. 11, no. 4 (Jul 1903), 6.
40 Ibid., vol. 10, no. 9 (Dec 1902), 9.
41 Ibid., vol. 11, no. 3 (Jun 1903), 17.
42 Ibid., vol. 12, no. 4 (Jul 1904), 4.
43 Ibid., vol. 13, no. 1 (Apr 1905), 3.

Chapter 9

1 *Lyttleton Times*, 26 Feb 1905, unidentified page. Newspaper Cutting Book, Hocken MS-0464-3.
2 *Table Talk* (Melbourne), 20 Apr 1905, 'An Interview with Mrs Baeyertz'. Family Papers.
3 S. Watson, *From Darkness to Light*, pp. 151, 152.
4 *Christchurch Press*, 12 Nov 1905, unidentified page.
5 James Cowan, *Official Record of the New Zealand International Exhibition of Arts and Industries held at Christchurch 1906–7: a descriptive and historical account by J. Cowan*. Wellington: Govt. Printer, 1910, p. 16.
6 *Triad*, vol. 14, no. 10 (Jan 1907), 44.
7 *New Zealand Times*, 12 Sep 1906, 11.
8 *Triad*, vol. 14, no. 9 (Dec 1906), 42.
9 Ibid., vol. 14, no. 8 (Nov 1906), 42.
10 Ibid., p. 36.
11 *Bulletin*, vol 27, no. 1395 (8 Nov 1906), 23.
12 *The Exhibition Sketcher*, 1 Nov 1906, p. 5.
13 *Triad*, vol. 14, no. 8 (Nov 1906), 42.
14 Ibid., vol. 3, no. 10 (Dec 1895), 3.
15 Ibid., vol. 4, no. 1 (Apr 1896), 4.
16 Ibid., vol. 4, no. 9 (Dec 1896), 3.
17 J.M. Thomson, *The Oxford History of New Zealand Music*. Oxford: Oxford University Press: 1991, p. 45.
18 *Canterbury Times*, 'The *Triad* and its Methods of Criticism', 2 May 1906. Cited in *Triad*, vol. 14, no. 3 (Jun 1906), 9.
19 *Triad*, vol. 15, no. 2 (May 1907), 36.
20 Ibid., vol. 15, no. 1 (Apr 1907), 1.
21 Ibid., p. 5
22 Ibid., (Apr 1907) 3, 5, 6.
23 Ibid., vol. 15, no. 3 (Jun 1907), 4.
24 Ibid., vol. 14, no. 12 (Mar 1907), 13.
25 Ibid., vol. 14, no. 5 (Aug 1906), 11.
26 *The Philistine: A Periodical of Protest*, vol. 25, no. 5. (Apr 1908) Cover.
27 Ibid., vol. 18, no. 3. (Feb 1904) Cover.
28 *Triad*, vol. 15, no. 1 (Apr 1907), 6.
29 Ibid., vol. 15, no. 2 (May 1907), 3.
30 Ibid., vol. 15, no. 7 (Oct 1907), 9.
31 Ibid., vol. 14, no. 2 (May 1906), 35, 36.
32 Ibid., vol. 15, no. 2 (May 1907), 6.
33 Ibid.
34 Ibid.
35 Ibid., vol. 15, no. 4 (Jul 1907), 38.
36 Ibid., p. 35.
37 Ibid., vol. 15, no. 2 (May 1907), 5.
38 Ibid., p. 4.
39 Ibid., vol. 15, no. 4 (Jul 1907), 3.
40 Ibid.
41 Ibid., vol. 15, no. 3 (Jun 1907), 7.
42 Ibid., vol. 15, no. 6 (Sep 1907), 7.
43 *Australia*, cited in the *Triad*, vol. 15, no. 3 (Jun 1907), 5.
44 *Evening Star* (Dunedin), 22 May 1907, 6.

45 *Southland Daily News,* cited in the *Triad,* vol. 15, no. 5. (Aug 1907), 16.
46 Stanley Sadie ed., *The New Grove Dictionary of Music and Musicians,* 2nd edn. (New York: Grove, 2001), vol. 6, p. 688.
47 *Triad,* vol. 14, no. 8 (Nov 1906), 3–4.
48 Ibid., vol. 14, no. 3 (Jun 1906), 8, 3, 9.
49 *Southland Daily News,* no date. cited in *Triad,* vol. 15, no. 5 (Aug 1907), 16.
50 Ibid.
51 *The World,* 3 May 1893, cited in *Shaw's Music,* ed. Dan H. Laurence. London: Bodley Head: 1981, vol. II, p. 872.
52 *New Zealand Mail,* Aug 1907, unidentified page, cited in the *Triad,* vol. 15, no. 6 (Sep 1907), 10.
53 *Triad,* vol. 16, no. 1 (Apr 1908), 9.

Chapter 10

1 Letter from Morton to A.G. Stephens of 26 Feb 1906, ATL MS-Papers-0962-2.
2 Ibid., of 4 June 1906, ATL MS-Papers-0962-2.
3 Letter from Morton to A.G. Stephens of 6 Aug 1900, ATL MS-Papers-0962-2.
4 Ibid., of 19 Jan 1906, ATL MS-Papers-0962-2.
5 *Triad,* vol. 15, no. 6 (Sep 1907), 5, 10.
6 Ibid., vol. 15, no. 3 (Jun 1907), 35.
7 Ibid., vol. 13, no. 5 (Aug 1905), 39.
8 Ibid., vol. 15, no. 3 (Jun 1907), 35.
9 'Carreno, Teresa.' *Encyclopaedia Britannica.* 2006. Encyclopaedia Britannica Online. http://www.britannica.com/eb/article=90-20490.
10 *Triad,* vol. 15, no. 5 (Aug 1907), 39.
11 Ibid.
12 Ibid., 40.
13 Ibid., vol. 15, no. 6 (Sep 1907), 37.
14 Ibid., vol. 15, no. 9 (Dec 1907), 5, 6.
15 Ibid., vol. 15, no. 10 (Jan 1908), 6.
16 Ibid., p. 8.
17 Ibid., p. 5.
18 Letter from Morton to A.G. Stephens, 18 July 1907, ATL MS-Papers-0962-2.
19 Ibid., of 23 June 1905. ATL MS-Papers-0962-2.
20 *Triad,* vol. 15, no. 11 (Feb 1908), 7.
21 *New York World,* 5 Jul 1908, Unidentified page. Newspaper Cutting Book, Hocken MS-0464-3.
22 *Triad,* vol. 15, no. 11 (Feb 1908), 9, 11.
23 Ibid., vol. 15, no. 12 (Mar 1908), 9.
24 Ibid., vol. 16, no. 5 (Aug 1908), 4.
25 Ibid., vol. 15, no. 11 (Feb 1908), 5.
26 Ibid., vol. 15, no. 10 (Jan 1908), 10.
27 Ibid., vol. 15, no. 11 (Feb 1908), 5.
28 Ibid., vol. 16, no. 7 (Oct 1908), 29, 30.
29 Ibid., vol. 17, no. 12 (March 1910), 20.
30 Margaret Scott, ed., *The Katherine Mansfield Notebooks,* vol. 1. New Zealand: Lincoln University Press & Daphne Brassell Associates Ltd., 1997, p. 96.
31 Pat Lawlor, *More Wellington Days,* 'In the Days of *The Triad*'. Whitcombe & Tombs, 1962, p. 158. (Citing David McKee Wright.)
32 *Triad,* vol. 16, no. 1 (Apr 1908), 15, 20, 19.
33 Vincent O'Sullivan & Margaret Scott, eds, *The Collected Letters of Katherine Mansfield,* vol. 1. Oxford: Clarendon Press, 1984, pp. 44–5. (Letter to Vera Beauchamp of ?Apr–May 1908).
34 *Triad,* vol. 15, no. 9 (Dec 1907), 46.
35 Ibid., vol. 15, no. 11 (Feb 1908), 34, 35, 36.
36 Cited in the *Triad,* vol. 15, no. 12 (Mar 1908), 3.
37 Ibid., p. 9.
38 Cited in the *Triad,* vol. 16, no. 1 (Apr 1908), 6.
39 Ibid., vol. 16, no. 1 (Apr 1908), 10, 11.
40 Ibid., vol. 16, no. 3 (Jun 1908), 4.
41 Ibid., vol. 16, no. 6 (Sep 1908), 3, 4.
42 Ibid., vol. 16, no. 2 (May 1908), 8.
43 Ibid., vol. 16, no. 4 (Jul 1908), 46.
44 Ibid., vol. 16, no. 9 (Dec 1908), 23.
45 Ibid., vol. 16, no. 10 (Jan 1909), 6.
46 Letter from Richard Singer to Charles Baeyertz of 12 Dec 1909, ATL 77-067-6/22.
47 Letter from Richard Singer to Pat Lawlor of 29 Apr 1960, ATL-MS-77-067-6/28.
48 Letter from Charles Baeyertz to his wife, Bella, of 21 Jul 1909. Family papers.

Chapter 11

1 Letter from Charles Baeyertz to his wife, Bella of 21 Jul 1909. Family papers.
2 André Siegfried, translated by E.V. Burns, *Democracy in New Zealand.* Wellington: Victoria University Press with Price Milburn, 1982, p. 251.
3 R.F. Irvine & O.T.J. Alpers, *The Progress of New Zealand in the Century.* Toronto: Linscott, 1902, p. 383.

4   Pat Lawlor, *Old Wellington Days*. Wellington: Whitcombe & Tombs Ltd, 1959, p. 131.
5   Ibid.
6   *Triad*, vol. 17, no. 2 (May 1909), 34.
7   Ibid., vol. 15, no. 11 (Feb 1908), 17.
8   Letter from Charles Baeyertz to his wife, Bella, of 21 Jul 1909. Family papers.
9   *Triad*, vol. 18, no. 3 (Jun 1910), 20.
10 Ibid., vol. 18, no. 3 (Jun 1910), 21.
11 Ibid., vol. 18, no. 5 (Aug 1910), 46.
12 Frank Morton, *The Secret Spring*. Sydney: Privately printed, 1919.
13 *Triad*, vol. 17, no. 6 (Sep 1909), 4.
14 Frank Morton, *The Secret Spring*, dedication to Frank Harvey.
15 Ibid., part V, 5th page (unpaginated).
16 Letter from Charles Baeyertz to his wife, Bella, of 21 Jul 1909. Family papers.
17 Antony Alpers, *The Life of Katherine Mansfield*. London: Jonathan Cape Ltd., 1980, p. 293.
18 *Triad*, vol. 17, no. 3 (Jun 1909), 15.
19 Ibid., vol. 17, no. 5 (Aug 1909), 46.
20 Ibid., vol. 17, no. 5 (Nov 1909), 9, 10.
21 Ibid., vol. [18], no. 2 (May 1911), 10.
22 Ibid., vol. [18], no. 3 (Jun 1911), 21.
23 Ibid., vol. 18, no. 5 (Aug 1910), 19.
24 Ibid., vol. [18], no. 5 (Aug 1911), 48.
25 Ibid., vol. 18, no. 11 (Feb 1911), 6.
26 Ibid., vol. [18], no. 5 (Aug 1911), 3–4.
27 Ibid., vol. 17, no. 3 (Jun 1909), 4.
28 Ibid., vol. 17, no. 7 (Oct 1909), 12.
29 Douglas Pike, ed., *Australian Dictionary of Biography*, vol. 3. Melbourne: Melbourne University Press, 1969, p. 47.
30 *Triad*, vol. 17, no. 3 (Jun 1909), 4.
31 Ibid.
32 Ibid., vol. 18, no. 5 (Aug 1910), 6.
33 Ibid., vol. 17, no. 10 (Jan 1910), 42.
34 Ibid., vol. 14, no. 10 (Jan 1907), 8.
35 Ibid., vol. 17, no. 5 (Aug 1909), 9.
36 Ibid., vol. 16, no. 10 (Jan 1909), 9, cited.
37 *The New Zealand Magazine*, vol. 22, no. 5, Pat Lawlor, 'The Passing of C.N. Baeyertz', (Sep–Oct 1943), 13.
38 Alan Mulgan, *Great Days in New Zealand Writing*. Wellington: A.H. & A.W. Reed, 1962, pp. 122, 124.
39 *Triad*, vol. 17, no. 10 (Jan 1910), 3.
40 Ibid., vol. 17, no. 9 (Dec 1909), 11.
41 Ibid., vol. 7, no. 7 (Oct 1899), 16.
42 See Colin Henry Mitchell, 'The Arts in Wellington, 1890–1912: A Cultural and Social Study'. MA Thesis: Victoria University of Wellington, Feb 1959, pp. 12, 17.
43 *Triad*, vol. 17, no. 7 (Oct 1909), 3.
44 Ibid., vol. 17, no. 8 (Nov 1909), 20.
45 Ibid., vol. 16, no. 10 (Jan 1909), 39.
46 Ibid., vol. 18, no. 5 (Aug 1910), 7.
47 Ibid., vol. 18, no. 5 (Aug 1910), 9.
48 Ibid.
49 Ibid., vol. 17, no. 10 (Jan 1910), 3.
50 Ibid., vol. 18, no. 9 (Dec 1910), 11.
51 Ibid., vol. 17, no. 8 (Nov 1909), 10.
52 Ibid., vol. 18, no. 9 (Dec 1910), 5.
53 Ibid. vol. 16, no. 1 (Apr 1908), 10.
54 Ibid., vol. [18], no. 6 (Sep 1911), 56.
55 Ibid., vol. [18], no. 6 (Sep 1911), 53.
56 Ibid., vol. [18], no. 7 (Oct 1911), 6.

CHAPTER 12

1   Charles Baeyertz, Introduction to *Eight Musical Monologues composed and performed by Mildred Carey-Wallace*. London: Frederic Harris, 1920, ATL Music Score Collection, call no. Music Box CAR Mus 1919.
2   *Triad*, vol. 19, no. 13 (Apr 1912), 5.
3   Unidentified Wellington newspaper, early 1912, Newspaper Cutting Book, Hocken MS-0464-3.
4   *Triad*, vol. 18, no. 11 (Feb 1912), 4.
5   Letter from Rosina Buckmann to Bella Baeyertz of 7 Jul 1912. Family papers.
6   John Baeyertz, 'Baeyertz and his Triad', typescript, citing Maida, ch. 7, p. 4. Family papers.
7   Unidentified newspaper cutting. Newspaper Cutting Book, Hocken MS-0464-3.
8   *Triad*, vol. 22, no. 2 (May 1914), 255.
9   Letter from Richard Singer to Pat Lawlor of 29 Apr 1960, p. 5, ATL 77-067-6/28.
10 *Triad*, vol. 20, no. 9 (Dec 1912), 46.
11 Ibid., vol. 21, no. 8 (Nov 1913), 287.
12 Ibid., vol. 20, no. 9 (Dec 1912), 46.
13 Ibid., vol. 22, no.1 (Apr 1914), 206.
14 Ibid., vol. 21, no. 1 (Apr 1913), 3, 4.
15 Ibid., vol. 20, no. 9 (Dec 1912), 3.
16 Ibid., vol. 20, no. 3 (Jun 1912), 4.
17 Ibid., vol. 22, no. 3 (Jun 1914), 316.
18 Ibid., vol. 17, no. 10 (Jan 1910), 20, 21.
19 Ibid., vol. 19, no. 13 (Apr 1912), 5.
20 Ibid.
21 Ibid., vol. 22, no. 2 (May 1914), 244.

22 Ibid., vol. 21, no. 9 (Dec 1913), 303.
23 Ibid., vol. 20, no. 4 (Jul 1912), 4.
24 Ibid., vol. 19, no. 13 (Apr 1912), 57.
25 Ibid., vol. 20, no. 8 (Nov 1912), 57.
26 Ibid., vol. 20, no. 9 (Dec 1912), 50.
27 Ibid., vol. 20, no. 12 (Mar 1913), 4.
28 Ibid., vol. 21, no. 11 (Feb 1914), 71.
29 Ibid., vol. 17, no. 8 (Nov 1909), 20.
30 Ibid., vol. 22, no. 2 (May 1914), 263, 264.
31 Ibid., vol. 20, no. 2 (May 1912), 50.
32 Ibid., vol. 21, no. 9 (Dec 1913), 305.
33 Ibid., vol. 20, no. 12 (Mar 1913), 4.
34 Ibid., p. 6.
35 Ibid., vol. 21, no. 6 (Sep 1913), 146.
36 Ibid., vol. 21, no. 6 (Sep 1913), 144.
37 Ibid., p. 163.
38 Ibid., vol. [18], no. 11 (Feb 1912), 3.
39 Ibid., vol. 19, no. 12 (Mar 1912), 12, 15, 16.
40 Cited by David Dowling, 'Bruce Mason', *Dictionary of New Zealand Biography*, vol. 5. Auckland University Press & Dept. of Internal Affairs, 2000, p. 340.
41 *Dominion*, 12 Apr 1975, Bruce Mason, 'Post Television Roundabout', p. 4.
42 *Triad*, vol., 19, no. 13 (Apr 1912), 10.
43 Ibid. vol. 22, no. 2 (May 1914), 264.
44 Ibid., vol. 18, no. 5 (Aug 1911), 9.
45 Ibid., vol. 20, no. 9 (Dec 1912), 38.
46 Ibid., vol. 20, no. 10 (Jan 1913), 9.
47 Ibid., vol. 21, no. 9 (Dec 1913), 306.
48 Ibid., vol. 22, no. 2 (May 1914), 245.

Chapter 13

1 *Triad*, vol. 21, no. 11 (Feb 1914), 63, 64.
2 Ibid., vol. 22, no. 2 (May 1914), 255, 256.
3 Ibid., pp. 256, 257.
4 Ibid., vol. 22, no. 10 (Jan 1915), 15.
5 Ibid., vol. 1, no. 1 (Apr 1893), 3.
6 Ibid., vol. 20, no. 6 (Sep 1912), 47.
7 Ibid., vol. 18, no. 6 (Sep 1911), 6.
8 Ibid., vol. 22, no. 4 (Jul 1914), 363, 364.
9 Ibid., vol. 20, no. 7 (Oct 1912), 39, 41.
10 Ibid., vol. 21, no. 9 (Dec 1913), 315.
11 Ibid., vol. 21, no. 5 (Aug 1913), 67.
12 Ibid., vol. 18, no. 1 (Apr 1910), 3, 4.
13 Ibid., vol. 18, no. 5 (Aug 1910), 37, 39, 40.
14 Ibid., vol. 19, no. 12 (Mar 1912), 5.
15 Ibid., vol. 17, no. 7 (Oct 1909), 9–10.
16 Ibid., vol. 17, no. 12 (Mar 1910), 5.
17 Ibid., vol. 18, no. 12 (Apr 1911), 5.
18 Ibid., vol. 14, no. 3 (Jun 1906), 10.
19 Ibid., vol. 18, no. 2 (May 1911), 51.

20 Ibid., 18, no. 9 (Dec 1910), 3.
21 Ibid., vol. 18, no. 8 (Nov 1911), 8.
22 Ibid., vol. 22, no. 4 (Jul 1914), 371.
23 Ibid., vol. 17, no. 8 (Nov 1909), 4.
24 Ibid., vol. 18, no. 9 (Dec 1910), 3.
25 Ibid., vol. 17, no. 8 (Nov 1909), 4.
26 Ibid., vol. 22, no. 4 (Jul 1914), 373.
27 Ibid., p. 371.
28 Ibid., vol. 22, no. 7 (Oct 1914), 552.
28 Ibid., p. 553.
30 Ibid., vol. 22, no. 5 (Aug 1914), 424.
31 Ibid., p. 445.
32 Ibid., vol. 22, no. 8 (Nov 1914), 643.
33 Ibid., vol. 23, no. 2 (May 1915), 263.
34 Ibid., vol. 22, no. 11 (Feb 1915), 63.
35 Ibid., vol. 22, no. 12 (Mar 1915), 126.
36 Ibid., p. 180.
37 Ibid., vol. 22, no. 7 (Oct 1914), 576.
38 Ibid., vol. 22, no. 5 (Aug 1914), 442.
39 Ibid., vol. 22, no. 12 (Mar 1915), 178, 179.
40 Ibid., vol. 23, no. 6 (Sep 1915), 516.
41 Ibid., vol. 22, no. 7 (Oct 1914), 576.
42 *The Little Review*, (New York & London), vol. 5, no. 10, Feb 1918. Intro.
43 *Triad*, vol. 20, no. 9 (Dec 1912), 57, 58.
44 Wilfrid Scawen Blunt, *My Diaries, being a personal narrative of events, 1888–1914*. London: Martin Secker, 1932, p. 743 (Entry for 15 Nov 1910).
45 *Triad*, vol. 20, no. 9 (Dec 1912), 58.
46 Ibid., vol. 25, no. 3 (Jun 1917), 62.
47 Ibid., vol. 22, no. 7 (Oct 1914), 552, 553, 554.
48 Ibid., vol. 22, no. 8 (Nov 1914), 661.
49 Ibid., vol. 23, no. 1 (Apr 1915), 228.
50 Ibid., vol. 23, no. 3 (Jun 1915), 303–4.
51 Ibid., vol. 22, no. 10 (Jan 1915), 23.
52 Ibid., vol. 23, no. 2 (May 1915), 288.
53 Ibid., vol. 23, no. 3 (Jun 1915), 350.

Chapter 14

1 *Triad*, vol. 23, no. 11 (Feb 1916), 51, 52.
2 Ibid., p. 23.
3 Ibid., vol. 23, no. 13 (Apr 1916), 3.
4 Ibid., vol. 23, no. 4 (Jul 1915), 363–4.
5 Ibid., vol. 23, no. 10 (Jan 1916), 57.
6 Ibid., vol. 24, no. 3 (Jun 1916), 26.
7 Ibid., vol. 25, no. 2 (May 1916), 63.
8 Ibid., p. 61.
9 Ibid., vol. 24, no. 3 (Jun 1916), ii.
10 Ibid., vol. 24, no. 8 (Nov 1916), 54.
11 Ibid., p. 65.

12 Ibid., vol. 23, no. 12 (Mar 1916), 67.
13 Ibid., vol. 23, no. 11 (Feb 1916), 45.
14 Ibid., vol. 23, no. 7 (Oct 1915), 11.
15 Ibid., vol. 23, no. 4 (Jul 1915), 410.
16 Ibid., vol. 22, no. 7 (Oct 1914), 543.
17 Cited in the *Triad*, vol. 24, no. 11 (Feb 1917), 45.
18 Cited in the *Triad*, vol. 24, no. 12 (Mar 1917), 9.
19 Ibid., vol. 25, no. 11 (Feb 1918), 3.
20 Ibid., vol. 25, no. 2 (May 1917), 14.
21 Ibid., vol. 25, no. 4 (Jul 1917), 24.
22 Ibid., vol. 26, no. 8 (Nov 1918), 13.
23 Ibid., vol. 24, no. 7 (Oct 1916), 44.
24 Cited in the *Triad*, vol. 24, no. 7 (Oct 1916), 68.
25 Ibid., vol. 25, no. 11 (Feb 1918), 42.
26 Ibid., vol. 24, no. 10 (Jan 1917), 43.
27 Ibid., vol. 24, no. 9 (Dec 1916), 17.
28 Ibid., vol. 25, no. 11 (Feb 1918), 43.
29 Ibid., vol. 26, no. 1 (Apr 1918), 14.
30 Ibid., vol. 24, no. 10 (Jan 1917), 3.
31 Ibid., vol. 23, no. 9 (Dec 1915), 4.
32 Ibid., vol. 24, no. 7 (Oct 1916), 6.
33 Ibid., vol. 24, no. 2 (May 1916), 3.
34 Cited by Rudolph Baeyertz in 'Baeyertz and his "Triad"', Hocken, MS-0464-2, p. 27.
35 *Triad*, vol. 23, no. 13 (Apr 1916), 72.
36 Ibid., vol. 24, no. 9 (Dec 1916), 44.
37 Ibid., vol. 25, no. 8 (Nov 1917), 51, 53.
38 Letter from Richard Singer to Pat Lawlor of 29 Apr 1960, ATL 77-067-6/28, p. 5.
39 Ibid., p. 4.
40 Letter from Richard Singer to Pat Lawlor of 29 Apr 1960, ATL 77-067-6/28, p. 4.
41 *Triad*, vol. 24, no. 2 (May 1916), 3.
42 Ibid., vol. 24, no. 4 (Jul 1916), 7.
43 Ibid., vol. 26, no. 6 (Sep 1918), 8.
44 Ibid., vol. 26, no. 8 (Nov 1918), 37.

CHAPTER 15

1 Rudolph Baeyertz, 'Baeyertz and his "Triad"', Hocken MS-0464-2, p. 14.
2 Letter from Charles Baeyertz to Rudolph Baeyertz of 5 Dec 1933. Family papers.
3 *Evening Star* (Dunedin), 1 Aug 1919, p. 6.
4 *Triad*, vol. 26, no. 9 (Dec 1918), 4.
5 Ibid., vol. 26, no. 11 (Feb 1919), 3.
6 Ibid., vol. 26, no. 12 (Mar 1919), 5.
7 Ibid., vol. 27, no. 2 (May 1919), 3.
8 Diary of Charles Baeyertz. Family papers.
9 Charles Baeyertz, Introduction to *Eight Musical Monologues composed and performed by Mildred Carey-Wallace*. London: Frederick Harris Company, 1920, ATL Music Score Collection, call no. Music Box CAR Mus 1919.
10 *Triad*, vol. 27, no. 6 (Sep 1919), 33, 34, 36.
11 Ibid., vol. 28, no. 4 (Jul 1920), 22.
12 Ibid., vol. 27, no. 12 (Mar 1920), 5.
13 Ibid., vol. 27, no. 6 (Sep 1919), 33.
14 Ibid., vol. 27, no. 11 (Feb 1920), 29. Lewis Rose Macleod, 'A Critic from "Down Under"'. Reprinted from the *Daily Mail*, 22 Oct 1919.
15 *Triad*, vol. 27, no. 11 (Feb 1920), 27.
16 Letter from Lord Northcliffe, 16 Oct 1919. Family papers.
17 *Triad*, vol. 27, no. 12 (Mar 1920), 6.
18 Ibid., vol. 28, no. 1 (Apr 1920), 13.
19 Ibid., pp. 11, 12.
20 Ibid., pp. 12, 14.
21 Ibid., vol. 28, no. 8 (Nov 1920), 19.
22 Ibid., vol. 29, no. 7 (Oct 1921), 7.
23 Ibid., vol. 27, no. 4 (Jul 1919), 10.
24 Robin Hyde, *Journalese*. Auckland: The National Printing Company Ltd., 1934, pp. 20 & 21.
25 *Triad*, vol. 28, no. 4 (Jul 1920), 48.
26 Ibid., vol. 28, no. 9 (Dec 1920), 22.
27 Ibid., vol. 29, no. 8 (Nov 1921), 7.
28 Ibid., vol. 30. No. 1 (Apr 1922), 5.
29 Ibid., vol. 29, no. 6 (Sep 1921), 35.
30 Ibid., vol. 30, no. 4 (Jul 1922), 5.
31 Ibid., vol. 28, no. 5 (Aug 1920), 19.
32 Ibid., vol. 30, no. 3 (Jun 1922), 69.
33 Ibid., vol. 30, no. 11 (Feb 1923), 5.
34 Ibid., vol. 30, no. 7 (Oct 1922), 6.
35 Ibid., vol. 31, no. 6 (Sep 1923), 60.
36 Ibid., vol. 20, no. 4 (Jul 1912), 57.
37 Ibid., vol. 25, no. 8 (Nov 1917), 49, 50.
38 Ibid., vol. 26, no. 12 (Mar 1919), 15.
39 Ibid., vol. 23, no. 1 (Apr 1915), 185.
40 Ibid., vol. 8, no. 9 (Dec 1900), 9.
41 Ibid. vol. 28, no. 1 (Apr 1920), 10.
42 Diary of Charles Baeyertz. Family papers.

CHAPTER 16

1 Diary of Charles Baeyertz, p. 348. Family papers.
2 *Triad*, vol. 28, no. 6 (Sep 1920), 11.
3 Letter from Charles Baeyertz to L.L.

Woolacott of 1 Sept 1920, ATL MS-Papers-8765.
4   Ibid.
5   *Triad*, vol. 28, no. 8 (Nov 1920), 6.
6   Ibid., vol. 28, no. 6 (Sep 1920), 45.
7   *Otago Daily Times*, 7 Jan 1921, 3.
8   *Bulletin*, 29 June 1949, 29.
9   *Triad*, vol., 29, no. 8 (Nov 1921), 45.
10 Ibid., vol. 29, no. 2 (May 1921), 14.
11 Letters from Charles Baeyertz to his wife, Lillian, Aug 1931 & Sep 1938. Family papers.
12 *Wireless Weekly*, 'Wings of Exactitude, Hooves of Correction', 27 Sep 1929, 7. Newspaper Cutting Book, Hocken MS-0463-3.
13 *Triad*, vol. 30, no. 1 (Apr 1922), 5, 6.
14 Ibid., vol. 30, no. 9 (Dec 1922), 23.
15 Ibid., vol. 30, no. 11 (Feb 1923), 20.
16 Ibid., vol. 31, no. 2 (May 1923), 24.
17 Ibid., vol. 27, no. 12 (Mar 1920), 37.
18 Ibid., vol. 28, no. 4 (Jul 1920), 7.
19 J.M. Thomson, *Oxford History of New Zealand Music*, p. 155.
20 *Triad*, vol. 23, no. 3 (Jun 1915), 309.
21 Ibid., vol. 30, no. 8 (Nov 1922), 22.
22 Ibid., vol. 31, no. 1 (Apr 1923), 41.
23 Ibid., vol. 30, no. 8 (Nov 1922), 6.
24 Ibid., vol. 30, no. 11 (Feb 1923), 35.
25 Ibid., vol. 31, no. 7 (Oct 1923), 7.
26 Ibid., vol. 31, no. 9 (Dec 1923), 3.
27 Ibid., vol. 31, no. 1 (Apr 1923), 11.
28 Ibid., vol. 31, no. 3 (Jun 1923), 13.
29 Ibid., vol. 31, no. 4 (Jul 1923), 23.
30 Death Certificate of Frank Morton, Papers of Dennis McEldowney, Notes and Correspondence re *Dictionary of New Zealand Biography*, ATL MS-Papers-7777-131
31 *Triad*, vol. 31, no. 10 (Jan-Feb 1924), 6.
32 Letter from Frank Morton to A.G. Stephens 12 Jun 1907. ATL MS-Papers-0962-3.
33 Letter from Frank Morton to Richard Singer, 17 Feb 1909. ATL 77-067-6/24.
34 *Triad*, vol. 30, no. 1 (Apr 1922), 6.
35 Ibid., vol. 17, no. 6 (Sep 1909), 4.
36 Ibid., vol. 31, no.10 (Jan-Feb 1924), 70.
37 Ibid., vol. 31, no. 12 (Apr 1924), 6.
38 Ibid., vol. 32, no. 8 (Dec 1924), 68.
39 Ibid., vol. 17, no. 4 (Jul 1909), 38.
40 Pat Lawlor, *Confessions of a Journalist*. Wellington: Whitcombe & Tombs Ltd., 1935, p. 236.
41 *New Zealand Magazine*, vol. 22 no. 5, Pat Lawlor, 'In the Days of The Triad', vol. 22, no. 5 (Sep/Oct 1943), 14.
42 *Triad*, vol. 31, no. 12 (Apr 1924), 18.
43 Ibid., vol. 33, no. 3 (Jul 1925), 28.
44 Ibid, vol. 32, no. 9 (Jan 1925), 5.
45 Ibid., vol. 27, no. 1 (Apr 1919), 12.
46 Ibid., vol. 33, no. 1 (May 1925), 28.
47 *New Triad* (Sydney), vol. 1, no. 1 (Aug 1927), 10.
48 *New Triad* (Wellington), vol. 1, no. 1 (20 Aug 1937), 1 .

Chapter 17

1   *Wireless Weekly*, 27 Sep 1929, unsigned (?Ronald McCuaig), 'C.N. Baeyertz: Wings of Exactitude: Hooves of Correction', pp. 7.
2   Ibid., pp. 7–8.
3   K.S. Inglis, *This is the ABC: The Australian Broadcasting Commission 1932–1983*. Melbourne: Melbourne University Press, 1983, p. 14.
4   'Australian Chapter – By an Admirer', unsigned typescript, Hocken MS-0464-1, p. 3.
5   *Wireless Weekly*, 22 May 1931, 6.
6   Letter to unidentified newspaper, 'Why not a Sponsor', signed Ludwig Wagner, Bondi, (11/3/35). Family papers.
7   *Bulletin*, vol. 64, no. 3306, 23 Jun 1943, 9.
8   Ibid., vol. 70, no. 3620, 29 Jun 1949, Ronald McCuaig, 'Baeyertz and Lucifer', 29 Jun 1949, 32.
9   *Evening Post*, 18 Aug 1931, 14.
10 Ibid. Unidentified date. Newspaper Cutting Book, Hocken MS-0464-3.
11 Ibid., 15 Aug 1931, 4.
12 Ibid., 20 Aug 1931, 6.
13 Letter from Charles Baeyertz to his wife Lillian of 16 Aug 1931. Family papers.
14 Ibid.
15 Ibid.
16 Ibid.
17 Cited by Rachel Barrowman, *Mason – The Life of R.A.K. Mason*. Wellington: Victoria University Press, 2003, p. 47.
18 *Phoenix*, vol. 1, no. 1, 'The Cause of it all' (Mar 1932) unpaginated.
19 *Art in New Zealand*, vol. vi, no. 4, A.R.D. Fairburn, 'Some Aspects of N.Z. Art & Letters' (Wellington: Harry H. Tombs Ltd), 218.

20 Letter from Charles Baeyertz to his wife Lillian of 23 Aug 1931. Family papers.
21 *Evening Post*, 4 Sep 1931, 9.
22 Ibid., 7 Sep 1931, 9.
23 Letter from Charles Baeyertz to his wife Lillian of 17 Apr 1939. Family papers.
24 Letter from Charles Baeyertz to his wife Lillian of 15 Apr 1939. Family papers.
25 Ibid.
26 Inglis, *This is the ABC*, p. 184.
27 John Baeyertz, 'Interview with Bruce Webber'. Family papers.

Epilogue

1 *Herald* (Melbourne), 'Rouseabout' (July 1943). Newspaper Cutting Book, Hocken MS-0464-3.
2 *New Zealand Magazine*, vol. 22, no. 5, Pat Lawlor, 'The Passing of C.N. Baeyertz' (Sep/Oct 1943), 12–5.
3 Ibid., vol. 22, no. 6, Pat Lawlor 'In the Days of "The Triad"' (Nov/Dec 1943), 12.
4 Ibid.
5 J.M. Thomson, ed., *The Attentive Ear: A Workbook on Music Criticism*. Wellington: Centre for Continuing Education, VUW, 1987, p. 12.
6 Text by Hamish Keith, picture research by William Main, *New Zealand Yesterdays: A look at our recent past*. Sydney, NSW: Reader's Digest Services, 1984, p. 168.
7 *Landfall*, vol. 23, no. 1, K.K. Ruthven, 'Ezra Pound, Alice Kenny & the 'Triad' (Mar 1969), 76.
8 Patrick Evans, *Penguin Book of New Zealand Literature*. Auckland: Penguin, 1990, pp. 31–2.
9 Letter from Leone Flemons to Joanna Woods, 8 May 2007 (Author's papers).
10 Letter from Charles Brasch to Rudolph Baeyertz of 13 Nov 1957. Hocken MS-0996-003/130.
11 Jane Stafford & Mark Williams, *Maoriland: New Zealand Literature 1872–1914*. Wellington: Victoria University Press, 2006, p. 10.

Selected Bibliography

1. Unpublished Manuscripts

Alexander Turnbull Library, Manuscripts and Archives Section

Baeyertz, J. fl 1996. Correspondence relating to record of C.N. Baeyertz and his *Triad*. MS-Papers-5571.
McEldowney, D. Papers, notes and correspondence re Dictionary of New Zealand Biography. MS-Papers-7777-131.
Morton, F. 1869–1923. Papers, 1897–1909, 1919. MS-Papers-0962.
—. Correspondence relating to the *Triad* [1909–16]. 77-067-6/22
Singer, R.A. Miscellaneous Papers [1909–10]. 77-067-6/23
—. Correspondence between R.A. Singer and Frank Morton, 1908–16. 77-067-6/24
—. Letters from Frank Morton, 1909. 77-067-6/25
—. Correspondence relating to the *Triad* [1943]. 77-067-6/26
—. Correspondence relating to the *Triad* [1908–14]. 77-067-6/27
—. Papers relating to the *Triad*, 1943–61. 77-067-6/28
—. Papers relating to the *Triad* [1908–56]. 77-067-6/29
Pound, E. 1885–1972. Letters to the *Triad*, 21 Dec 1914. MS-Papers-3015.

Baeyertz Family Papers (donated to Alexander Turnbull Library in June 2007).

Letters, photographs, miscellaneous papers and unpublished typescript by Dr John Baeyertz.

Hocken Library Archives

Baeyertz, R.E. Papers relating to his father Charles Nalder Baeyertz. MS-0464-1
—. 'Baeyertz and his "Triad" by his son R.E. Baeyertz'. MS-0464-2
—. Newspaper cuttings book, 1881–1943. MS-0464-3
—. 'The Reading of Shakespeare's Blank Verse'(lecture notes). MS-0464-4
—. 'The Melody of Speech'(lecture notes). MS-0464-5
—. Autograph Book, 1908–9. MS-0464-7
Brasch, C. Literary and personal papers (ARC 0124). MS-0996-003/130
Thomson, J. Papers relating particularly to *Southern People. A Dictionary of Otago Southland Biography*, ed. J. Thomson. MS-1926/077

2. Selected Theses

Baughen, G.A.K. 'C.N. Baeyertz and the Triad 1893–1915'. Thesis (B.A. Hons). University of Otago, 1980.
Evans, G.C. 'Colac and District, 1860–1890'. Thesis (M.A.). University of Melbourne, 1968.
Hamilton, S.D. 'New Zealand English Language Periodicals of Literary Interest Active 1920s–1960s'. Thesis (Ph.D. English). University of Auckland, 1996.
Mann, S. 'F.C. Gibbs: His Influence on the Social History of Nelson, 1890–1950'. Thesis (M.A. History). Victoria University College, 1954.
May, J.M. 'Thus Spake the *Triad*: a view of music in New Zealand 1893–1915'. Thesis (M.A. Music). University of Auckland, 1991.
May, J.M. 'An index of musical activities in New Zealand: reported in the *Triad*,

1893–1927'. Compiled by Judith M. May as part of her M.A. in Music. University of Auckland, 1993.

Mitchell, C.H. 'The arts in Wellington, 1890–1912: a cultural and social study'. Thesis (M.A.). Victoria University College, 1959.

Moriarty, J. 'Wellington's music in the first half century of settlement: a particular aspect of Victorian New Zealand'. Thesis (M.A.). Victoria University of Wellington, 1967.

3. ARTICLES

'The Law and the Critics' (unsigned). *New Zealand Listener*, 22 Oct 1943: 4–5.

Dunmore, J. 'Charles Nalder Baeyertz and "The Triad"'. *New Zealand Legacy*, vol. 14, no. 1: 16–7 (2002).

Fitchett, D. 'Musicians and musical taste in Australasia'. *Review of reviews*, vol. 7, no. 7: 29–36 (Jul 1895).

Holcroft, M. 'Baeyertz of the *Triad*'. *New Zealand's Heritage*, vol. 5, part 69: 1924–8 (1972).

Keith, H. 'State of the opera'. *New Zealand Listener*, 21 Oct 1978: 28–9.

Lawlor, P. 'The passing of C.N. Baeyertz'. *New Zealand Magazine*, vol. 22, no. 5: 13–5 (Sep/Oct 1943).

—. 'In the days of the *Triad*'. *New Zealand Magazine*, vol. 22, no. 6: 12 (Nov/Dec 1943).

Mason, B. 'Post Television Roundabout'. *Dominion*, 12 Apr 1975: 4.

May, J.M. 'Charles Baeyertz: The Golden Years of the *Triad*'. *Music in New Zealand*, no. 20: 54–8. (Autumn 1993).

—. 'New Zealand Music as seen by the *Triad*'. *Crescendo*, no. 32: 3–7 (Aug 1992).

Phillips, J. 'Musings in Maoriland', *Historical Studies*. Dept. of History, University of Melbourne, vol. 20: 520–35 (Apr 1982–Oct 1983).

Ruthven, K. 'Ezra Pound, Alice Kenny and the *Triad*'. *Landfall*, vol. 23, no. 1: 73–84 (Mar 1969).

Seaman, G. 'Early Musical Periodicals in New Zealand'. *Continuo*, vol. 6, no. 1: 4–14 (Jun 1976).

Water, B. 'The Critic and the Contralto'. *Crescendo*, no. 64: 14–9 (Apr 2003).

4. ELECTRONIC RESOURCE

Dictionary of New Zealand Biography (Wellington: Ministry for Culture and Heritage, 2001). http://www.dnzb.govt.nz/dnzb/

5. PERIODICALS

New Zealand and Australian

Australian Journal (1865–1962), Melbourne.
Bookfellow (Jan–May 1899, 1911–25), Sydney.
Bulletin (1880–), Sydney.
Citizen (Jan–Nov 1909), Wellington.
Critic (Jun–Oct 1899), Wellington.
Current Thought (1908–9), Christchurch.
Islands (1972–), Christchurch.
Landfall (1947–), Christchurch and Dunedin.
Listener (1973–), Wellington.
Lone Hand, (1907–21), Sydney.
Maorilander (Feb–Mar 1901), Auckland.
Melbourne Punch (1855–1900), Melbourne.
Monthly Review (1890–1), Wellington.
Native Companion (Jan–Dec 1907), Melbourne.
New Triad (Aug 1927–Jun 1928), Sydney.
New Triad (1937–42), Wellington.
New Zealand Illustrated Magazine (1899–1905), Auckland.
New Zealand Listener (1939–73), Wellington.
New Zealand Magazine (1930–?1952), Wellington.
New Zealand Magazine (Jan 1876–Oct 1877), Dunedin.
New Zealand Musical Monthly (Jan 1888–Nov 1890), Balclutha.
New Zealand Railways Magazine (1926–40), Wellington.
Phoenix (Mar 1932–Jun 1933), Auckland.
Red Funnel (1905–9), Dunedin.
Review of Reviews, Australian edition (1892–1900), Melbourne.
Spilt Ink (1932–7), Wellington.
Table Talk (1885–1939), Melbourne.
Tomorrow (1934–40), Christchurch.
Triad (1893–1927), Dunedin, Wellington and Sydney.
Zealandia (Jul 1889–Jun 1890), Dunedin.

American and British

Athenaeum (1830–1921), London.
Atlantic Monthly (1857–), Boston.
Blackwood's Edinburgh Magazine (1817–1905), Edinburgh and London.
Cassell's Family Magazine (1874–97), London.
Cornhill Magazine (1860–1975), London.
Edinburgh Review (1802–1929), Edinburgh.
Etude (1883–1954), Philadelphia.
Graphic (1869–1932), London.
Harper's Weekly (1857–1916), New York.
Household Words (1881–1905), London.
Lady's Home Journal (1883–), Philadelphia.
Lancet (1823–), London.
London Illustrated News (1842–), London.
McClure's Magazine (1893–1929), New York.
Munsey's Magazine (1889–1929), New York.
Musical Times (1910–), London.
Nineteenth Century (1877–1900), London.
North American Review (1815–1940), New York.
Poetry Magazine (1912–), Chicago.
Punch (1841–2002), London.
Scribner's magazine (1887–1939), New York.
Smart Set (1900–29), New York.
Spectator (1828–), London.
Studio (1893–1964), London.
The Dial (1880–1929), Chicago.
The Idler (1896–1911), London.
The Philistine (1895–1915), New York.
Windsor Magazine (1895–1939), London.

6. New Zealand Newspapers and Weeklies

Auckland Star (1887–1991), Auckland
Canterbury Times (1865–1917), Christchurch.
Dominion (1907–), Wellington.
Evening Post (1865–2002), Wellington.
Evening Star (1863–1979), Dunedin.
Fair Play (Nov 1893–Nov 1894), Wellington.
Lyttleton Times (1851–1929), Christchurch.
New Zealand Herald (1863–), Auckland.
New Zealand Mail (1870–1907), Wellington.
New Zealand Observer: and Free Lance (1890–1954), Wellington.
New Zealand Times (1874–1927), Wellington.
Otago Daily Times (1861–), Dunedin.
Otago Witness (1851–1932), Dunedin.
Press (1861–), Christchurch.
The Auckland Weekly News (1877–1934), Auckland.

7. General Reading

Alpers, A. *The Life of Katherine Mansfield* (London: Jonathan Cape Ltd., 1980).
Baeyertz, C. *Guide to New Zealand: The Scenic Paradise of the World* (Dunedin: Mills, Dick & Co., 1902).
—. *Voice Culture and Practical Suggestions to Singers* (Dunedin: Stone & Co., 1892).
Barrowman, R. *Mason – The Life of R.A.K. Mason* (Wellington: Victoria University Press, 2003).
Bennett, B., ed. *Cross Currents: Magazines and Newspapers in Australian Literature* (Melbourne: Longman Cheshire, 1981).
Blunt, W. *My Diaries, being a Personal Narrative of Events, 1888–1914* (London: Martin Secker, 1932).
Brasch, C. *Indirections: A Memoir 1909–1947* (Wellington and New York: Oxford University Press, c. 1980).
Buchanan, I., Dunn, M., Eastmond, E. *Frances Hodgkins: Paintings and Drawings* (Auckland: Auckland University Press, 1994).
Cambridge, A. *Thirty Years in Australia* (London: Methuen & Co., 1903).
Campbell, M. *Music in Dunedin: An Historical Account of Dunedin's Musicians and Musical Societies from the Founding of the Province in 1848* (Dunedin: Charles Begg & Co., Ltd., 1945).
Cantrell, L., ed. *Bards, Bohemians and Bookmen: Essays in Australian Literature* (St. Lucian, Q: University of Queensland Press, 1976).
Coe, L. *Wireless Radio: a Brief History* (Jefferson, N.C.: McFarland, c.1996).
Day, P. *The Making of the New Zealand Press 1840–1880* (Wellington: Victoria University Press, 1990).
De Serville, P. *Pounds and Pedigrees: the Upper Class in Victoria 1850–1880* (South Melbourne: Oxford University Press, 1991).

Downes, P. and Harcourt P. *Voices in the Air: Radio Broadcasting in New Zealand, a Documentary* (Wellington: Methuen [in assoc. with] Radio New Zealand, 1976).

Drayton, J. *Frances Hodgkins: A Private Viewing* (Auckland: Godwit, 2005).

Dunn, M. *A Concise History of New Zealand Painting* (Auckland: David Bateman; Roseville East, NSW: Craftsman House, 1991).

—. *Nerli: an Italian Painter in the South Pacific* (Auckland: Auckland University Press, 2005).

Evans, P. *The Penguin History of New Zealand Literature* (Auckland: Penguin, 1990).

Foster, R. *Come Listen to my Song* (London: Collins, 1949).

Gill, L. *Letters of Frances Hodgkins* (Auckland: Auckland University Press, 1993).

Grace, A. *Hone Tiki Dialogues* (Wellington [N.Z.]: Gordon & Gotch, 1910).

—. *Maoriland Stories* (Nelson: Alfred H. Betts, 1895).

—. *Tales of a Dying Race* (London: Chatto & Windus, 1901).

Grant., J. and Serle, G. *The Melbourne Scene 1803–1956* (Sydney: Hale & Iremonger, 1983).

Greenop, F.S. *History of Magazine Publishing in Australia* (Sydney: K.G. Murray Pub. Co., 1947).

Harvey, D.R. *A Bibliography of Writings about New Zealand Music Published to the End of 1983* (Wellington: Victoria University Press, 1985).

Harvey, R, Kirsop, W. and McMullin, B.J., eds. *An Index of Civilisation: Studies of Printing and Publishing History in Honour of Keith Maslen* (Melbourne: Centre for Bibliographical and Textual Studies, Monash University, 1993).

Hebb, I. *The History of Colac and District* (Melbourne: Hawthorn Press, 1970).

Hurst, M. *Music and the State in New Zealand: A Century of Entertainment 1840–1943* (Auckland: Charles Begg & Co.Ltd., 1944).

Hyde, R. *Journalese* (Auckland: The National Printing Company Ltd., 1934).

Inglis, K. *This is the ABC: The Australian Broadcasting Commission 1932–1983* (Melbourne: Melbourne University Press, 1983).

Irvine, R., and Alpers, O. *The Progress of New Zealand in the Century* (Toronto: Linscott, 1902).

Keith, H. and Main, W. *New Zealand Yesterdays: A Look at our Recent Past* (Sydney: Reader's Digest Services, 1984).

Keith, H. *Painting 1827–1967* (Wellington: A.H. & A.W. Reed, 1968).

King, M. *The Penguin History of New Zealand* (Auckland, Viking, 2004).

Laurence D., ed. *Shaw's Music: The Complete Music Criticism in Three Volumes* (London: Max Reinhardt, the Bodley Head, 1981).

Lawlor, P. *Confessions of a Journalist* (Wellington: Whitcombe & Tombs, Ltd., 1935).

—. *More Wellington Days* (Wellington: Whitcombe & Tombs, Ltd., 1962).

—. *Old Wellington Days* (Wellington: Whitcombe & Tombs, Ltd., 1959).

Maconie, J. *Landmarks in New Zealand Writing to 1945* (Wellington: New Zealand Book Council, 1990).

McCormick, E. *Letters and Art in New Zealand* (Wellington: Dept. of Internal Affairs, 1940).

—. *New Zealand Literature: A Survey* (London: Wellington: Oxford University Press, 1955).

—. *Portrait of Frances Hodgkins* (Auckland: Auckland University Press, 1990).

McLintock, A. *History of Otago: The Origins and Growth of a Wakefield Class Settlement* (Christchurch: Capper Press, 1975).

Morton, F. *Secret Spring* (Sydney: Privately printed, 1919).

—. *Angel of the Earthquake* (Melbourne: Atlas Press, 1909).

—. *Laughter and Tears: Verses of a Journalist* (Wellington: The New Zealand Times Co, 1908).

Mulgan, A. *Great Days in New Zealand Writing* (Wellington: A.H. & A.W. Reed, 1962).

—. *The Making of a New Zealander* (Wellington: A.H. & A.W. Reed, 1958).

Oliver, W. *The Story of New Zealand* (London: Faber and Faber, 1960).

O'Sullivan, V., and Scott, M., eds. *The Collected Letters of Katherine Mansfield*, vol. 1 (Oxford: Clarendon Press, 1984).

Olssen, E. *A History of Otago* (Dunedin, McIndoe, 1984).

Park, I. *New Zealand Periodicals of Literary Interest* (Wellington: Library School,

National Library Service, 1962).

Pember Reeves, W. *The Long White Cloud: Ao Tea Roa* (London: George Allen & Unwin Ltd., 1898).

Pike, D., ed. *Australian Dictionary of Biography* (Melbourne: Melbourne University Press, 1969).

Reed, A. *The Story of New Zealand* (Wellington: A.H. & A.W. Reed, 1945).

Reed, D. *The Popular Magazine in Britain and the United States, 1880–1960* (Toronto: Buffalo: University of Toronto Press, 1997).

Rice, G. *Black November: The 1918 Influenza Pandemic in New Zealand* (Christchurch: Canterbury University Press, 2005).

Sadie, S., ed., and Tyrell, J. exec. ed. *The New Grove Dictionary of Music and Musicians*, 2nd ed. (New York: Grove, 2001).

Scholefield, G. *Dictionary of New Zealand Biography* (Wellington: New Zealand Department of Internal Affairs, 1940)

Scholefield, G. *Newspapers in New Zealand* (Wellington: A.H. & A.W. Reed, 1958).

Scott, M., ed. *The Katherine Mansfield Notebooks*, vol. 1 (New Zealand: Lincoln University Press and Daphne Brassell Associates Ltd., 1997).

Serle, G. *The Rush to be Rich: A History of the Colony of Victoria, 1883–1889* (Melbourne: Melbourne University Press, 1971).

Shaw, G. *Pygmalion*, definitive text (Harmondsworth: Penguin Books, 1941).

Siegfried, A. *Democracy in New Zealand*. Trans. E. Burns. (London: Bell 1914).

Simpson, A. *Opera's Farthest Frontier: A History of Professional Opera in New Zealand* (Auckland: Reed Publishing (NZ) Ltd., 1996).

—. ed., *Opera in New Zealand: Aspects of History and Performance* (Wellington: Witham Press, 1990).

Sinclair, K. and Harrex, W. *Looking Back: A Photographic History of New Zealand* (Wellington; New York: Oxford University Press, 1978)

Sinclair, K., ed., *The Oxford Illustrated History of New Zealand* (Auckland: Oxford University Press, 1990).

Stafford, J. and Williams, M. *Maoriland: New Zealand Literature, 1872–1914* (Wellington: Victoria University Press, 2006).

Stephens, A. and Lindsay, N. *Oblation* (Sydney: A.G. Stephens and N. Lindsay, 1902).

Stephens, A. *The Red Pagan* (Sydney: Bulletin Newspaper Co., 1904)

Stuart, L. *Nineteenth Century Australian Periodicals: an Annotated Bibliography* (Sydney: Hale & Iremonger, 1979).

Sturm, T., ed. *Oxford History of New Zealand Literature in English* (Auckland: Oxford University Press, 1991).

Thomson, J., ed. *Southern People: A Dictionary of Otago Southland Biography* (Dunedin: Longacre Press in association with the Dunedin City Council, 1998).

Thomson, J.M. *A Distant Music: The Life and Times of Alfred Hill, 1870–1960* (Auckland: Oxford University Press, 1980).

—. *The Oxford Dictionary of New Zealand Music* (Auckland: Oxford University Press, 1991).

—., ed. *The Attentive Ear: A Workbook of Music Criticism* (Wellington, Stout Research Centre, 1985).

Trollope, A. *New Zealand* (London: Chapman & Hall, 1874).

Twopeny, R. *Town Life in Australia* (London: Elliot Stock, 1883).

Vogel, J. *Anno Domini 2000, or, A Woman's Destiny* (London: Hutchinson, 1889).

Watson, S. *From Darkness to Light* (London: 26 Fore St., c. 1900).

Webb, B. *Visit to New Zealand in 1898: Beatrice Webb's Diary with Entries by Sidney Webb* (Wellington: Price Milburn & Co., 1959).

Wilson, A. *Wire and Wireless: A History of Telecommunications in New Zealand, 1860–1987* (Palmerston North: Dunmore Press, 1994).

INDEX

A number in **bold** indicates an illustration. A number followed by *n* indicates a footnote. An en dash (–) between two numbers indicates continuous treatment of a topic, a tilde (~) indicates that a topic is referred to on each page in the range. Throughout the index 'B' denotes Charles Nalder Baeyertz.

Aborigines (Australia) 28
Academy of Fine Arts (Wellington) 56
accents 66, 101, 140–41, 160, 161, 211, 216
Adams, Arthur 81, 82, 98, 110, 120, 135–6, 151, 180; on *Triad* art supplements 181–2
Adelaide 24, 25, 27, 28, 41, 101
Adelaide College of Music 24
Alexander Turnbull Library 82*n*, 219
Alfred, Prince 17
Algie, J. Stewart 52
Alien Enemy Teachers Act 164
Allen, Maud 154–5
Alpers, Oscar 129
Altschuler, Modest 116
Andersen, Johannes 81, 82, 103–4; 'Exhibition Ode' 103
Andrews, E.W. 160
anti-Semitism 13–14
ANZACs 175; Ettie Rout's safe sex efforts 192
Aorangi (ship) 110
Archibald, Jules François 34, 135
Argus 31, 133
Arndt, Mina 194
Aronson, Frederick 21
Aronson, George 16, 21, 32
Aronson, John 15
Aronson, Mrs Frederick 123
Aronson, Saul 21
Art Club (Wellington) 56
Art in Australia 207
Art in New Zealand 213
Auckland 70
Auckland Amateur Operatic Society 158
Auckland Choral Society 178
Auckland Competitions 143, 155
Auckland Liedertafel 163
Audran, Edmond 55; *La Mascotte* 55, 83
Australasian accents 66, 101, 140–41, 160, 161, 211, 216

Australian Journal 33, 34
Australian literary nationalism 34, 135
Australian Women's Weekly 214

Baeyertz, Bella 32, 43, 59, 142, 171; children 34, 36, 63, 128; children's weddings 144–5; cooking 33, 76, 131, 140; death 209; death of Estelle 59, 60; marriage strains & break-up 128, 129, 131, 132, 144; qualities 32–3, 131; refuses divorce 145, 146, 171; wedding 32
Baeyertz, Charles (eldest son, 'Carl') 13*n*, 59, 76, 174; birth 34; death 218; marriage 144; *Triad* employment 144, 169
Baeyertz, Charles (father) 16, 17; death 13, 18
Baeyertz, Charles (grandfather) 13*n*, 14, 32
Baeyertz, Charles (youngest son, 'Charlie') 13*n*, 184, 186, 195, 198, 212, 214, 215; birth 171; death 218; prisoner of war 216
BAEYERTZ, CHARLES NALDER: ancestry 14–15, 18, 165, 168; death & tributes to 216, 217–18; early business enterprises 36, 42; fancy dress ball outfit 205; finances 36, 59, 91, 156, 183, 202, 214; *Guide to New Zealand: The Scenic Paradise of the World* 97; illnesses 28, 117, 196, 216; influence of Methodism 22; journalism 44–5, 208, 214; libel action 164, 167–9; Maori 23, 76–7, 78, 93; Melbourne period 30–36; motor car 183; move to Dunedin 37, 38, 43; move to Sydney 162–3; move to Wellington 127, 129, 130; name problems in WWI 164, 165, 168, 179; overwork 172, 214; post-*Triad* employment 208–10, 213–16; property speculation 33, 36, 42; relations with Frank Morton 115, 118, 120, 150, 181, 196–7, 199–200, 204
ART 56, 150; artistic tastes 91–2, 138, 139, 194; *painters*: C.N. Worsley 92, 137,

139, 194; Goldie 100; James Nairn 56; Mina Arndt 194; Nerli 54; O'Keeffe 54; van der Velden 55, 91
CHARACTER & ATTRIBUTES 150, 188, 217; abilities 35; appearance 58, 137, 162; business sense 15; caricatures of 74, 86, 87, 95, 113, 133, 149, 159; cosmopolitanism 15, 34, 44, 131; cultural mission 53, 57, 58, 62, 67, 86, 93, 161; Edwardianism 86; enthusiasm for gadgets & novelties 75; 'fallen' 211; flamboyance 17; Jewish background 13, 15, 109; love of children 76–7; moneymaking interest 21; photographic memory 22–3; 'Pooh-Bah' 111; public speaking 15; relation to mother 30, 101, 102; religion 44, 53, 58; reputation 86, 136, 137, 190; scientific interests 54, 75, 91, 208; sense of humour 25, 30, 53, 70; sportsman 31; strength 67
CHILDHOOD: birth 13; Colac period 13, 16, 18; death of father 13, 18, 19; father figure 26–7; mother's evangelism 27–8; musical interests 24, 25; school magazine 25–6; schooling 20, 21–2, 23, 24–7; typhoid 28
CRITICAL ACTIVITIES 30–31, 71, 205; acknowledgements of 212; advantages of name 30; appraised 111, 161; attacked 179; Australian sensitivity 199; bluntness 22, 25–6, 93–4; clash with 'Civis' 45–7; critic's role 112; dance 154–5; defence of 111, 125, 172; encouragement to performers 94; for *Otago Daily Times* 45; 'Pooh-Bah' 111; relinquishes *Triad* reviewing 179; renews *Triad* reviewing 195; Shavian comparison 112–13
LANGUAGE, LITERATURE, DRAMA: as actor/entertainer 45, 47, 158; Australasian accents 66, 101, 140–41, 160, 161, 211; Australian Aboriginal language 28; Competitions judge 95–6, 117, 140, 141, 211, 214; drama 158; enunciation & pronunciation 21–2, 66–7, 93, 110–11, 117, 141, 155, 218; French, German, Greek languages 43; linguistic ability 22–3; literary tastes 57, 93; Maori language 23, 76–8, 120; 'Masterly English' course 203; misspellings 63; poetry tastes & criticisms 82–3, 166–7; Shakespearean enunciation 154, 198; teaching 43; 'The Melody of Speech' 210, 212; verses for *Triad* 198; *Voice Culture* 45, 56; <u>reviews of</u>: Alfred Grace's stories 79–80; Arthur Adams's poems 82–3; Harry Vogel's novel 81; H.B. Irving as Hamlet 154; Marie Fix's (Ney's) acting 158, 160

LIFE WITH BELLA 32–3, 75, 76; absences 98, 128, 130, 131; children 34, 36, 55, 63, 76, 128, 184; children's weddings 144–5; death of Estelle 59; Dunedin lodgings 42, 45, 59, 75, 90; marriage strains & break-up 128-31, 144-5; move to Dunedin 37, 43; move to Wellington 127, 129, 130; musical evenings 92, 144; musicians invited home 90, 91, 93, 140; neglect of family 130, 171; Rudolph's cycling accident 128; visits mother 101, 102; wedding 32; Wellington lodgings 127, 144, 145

LIFE WITH LILLIAN 171, 195, 196, 198, 212, 214, 215; concern for Charlie 215; gardening 215; Maida joins them 214; marriage 209

LIFE WITH MILDRED 168, 183, 184; affair 141–5; ménage à trois 171; Mildred's death 186; move to Sydney 162–3; seeks divorce from Bella 145–6; shaves off beard 162; son's birth & early life 171, 172, 195

MUSIC 42–3; as organist 27, 30, 37, 42, 43, 45, 47, 48; as choirmaster in Melbourne 30; as music director in Dunedin 47–8; audiences 56, 57, 198; Competitions judge 117, 140, 198; defends German music 164; enjoyment of radio broadcasts 215; Fuller libel case 151–2; gains L.Mus. L.C.M. 68–9; grades composers 62; London 188–9; music in NZ 67–8, 158; musicians invited home 90, 91, 93, 140; New York 107–8; New Zealand orchestras 102–3, 104, 116, 158; Parry's *Job* 112; Rimsky-Korsakov's *Scheherazade* 189; Sheffield Choir 155; Strauss's *Symphonia Domestica* 108; Sydney 172–3; teaching 43, 45, 58; trans-Tasman comparisons 101; Wagner's music 85, 168; <u>musicians</u>: Albert Friedenthal 91; Albert Mallinson 130; Alfred Hill 90, 201; Amelita Galli-Curci 207; Amy Castles 150n; André Skalski 200; Baxter Buckley 144; Cherniavski brothers 140; Clara Butt 123-5, 140, 155; Elgar as conductor 108; Emma Calvé 140; Enrico Caruso 111, 189; Fritz Kreisler 207; Geraldine Farrar 189; Gustav Slapoffski 117; Henri Verbrugghen 172-3, 201; Jan Kubelik 125; Jascha Heifetz 189; John

McCormack 153–4; Leopold Godowsky 189; Lilian Irvine 93; Louise Kirkby-Lunn 155; Marcella Sembrich 110–11; Marion Mitchell 84; Marion Watson 94; Mark Hambourg 91; Melba 89, 90, 108, 111, 130, 135, 168; Michael Balling 160; Paderewski 92, 93; Philip Newbury 197; Rachmaninov 189; Raffaello Squarise 57, 116; Rosina Buckmann 90, 125, 140, 189; Sir Henry Wood 189; Teresa Carreño 116; Watkin Mills 91
OPINIONS: A.G. Stephens 130*n*; American newspapers 107; Aucklanders 70; Australia 161; Australian literary nationalism 135; Australia/NZ comparisons 199, 200; Boer War sentiments 163; David Low 148–9; English bookshops 188; Christchurch 104; Dunedin 169; Ettie Rout 192; film censorship 147; genetic consequences of war 175; labour movement 148; Mark Twain 69–70; New York 109; Niagara Falls 107; NZ scenery 39, 97, 117; Sydney 162–3; *Triad* 209; William Massey 148
RADIO BROADCASTING 208–10, 213, 217; advertising 210, 211; 'fallen' 211; music programmes 210–11; simulated cricket commentaries 210; voice tutor for ABC 215–16
TRAVELS: Australia 101, 132–3, 140; England 187–8; New York 107–10; United States 105–10, 187, 189; *Triad* business 55–6, 61–2, 63, 65, 67, 98, 187–8; voyage to Dunedin 38; Wellington return 211–12, 213; with Maida 105, 110; with Mildred 184, 186
Baeyertz, Emilia (mother) 15–17, 20–24, 26, 30, 32, 36, 187; as public speaker 15, 37; conversion to Christianity 19–20; death of husband 18, 19; evangelism 20, 21, 23–4, 27–8, 37, 101–2; evangelistic service described 27–8; Jewish background 13, 15; marriage 15–16; visit from B & family 101
Baeyertz, Estelle 55, 60, 128; drowning 59
Baeyertz, John 32
Baeyertz, Leone 218
Baeyertz, Lois 216, 218
Baeyertz, Maida 59, 76, 144, 214, 218; American trip with B 105, 110; birth 36; joins B in Sydney 214; nurses B 216; *Triad* contribution 105, 214; wedding 144–5

Baeyertz, Marion 16, 23, 37, 101; birth 19
Baeyertz, Mary 14
Baeyertz, Rudolph 22, 35, 76, 90, 93, 171; birth 63; coolness of B towards 184, 214, 218; cycling accident 128, 130; memoir of father 171, 184, 219; war service 174, 184
Balfe, Michael William: *The Bohemian Girl* 85
Ballance, John 49
Ballarat 24, 31, 32, 152, 156, 161; Competitions 95, 132, 140, 141, 152
Balling, Michael 65–6, 160
Barkly, Sir Henry 13–14
Barnett, Maughan 72, 144
Baughan, Blanche 121, 122, 151
Beardsley, Aubrey 134–5
Beauchamp, Sir Harold 206*n*
Bedford, Randolph 136
Beecham, Thomas 189
Beethoven, Ludvig van: 'Moonlight Sonata' 72; third symphony 71
Berlioz, Hector: *La Damnation de Faust* 107
Besant, Annie 114
Best, Elsdon 81
Bickerton, Alexander 75–6, 81
Bird, Violet 127
Bisson, Edouard 139
Bizet, Georges: *Carmen* 84
Blaikie, Rev. James 32
Blast 166
Blunt, Wilfred 167
Boehm, T.W. 24, 26
Bohemianism 114, 122, 180, 191, 204
Bolitho, Hector 126, 193, 204, 205
Book Lover 133
Bookfellow 110, 130, 151, 202
Booth, General 110
Booty, Fred 113
Boston Symphony Orchestra 108
Bouguereau, William-Adolphe 99, 139
Bracken, Thomas 78; *Musings in Maoriland* 78
Bradman, Don 210
Brasch, Charles 18*n*, 170, 219
Brennan, Christopher 127*n*
Bristol Piano Company 164
Brodsky, Maurice 34
Brooke, Rupert 166
Buckley, Baxter 144
Buckmann, Rosina 90, 94, 125, 140, 144; career in Britain 144, 189

Bulletin 33, 79, 98, 118, 136, 191, 218; and B 82, 89, 103, 157, 211, 217; cartoonists 148, 149, 180; 'Ladies Page' 134; on Clara Butt 124; 'Red Page' 82, 110, 135, 180; style 115, 157; taps Australian nationalism 34, 135; war cartoons 180; *see also Lone Hand*; Stephens, A.G.
Butler, George E. 138
Butler, O'Brien 143, 169, 186; *Muirgheis* 143, 186
Butt, Clara 89, 123–4, 125, 140, 155, 218

Calvé, Emma 90, 140
Cambridge, Ada 35–6
Cameron, Lily 48
Canberra 163
Candler, Samuel 13
Canterbury Art Society 150
Canterbury Times 93, 161
Carey-Wallace, Mildred 168, 183; affair with B 141–5; appearance 143, 184; birth of son 171; compositions 143, 171, 195, 196; death & burial 186–7; friendship with Lillian Price 145; musical abilities 143; performances 141, 143, 184; to Sydney with B 162
Carl Rosa Company 84
Carpenter, Edward 146, 147
Carreño, Teresa 116, 140, 143
Carrière, Eugène 139
Caruso, Enrico 154*n*, 108, 110, 153, 155, 189, 201
Castles, Amy 89, 140, 150
cellists 88
Centennial International Exhibition (Melbourne) 35–6, 40
Cézanne, Paul 167
Champion, Henry 133
Chapple, Frederic 26–7
Cherniavski brothers 140
Choral Society (Wellington) 72
Christchurch: B's dislike 104; Hagley Park 102; NZ International Exhibition 102
Church, Hubert 98
Citizen 126
City of Sydney Eisteddfod 214
'Civis' 57, 67, 68; clash with B 45–7
Clarke, Marcus: *For the term of his Natural Life* 33
C.N. Baeyertz Institute 203, 209
Cohen, Edward 15*n*
Colac (Victoria) 13, 16-19, 34
Colborne-Veel, Mary 202
Collegian Herald 25

Colonial Museum (Wellington) 104
Competitions: B as judge 95–6, 117, 140, 141, 152, 155, 198, 211, 212, 214; Auckland 143, 155; Ballarat 95, 132, 140, 141, 152; Dunedin 94–6, 117, 132, 143; Greymouth 158; Invercargill 141; Ipswich-Blackstone 198; Melbourne 198; Napier 158; Sydney 214; Wellington 152, 211–12
conductors *see* Altschuler, Modest; Balling, Michael; Coombs, James; Elgar, Sir Edward; Slapoffski, Gustav; Squarise, Raffaello; Verbrugghen, Henri; Wielaert, Johannes
Conried, Heinrich 107
conscription 174–5, 181
Coombs, James 116
Cottle, Thomas 80, 81, 100
Cowan, James 81
Cowen, Frederic 35
cricket 101, 208*n*: simulated Ashes broadcasts 210
Crosland, Thomas 147
Cross, Zora 180; *Songs of Love and Life* 180
Crossley, Ada 89
Cubism 167
cultural journals: Australia 33, 34, 118, 135–6; New Zealand 50–51, 80–81, 117, 122
Current Thought 122

Daily Mail 188
Daly, Victor 136
Darwin, Charles 75
Daudet, Alphonse 80
Davis, Ernest 84
Davis, Lady (Marion) 84
Davison, Emily 146
Deakin, Alfred 132
Deamer, Dulcie 191
decadence 118, 119, 122, 123, 133, 135
Dickens, Charles 34
Dolores, Antonia (formerly Antoinette Trebelli) 131
Domett, Alfred: *Ranolf and Amohia* 78
Dominion 126, 190
Donizetti, Gaetano: *Don Pasquale* 108
Donne, Thomas Edward 106
Douglas, Lord Alfred 147
Dresden Piano Company 52–3, 58; name change 164
Dunedin 37, 39, 42; architecture 39–40; art groups 54, 55, 64, 65; B's opinion of 169;

exhibitions 40–41, 54; Jewish community 52; London Street 42; Popular Concerts 47–8; poverty 41; Presbyterianism 43–4; Royal Terrace 42; Vauxhall Gardens 44; wartime amusements 173–4
Dunedin Competitions 94–6, 117, 132, 143
Dunedin Liedertafel 52*n*, 84, 93
Dunedin Orchestral Society 71; concert reviewed by B 116
Dunedin School of Art 54, 65
Dunedin Star 85
Dyson, Edward 181

Easel Club (Dunedin) 65
Echo 161
Elgar, Sir Edward 108
Eliot, George 121
Elman, Mischa 155
Elsley, A.J. 139
Escoffier, Auguste 88
Evans, Graham 22
Evans, Patrick: on B & *Triad* 218
Evening Post 130, 211, 212
Evening Star 111, 217

Fabian Society 49
Fairburn, A.R.D. 213
Farley, Henry 44
Farrar, Geraldine 189
Federation of Labour 148
Fels, Willi 42
Fenwick, George 45
Ferguson, Mary 59
Feruzzi, Roberto 139
Fielding Choir 158
Finck, Henry 111, 112
Findlay, David 156*n*, 202*n*, 171
Findlay, Sir John 152
Fitchett, Frederick 45
Fitchett, Very Rev. Alfred 67–8
Fix, Marie 158, 160
Flynn, Father 140–41
Franck, César: 'The Beatitudes' 197
Fraser, Peter 148
Free Lance 98
Freeth, P.C. 144
Freyberg, Bernard 178
Friedenthal, Albert 91
Frohman, Charles 186
Fry, Roger 167
Fuller, John 151, 197, 202; libel action 151–2
Futurism 139, 165, 194

Galli-Curci, Amelita 207
Gallipoli campaign 165, 168, 173, 177
Gauguin, Paul 64
Geelong 20–21
Genée, Adeline 154
George V, King 209
Gerardy, Jean 88
Gibb, Wiliam 194
Gilbert and Sullivan operettas 31, 83; *HMS Pinafore* 58, 83; *Patience* 83; *Pirates of Penzance* 83; *The Mikado* 31, 111*n*
Glasgow Boys 56
Glee and Madrigal Society (Wellington) 84
Godowsky, Leopold 189
gold rushes: Victoria 14
Goldie, Charles 99–100
Gonsalez Italian Grand Opera Company 178–9
Gore 58
Gounod, Charles: *Faust* 84, 91; *Romeo and Juliet* 107
Grace, A.A. (Alfred) 78–9, 126, 133, 192; *Maoriland Stories* 79; on *Triad*'s move to Australia 157; *Tales of a Dying Race* 79–80; *Triad* stories 79
Grand National Eisteddfod (Ballarat) 132
Grand Opera Company (George Musgrove) 84, 116–17
Grand Opera Company (J.C. Williamson) 140
Great Depression 209–10, 213–14
Grey, Sir George: *Polynesian Mythology* 78
Greymouth 158
Grossmann, Edith Searle (Edith Grossman) 81, 137

Hahndorf 24, 26
Hallé Orchestra 66, 160
Hallenstein, Bendix 42
Hambidge, George 177
Hambourg, Mark 91, 92, 125
Hamilton, Augustus 78, 81; Maori art 104
Hamilton, Sir Ian 175
Hammerstein, Oscar 107
Hardy, Thomas 63
Harmonic Society (Nelson) 65
Harris, Dick 133–4
Hauroto (ship) 38, 141
Hawaii 105–6
Hawera 58–9
Hawera Operatic Society 158
Hebb, Isaac 16
Heifetz, Jascha 189

Henderson, W.J. 111, 112, 125
Henry, O. 76, 118
Herald (Melbourne): tribute to B 217
Hill, Alfred 53, 72, 73, 100, 102, 201; *A Moorish Maid* 90; *Australia* 201*n*; 'Exhibition Ode' 103; *Hinemoa* 72–3, 82, 90; *Joy of Life* 201*n*; *Tangi* 201; *Tapu* 102; *Waiata Poi* 90, 100, 201; *Welcome* overture 201*n*
Hiroti, Haimona 77
Hiscocks, Fred 148, 149, 153, 182; *The Gunner* 165; war service 165, 170
Hobart 101
Hocken Library 210, 219
Hocken, Thomas Morland 41
Hodges, Hamilton 101
Hodgkins, Frances 41, 42, 64, 65, 81, 99, 100; 'Goose Girl' 64; 'In Maiden Meditation Fancy Free' 64; Modernist influences 194; Nerli as teacher 54–5, 64
Hodgkins, Isabel 54, 55
Hodgkins, William 41, 54, 55; death 99
Holcroft, Monte: on B & *Triad* 217
Holland, Harry 148
Hood, Thomas 83
Hubbard, Elbert 106, 107
Humperdinck, Engelbert: *Hänsel und Gretel* 107
Huneker, James 111
Hunt, Holman: *Light of the World* 139
Huntly Orchestral Society 158
Hutton, David Con 54
Huxley, Thomas 75
Hyde, Robin 190; on B & *Triad* 190, 192

Illustrated Magazine see *New Zealand Illustrated Magazine*
Imagism 150–51, 166
Impressionism 56, 99
Industrial Exhibition (Wellington) 72
Industrial Workers of the World 181
influenza epidemic 185–6
Inglis, K.S. 210, 216
Invercargill Competitions 141
Ipswich-Blackstone 'Eisteddfod' 198
Irvine, Lilian 93
Irving, Ethel 154
Irving, H.B. 154; *Hamlet* 154
Izett, James: *Maori Lore* 93

Jacobowski, Edward: *Erminie* 125
Jacobs, S. 62
Jerome, Jerome K. 57*n*

Joel, Grace 64–5, 100
Johnston, Isabella Delgarno see Baeyertz, Bella
Johnston, Rev. Kerr 32
Jones, Shàdrach 44
Joubert, Jules 41*n*
Jowett, Dr 63

Keith, Hamish 7, tribute to B & *Triad* 218
Kelly, A.L. 179, 196, 200, 201
Kenny, Alice 81, 121, 134, 166, 170*n*, 190*n*
Kernot, Gladys 134, 151, 167, 190*n*,
King, Charles 161
Kirkby-Lunn, Louise 155
Kitchener, Lord 168, 208
Kontski, Chevalier de 72
Krehbiel, Henry 111
Kreisler, Fritz 207
Kubelik, Jan 125

Labour Party
Lamb, Charles 109, 123
Lamb, Mary 109
Lambs' Club (New York) 109, 110, 189
Lancaster, G.B. 81, 122
Landfall 18*n*, 170, 219
Lauder, Harry 178
Lawlor, Pat 35, 130, 202, 204; *Confessions of a Journalist* 126*n*; *More Wellington Days* 119; *Old Wellington Days* 159; on *Triad*'s heyday 136; tribute to B 217
Lawson, Henry 34, 115, 136, 202
Lawson, Will 177, 178; 'Irish Girls' 178
Lazarus, Maria 15
Le Gallienne, Richard 118, 123
Le Ménestrel 51
Lefebvre, Jules: 'Chloe' 30
Lewis, Wyndham 166
Liberal Government 41, 49, 70, 102, 130, 147, 148
Liliputian Opera Company 55, 84
Lilley's Magazine 135
Lindsay, Norman 99, 180, 181
Littlejohn, Emma 210
London College of Music 68, 69
London Mercury 213
Lone Hand 118, 135–6; tribute to *Triad* 136
Los Angeles 106
Low, David 103*n*, 133, 148
Lowell, Amy 166
Lusitania (ship) 169, 186
Lyster, William 31
Lyttelton, Edith 122*n*

Mackay, Jessie 81, 120–21, 122, 151
Magny, Olivier de 115
Mallinson, Albert 130
Maloga Mission Station 28
Manapouri (ship) 43
Mander, Jane 137–8, 193; *The Story of a New Zealand River* 137; *The Strange Attraction* 193
Manhattan Opera House 107, 108
Mansfield, Katherine 91, 122–3, 206n: favourite foods 131–2; 'The Death of a Rose' 123; *The Garden Party* 193
Manson, Mabel 71
Maori 93, 98, 134; Alfred Hill's music 72, 90, 100, 201; art 104; deity Rongomatane 120; Goldie portraits 100
Maori contingent 177
'Maoriland' 77
Mararoa (ship) 61
Marinetti, Filippo 139, 150
Marsh, Edward: *Georgian Poetry* 166
Masefield, John 166; *Gallipoli* 175
Mason, Bruce 154
Mason, R.A.K. 213
Massey, William 148, 185
Matisse, Henri 167
Maugham, Somerset 179
McCay, Adam 204
McCormack, John 144, 153–4
McCrae, Hugh 207, 208
McCrae, Mahdi 207
McEldowney, Dennis 131n
McIntosh, Hugh 180–81, 208
McIntyre, Raymond 194
Melba, Nellie 31, 53, 88–9, 90, 108, 110, 130, 189; memoirs 135
Melbourne 13–14, 101, 132, 133, 163; art 30, 36; Competitions 198; exhibitions 29–30, 35–6, 40; financial collapse 36; gold rush period 29–31, 33–4, 35; Jewish community 15, 23; journals 33–4; musical life 30–31, 35; property boom 33; schools 21, 22, 64
Melbourne Punch 33
Mencken, H.L. 213
Mendès, Catulle 118, 123
Merton, Owen 194
Methodism 22, 31
Metropolitan Opera (New York) 107–8
Mills, Dick and Co. 62
Mills, Watkin 91
Mitchell, Colin 138
Mitchell, Marion 84
Modernism 166, 194, 217, 219

Mohwinkel, Hans 117
Monowai (ship) 62, 85
Monroe, Harriet 150, 166, 167
Montague, J.F. 158
Montez, Lola 31
Monthly Musical Record 51
Monthly Review 50
MORTON, FRANK 113, 114–15, 116, 133; appearance 127, 149–50, **119**, **182**; Bohemianism 180; breakdown 180, 181; death 203, 205; departs Dunedin 118; drinking problem 114, 115, 118, 196; family life 204; literary tastes 118; moves to Sydney 169; self-destructive 118; sensualist 115; Sydney socialising 180–81; role in NZ's cultural life 158; tributes to 204; views on sex 131
PROFESSIONAL LIFE: aliases 170, 190, 205; art appreciation limited 194; Assistant Editor of *Triad* 118; Associate Editor of new *Triad* 203; attack on women writers 120–22; book & other reviews 145, 150, 151, 154–5, 177, 192, 193; cocktail recipe 147; disputes 126–7; Ezra Pound dispute 166–7, 192, 218; food writings 131–2, 138; on Australian authors 136; on Clara Butt 124; on divorce 145–6; on homosexuality 147; on Yeats 151n; output 151; M's poetry appraised 151, 161; poetry selections for *Triad* 192; poetry tastes 115, 122, 150, 151; relations with Arthur Adams 180; relations with B 115, 118, 120, 150, 181, 196–7, 199–200, 204; relations with David McKee Wright 180; *works*: *Exultant Bride* 190; *Naked Notorieties* 190; *The Angel of the Earthquake* 131; 'The Compleat Gastronomer' 131, 147; 'The Kingdom of Bohemia' 122; 'The Luck of Harris Temple' 119n; 'The Man in Red' 118–19; *The Secret Spring* 131, 190; 'The Song of the Lady Elocutionist' 142; *Widows Wistful* 190
WAR: anti-German outbursts 165; conscription advocacy 174–5, 181; genetic consequences of 175; NZ Expeditionary Force 175; on horrors of war 164–5; soldier sons 174, 175–6; tirades 179
Morton, Louise 204
Mulgan, Alan 136, 154, 217; appraises B 136–7; *Great Days in New Zealand Writing* 217
Municipal Orchestra (Wellington) 158
Murdoch, Walter 133

Murphy, Amy 94, 101
Musgrove, George 83n, 31, 84, 85, 117; opera company 31, 84, 116
music in New Zealand 58–9, 67–8, 70-72, 83-5
musical journals 51, 52
Musical Times 51
musicians *see* cellists; conductors; pianists; singers; violinists
Musin, Ovid 72

Nairn, James 56, 64, 99, 138
Napier 61; Competitions 158
Napier Boys High School 160
Napier City Band 61
National Art Gallery 206n
National Council of Women 146n
National Gallery School (Melbourne) 64
Nelson 65, 66; Harmonic Society 65
Nerli, Girolamo 41, 54, 56, 65, 99; *Bacchanalian Orgie* 54; Dunedin influence 54–5; Otago Art Academy 64; Robert Louis Stevenson portrait 54
New Plymouth 70
New Triad 207
New York 107–10; opera 107–8
New York World 110
New Zealand: scenery 39, 97, 117; transport 61, 63
New Zealand and South Seas Exhibition 40–41, 54
New Zealand Competitions Society 152
New Zealand Expeditionary Force 175
New Zealand Herald 88, 177
New Zealand Illustrated Magazine 80–81, 82, 86, 100, 117, 120, 134
New Zealand Listener 113n, 217, 218
New Zealand Magazine 50; tribute to B 217
New Zealand Mail 56, 113, 115
New Zealand Medical Corps 174
New Zealand Musical Monthly 52
New Zealand Symphony Orchestra 103
New Zealand Times 102, 144, 150, 180
Newbury, Philip 57, 197–8
Ney, Marie 158, 160
Niagara (ship) 185
Niagara Falls 107, 117
Northcliffe, Lord 188, 190, 202
NZ Observer and Freelance 70, 74

Oamaru 58
O'Farrell, James 17n
O'Keeffe, Alfred 54, 55, 65
operas & operettas 83, 84, 85; Melbourne gold rush period 31; New York 107–8; *works*: *A Moorish Maid* 90; *Aïda* 107; *Barber of Seville* 53; *Bohemian Girl* 85; *Carmen* 84; *Don Pasquale* 108; *Erminie* 125; *Faust* 84, 91; *Flying Dutchman* 84; *Hänsel und Gretel* 107; *Il Trovatore* 84; *La Bohème* 107, 189; *La Damnation de Faust* 107; *La Mascotte* 55, 83; *La Poupée* 83; *La Traviata* 108; *Les Cloches de Corneville* 83; *Lohengrin* 84, 107; *Madame Butterfly* 107, 140; *Maritana* 85; *Rigoletto* 31; *Roméo et Juliette* 107; *Salome* 108; *Tannhäuser* 84, 107; *Tapu* 90, 102; *The Belle of New York* 84; *The French Maid* 83; *Tosca* 107; *see also* Gilbert and Sullivan operettas
Orchard, Arundel 198, 201
Orchestral Society (Wellington) 72
orchestras: Boston Symphony Orchestra 108; Hallé Orchestra 66, 160; New Zealand 102–3, 104, 116, 158; Philadelphia Orchestra 189; Russian Symphony Orchestra 116
Otago Art Academy 64
Otago Art Society 55n, 54, 65, 99, 100
Otago Conservatorio of Music 43
Otago Daily Times 18n, 37, 38, 41, 45, 52, 198, 217; B's clash with 'Civis' 46; editors 29, 41, 45; employment of Frank Morton 114, 115, 118; Nerli advertises 64; on B as competions judge 96
Otago Witness 28, 56–7, 208; B's articles on music 44–5; 'Civis' 57; 'Civis' and B clash 45–6
Otira Gorge 117

Paderewski, Ignacy Jan 53, 92, 200
Page, Bernard 163
Pago Pago 105; Mildred's death & burial 186
painters *see* Bouguereau, William-Adolphe; Butler, George E.; Gauguin, Paul; Goldie, Charles; Hodgkins, Frances; Hodgkins, William; Joel, Grace; Nairn, James; Nerli, Girolamo; O'Keeffe, Alfred; Perrett, John; Richardson, Mollie; van der Velden, Petrus; Wilson, Laurence; Worsley, C.N.
Palmerston North 84
Pankhurst, Emmeline 146
Parker, Robert 55, 72
Parry, Hubert: *Job* 112
Paterson, Banjo 115
Pelorus Jack 109–10
Perrett, John 64
Philadelphia Orchestra 189

Philharmonic Society (Dunedin) 116
Philistine 106
Phoenix 213, 217
photo-engraving 138
pianists *see* Buckley, Baxter; Carreño, Teresa; Friedenthal, Albert; Godowsky, Leopold; Hambourg, Mark; Kontski, Chevalier de; Paderewski, Ignacy Jan; Rachmaninov, Sergei; Skalski, André
Plançon, Pol 111
Planquette, Robert: *Les Cloches de Corneville* 83
Plimmer, Harry 158
Plimmer-Denniston Company 158
Poetry 150, 151, 166
poets *see* Adams, Arthur; Baughan, Blanche; Brennan, Christopher; Church, Hubert; Kenny, Alice; Kernot, Gladys; Lawson, Will; Mackay, Jessie; Pound, Ezra; Wall, Arnold; Yeats, W.B.
Pollard, James 55*n*
Pollard, Tom 55*n*, 84, 102, 158, 202
Polynesian Society 78, 81, 120; *Journal* 78
Post-Impressionism 167
Pound, Ezra 134, 150, 166, 170*n*, 192; *Cathay* 192; dispute with Morton 166-7; on *Triad* 167, 192; Vorticism 166
Price, Lillian 145, 171, 195, 198; appearance 145; death 218; marriage to B 209; ménage à trois 171
Prince Alfred College (Adelaide) 25, 26, 28, 32, 33, 101
Prince Alfred College Chronicle 26
Puccini, Giacomo 107; *La Bohème* 107; *Madama Butterfly* 107, 140; *Tosca* 107
Pulitzer, Joseph 110

Quale, Jack 206
Quarterly Review 86

Rachmaninov, Sergei 189
radio 208-9; commercial possibilities 210; short wave 215
radio stations 210-12; ABC 215-16
rail travel 61, 63; refreshments 63
Ramsay, Jeanne 101
Rayner, Fred 103; *Exhibition Sketcher* 103; *Sketcher Competition* 86
recordings 153
Red Funnel 117
Red Lion Brewery 64
Reeves, William Pember 49
Reform Government 148
Reimann, Adolph 24
Review of Reviews 51, 65, 67

Riccardi Company 83
Richardson, Mollie 138
Richmond, Dorothy 194
Riego, Teresa del 184
Rigoletto 31
Rimsky-Korsakov, Nikolai: *Scheherazade* 189
Rippmann, Walter 122
Robertson, William 17
Rodin, Auguste 139
Rosenthal, David 32
Rotorua 98
Rout, Ettie 191-2
Royal Dunedin Male Choir 52*n*
Royal Opera Company 83
Royal Wellington Choral Society 173
Roycroft Press 107
Rumford, Kennerly 123-5, 140, 155, 218
Runciman, John 89
Russian Symphony Orchestra 116
Rutherford, Ernest 75
Ruthven, K.K. 170; on *Triad*/Ezra Pound dispute 218
Rylstone (Australia) 216

Salvation Army 110
San Francisco earthquake 106
Sandhurst (now Bendigo, Victoria) 23
Sandow, Charles 67, 75
Saturday Review 89
Savage, Michael 148
Science Siftings 75
Seddon, Richard 49, 70, 102, 103, 147, 217
Sembrich, Marcella 108, 110-11
Semple, Bob 148
Shackleton, Ernest 177
Shakespeare, William: *Hamlet* 154
Shakespearean Society of New South Wales 198
Shakspere Society 158
Shaw, George Bernard 123, 154; as music critic 112, 113; *Captain Brassbound's Conversion* 158; *Pygmalion* 66
Sheffield Choir 155, 158
Sheppard, Kate 146*n*
Siegfried, André 129
Singer, Richard 35, 100, 127, 133, 134, 145, 152, 171, 181, 204, 217
singers *see* Buckmann, Rosina; Butt, Clara; Calvé, Emma; Caruso, Enrico; Castles, Amy; Dolores, Antonia; Farrar, Geraldine; Fuller, John; Galli-Curci, Amelita; Hodges, Hamilton; Irvine, Lilian; Kirkby-Lunn, Louise; Lauder, Harry; Manson, Mabel;

McCormack, John; Melba, Nellie; Mills, Watkin; Mitchell, Marion; Mohwinkel, Hans; Murphy, Amy; Newbury, Philip; Plançon, Pol; Ramsay, Jeanne; Rumford, Kennerly; Sembrich, Marcella; Sorel, Bel; Trebelli, Antoinette; Watson, Marion
Skalski, André 198, 200, 201
Skeyhill, Tom: *Soldier Songs from Anzac* 174
Slapoffski, Gustav 84, 116
Smart Set 213
Smith, Goldwin 71
Smith, Stephenson Percy 78
Soady, Rose 181*n*
Sonoma (ship) 186, 187, 189
Sorel, Bel 140
Souter, David 135
Southland Daily News 111, 112
Spencer, Herbert 75
Spilt Ink 207
Squarise, Raffaello 41, 43, 53, 116; *Barber of Seville* performance 57
Stanley, Coralie 191
Star (Auckland) 201
Stead, W.T. 51
Stephens, A.G. 79, 82, 89, 110, 114, 115, 151, 202, 204; move to Wellington 130; on NZ poets 151; poems reviewed by B 98–9
Stevenson, Robert Louis 54
Stewart, Nellie 31
Stoddart, Margaret 194
Stone's Otago & Southland Directory 43
Stout, Anna 146, 178
Stout, Sir Robert 41, 42
Strauss, Richard: *Salome* 108; 'Symphonia Domestica' 108
Strong, Archibald 133
Stuart, Rev. D. M. 44
Studio 118
Sunday Sun and Guardian 214
Sunday Times: B becomes editor 208
Sydney: B's approval 162–3; musical life 172
Sydney Conservatorium of Music 170, 173, 198, 201, 214
Sydney Liedertafel 90
Symons, Arthur 118, 123

Table Talk 33, 34, 168; describes Emilia 101
Tagore, Rabindranath 150
Taki Taki 77
Tapanui Courier 66, 140, 164; on *Triad* 124
Tatler 161
Te Tuhi, Patara 100
Tempest, Marie 179, 200
Terry, Ellen 154
The Academy 147
The Christian 101
The Gunner 165
The Lancet 75
The Magazine of Music 53
The Penguin History of New Zealand Literature 218
The Southern Cross 101
The Strangers' Vade-Mecum or South Island Guide 40
The Triad Magazine Ltd 156*n*, 179, 202
Theatre Magazine 164, 165, 201
theatres: dimming of lights 146
Theomin, David: sponsorship of *Triad* 52–3
Theomin family 42, 52
Thompson, Sydney 194
Thomson, John Mansfield 104; on B's role as critic 218; *The Attentive Ear* 218
Travers, Pamela 191; *Mary Poppins* 191
Treaty of Waitangi 177
Trebelli, Antoinette (later Antonia Dolores) 71, 131*n*
Tregear, Edward 78, 120
TRIAD 21, 22, 24-6, 30, 31, 217; 5th anniversary 73; 12th anniversary 100; 15th anniversary 124; 30th anniversary 199; disputes 126–7; 'Frank Morton Memorial Number' 204; Morton/Baeyertz contributions weighed 204–5; Morton/Baeyertz relationship 115, 118, 120, 150, 181, 196–7, 199–200, 204
ADVERTISING & ADVERTISERS 55, 56, 58, 62, 63, 156, 163, 173, 189, 195; corsetry 96–7; Northcliffe's testimonial 188; overload 169–70
ART 55, 64, 100, 118, 138–9, 181–3; caricatures & cartoonists **113**, **133**, 139, 148, **149**, 165, **182**; incomprehension of modern movements 167, 194; Maori 78; supplement 100, 137-9, 181–2, 183; *artists*: Alfred Walsh 194; Aubrey Beardsley 134–5; Charles Goldie 100; Dorothy Richmond 194; Frances Hodgkins 64, 194; Frank Wright 194; Goldie 138; Grace Joel 65; James Nairn 99; Margaret Stoddart 194; Mina Arndt 194; Nerli 64; Nugent Welch 194; Raymond McIntyre 194; Sydney

Thompson 194; Walter Wright 194; Wiliam Gibb 194; Worsley 139
AUSTRALASIAN EDITION 156, 164, 169; debut 170; NZ content 173, 177, 192, 205; trans-Tasman differences 172, 206–7
COLUMNS, CONTRIBUTORS, CORRESPONDENTS 51, 65, 115, 118, 134, 205; 'A Woman hits back' 191; 'Allegro' 72; 'Answers to Correspondents' 57; 'Art Notes' 54, 81; 'Criticus' 99; 'Diapason' 72; 'Editors Note Book' 57, 63; 'Epistemon' 120, 170, 205; 'Fantastika' 133*n*; 'Lalie Seton Cray' 190–91; 'Obiter Dicta' 63, 97, 106, 111–12, 120, 146, 148, 156, 161, 163, 185; 'Oliver Pageant' 193; 'Pan Optes' 133*n*; 'Rosemary June' 190, 191; 'Science Jottings' 98; 'Selwyn Rider' 170, 205; 'Susan Gloomish' 190, 200, 201; 'T.F. Monk-Orran' 170, 205; 'Things Visble' 119, 120, 124, 127, 179; 'Wireless Whispers' 208; A.A. Grace 126, 133; A.G. Stephens 170; Adam McCay 204; Alice Kenny 133; C.N. Worsley 139; Coralie Stanley 191; David McKee Wright 135; Dick Harris 133; Dora Wilcox 202; Dulcie Deamer 191; Frank Morton 118-22, 133; Fred Hiscocks 170; George Hambidge 177; Gladys Kernot 134; Godfrey Turner 126, 133, 192–3; Hector Bolitho 193, 204; Katherine Mansfield 123; L.L. Woolacott 192; Lillian Price 145, 171; Pamela Travers 191; Richard Singer 106, 133; Will Lawson 177
DRAMA & LITERARY CONTENT 79–80, 83, 98, 117, 118–19, 120, 133, 134, 192; advent of Morton 118; dispute with Ezra Pound 166–7; Futurism manifesto 139; humorous verses by B 198; Maori 192; post-war Oxford poets 192; role of sex in love poetry 131; wartime 174, 176–7, 179; *Wheels* 192; Yeats 134; *people*: Edith Searle Grossmann 137; Jane Mander 193; Katherine Mansfield 193; Marie Tempest 179; Somerset Maugham 179; Zora Cross 180
EDITORIAL & PRODUCTION: appearance & size 53, 73, 98*n*, 199, 202; Australasian edition 156, 164, 169, 170; Australian office 163; circulation 55, 58, 63, 68, 86, 124, 126, 137, 195; critical independence 141; directors 156*n*, 190*n*, 202*n*; dumbing down 203, 205, 206; Dunedin office 62; early distribution methods 58; early sponsorship 52, 58, 62; editorial intentions 51, 52, 60; editorial rejections 57, 58; editorial staff 62, 118, 156–7, 205, 207; financial arrangements 156, 179, 183; high-brow/low-brow balance 48, 206; launched 48–51; libel actions 151–2, 153, 197–8; Morton's appointment 126–7; Morton's breakdown 181; Morton's death 205, 206; liquidation 202; move to Sydney 156–7, 162-4, 169; move to Wellington 129; national coverage 56; ownership changes 207; price 53, 56, 57, 157, 199; printers 62; printing works fire 203; profitability 91; The Triad Magazine Ltd 156*n*, 179, 202; title explained 53; Wellington office closure 169

GENERAL CONTENT: Australian content 135–6, 163; book reviews 145, 150, 192, 193; clippings from other journals 96; competitions & prizes 51, 57, 62, 79, 93; contents of early issues 34, 53, 57; corsetry articles 96; education 106; food writing 131–2, 147; letters page 160–61, 183; Maori 77, 78, 138; obituaries 201, 202, 204; Queen Victoria 86; radio 208; science coverage 54, 64, 75–6, 98, 118, 208; society gossip 190; supplements 62, 77, 169; pictorial 62; travel writing 97–8, 105, 107, 109, 120; wartime 173–4, 179; women's market 202–3

ILLUSTRATIONS 109, 126, 135, 138, 168, 181; art supplement 100, 137-9, 181–2, 183; art works 99, 134, 138, 139; caricatures 133; Goldie's studio 100; Maori subjects 77, 100, 138; musicians 84, 85, 91, 94, 123, 138, 140; policy 138, 139, 181; scenery 97, 138

MUSIC 65, 66, 67, 71, 72, 158, 200; Clara Butt furore 123–4, 218; controversies 67–8, 70; Harry Lauder 178*n*; Henri Verbrugghen 170; International Exhibition (Christchurch) 102; interviews 91, 92; L.C.M. exams promoted 69; Mildred Carey Wallace 196; Philip Newbury 197–8; *Salome* controversy 108; significance of criticism 89, 91; music supplement 56, 57, 81, 144, 170, 171; Wagner 85

ROLE, REPUTATION, READERSHIP: Australasian reputation 136, 137; Australian readership 133, 199; Australian appraisals 162; critical independence 141; female readership 57, 121, 189–91, 199; Morton's initial appraisal 115; NZ reputation 119, 120; readers' appraisals 117, 157, 161; rival

magazines 56, 80–81; role in NZ 157–8; successors of 213
SOCIAL & POLITICAL CONTENT: dimming of theatre lights 146–7; Ettie Rout defence 191–2; homosexuality 147; influenza epidemic 185–6; marriage & divorce 145–6, 198; politics 147, 148, 157; women's suffrage 146; war coverage 164–5, 168, 175–8
Trimnell, Thomas 72
Tripe, Mary Elizabeth see Richardson, Mollie
Trollope, Anthony 39, 40
Truth and Progress 27, 28
tuberculosis 15, 135, 193, 202, 214
Turner, Godfrey 126, 133, 192–3, 201–2; defence of Ettie Rout 191
Twain, Mark 69–70, 110
Twopeny, Richard 29, 41

Ulimaroa (ship) 162
Union Steam Ship Company: *Red Funnel* 117

van der Velden, Petrus 55, 56, 91, 99, 206; *Old Jack* 55
Van Dongen, Kees 167
Van Norden's Magazine 129
vaudeville 117
Ventura (ship) 105
Verbrugghen, Henri 170, 172, 173, 198, 200–201
Verbrugghen Quartet 172
Verdi, Giuseppe: *Aida* 107; *Il Trovatore* 84; *La Traviata* 108
Victor Talking Machine Company 153
Victoria, Queen 17, 85–6, 88, 100
Victorian gold rush 14
violinists *see* Elman, Mischa; Heifetz, Jascha; Hill, Alfred; Kreisler, Fritz; Kubelik, Jan; Musin, Ovid; Verbrugghen, Henri
Vogel, Harry 81–2; *Maori Maid* 82
Vogel, Julius 18n, 52, 81; *Anno Domini 2000* 82
von Zedlitz, George 164
Vorticism 165–6, 192, 194

Waddell, Rutherford 41
Wagner, Richard 53, 85, 117, 168; *Flying Dutchman* 84; *Lohengrin* 84, 85, 107; *Tannhäuser* 84, 85, 107
Waipukurau 73
Wall, Arnold 122
Wallace, (William) Vincent: *Maritana* 85

Walsh, Alfred 194
Wanganui 63, 77, 105, 120, 164
Wanganui Garrison Band 141
Ward, Sir Joseph 103, 147, 185
Watson, Marion 94
Watson, Sydney 15, 17, 18, 20, 21, 24, 102
Watt, Ernest 207
Webb, Beatrice 49–50
Webb, Sidney 49–50
Webber, Bruce 216
Weekly News 56
Welch, Nugent 194
Wellington 119–20, 129–30; art 56; Competitions 152, 211–12; Industrial Exhibition 72; music 55, 58, 71–2, 129
Wellington Competitions Society 211
Wellington Liedertafel 163
Wellington Male Choir 163
Wellington Orchestral Society 53
Wellington Savage Club 212-14
Wellington School of Design 56
Wells, H.G. *The Time Machine* 63
Wesley College (Melbourne) 21, 23, 24
Wesley, John 27
West Coast 97
Whangarei 137
Whitcombe and Tombs 121
Whyte, Arthur 156n, 202n
Wielaert, Johannes 164
Wilcox, Dora 81, 202
Wilde, Oscar 76, 80, 108, 118, 122, 134, 147
Wilkinson, Iris *see* Hyde, Robin
Williamson, J.C. (James Cassius) 31, 83, 126, 140, 189; Grand Opera Company 140; opera company 31
Wilson, Charles 134
Wilson, Laurence 64
Wireless Weekly 210; interviews B 209
women's rights & suffrage 49, 57, 82, 120, 137, 146
Wood, Sir Henry 189
Woolacott, L.L. 192, 196, 197; Associate Editor of *Triad* 205; purchases *Triad* 207
World War I: anti-German feeling 163, 168; B defends German music 164; cultural activities 178; fundraising carnivals 173; Gallipoli campaign 165, 168, 173, 177; name changes 163, 164
Worsley, C.N. 92, 137, 139, 194, 202
Wright, David McKee 135, 180
Wright, Frank 194
Wright, McGregor 54, 138
Wright, Walter 194

writers *see* Bedford, Randolph; Daly, Victor; Eliot, George; Grace, Alfred; Grossmann, Edith Searle; Hardy, Thomas; Henry, O.; Lawson, Henry; Lyttelton, Edith; Mander, Jane; Mansfield, Katherine; Symons, Arthur; Wells, H.G.; Wilde, Oscar

Wyinks, Heron 145

Yeats, W.B. 134, 150, 151

Zealandia 50–51, 52, 80